visit a flying to New Brighton

The Pier. New Brighton The

8th DECEMBER, 1965 ★ 7 - 11 P.M.

FREE · FREE · FREE TO CAROLINE CLUB MEMBERS

YARD BIRDS ★ THE 4 PENNIES

BRIAN POOLE AND THE TREMELOES

THE HONEYCOMBS ★ TWINKLE

PAUL & BARRY RYAN

GARRY FARR & THE T BONES

AND MANY ★ MORE ★ BIG NAMES

THE TOWER New Brighton

Proudly Announces the Opening of the New

ZOO

With the Greatest Collection of Animals, including Lions Leopards, Bears, Wallabys, Llamas, Monkeys, Baboons and many others. Also Kiddies' Pet Corner.

Admission 6d.

AND

CARTOON CINEMA

45 MINUTES SHOWING OF THE LATEST CARTOON FILMS, POPEYES ANITOONS PUPPETOONS Etc.

Admission 6d.
— OPEN DAILY —
from 21st MAY, 1950

Also CAPTAIN S. HOWES' SENSATIONAL STAGE PRESENTATION PERFORMING LIONS' ACT DAILY at 2 p.m., 4 p.m. and 6 p.m.

BIG BEAT SESSIONS

EVERY FRIDAY at the

TOWER BALLROOM, NEW BRIGHTON

FRIDAY, 1st DECEMBER 1961

Another Great Six Band Line Up –

THE BEATLES · · RORY STORM AND THE HURRICANES
DALE ROBERTS AND THE JAYWALKERS · DERRY AND THE SENIORS
KINGSIZE TAYLOR & THE DOMINOES · STEVE DAY & THE DRIFTERS

First Heat "Mr. Twist" Competition

7-30 p.m. to 1-00 a.m.   Licensed Bars (until 11-30 p.m.)

LATE TRANSPORT (Liverpool, Wirral and Cheshire)

Excursions Leaving St. John's Lane (Lime Street) 7-30 p.m. to 9-00 p.m.

TICKETS 4/6

OPEN DAILY.

Old English Fair Grounds,   Switchback,
Japanese Tea House,   Wonderful Japanese Per
Animated Photographs,   formers,
Dancing Platform,   Magnificent Band,
Quinette's Grand Circus.   Grand Water Chute,

ON WEDNESDAY NEXT, JUNE 16,
The LIVERPOOL WHEELERS will hold their Meeting on
Athletic Grounds,
25 Miles Handicap at 7 p.m.
Special Prize for Track Record.

ON SATURDAY NEXT, JUNE 19,
GRAND COMMEMORATION ATHLETIC SPORTS,
Under A.A.A. Laws and N.C.U. Rules.

£120 IN PRIZES

Illuminations at Dusk,
100 Electric Lights,
10,000 Lamps.

Sports commence at 2 p.m.

1

Introduction

My book tries to focus on some of the main events that occurred in the history of New Brighton Tower and grounds, from the visiting celebrities and the stories that helped shape its very existence.

From newspaper cuttings to personal recollections, I hope to bring the building back to life. It has been an honour to delve into its past.

Millions have visited its shores, for romance or just a family day out. The ghost of the place lives in the very fabric of our souls.

Even now when I walk over the site I can hear the laughter, and smell of candy floss, but my emotions are mixed with sadness that it no longer graces the skyline with the tallest building in England.

Many people have helped me in this quest to name but a few,

Mr Alan Clay for his photographs, recollections and proof reading.

Mr Ken Clark for some fantastic photographs. Also the many whose help and advise proved to be invaluable on my Facebook pages, including Mr Steve Parry, Belita Leyland Howell, Pamela Ann Boddy Fair, Harry Colville, Dawn Lowery, and not forgetting Mr Hugh Rowland for access to the C.W Binks archive. The New Brighton Heritage and Information Centre and Shirley Ashton along with the staff at the Wallasey Central Library (Reference Section) in Earlston Road, even with staff cuts they managed to dig out some nuggets of information.

My connection with New Brighton Tower goes back through many generations of my family. From fireman John Dutton who helped to extinguish the fire in 1898, when James Shone met such a tragic death. To Inspector Dutton who helped investigate the suicide of George Price who worked for Colonel Cummins Wild West Show. And my sister who met Keith Menefee an American serviceman in the Tower ballroom during the 2nd World War and went on to become a GI bride. And not forgetting Ted Dutton secretary of the Rakers Football Club., and finally to my own escapades watching some of the most iconic pop groups perform in the swinging sixties. This is my contribution to the memory of the Tower, I hope you enjoy the trip back in time.

Contents

THE IDEA IS BORN

With the lure of millions of Victorian holiday makers to the seaside, and the rapidly-expanding working-class holiday market offering so many attractions. The scene was set for dubious investment schemes.

It did not take long before our first enterprise took shape in the form of the New Brighton Aquarium, Baths, and Hotel Company Limited, founded in 1872. The original idea of a hotel and aquarium, sounded a good idea on paper but faltered in the directors remuneration department, and the company received its marching orders with a winding-up order in 1879, with a total loss to the shareholders.

Not to be deterred the same site next to the Palace was to be the location for The New Brighton Graydon Great Wheel and Tower Company Ltd.

A bit of a mouth full, but still determined to help shareholders part with their money. Formed in 1896 with a capital of £140,000.

The prospectus informed "Of the annual 11 million visitors if only 50 per cent of visitors rode the wheel, a profit of 50 per cent was possible"

Graydon was a U.S. Navy lieutenant who invented the type of mammoth wheel New Brighton hoped one day to boast.

It was intended that the local wonder would be almost 600 feet high – that is, almost as high as the tower actually build at New Brighton a few years later. From carriages attached to it, passengers would have an "unsurpassed view of miles around".

Not all was well. Walter Basset went to court, claiming he had signed an agreement with Graydon on the 10th August 1895 which gave him exclusive rights. The case went to litigation and dragged on and on, and eventually the project was axed. It took a while before New Brighton Tower was to rise like a Phoenix from the ashes of these previous unsuccessful enterprises.

The Press cutting of 1896 informs the public that the first sod has just been cut on the Rock point estate, New Brighton, in "preparation for the excavations and drilling prior to the foundations of the new Eiffel Tower being commenced." A "great enterprise has already been commenced upon a scale which will place New Brighton to the front of many of the great popular watering places to which the Lancashire millions now flock." The New Brighton Tower & Recreation Company incorporated in July 1896 purchased the Rock Point Estate, the former home of the late Captain Molyneux for £50,000, the land had been previously purchased by The Tower Estates Syndicate for £30,000. So along with the £20,000 profit plus £125,00 worth of shares in the new company, the syndicate did quite well out of the arrangement.

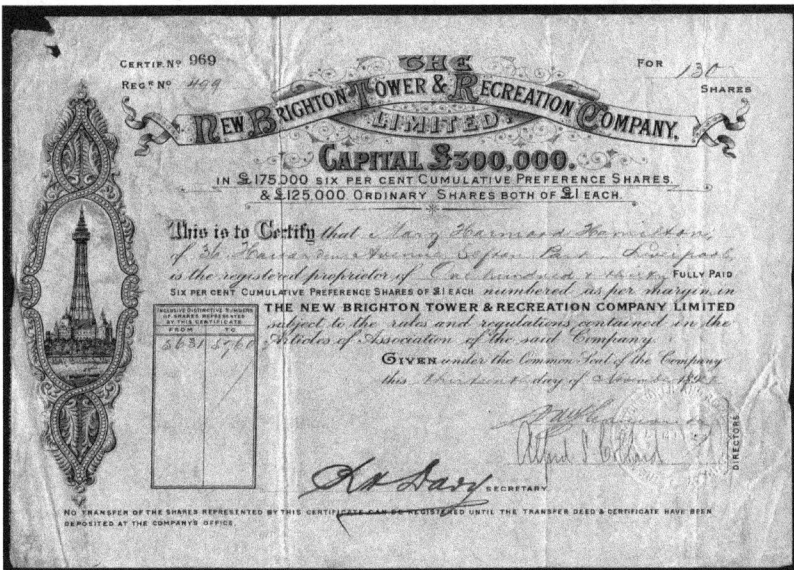

A leading figure in both ventures was Robert P Houston, a Liverpool ship-owner and Unionist M.P., In 1877 he bought a share in a packet steamer with his inheritance. He used the profits to start up his own management company in 1880, R. P. Houston & Company.

Later to become Sir Robert Paterson Houston, 1st Bt., Member of Parliament for West Toxteth, and a shipping magnate. Robert Houston is described in the Oxford Dictionary of National Biography as "a hard, ruthless, and unpleasant man."

His third and final marriage, to Lucy Houston on December 12, 1924, was an interesting affair, they lived as tax exiles on the island of Jersey.

When Sir Robert showed Lucy his will, she tore it up telling him that one million pounds was not good enough. Sir Robert then suffered a series of mental disorders and Lucy employed a food-taster to ensure that he was not being poisoned. Even so Sir Robert mysteriously died on his yacht Liberty on 14 April 1926, leaving his widow roughly £5.5 million.

The Tower was to be the highest in the realm at 621 feet, with a music hall, theatre, seaside curiosities and a menagerie together with refreshment rooms and an outside cycle track. Shares were £1 each and the Architects Maxwell & Turk of Manchester, who had already designed the Blackpool Tower at only 518 feet 9 inches tall were employed..

APPOINTMENT OF MR HOLLINGSHEAD

Hollingshead has just taken on the organisation and management of the New Brighton Tower and Grounds Co. - Mr Houston's property. The tower and grounds are situated within a ring fence and comprise 25 acres of finely wooded and undulating grounds with sea and river views, and it is hoped that they will concentrate all the attractions of Blackpool, not to mention adding to them. Half a million sterling has already been expended, and about a thousand men are employed in preparing the place. Mr. Hollingshead will be 70 in September, but there are few of the younger generation who could complete with him in pluck and energy. Had he been in the Government service, he would have been superannuated years ago.

Plans dated January1896

Molyneux Estate 1894
Before the promenade or New Brighton tower construction

On the high ground, which later became known as the Tower Grounds, was Rock Point House which was sometimes known as Rock House. The mansion was once the home of Lord and Lady Houston and their family. Captain W.H. Molyneaux R.N had been a successful officer in the Royal Navy. The families wealth being generated by prize money obtained from the capture of a French Frigate, and other profitable endeavours including his marriage to the daughter of Admiral Sir Andrew Mitchell, KB. in June 1837. The eldest son Andrew Mitchell Molyneux, Captain 23rd Royal Welsh Fusiliers, and J.P. for Cheshire, was to inherit the property in 1873.

An interesting footnote to the family history Captain W.H. Molyneaux on the sailing ship "Tagus" was the first ship to locate the mutineers of the Bounty on visiting the Pitcairn Islands.

The original Rock Point House was converted by the Tower Company into the Rock Point Castle Restaurant.

The large house near the entrance gates to the Tower at the bottom of Egerton Street was originally a separate property called West Bank owned by Mr T. Addison, it was acquired by the Tower Company for use as a Manager's house and offices.

Mr Thomas Addison had a long association with the Royal National Lifeboat Association, and helped to raise funds for "The Rescue" a 42 ft tubular lifeboat, launched on the 24th January 1863.

8

Eiffel Tower For New Brighton
Commencement of Operations

There can be no doubt that the efforts being put forward by public bodies and private individuals to make New Brighton one of the most - attractive seaside resorts in the north will meet with the approval, not only of visitors, but of the majority of the residents in the district. We announced in our columns a few weeks ago that a scheme had been decided upon for the establishment of a pleasure resort at New Brighton and on lines somewhat similar to those at Olympia in London. That project has now assumed definite shape, and the site - the estate of the late Captain Molyneux on Rock Point - has been secured by a company (at the head of which is Mr. R. P. Houston, M.P.) who has paid a deposit of over £2000 to the trustees of the property. The grounds, as already indicated, are about 500 yards to the south of the pier, and are bounded on the east side by the river. The promenade, which is to be extended from the Magazines, Egremont, to New Brighton, will give convenient access to the grounds, whilst an upper entrance will be provided in Rowson Street. One of the principal features of the scheme will be the Eiffel Tower, such as was erected in Blackpool, and it will be interesting to the public to know that at the present times excavating operations are in progress in order to prepare the foundations of the tower. That the scheme is one of immense proportions and will be readily realised when it is stated that it is the intention of the company to spend some thing like a quarter of a million of money in providing grounds, in which will be found attractions of every conceivable character. We understand that the company have also acquired the lease and interest of the Royal Ferry Hotel, close by the pier, with which establishment, we believe, Captain Walters has for some time been connected. With a gentleman of enterprise like Mr. Houston at the head of affairs, it is expected that the scheme will be a great success. There seems to be no reason to fear that the pleasure grounds will injure the Palace, for there will doubtless, be generous support given to both places by the increased number of visitors who are sure to find their way to New Brighton. It should be added that the new company have spared no pains to secure every possible advantage in order to make the scheme as popular as possible. Indeed, it is stated that they recently approached the Wallasey District Council with a request that the present landing pier might be removed to a position directly opposite the grounds. This request they backed up with an offer to build the new pier if the council approved of the idea. That matter, however, we find, fell through, as the council could not see their way to interfere with the present position of the landing pier, which they pointed out was directly in a line with Victoria Road, the principal thoroughfare of the district.

Liverpool Mercury 10th February 1896

In July 1896, the New Brighton Tower and Recreation Company Limited issued a prospectus that invited 175,000 subscriptions at £1 each to fund the building of a resort on thirty-two acres of land it had recently acquired. The number of visitors to New Brighton vary, according to the Evening Express on 26 November 1896, 11 million people 'ferried to New Brighton annually'; by 1899 the Wallasey News estimated the number of passengers carried on Wallasey Ferries to New Brighton in that year was 15,087,680, and this does not include the railways. In 1897 there were 285 arrests for drunkenness. By coincidence, the very day that this statistic was reported a liquor licence was refused for the Japanese cafe. It was no wonder that the Tower Management faced fierce opposition to their concerts from local magistrates who issued the licenses. The publication Music Hall stated on the 10 June: "In the present moment, Mr. Bantock is waging war with the local magistrates, the Wirral Salons, as the Liverpool Review dubs them, who have refused to grant a seven days' music license, whereby the people for whom the concerts were primarily intended-those who cannot find time for the enjoyment of music during the busy week-are deprived of its solace on the seventh day. One may well ask why so many of the powers that be deem in their wisdom that there is something immoral in Sunday music. The idea is too childish for words".

Adverse publicity appears to have swayed the magistrates, for just five days later a licence was granted at the Wallasey Petty Sessions for twelve months for theatre and for 'singing and dancing ... for "serious and classical" music for two hours on Sunday.'

The Music Hall reported the good news on 24 June describing the licence as 'enlightened policy of providing harmless entertainment on the Sunday.' One of the grandest rooms inside the Tower was a magnificent ballroom, constructed to harness the enthusiasm for dancing identified by the Birkenhead News on 3 June 1896 as 'the favourite diversion of visitors' to the New Brighton Palace and promenade. The Birkenhead News reported on the 25th July 1896, that the ballroom was decorated in white and gold with emblems depicting various Lancashire towns and its floor was constructed from '11,690 superficial feet in oak parquetry.

With over one and a half million visitors to the Tower grounds each year, the company struggled to balance the books. On 8 June 1898 the City Press declared that 'It is useless wasting sympathy on people who are foolish enough to subscribe for shares on this prospectus'; the Pall Mall Gazette, on the same day, described the property as 'over-capitalised' and, furthermore, that the directors were 'ignorant of the "leisure business."'

This report also suggested the insufficient number of ferries allocated to New Brighton and the location's 'always stormy' weather, suggesting that not only was travelling to the resort a problem, but that it was built in an unsuitable region, given its reputation for inclement weather.

Reference: Paul Watt, City Press, Birkenhead News.

Robert Harold Davy was born June 4, 1868 in Ramsbottom, Bury, Lancs., and died June 23, 1936 in Cottage Hospital, Hoylake, Merseyside.

He married Annie Lazarus on 1890 in Ramsbottom, Lancs. It was during this time that he was employed by the Manchester Ship Canal Company whilst working in the Secretaries office, on the construction of the Liverpool to Manchester Canal. Thirty-six miles in length, with its five sets of locks, a true marvel of Victorian engineering.

In 1892, Mr. Davy became Assistant Secretary to the Blackpool Tower Co Ltd., and in 1896 took up an appointment with New Brighton Tower Co.

From the Weekly News of 3rd November 1905: "New Brighton Tower's new Manager. Mr R. H. Davy, who for six years has had the management of the athletic meetings held at New Brighton Tower, and who has also performed the secretarial duties in connection with that place of amusement, has been appointed manager of the Tower grounds in succession to Mr Albert Bulmer."

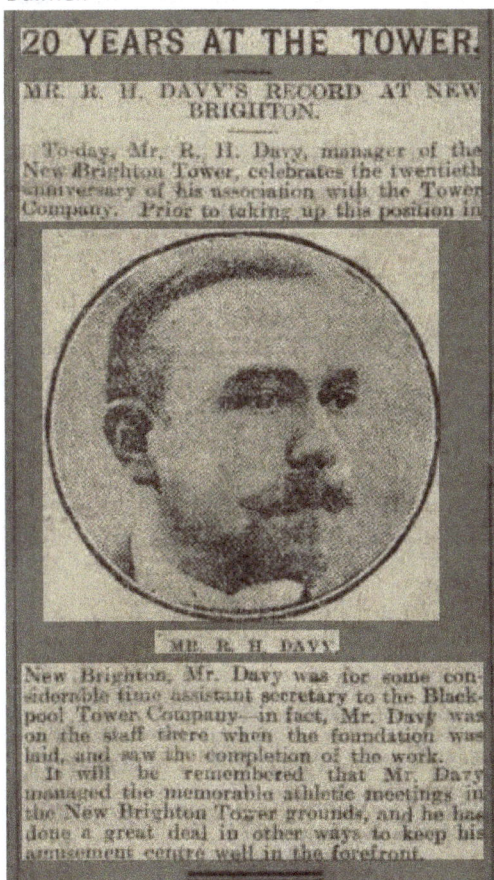

20 YEARS AT THE TOWER!

MR. R. H. DAVY'S RECORD AT NEW BRIGHTON.

To-day, Mr. R. H. Davy, manager of the New Brighton Tower, celebrates the twentieth anniversary of his association with the Tower Company. Prior to taking up this position in

MR. R. H. DAVY

New Brighton, Mr. Davy was for some considerable time assistant secretary to the Blackpool Tower Company—in fact, Mr. Davy was on the staff there when the foundation was laid, and saw the completion of the work.

It will be remembered that Mr. Davy managed the memorable athletic meetings in the New Brighton Tower grounds, and he has done a great deal in other ways to keep his amusement centre well in the forefront.

Liverpool Echo 28th Aug 1916

The supervision and responsibility of such a large project as the New Brighton Tower does not leave much time for recreation. Walking around the 35 acres of site which he controlled left little time for him to enjoy his favourite sport of fishing and golf.

At billiards he was regarded as a brilliant "cueist", the occasional game could be enjoyed in the Tower. He was a Fellow of the Chartered Institute of Secretaries.

Annie passed away on the 26th July 1913 after a severe illness and operation at the Hospital for Women in Liverpool. Interred in Broad Green Cemetery, Liverpool. At the time the couple had been living at "Church Lea" New Brighton, her occupation shown as Boarding House Keeper.

11

The contract to build New Brighton Tower was awarded to Handyside & Company of Derby. Over a 1000 tons of mild steel was used, at a cost of £120,000, in contrast to the earlier Blackpool and Eiffel towers, both constructed using wrought iron. Mild steel can last up to 60 years with suitable galvanising. Wrought iron is known for its durability and will last many hundreds of years, its unique properties allow it to resist corrosion.

The foundation stone of Blackpool Tower was laid on 25 September 1891 and a time capsule was buried beneath it. New Brighton Tower had a much less auspicious opening ceremony on 22nd June 1896 the first piece of turf was cut at the Tower grounds' site and the building of the tower started in earnest. The octagonal building at the base was built in the same red Ruabon brick as the Blackpool building. Within the legs stood the 3,000-seat Grand Tower Theatre, and there was a ballroom which could accommodate a thousand couples. It opened incomplete for the Whitsuntide holiday of 1897. Below is the story of its construction and the heavy toil it took on the workers that built this superb structure.

With the help of a notebook which contains photographs, notes, drawings and blueprints taken during the construction of the New Brighton Tower between 1896-1897.

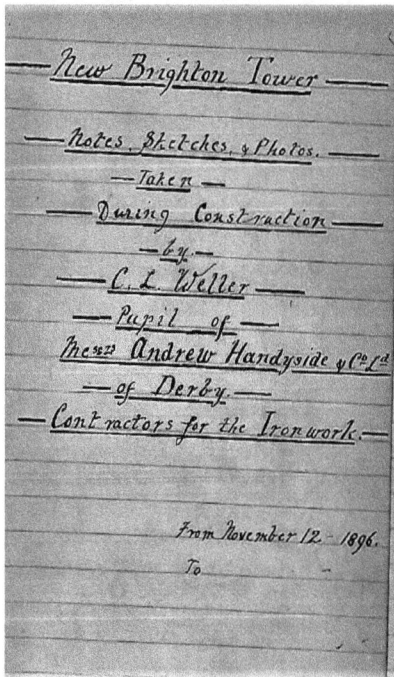

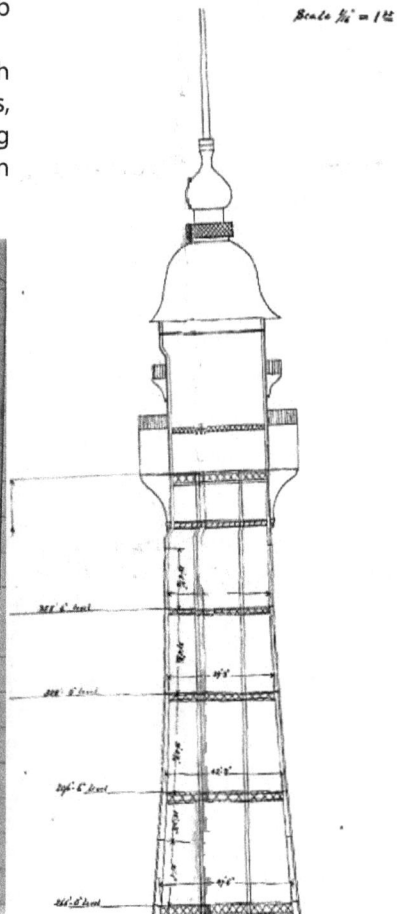

The following section describes the complicated and risky business of the construction of the tallest building in the land. Included are several newspaper clippings concerning workers who fell to their deaths during the construction in 1897. In his notes, Weller talks about these deaths and some of the photographs show the scenes of the accidents.

What happened to Mr Weller is a complete mystery the diary is unfinished and covers the period up to 21st August 1897.

The mid-nineteenth century was a period when a series of changes took place in the construction industry, with the introduction of new materials and the need for new building types, especially in that part of the industry concerned with the design and erection of iron structures. With the proliferation of professional organisations, alternative views were developing about the provision of education and training for designers. It was not until 1892 that a design manual, was published by Redparth Brown and Co this contained safe load tables, provided on the assumption that there were very few engineers who would be able to produce calculations to justify the size of the beam to be used. It was within this frame work that Mr Weller was to be encouraged to take notes and photographs of the companies work in the construction of New Brighton Tower.

Handyside began manufacturing arched structures, such as the train sheds for railway stations in the 1850's, one of the largest structures built by Handyside, was said to be the largest hall in the kingdom, was the 1886 National Agricultural Hall in London, now known as Olympia. With its own foundry and fabrication workshops the company was well placed to deliver a complicated structure in parts to the site at New Brighton. Mr Weller was a pupil of Andrew Handyside Co Ltd he would have been allowed to attend classes in the daytime to further his education. Our apprentice structural engineer arrived on site in the winter of 1896 from his note book dated the 12th November entitled "Condition of work" he made the following observations:

"Of the eight foundation holes for the legs. One was concreted ready for the base except that the bolt holes required de-greasing, of the other holes, one was partly concreted and the others in a more or less complete stage of being dug. All this work however was not being done by A.H & Co. The work done this day, was one base unloaded from a wagon onto the ground by means of a pair of legs and a winch worked by four men. Its weight was 5 tons 7 cwt. Height of legs 20 ft.

A road was also being made of sleepers laid on the ground from the gate to the site of the Tower".

13

The first photograph dated 30th November 1896 with handwritten title "From South showing pillar in centre for theodolite" on close examination the operator can be seen standing behind the theodolite, which must be precisely placed vertically above the point to be measured. It was vital to establish all the angles and measurements of the metal components. In the background can be seen a steam winch, used to assemble the legs. With the vertical brick walls well under construction.

The eight tower legs A,B,C,D,E, F & H have all been allocated a foundation hole each attached to a base plate.

Ring girders are installed at various intervals all the way up to the top with Six ring girders above the dome and two below.

The whole of the steel used was produced by Andrew Handyside Co Ltd in their Brittania Foundry. The construction of the steel work, its erection and fabrication and all the engineering work in connection with the completion of the Tower, were undertaken by the firm's engineers.

Most of this great mass of metal was shipped to the tower site from Derby a journey of

607. Nov 19. From West looking across arena

nearly ninety-five miles. The massive size of the structure was by no means the only difficulty with which the engineers had to contend.

Weight alone called for the most exacting accuracy in calculating the proportions of the various girders and components, and the provision of massive foundations deep in the solid sandstone. The effect of the wind had to be countered by a system of ring girders and cross-bracing. The effects of rust and corrosion were guarded against by a layer of red lead and then several coats of paint. All the parts of the Tower had to be accessible for inspection and painting.

The photograph above reads "Nov 19 - From West looking across arena."

Note book records: Leg A & B riveted to base with brackets bolted on same. The hole in the centre had a depth of 8 feet and a diameter of 42 ft.

The same size as the Circus shown on the Building News Plan dated December 29th 1899.

Heat and cold were factors that required the most careful consideration.

The tower is composed of eight main pillars, rising from the ground. The lower construction much larger and heavier in section. With very long rectangular steel riveted boxes being tapered and placed end to end. With special consideration made to facilitate handling by the cranes down the centre of the construction; a final ring girder was made when the eight portions were in position, to facilitate the viewing platform.

The Tower was finally completed in August 1898, a major engineering achievement which rivalled Blackpool Tower. Six men had died in the construction of this giant structure, whose useful life was to last only 16 years, before the metal structure was demolished.

15

Dec 14-96   From South. showing 2nd Piece of leg ready for hoisting

Above photograph is dated 14th December 1896 with the following note:
"From South showing 2nd piece of leg ready for hoisting."
In the background a steam traction engine , and the A frame used to lift
the leg into position. Below drawing used to construct the A frame.

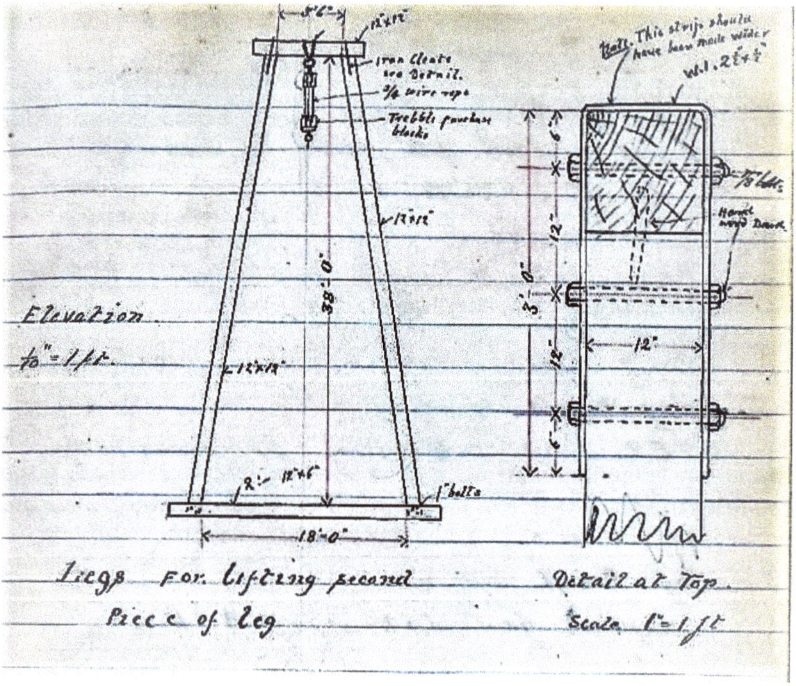

16

Steady progress had been made in the construction of the Tower with no delays. Then disaster struck with the first of many fatalities.

From the note book entry dated Wednesday 13th January 1897. "While lifting the ring girder D/E the hook of the 10 ton crane broke. The girder and sling chains weighing 9 ton 18 cwt. Fell to the ground, bringing with it the platform attached to the leg, there were six men working at the time, of these two were killed instantly, the other lies in a critical condition. The girder is so much bent that a new one will have to be made. "

Work on site stopped, while waiting for the results of the inquest.

The inquest was held on the 18th Jan verdict "Accidental death" Work resumed later that day. The local newspaper reported a few days later that John Daly had now recovered consciousness and was doing wonderfully well, in Seacombe Cottage Hospital.

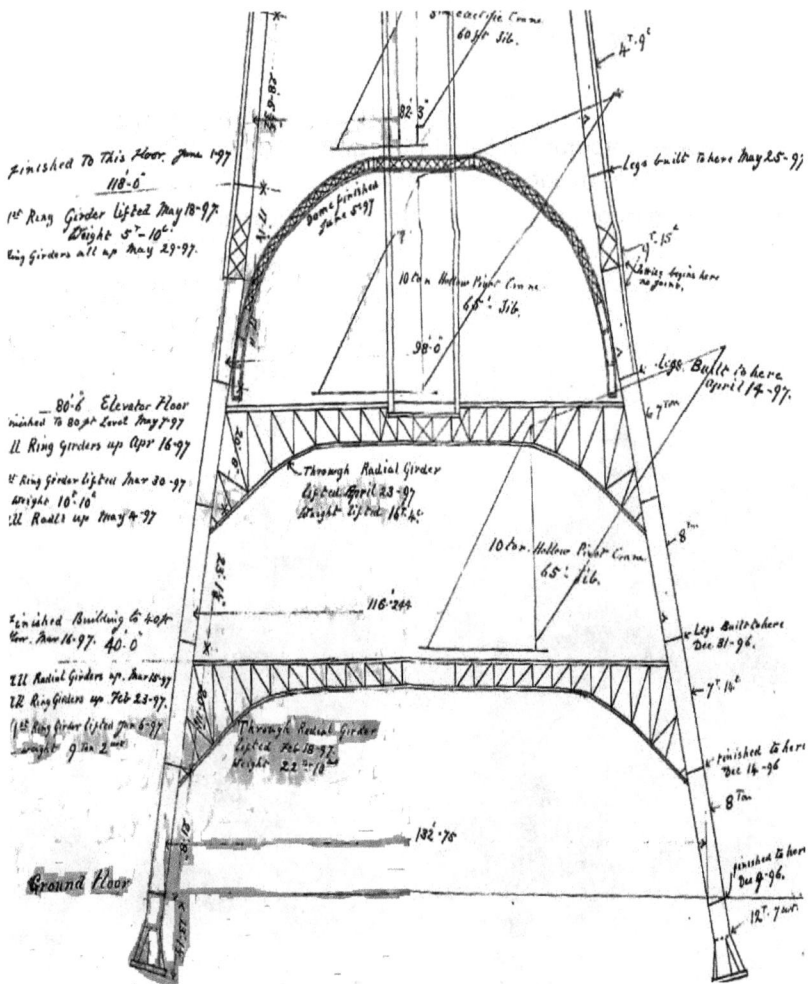

614. Jan 13 - 97. Fallen girder from entrance of arena

The above photograph is dated 13th January 1897.
"Fallen girder from entrance of arena."
Below Broken Hook , and platform from were the men fell.

E. Jan 13 - 97. Fallen girder from north. Legs D & E

The Fatality at New Brighton Tower

Mr Churton, coroner for Birkenhead opened an inquest yesterday at the New Brighton Hotel on the bodies of Alexander Stewart 21 years of age, belonging to Derby, and John Richardson 45, who hailed from Cardiff, and who were killed on Wednesday at the New Brighton Eiffel Tower works by the collapse of a crane hook on which was suspended an iron girder weighing about nine tons. The girder had been raised to a height of nearly fifty feet, and was being placed in position between the upright leg or pillars of the Tower, when the hook snapped. In its fall the girder carried away positions of the platform on which the deceased men and others were working, Stewart and Richardson were thrown down a distance of 35 feet, and fell upon the iron girder obtaining injuries which caused instant death. When the jury had assembled the coroner was handed a telegram from the Government Inspector of factories, Mr Richmond requesting information about the inquiry. Inspector Bowyer stated that the police had not communicated with the Government inspector, and the coroner then informed the jury that it was necessary the Government representative should be present, and in order that he might attend the inquest it would have to be adjourned to some day which would be convenient for him to do so. The jury then proceeded to view the bodies of the deceased men and the scene of the accident. Also John Daly, who lies in the Seacombe Cottage Hospital suffering from injuries sustained in the accident.

The Cheshire Coroner and his Duties - Extraordinary incident

Mr Henry Churton West Cheshire coroner, who is a very old gentleman, remarked that he was unable to go upstairs to view the bodies, being held in a room in the mens lodgings in Seymour street. The coffins had to be removed downstairs. More controversy followed when it was found that the deaths had not been recorded as an industrial accident.

7. Fallen girder from North.

The Liverpool Courier
January 16th, 1897

19

Appalling Fatality at the Tower
A man smashed to Atoms

Another appalling fatality took place on Tuesday evening last at the Tower Works, New Brighton, the cause of which was an accident whereby a young labourer, named John Jackson, fell from near the top of the tower to the earth, and was literally smashed to a pulp.

The Inquest was held by Mr Bates, at the Boathouse Hotel, Magazines on Thursday. Mr William Buchan, H.M.Inspector of factories: and Inspector Bowyer were in attendance as was also Mr. Ashley representing the Tower Co. Harry Savory, the first witness stated that he was one of the foreman at the Tower works, and Jackson, who was a labourer of 32 years of age, belonged to his gang. On Tuesday evening, at 7-30, when at work on the top stage of the Tower, he sent the deceased down to the 80-ft level to sling out to the road a piece of timber, which the men had been working on and had carried over the lift hole. He wanted the timber moving from over the lift, so that they might lift the next girder up. After giving the order, he did not see the deceased again, and, looking down the hole, the timber was still there, but the man was missing. He then sent another man to see about it, thinking that the deceased must have misunderstood him, but the next moment he received a telephone message saying that Jackson had fallen to the bottom.

Deceased, whose usual occupation was that of an ironworker, had been employed on the Tower from the start, but had been absent a few weeks ago owing to his ribs having been fractured by a kick. He (deceased) was quite used to the work and would go anywhere on the structure. He was the last man one would expect to fall, as he was always the first to be at the top. He was quite sober at the time.

The Coroner: Could you suggest anything which could prevent such accidents?- Witness: No, I really could not.

Do you think it would be practicable to sling a net underneath the men? That would not do any good, and a net could have no hold at all to prevent such an accident as this one.

It would not be possible to have one?: No sir.

The Foreman (Mr.F.Storey): Would a lift be possible?

Witness: There is a lift, but the ironwork has to go straight through the floors. The deceased had very bad boots on with the sole half hanging off one, and he had to borrow a knife to cut a piece of leather away.

The Foreman: I want to know about the lift - if it would not be more convenient and calculated to save life if there was a lift for the men to go up and down in, instead of the ladders? - There is a lift now.

How did the deceased go down?- He went down the ladders. The lift is not at work; it is not quite finished yet as they can't work it until they get to a certain height.

20

There is another thing-the hours he had worked that day; how many where they! - He had started at six in the morning. And it was seven when he stopped? - Yes half past seven. We have three shifts: one goes on at 3-30 and works till 8-30 in the afternoon; another goes on at 8 and works until 9 at night, and the ordinary one goes on at 6 and knocks off at 5-30, Deceased was in the ordinary shift, but had been working 2 1/2 hours overtime on Tuesday night.

The Coroner: Is it compulsory? - Oh, no! the men will simply ask me to let them work late to make the money up.

The Foreman: Deceased was working 13 1/2 hours.

A juror : Is there any protection on the ladders? - No, there is not ,but he didn't fall from the ladder.

The next witness, William Lee, labourer, stated that he was, on Tuesday evening working on the first floor when he heard the rattle of chain.

He looked up and saw Jackson in the act of falling backwards over a girder, over which he turned a somersault and fell face forward, striking another before he reached the ground. He didn't think deceased was careless.

The Coroner: He was not venturesome? Well, were all venturesome after a fashion. It is the nature of the occupation, I suppose; and deceased was one of the most venturesome? - Yes.

Would it be possible to protect the man when working? - Not more than has been done.

The Foreman: Did you work the same number of hours as deceased? Witness: Yes, sir.

Do you consider such hours right, when working at such a height? - Will the men have privilege of knocking off if they like: it is for their own choice.

Do you think a man having worked so long, is in a position to safeguard his life, just as if he had worked the ordinary hours-what are the ordinary hours?-Ten hours a day.

Do you think a man working 13 1/2 hours, is in as good a position to safeguard his life as one who has only worked 10? - I think I am.

We have so much time allowed for tea.

Witness added that he did not know from what height Jackson fell, and that he thought when he saw him falling over the girder, that it was a bag tumbling down.

Mr Ashley, on behalf of the Company. Observed that the 13 hours included a half hour for breakfast, and an hour for dinner.

Mr William Stuart who represented the contractors at the grounds said this had been the first accident of its kind since the worked started.

The Coroner: Would it be possible to protect the men working in other parts of the Tower besides the lift hole? - We do as far we can.

There is plenty of stage, and for all outside work we have scaffolding and a platform travelling round each leg.

Have you had any complaints? - None, I always tell the men if the stage is not right, for them to have it made right, and all my foreman are instructed to this effect.

It has been suggested that a net should be placed under the place where the men are working?-

It would not be practicable because we could not put a net on the lift hole. Would it be possible to put it in another position?- The other position are well staged.

The only danger in the Tower are the lift holes, and the outside position?- Yes, but the outside stages are railed around.

And nothing has suggested itself to you for the better preservation of life than what you have done?- Nothing at all.

The Foreman: We don't want to interfere with the practice, but there have already been three lives lost, and it behoves the jury to take steps to prevent further accidents.

A Juror: Did you see the torn shoe referred to? - Witness: Yes, and I should think it tripped the deceased and caused the accident.

The Foreman: Do you think a man engaged for the length of time spoken of at this work is safe? - Yes I think it is perfectly safe: and of course the overtime is not compulsory.

You would not threaten to discharge a man because he did not work overtime?- No; not at all. We have never discharged a man for that.

The Coroner: That appears to be all the evidence. There is no doubt that you will bring in a verdict that the deceased was accidentally killed, but there is the consideration whether you could make any suggestion to the contractor or the Company for the protection of life.

When considering that, you will have to be very careful what you do, as it is but an easy thing to instruct a firm of contractors for they certainly know their business better than you can, and therefore, whatever suggestions you make must be practicable. I don't think that, in this case anything could have been done to save the man's life. He appears to have fallen down what is used as a hoist, and it would be impossible to protect that. The other places are all closely planked across, and be could not fall in any other place, except down the lift hole, when he must, of necessity, fall to the bottom.

After consideration, the jury agreed that the death was purely accidental, and that no one was to blame. They added the opinion that the accident was very probably brought about by the broken sole of the man's boot.

Complaint about the Mortuary.

The Foreman said the jury also wished to refer to the mortuary there.

It was in a bad sanitary condition and had neither light nor water; and he believed the want of these two elements made it inconvenient for the police and others, who had to take bodies there.

The Coroner observed that the building had to be used occasionally for post-mortem examinations, which could only be conducted with great difficulty in a place without light and water; and besides this a good many of the jury had complained of the smell of the place. Inspector Bowyer stated that he had reported the matter previously to the District Council, but no remedy had been applied up to now.

The Wallasey Times July 31, 1897

The drawing above shows the construction used to cover the excavated hole in the centre of the site.

Work continued at a pace with the following notes worthy of mention:

Dec 22 - On moving the crane between E&F bottom casting cracked, clips of 2x1" iron made to go around it.

Jan 20 - Fallen girder all cut up and sent away to Derby.

Jan 26 - Snowed all day work stopped.

Feb 24 - Use of steam winch much quicker than by hand.

Mar 10 - Radial girder F was being built up. 10 ton crane put up at 40ft level opposite leg A.

Mar 11- The connection of radial F, which had been bent by falling, were made hot and straightened.

Mar 23 - Ring girder (80ft) C/D built complete.

Apr 8 - Riveting 80ft ring girders 2 sets & Leg C at 40 ft., using 10 ton crane.

Apr 10 - Moving 10 ton crane No 2 by hand and fixed. 80 men now working on job. All 80 ft ring girders riveted ready for lifting.

Apr 16 - Good Friday working as usual. No riveters turned up.

Apr 17 - No riveting. The number of men now employed on the job are: exclusive engineering staff 4 week paid, with 93 time paid. The hours worked as follows:

One gang comes on   4:30 am to 4:00 pm
        Breakfast   8:30 - 9:00   Dinner 1 to 2
Other gang comes on 8:30 am to 8:00 pm
        Breakfast first   Dinner 12 to 1

Apr 23 - A/E lifted by means of two 10 ton cranes one at each end.

Apr 26 - Hours of working:

        Early gang 4 am to 8 am, 8:30 am to 12:00, 1pm to 3:30 pm

        Late gang   8 am to 1 pm   2pm to 8.0 pm

        Paid - time and a half before 6 am

        Paid - time and a quarter after 5:30 pm

May 7 - Legs B6, A6 & C6 lifted by means of 10 ton crane.

        No1 & Steam winch used total weight 9 Ton 8 cwt.

May 8 - Waiting for 118 ft ring girders, work stopped at 12 noon.

May 12 - Very windy. All the bracing of ring girders cut to size.

May 21- 118 ft ring girder H/A lifted with crane.

        This girder was riveted complete by 3 sets in 9 to 10 hours.

        The riveters were paid £1 a hundred 7/8 rivets.

June 3 - Work stopped on account of rain.

June 4 - Building Dome.

June 7-8 Holidays nothing done.

June 10 - Lift guide finished. Timbering top of dome for electric crane.

        The lift guards were riveted on the ground in one piece.

June 12 - The hours worked as follows:

        Early gang 3 am to 8 am , 8:30 am to 1pm. 2pm to 3pm.

        Late gang 8 am to 12 noon. 1pm to 8:30pm.

        No of men employed =   63 time paid

                       5 sets Riveters & 6 week paid men

June 16 - Very wet & windy. No riveting done, very little work of any kind.

June 17 - Still windy. No riveters out. 1st floor Metz. floor with

        30 cwt crane standing on 40ft floor.

June 18 - Still very wet and windy. Nothing done.

June 19 - Riveting 40ft 1 set, 60ft 1 set & 80ft 1 set. Building Ellipticals.

June 22 - Jubilee day no work done.

June 23 - Finishing gutters around dome. Electric crane working 2 legs lifted No7 weigh 4 ton 15cwt each. Works easily 110 volts about 50 amps.

The last entry in the note book dated the 24th June followed by a newspaper cutting of the accident on the 31st July 1897.

Probably Mr Weller produced more than one volume of notes but the others are missing. I feel privileged that we can have an insight into the building of this fantastic structure.

Throughout the notes each day describes in detail the installation of each section. The legs numbered A to H. The movement of cranes between the different levels. Then each prefabricated boxed section has a number. Special attention was paid to the hours worked. The labour force worked a six day week, Sunday a day of rest. The working day was a minimum of 12 hours, with overtime on top. Long hours of work the weather and lack of safety equipment all contributed to a high accident rate. With no health and safety considerations. Speed was of the essence.

The Tower Fatality
Proceeding at Inquest.
The foreman and life saving appliances.

On Saturday morning, at the New Brighton Hotel, Victoria Road the coroner for West Cheshire Mr J.C. Bate held an inquiry in the circumstances attending the death of Thomas McGrant, aged 36, of 16 Richmond Street, New Brighton. Mr William Buchan Inspector of factories was in attendance. Mr Francis Storey D.C. was appointed foreman of the Jury. Mrs McGrath, mother of the deceased, living at 69, John Street, Derbys stated that her son had been a riveter for twenty years during which time he had always been sober and steady, and sound in health.

Joseph Clarke stated that he was a riveter employed at the New Brighton Tower. On Thursday last he was working with the deceased on the girder immediately below the 80 foot platform.

They riveted one side, then moved their stage and commenced to work at the opposite side. They had put in a number of rivets on this side, when the work was delayed for a few minutes, whilst another workman was dispatched for a new strap to continue the riveting. During this time the deceased, taking with him a hammer, made his way from the scaffold to the side they had completed. Witness saw him reel over the plank and fall backwards. Witness could see no reason why he should have gone; he had examined the side the same afternoon and as far as he knew the deceased had no occasion to leave the stage.

He did not hear the hammer being used.

Witness could not say whether his foot slipped. Deceased was not a "venturesome" man. He was always careful.

The Coroner; I believe the place on which you were working was practically over the lift hole? - We were working near the lift hole.

Could you form any idea as to how he came to fall? - He must have overbalanced. That is all I can make it out to be.

Did he fall directly to the ground? - He caught against the first floor and then bounced off that onto the ground.

Was he dead when you went down? - I went down immediately. He was close on dead then.

Mr Buchan: Is anything you can suggest which might have prevented this accident?

- I don't think it could have been prevented.

The Foreman of the jury: Did he fall through the lift hole? - Yes.

Was there no foreman in charge of the gang?- There were three of us working together, but the foreman was up above at the time.

By a Juror: He walked back on a plank. He did not walk on a girder.

The Foreman: Were his boots all right? - Witness: I didn't notice.

The Foreman explained that the reason of his question was that the cause of the previous accident was said to have been the unsound state of the boots worn by the victim.

William Stewart stated he had charge of the work at the Tower, on behalf of the contractors. The foreman of the riveters would have four gangs of workmen to look after that morning. Witness had examined the place from which the deceased fell before any alterations were affected. He could not say why the deceased went across to the side he had been working on.

Mr Buchan: If the snap was bad would not rivets on that side be rather rough?- Witness: The snap goes suddenly sometimes. I think that is what must have happened. I think that if it was a bad snap and it was wrong when they were at the first end of the girder, they would have changed it when they were moving the stage.

Witness: had never seen netting used in such work. To prevent accident there was nothing better than giving the men plenty of scaffolding to work on, and that was what they did at the Tower.

The Foreman: In view of the number of lives lost, does nothing suggest itself to you by which the accidents might be prevented?- We do all we can.

Foremen: Who was to see that everything is right. Deceased was the leading man of the gang, thoroughly trustworthy, and not likely to make mistakes. We do all in our power to secure the men's safety. In some instances where men are working at a great height they have ropes attached to them. Would not that be a good thing? If we tried that, I am afraid the men would he oftener without than with the ropes.

Would it be practicable? - No, I don't think so, because the men have so much running about to do.

I understand the system is employed in the work of the Dock board?- Well, I have never heard of it and have not seen it.

The Foreman: Well, it could be made compulsory. This loss of life is a dreadful thing, and if the accidents continue, it will be a kind of perpetual nightmare to the people.

The Coroner thought that in the instances the foreman had referred to, the men would be fixed at one stage. But in this case where the men were continually going up and down, he did not think the system would be practicable.

Witness: the riveters would find it very cumbersome.

The Foreman: It would be better for him to make his life safe.

At this stage the boots worn by the deceased at the time of the fatality were produced. They were very much worn, half the sole of the right boot being completely gone.

A Juror: Those are not fit to work in on the Tower.

The Coroner (addressing the jury): I think you will have no doubt in saying that the deceased was killed accidentally. But I do not know whether you will think it advisable to add anything to your verdict. At the inquest held a fortnight ago the same questions were raised as have been today. I think it would be almost impossible to devise any scheme that would entirely protect a man at this work. It appears from observations of the Tower that a man might be in a position a hundreds times in a day in which if he made a false step he would be killed, and seeing that this is the case it appears to me that accidents of this kind are simply the results of a dangerous occupation, and hard to avoid. But if you have any scheme or recommendation to make to the contractors I am sure they will be very willing to fall in with the suggestion if it can be carried out.

Evidence was then given by Henry Thomas White, resident engineer at the Tower. Who did not think either nets or ropes would be feasible as they were lifting things all over the Tower.

The jury returned a verdict of 'Accidental death.' In announcing the decision, the Foreman and the jury were pleased to learn that attention was being directed to the boots of the workmen, and hoped this would continue as it might be the means of preventing a further fall, Mr Stewart intimated that the matter should have his closest attention.

Wallasey Times, August 21, 1897

Showing Ring Girders
in postion- 19 Jan 1897

Taken Jan 19.97. From SE. shewing 3,40 ft Ring Girders in place.

27

Apr 2. 97. From moveable stage on Leg B. Shewing stages on Legs A & H

Above: April 2nd 1897. Showing the staging on Legs A & H. The pier can be seen in the distance.

Below: April 30th 1897. From S.W Tower built up to 80ft all but two Radial girders on 40 ft. Ready to be lifted

April 1897 - June 1897 Tower Construction

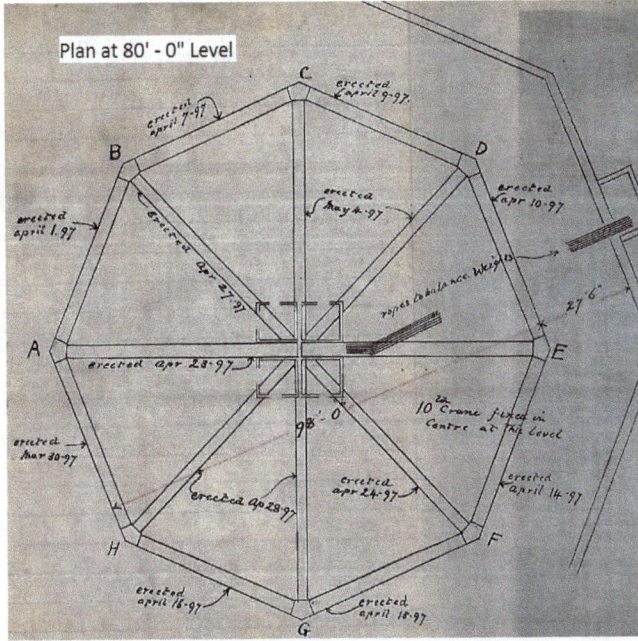

Plan at 80' - 0" Level

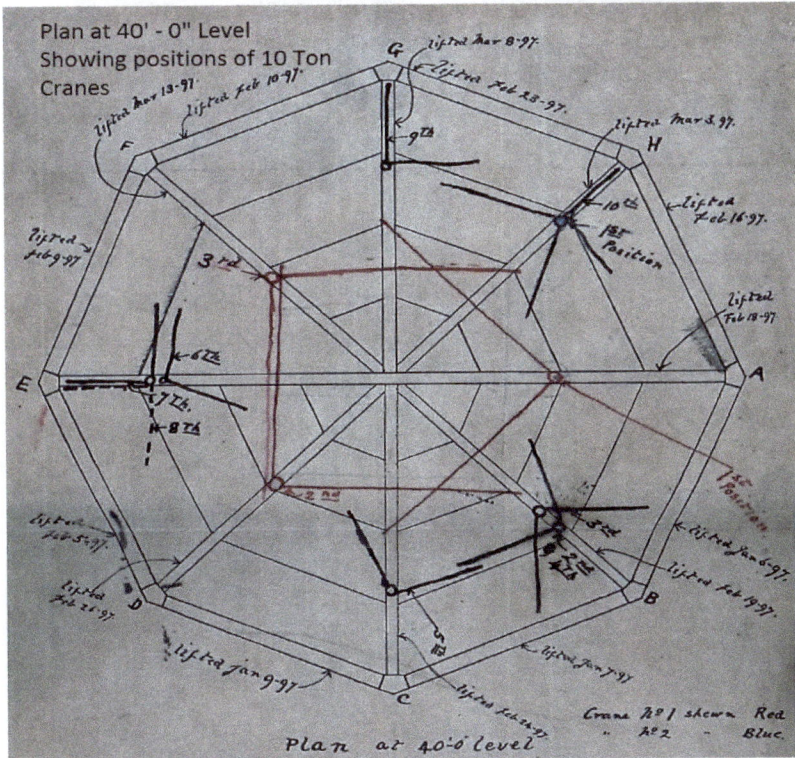

Plan at 40' - 0" Level
Showing positions of 10 Ton
Cranes

Plan at 40'-0 level

Crane no 1 shewn Red
  " no 2 " Blue.

Top: April 30th - From West looking across lake, 80ft Radials put in place.
Bottom: May 26th -From S. W Legs built up to 118ft, Four guiders in place.
Opposite Top: No date construction shown looking across the race track.
Opposite Bottom: No date construction shown outside Managers Office.

April 1897 - June 1897 Tower Construction

31

The sea wall and promenade from Holland Road are still to be built

Before the Tower was completed a decision was made to open the grounds for the Whitsuntide holidays. The gardens covered 25 acres, with many attractions and live acts dotted around the complex. With a large Japanese Cafe next to the lake, where Venetian Gondolas could be viewed sailing past. A seal pond in the old quarry, with an alpine rockery. An up market restaurant called 'The Rock Point Castle', situated in the wooded area close to the promenade. With an outdoor dancing platform which could hold over a thousand dancers music supplied by Military Band's, and above a high wire for tight-rope walking, with no safety net. Then there was the Old English Fairground on the higher level were the start of the water chute was located, in later years, it became the motor coach park. The Himalayan Switchback Railway was in high demand and a firm favourite.

THE ERA

OPENING OF THE
NEW BRIGHTON TOWER GROUNDS.
WHITSUNTIDE HOLIDAYS.

MEISTER GLEE SINGERS

LAVATER LEE

The COLIBRIS MIDGETS

RANDY AND DANDY

THE LORENZ SVENGALI TRIO
MIMICRY, MUSIC, and MYSTERY.

MARCELINE

Miss Marie Finney

Mr. JAMES FINNEY

Robertus

TWICE DAILY AT 2 AND 8

21 FOR

OPENING OF THE
NEW BRIGHTON TOWER GROUNDS.
WHITSUNTIDE HOLIDAYS.

AMATEUR CYCLE RACES.   FLAT RACING.

£150 IN PRIZES.

On WHIT-MONDAY and TUESDAY.

N. C. U. CHAMPIONSHIP ON MONDAY.

Old English Fair Grounds,	Quinette's Grand Circus,
Grand Water Chute into Lake,	Switchback,
Japanese Tea House,	Animated Photographs,
Wonderful Japanese Performers.	

DANCING PLATFORM. MAGNIFICENT BAND.

ILLUMINATIONS AND A THOUSAND OTHER HOLIDAY ATTRACTIONS.

Through Tickets, including Admission, from all Railway Stations.   15177G

The Tower Grounds opened on Whit Monday 7th June 1897, although the Tower itself was not completed. The General Manager Mr John Hollingshed had been under pressure to locate suitable acts for the Grand opening. He was a successful theatrical impresario, Hollingshead managed the Alhambra Theatre and was later the first manager of the Gaiety Theatre, London. During his tenure at the Alhambra, Hollingshead introduced London audiences to the Can-Can. Burlesque and risqué operettas were the normal fare at the Gaiety. Hollingshead called himself a "licensed dealer in legs, short skirts". Some impressive acts had been booked for the opening. James Hardy, a Canadian tightrope walker, who had walked across Niagara Falls. Only this time his task was walking over the heads of spectator's gathered on the open air dancing platform, whilst cooking a pancake on the high wire. With adverts placed in all the local newspapers "See his wonderful tricks on the high wire, at 130 feet above the ground. The management are now providing - The Greatest Sight on Earth"

An ensemble of natives from Mandalay in Burma had been shipped in along with bamboo huts to make up a village, accompanied by a Burmese Princess. The Victorian fascination with "circus freak" shows had developed a taste for the exotic. With Quinette's Grand Circus, several excellent performances were given during the day. Other circus acts of interest included Chiyokichis the Japanese high bamboo performers, and Theo the Ladder King. In addition there are switchbacks and swings, and in the evening the grounds, are lighted up with innumerable fairy and electric lights, which present a most enchanting appearance.

A grand Water Chute into a Lake, a Japanese tea house. And don't forget the Amateur Cycle Races with £150 in prizes. The cycle track is surrounded by a splendid cinder path for foot racing, and forming the centre a magnificent football ground, leased by the New Brighton Tower Football Club, Limited.

Important Notice.
New Brighton Tower Company, Cheshire.
General Manager, JOHN HOLLINGSHEAD.
Opening of Athletic Grounds and Dancing Platform, Whit Monday, June 7th. Two Full Orchestras. Twenty-five Acres, Wooded Grounds. Sea and River View. Summer Season, June 7th to Oct. 15th Sports to follow. Attractions in Preparation :—Eiffel Tower, the highest out of Paris; Cycle Track, with Sea View, the Largest in the World; Running Track; Theatre and Circus, seat 3,000; Ball-room for 3,000 Dancers; Lake, Water Chute, Fair Grounds, Menagerie, Club, &c.
WANTED, Large Open-Air Attractions. Acrobatic and Athletic. Small Things no good.
Wanted, to Buy, Two Band Kiosks, to Seat Forty-two Men each.
Wanted, Big Fair Attractions of all Kinds.
New Brighton Tower and Grounds,
JOHN HOLLINGSHEAD,
General Manager.
Letters answered promptly. If not, the usual

A Burmese Princess.

Special, costly, and important engagement, direct from Japan, of the

CHIYOKICHIS,

Slack Rope, Swinging Bamboo, Sword Walking extraordinary.

Real Native Male and Female Japanese Performers! Their first appearance in this town. Marvellous Performance on a Perpendicular Rope fixed 30 feet high.

ATANELLO,

The India-Rubber Demon! The man of 1,000 forms! The Boneless being of Bohemia! Truly a wonder.

NELLIE & ROSE,

Character Duettists and Song and Dance Artistes.

MISS ROSE ALLAN,

The favourite Balladist and Burlesque Actress.

[Webb, Photo.]   The Water Chute.

WATERCHUTE TOWER GARDENS.

SCENIC RAILWAY
NEW BRIGHTON.

NEW BRIGHTON TOWER. - OPENING ARRANGEMENTS.

By the opening of the New Brighton Tower Grounds, which will take place on Monday, the most, complete pleasure and recreation resort in the north of England if not the whole country will be placed at the disposal of the public. Much indeed remains to be done before the grounds or the tower itself are completed, but sufficient progress has been made with the undertaking to enable one to form a judgment of the enterprise as a whole, and to justify the management in fixing, upon Whit Monday as the opening day. Although the main essential of the scheme-the tower-has been erected to only about a quarter of its height, namely, 150 out of 600 feet, the portion constructed already forms the dominating feature in the scenery at the mouth of the Mersey, and its bold and massive proportions may be seen for miles around.

With £300,000 at its back the company which is constructing the tower is proceeding with the work in no niggardly or uncertain fashion. Since the original site was purchased further plots of the adjoining land have been secured, and the extent of the grounds now covers an area of over 25 acres. The site, when purchased by the company, was one of the prettiest, well-wooded estates in the district, end although it was found necessary to cut down some 300 trees and saplings, sufficient timber remains to give to the grounds a charming rural aspect. Under the energetic superintendence of Messrs. Maxwell and Tuke, the architects, and Mr. John Hollingshead, the manager, the work is being pushed on with extraordinary rapidity. The tower has reached the second storey, and will soon be available both for dancing and theatrical and circus performances.

The basement will be utilised as a, theatre or a circus, capable of seating 3000 people, and above the circus, will he placed the great ballroom, in which 4000 dancers may find space to enjoy their pastime. The roof of the ballroom will be formed into a beautiful promenade garden, from which magnificent views of the surrounding country may be obtained. These attractions, it will be understood, will not be immediately available, but the management have prepared a list of attractive features, which will, no doubt, prove sufficiently alluring to procure a liberal share of Whit Week holiday patronage. A large pond which stood in the grounds has been enlarged and deepened, and now forms one of the prettiest miniature lakes in the neighbourhood. Running into the lake there has been constructed a water chute, and visitors will be enabled to partake of an excitement akin to that enjoyed in the process of shooting the rapids.

Liverpool Mercury - Saturday 05 June 1897

A dancing platform has been constructed, with an area of 14,000 square feet, so that given fine weather, those partial to this amusement will be able to indulge in the enjoyment of it in the open air, free from the stuffiness of a crowded dancing hall. A carefully selected orchestra, under the conductor-ship of Mr. Granville Bantock, will give two concerts daily. A switchback railway has not, been omitted from the list of amusements, and on the pleasure and recreation ground, between the lake and the athletic grounds, various amusements will be provided, including a, circus, cinematograph, Japanese performers. &c. The athletic sports, on the cycle and running grounds, will form a principal feature of the days amusements on Monday and Tuesday next. Unfortunately the running track, owing to its newness, has not met with the approval of the N.C.A.A and consequently the directors have decided to augment Monday's programme by giving three handsome prizes in the 20 mile invitation race. Numerous invitations have been issued, and a good race between the best of the northern cyclists will, no doubt, be as satisfactory to the sport-loving public as the events which have been prescribed. The entries for the events on Tuesday are quite enough to occupy the whole of the afternoon. It may be added that the cement cycle track, three laps to the mile, is quite completed, and forms one of the best of its kind in the country. The arcade under the east end of the cycle track will be turned into a bazaar with various side shows. In the evening the grounds will be lighted with electricity and by 10,000 Vauxhall lamps. Among the future attractions promised are a high-wire contest from the 150-feet tower level, baseball matches between American ladies, glove contests between American champions, and Greek and Turkish wrestlers.

The Japanesse
Tea House

The Grand Stand in the
Athletic Grounds

New Brighton certainly required some sophistication with its brash and vulgar 'Ham-and-Egg' parade of side-shows, cafés and boarding houses, it was an up and coming resort seeking to emulate Blackpool's success.

In 1897 Granville Bantock became conductor at The Tower in New Brighton. The appointment was to prove a turning point in his life.

On a personal level he married a beautiful artist and poetess, Helena von Schweitzer, on 9th March 1898. The couple set up home at Liscard overlooking the Mersey. The Photograph with the couple's eldest sons, Angus and Raymond, taken in the garden at Holly Mount, Liscard on the Wirral.

When he arrived at New Brighton the Tower was incomplete but nevertheless, he was expected to conduct in the large ballroom at its base, which was also used for Liverpool Orchestral Society concerts. Some of the great soloists of the day were to be heard there.

At his disposal, a 33-piece military band whose chief function was to provide dance music in the evenings and during the day. With concerts in the open air alongside, a menagerie a fairground and tight-rope exhibitions by Blondin, and not to forget the numerous exhibitions of foreign and exotic cultures. Dancing at the Tower Ballroom had become so popular that the authorities sought a Musical Director. By the time Bantock reached his new post he was already a composer with a number of successful works and performances to his credit. A man of exceptionally wide culture, boundless curiosity, and unlimited energy, Bantock was a composer of works that were not only on the largest scale, but also heroic and exotic in theme.

Music for the evening dancers included the usual waltzes, polkas, gallops and marches whilst in the open air, Sousa and Suppé provided the fare.

Bantock carried out his duties conscientiously, providing music for five or six hours each day but he had ambitions beyond dance music. He had ambitions for British Music and a better class of audience, so he was pleased to find that he had a band of accomplished musicians who worked with him enthusiastically. The personnel of the dance band in the evenings were identical to his open air military band. Bantock's miracle was truly amazing he turned a municipal band into a first rate orchestra for serious modern classical music.

He soon set about trying to convince the authorities that good music would benefit the resort and suggested improved and extended programmes. The directors took a look warm response to his suggestions but Bantock was already using afternoon rehearsal time to practice more serious music.

Within a year of his appointment, and with the assistance of Mr. de Ybarrondo, a sympathetic member of the tower board of directors, a full orchestra of about 60 players was assembled and Bantock was conducting regular Sunday concerts at which he presented works by all the great composers whilst still conducting the dance band every evening from 7.30-10.00, offering a wider choice of programme. New Brighton quickly began to acquire a nation-wide reputation as a centre of pioneering musical excellence, visited by some of the major composers and performers of the day. In late 1898 he formed the New Brighton Choral Society, to augment the musical compositions. The subscription for 18 Sunday afternoon concerts was 10s. 6d.

He went on to arrange special Friday concerts with his full orchestra, the programmes always including a full symphony. There were Beethoven and Mozart symphonies, Dvorak's New World, Tchaikowsky's Pathétique and Rubinstein's huge, seven movement Ocean Symphony.

Having had such good audiences for the symphony concerts, it seems that it was not too difficult for Bantock, supported yet again by Mr de Ybarrondo, to persuade the directors to allow a further series of concerts and by 1899 his plans to include music of living British composers started to come to fruition.

Sir Frederick Cowen was invited to conduct a concert of his own works on 28 May 1899 and Stanford came to New Brighton on 25 June for the same reason. They were soon to be followed by Parry (9 July), Elgar (16 July), Corder (23 July), Wallace (30 July), German (20 Aug) and Mackenzie (3 Sept). William Wallace conducted the first performance of his Symphony, 'The Creation' and Bantock presented an all-British concert, a Tchaikowsky concert and a Liszt concert.

Edward Elgar came on the 14th July 1899, to attend the first performance of his "Minuet" In a series devoted to modern English composers and their work. Edward and Alice stayed with Bantock and his young wife Helena.

When Edward felt unwell with a slight chill, Helena wrote: Edgar was somewhat delicate and many arrangements were necessary for his comfort. Edgar's wife Alice was absolutely devoted to him and surrounded her husband with a ring-fence of attention and care that was pathetic...I am sure, awed by Mrs Elgar, with her array of rugs, shawls and cushions, extra body-belts and knitted bed socks for Edward's comfort. One evening Helena noted with astonishment no less than seven hot water bottles being filled for his bed, on occasion of Elgar complaining of a chill. He did manage to conduct the orchestra on the 16th July.

The size of the orchestra increased for important events and with assistance from Vasco V. Ackeroyd of the Liverpool Philharmonic, Bantock had somewhere near 100 players at his disposal. The wind, brass and percussion came from the permanent Tower Band and were professionals. The string section included some amateur players. Despite this, it was reported that the ensemble was excellent. Nevertheless, the tower management committee were no longer sympathetic to Bantock's cause and after the resignation of Mr de Ybarrondo, who had been such a strong supporter of the orchestral concerts, his good work came to an end.

The fact that Bantock had managed to achieve so much at New Brighton in only three years, and at a price that visitors could afford, is remarkable. A sixpenny admission ticket to the tower grounds included admission to the gallery. Those paying a further sixpence could reserve a seat and half a guinea could buy a season ticket for a series of eighteen Sunday concerts.

Contributions to music continued in various forms after Bantock's exit but none measured up to his monumental effort. In 1900 he moved to the Birmingham and Midland Institute as Principal conductor.

Ref: Bantock At New Brighton By Stuart Scott
https://en.wikipedia.org/wiki/Granville_Bantock programme.

NEW BRIGHTON TOWER.

REFUSAL OF A DRINK LICENSE.

At the Wallasey Petty Sessions, yesterday, before Alderman James Smith, Messrs. R. W. Preston, F. Johnston, T. R. Bulley, F. Pooley, J. Joyce, and Dr. Bell, an application was made by Mr. Pugh (instructed by Messrs. Thompson, Hughes, and Mathieson), on behalf of Mr. Roll-wagen, of the Albion Hotel, New Brighton, for a license to sell intoxicating liquors for six days during the Whitsuntide holidays at the New Brighton Tower Grounds. Mr. Pugh explained that the places proposed to be licensed were the Japanese tearoom and other buildings where meals would be served, and a first and second class bar underneath the grand stand. He added that the capital invested in the tower and grounds was over £300,000.—Evidence was given in support of the application by Mr. John Hollingshead, the manager, and others, and no opposition was offered.—Mr. Pugh also applied on behalf of Mr. Hollingshead for a music and dancing license to the Tower Grounds.—Mr. Hollingshead and the architect for the undertaking (Mr. Maxwell) stated that an open-air dancing plat-form had been erected capable of accommo-dating 800 or 1000 people.—Alderman Smith inquired whether any certificate had been received from the Urban District Council as to the safety of the structure. — Mr. Pugh replied that such a certificate had not been procured, but they would get one if the application was adjourned.—Mr. Maxwell ex-plained that the stage was practically erected on solid ground, and it was in every sense safe.—The bench then retired, and on returning into court the Chairman said that the application for a drink license was refused, but with regard to the other matter they would adjourn that till Friday morn-ing. The chairman suggested to Mr. Danger, the clerk to the district council, who was in court, that that authority should in the meantime get some competent person to inspect the platform and certify as to its safety.

DAVID NICHOLSON'S

LIQUID BREAD

A PURE MALT EXTRACT

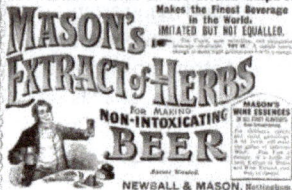

The Favourite Drink of the British Empire.

MASON'S EXTRACT of HERBS

Makes the Finest Beverage in the World.

IMITATED BUT NOT EQUALLED.

FOR MAKING NON-INTOXICATING BEER

NEWBALL & MASON, Nottingham.

H. CLAUSEN AND SON BREWING CO.

PHOENIX BOTTLING CO.

NEW BRIGHTON TOWER
GARDENS.

OPEN DAILY.

Old English Fair Grounds.
Japanese Tea House.
Animated Photographs.
Dancing Platform.
Quinette's Grand Circus.

Switchback.
Wonderful Japanese Performers.
Magnificent Band.
Grand Water Chute.

ON WEDNESDAY NEXT, JUNE 16,
The LIVERPOOL WHEELERS will hold their Meeting on Athletic Grounds.
20 Miles Handicap at 7 p.m.
Special Prize for Track Record.

ON SATURDAY NEXT, JUNE 19,
GRAND COMMEMORATION ATHLETIC SPORTS,
Under A.A.A. Laws and N.C.U. Rules.

£120 IN PRIZES.

Illuminations at Dusk.
1000 Electric Lights.
10,000 Lamps.

Sports commence at 2 p.m.
Admission by Molyneux-drive Entrance.
Prices 6d. to 2s.

QUINETTE'S Circus. -The well-arranged programme includes the Brothers Leonard, gymnasts, &c.; Mr H. Yelding, jockey and scene-act rider; the Levon troupe of acrobats, Little Hurst, clown; Madame La Place, on the rolling globe; Mons. and Madame Monti, clever and novel juggler; the Sisters Alma, on the tight-wire. Mr Yelding's jockey act, which followed, was extremely dashing. Not only did he perform the feats usually included in a "turn" of this sort, but he also threw a somersault off the horse backwards whilst going at speed, regaining a standing position by a similar feat. The audience's keen appreciation of Mr Yelding's efforts was shown by several rounds of cheering which summoned him back to the ring. A party of mounted ladies in jockey caps and jackets then went through the intricate evolutions of a manoeuvre à cheval; and a comic sketch entitled Mr and Mrs Brown's Visit to the Circus, in which an elderly lady and gentleman and their boy Billy come from amongst the audience and insist upon taking a riding lesson, and are allowed to do so with screamingly absurd results, concluded a programme which was capitally arranged, briskly carried out, and warmly received.'

The medallion was issued by the New Brighton Tower Company on 7th June 1897, to commemorate Victoria's Diamond Jubilee.

July 1897 - Programme

The New Brighton - TOWER GARDENS.
The enterprising company which has already made the New Brighton Tower
Grounds so popular, not only with residents in the immediate neighbourhood of
Liverpool, but also in towns farther afield, are sparing no efforts to push on with
the improvements in progress, and are making the most of the facilities already
at hand. Even at 'the present time the natural beauties of the ground and its
commanding position are such as to make it one of the most pleasant spots at
any seaside resort on the west coast, and week by week great progress is made in
placing it in an even more favourable position as an attraction to holiday-seekers.
The daily programme of amusements, provided shows that the management are
thoroughly alive to the necessity of providing something that is undoubtedly
excellent. A very good band is at hand for dancing purposes, and it also gives
recitals twice daily. In the afternoon and evening variety entertainments are
among the chief events, which also include two performances of Quinette'a
Circus, marionette performances, switchbacks, camera obscura, and fine water
Chute. There are also on appointed days sports on the splendid cycle track, some
noteworthy events being the half-mile and the 20 mile races of the Liverpool
Wheelers, on July 1 - the North Liverpool Wheelers' 20 mile race on July 15, the
Oxford Cycling Club one mile handicap and ten mile club championship race
on July 19, the Liverpool Gymnasium Cycle Club 25 mile race on July 22, and
others. A performance of a specially attractive nature commenced yesterday at
the grounds, and will be continued during the season. This is a daring high-rope
entertainment given by James Hardy, young Canadian, who has attracted much
attention in Canada and America by his performances. On many occasions he has
crossed the Niagara Falls, thus equalling the famous performance of Blondin, and
his last sensational feat in America consisted of crossing the Genesso Gorge, near
Rochester New York on a cable 1000ft in length. His first appearance in this
country was made last evening at the Tower Grounds, on a steel wire rope
stretched about 100ft. above the dancing platform. Upon this he went through
a marvellous performance, walking, running, sitting, and lying down upon the
rope with the greatest ease, and apparently as much at home upon his cable as
ordinary people are upon solid earth.
Liverpool Mercury - Thursday 01 July 1897

TILLER GIRLS - Appear on the Tower
By the late 1800's John's troupes were dancing in
ballet and pantomime performances all over the
world. At this time John was very excited by his
conception of The Mystic Hussars routine where
the girls dressed as cavaliers when performing
their dance routine, this was considered quite
revolutionary at the time as the girls were
connected to an electrical supply and their
swords lit up in the dark. John Tiller's first dancers
performed as 'Les Jolies Petites'. He originally
formed the group for the pantomime 'Robinson
Crusoe', , in 1890 at the Prince of Wales Theatre,
Liverpool. From this were founded the Tiller
School of Dancing and the Tiller Girl troupes.

August1897 - First Official Programme

Below we have a scan of one of the first official programme issued by the Tower. The acts booked for this opening season, being: Quinette's Circus. Camera Obscura and the World of Illusions - where seeing is not believing!. The camera Obscura room dark and mystical, a combination of education and entertainment. In the 19th century, with improved lenses that could cast larger and sharp images the camera Obscura flourished at the seaside and in areas of scenic beauty.

APPOINTMENT OF MR. W. H. SMITH.

We are pleased to record that Mr W. H. Smith, late agent for the Cambrian Railways at Liverpool, has been appointed secretary to the New Brighton Tower Company. This Company provides at New Brighton in its lovely grounds and gardens, sports, football, athletic festivals, cycling and racing, theatrical and gymnasium entertainments of the highest order, and, with the completion of the Tower and other buildings, these grounds can be recorded as second to none in the catering for public amusement, and a a cost quite within the reach of all.

Mr. Smith has been selected to specially organise the advertising and excursion business in this new undertaking, and such work could not have been placed in better hands, he having had a railway experience of some 23 years in traffic management and the other branches of railway work, and for the past four years has had much to do with the working up of excursion traffic to the Cambrian Coast, &c., with marked success. It will also be remembered by Mr Smith's old Oswestrv friends how well he organised from the start the Oswestry "Richmond" Building Society, and set new life and order in a very large and important Friendly Society at Oswestry, and when he relinquished the secretary- ship of those societies, he left them in a thoroughly solvent and up-to-date position.

In Mr. Smith the directors of the New Brighton Tower Company have secured a zealous officer, and we wish him every success in his new undertaking.

The Montgomery County Times and Shropshire and Mid-Wales Advertiser
    2nd October 1897

The Montgomery County Times

And Shropshire and Mid-Wales Advertiser.

WITH WHICH IS INCORPORATED

No. 817.	'THE SALOPIAN & MONTGOMERYSHIRE POST AND CARDIGAN COUNTY TIMES.	ESTABLISHED 1880.
No. 222. Vol. 5.	WELSHPOOL, Saturday, October 2, 1897.	Price One Penny.

.PROMOTION OF A RAILWAY OFFICIAL.

The numerous friends of Mr W H Smith, who during the last 18 months has occupied the position of secretary and manager to the New Brighton Tower Company with considerable distinction and credit, will be glad to hear that he has just been appointed to the position of London manager for Messrs Thompson, McKay, and Co., the well-known carriers in connection with the Great Central Railway Co's new depot in the metropolis.

Although but in the prime of life Mr Smith has spent nearly a quarter of a century in the railway world, and is held in the highest respect. He joined the Cambrian Railway Company in 1875 at their head- quarters at Oswestry, and there acquired experience of the duties of station work, traffic manager's office, claim's department, and then for six years chief clerk to the goods manager, after which he was appointed the Company's district agent for Liverpool, the north, and the Midlands. The position which Mr Smith has now accepted is a good one, and in keeping with his railway training, and he is to be highly congratulated on his success.

The Montgomery County Times and Shropshire and Mid-Wales Advertiser
    8th April 1899

The New Brighton Tower and Recreation Ground, which owes its origin to the enterprise of Mr. R. P. Houston, M.P., is progressing rapidly, and although the extensive works will not be completed in their entirety until Whitsuntide, 1898, the large portion allotted to athletic sports, the lake and water chute, with a huge open-air dancing platform, will be opened on Whit Monday, June 7th. Mr. John Hollingshead has been selected by the directors as their manager, and is bringing all his characteristic energy and vast experience to bear upon the undertaking.

NEW BRIGHTON TOWER GARDENS,

OPEN DAILY,

Old English Fair Grounds.	Switchback,
Japanese Tea House.	Wonderful Japanese Per-
Animated Photographs.	formers.
Dancing Platform.	Magnificent Band.
Quinette's Grand Circus.	

Illuminations—10,000 Lamps.

TO-MORROW (SATURDAY), 12TH INST., The NORTH LIVERPOOL BICYCLE CLUB will hold their MEETING on the ATHLETIC GROUNDS, and at 5 p.m. their 20-Mile Race will take place. Through Tickets, including Admission, from all Railway Stations. 15710d

NEW BRIGHTON TOWER GARDENS.

☞ THE MAGNIFICENT TOWER BAND ☜ (40 Performers).

In addition to the usual

GRAND VARIETY ENTERTAINMENT,

FREE TO ALL VISITORS,

The Management are now providing "THE GREATEST SIGHT ON EARTH,"

JAMES HARDY, THE MODERN BLONDIN, Who Daily Performs his Wonderful Tricks on the High Wire, at 130 feet above the Ground.

ONE WHOLE DAY'S ENJOYMENT FOR SIXPENCE.

THE BURMESE VILLAGE.

A most interesting Village direct from Further India. Admission Sixpence. d

THE NEW BRIGHTON TOWER AND RECREATION COMPANY.
MEETING OF SHAREHOLDERS.

The annual meeting of the shareholders of the company was held yesterday in the Japanese House, Tower Grounds, New Brighton. Mr Ybarrondo presided, and the other directors present were Messrs. Collard, Anderton, and Newbold. A telegram was read from the chairman, Mr. P. H. Chambers, regretting that he was unable to attend. The shareholders present were Messrs. R. P. Houston, M.P., Thomas E. Hassall, H. Hughes, J. Butcher, D. S. Hutchinson, Robert Dawson, George Hatton, George Dalton, C. D. M'Guinness, J. Garnett, Charles Pettiagell, John Roberts, John Ormrod, Edwin Kay, Donald Anderson, Thomas Morris. Hugh C. Hatton, Joseph Bromiley, W. Hewitt, and Hitchen and Squire, James Ashworth, and J. F. Wovenden. The report stated - In presenting the accompanying balance, sheet your directors have pleasure in reporting the satisfactory progress made with the undertaking since the inception of the company. The tower structure is practically finished, and there is every reason to expect that the main block of buildings, containing the theatre, ball, and concert room, winter gardens, &c., will be completed by next Easter. The athletic grounds, with the stands, are almost completed, the fairground has been laid out, the Japanese restaurant was opened to the public last season, and progress is being made with all other buildings on the ground. In addition to the original purchase of Rock Point estate, your directors deemed it advisable to purchase adjoining lands and property. These additions comprise about five acres. The whole area of the grounds is now about thirty acres, all of which is freehold. Since the formation of the company land in the neighbourhood has advanced very considerably in price. The whole undertaking will be complete in time for the opening of next season, and the principal attractions and artistes have been engaged. The cycle track was ready by Whitsuntide last year, and although owing to the building operations the pleasure grounds were in a chaotic condition, your directors determined to admit the public into such portions of the grounds as they were able to place at their disposal, and they have every reason to be satisfied with the course adopted. The cycle track and athletic grounds are pronounced to be the, finest in the kingdom, and have become most popular with the riders. The entries for the races which took place on August Bank Holiday proved to be the largest on record. The favourable opinions expressed by the public generally, by excursion agents and others, give your directors every real reason to look forward with confidence to the results of next season's working. Two directors Messrs. Philip H. Chambers and Wilfred F. Anderson, retire in accordance with the articles of association, and being eligible offer themselves for re-election. Since last meeting the directors have appointed Mr A. S. Collard a director of the company, and the directors will request the shareholders, to confirm this appointment. The auditors, Messrs. Harmood Banner and Son, retire, and being eligible offer themselves for re-election for the ensuing year.
Mr. W. H. Smith (secretary) having read the notice convening the meeting.
The Chairman said that although the grounds were in such an unfinished state the directors thought well to give the shareholders an opportunity of inspecting their property, and forming an idea of what the place would be like when completed. An account of one year's working could not be given, because the buildings, although progressing satisfactorily, were not complete, and only the Japanese house had been opened to the public. Although the directors

50

hesitated, on account of the unfinished state of the grounds, to open them to the public at Whitsuntide, they did not regret their action in opening, for nearly 200,000 visitors passed through the gates, and it was hoped they and others would all return next year, a favourable opinion having been unanimously expressed. The athletic grounds were almost complete for the opening, and had been the admiration of all who had visited them. (Applause.) Although not looked upon with favour by cyclists who had been in the habit of competing on older and better known grounds, they managed to obtain very numerous entries, and amongst them very many of the best amateurs and professionals in England, and one and all proclaimed the grounds and cycle track second to none.

The directors felt confident that the athletic grounds would prove a source of considerable revenue to the company. Referring to the tower, he said it would be completed in a few days. It was the highest structure in the United Kingdom, and commanded a unique view. The theatre, ballroom and Winter Gardens were well advanced, and the whole of the buildings would probably be completed in good time for next season's opening. In their report the directors referred to having purchased several lots of land over and above the original purchase of the Rock Point estate, and he thought he should explain that they had good reasons for doing so. The first purchase, and the only one which comprised a building of any consequence, was that known as " West Bank'" It not only gave them an extended sea front, but brought them considerably nearer the landing-stage, and learning that the property was for sale the directors thought these advantages were sufficient to induce them to purchase it at what they considered a moderate price, and by so, doing they have further avoided the possibility of any objectionable building or business being carried on there. It was intended to transfer the company's office to that building, and possibly provide accommodation for some of the company's employees. The other pieces of land were necessary to complete the athletic grounds in their present form, and to give the property a more symmetrical boundary line. In the original prospectus it was announced that the company had power to issue £125,000 four and a half per cent debentures, but that it was anticipated that not more than £100,000 would be required, and that the issue of this amount had been guaranteed. They would, however, be pleased to hear that their credit had improved since that date, and that the directors had made arrangements to issue £100,000 of debentures not at four and half per cent, as originally proposed, but at four per cent., and that those would be guaranteed both as to interest and the repayment of capital by one of the best and foremost guarantee and trust societies of London, thus constituting them a security of the highest class. The debentures would be issued this spring, and a large proportion of them had already been bespoken. Speaking of the accounts, he said they had been framed by the auditors in the simplest possible form. In view of the fact that neither the buildings nor the grounds were complete, and that the place was only opened tentatively, no profit and loss account had yet been opened, but both the receipts notwithstanding the unfinished and, he might well add, unattractive state, amounted to, £5005, a promising feature for future seasons. An item which called for an explanation was the large balance due on unpaid calls, viz., £7633 - 5s. The shareholders were aware that these accounts were made up to the 30th of October, and that the last call on the shares fell due that month. The bulk of that sum was, however, paid during the first days

51

of November, and the outstanding balance was but small, viz., under £600.The chairman concluded by proposing that the directors' report and statement of accounts, as presented be approved and adopted.

Mr. W. F. Anderton seconded the motion.The proposition was then unanimously carried. On the motion of the Chairman, seconded by Mr. A. S. Collard, Messrs. P. H. Chambers and W. F. Anderton were re-elected directors; and on the motion of the Chairman, seconded by Mr Newbold, the appointment of Mr. Collard on the board of directors was confirmed.- on the motion Mr. Hassall and Mr. Dalton, Messrs. Harmood Banner and Son were reappointed auditors for the ensuing year.- A vote of thanks to the chairman, on the proposition of Mr. I. P. Houston, M.P, brought the proceedings to an end.

Liverpool Mercury - Wednesday 29 December 1897

New Brighton Tower
SUNDAY CONCERTS
PROGRAMME
FIRST CONCERT, JUNE 3rd, at 3-30 p.m.
The Celebrated Tower Orchestra
Conductor: Mr. GRANVILLE BANTOCK.
Mr. ANDREW BLACK.
Programme and Book of Words, 3d.

New Brighton Tower
SUNDAY CONCERTS
PROGRAMME
SIXTEENTH CONCERT, Sept. 16th, 3-30 p.m.
The Celebrated Tower Orchestra
Kindly Conducted by Mr. A. E. RODEWALD.
Mr. E. C. Hedmondt.
Programme and Book of Words, 1d.

Bleak Financial Picture - Editors Note.
The Tower had large numbers of visitors and drunkenness was a major problem even with its own police force of 20 members it was still difficult to control. During the 1897 session there were 285 arrests for drunkenness with 242 convictions. *(Liverpool Mercury 27th August 1897)* By coincidence on the very same day the liquor licence for the Japanese cafe was refused.

The Tower Recreation Company struggled to balance its books even with an estimated 1.4 million visitors each year.

On the 8th June 1898 the City Press reported "It is useless wasting sympathy on people who are foolish enough to subscribe for shares on this prospectus", the *Pall Mall Gazette* on the same day described the directors of the company "ignorant of the leisure business". A modest profit of £2102 13s. 3d. was posted in late 1898. The following year the organisation needed to borrow another £25,000 to keep afloat. In 1904 a loss of £8,600 was recorded, followed by a larger loss the following year. The Towers fortunes did improve and by1907 with free admission to the grounds and additional attractions, which included a roof garden, and a road widening project, things started to improve. But many people viewed the enterprise as a white elephant.

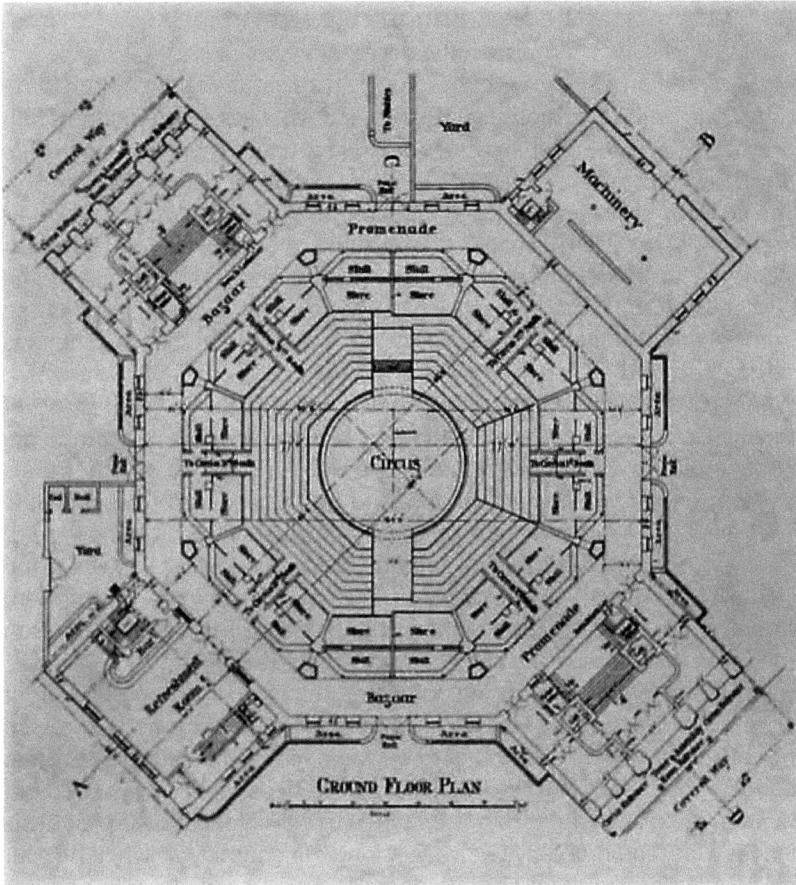

CROUND FLOOR PLAN

The whole of the building work was carried out by Messrs. W. A. Peters and Sons, contractors, Rochdale. All of the work was carried out within the short space of eighteen months, under the able superintendence of Mr John Ashley as clerk of works. With four main flights of stairs from the ground level to the top of the buildings, each 10ft wide, with numerous stalls and landing places therein. In the basement are large cellars, bottling stores and artists dressing rooms.

On the ground-floor level, immediately under the centre of the tower, there is a theatre arranged on the amphitheatre form, with one of the largest stages in the kingdom, with promenade gallery. There are refreshment-rooms. On the mezzanine floor are the kitchens and lavatories, with large storerooms. On the first floor is a large octagon dancing room, with stage capable of being used for variety performances, and opening out of the dancing room is a large refreshment-room. Above the dancing-room is the elevator hall, from which the ascent of the tower is commenced, which is all laid out with stalls in the form of a fancy fair, with shooting bungalows &c, and above this again is an open promenade, from which extensive views of the surrounding country can be obtained.

Ref : The Building News Dec 29, 1899.

The New Brighton Tower Fire.

Inquest on the deceased fireman.

Mr J.C. Bate, coroner for West Cheshire, held an inquiry at the Abbotsford Hotel, Seacombe, this morning into the circumstances attending the death of James Shone, the fireman who lost his life at the New Brighton Tower fire on Friday night last.

The first witness called was Ellen Shone, widow of the deceased who was greatly affected. Her husband was, she said, a bricklayer, and resided at Demesne Street. He was thirty-six years of age, and was a member of the Seacombe and Liscard fire Brigade. On Friday last he was at home suffering from incipient influenza or a heavy cold. About eight o'clock he was summoned by the fire Brigade bell, and he at once went out.

Witness begged of him not to go, but he said he felt better. Witness never saw him again alive. Henry Nightingale, a member of the Seacombe fire Brigade, said he knew the deceased very well. He assembled with the others on Friday night when the bell rang, and he seemed in his usual health. They went to the Tower, New Brighton and about an hour after their arrival I witness, another fireman, and the deceased ascended the tower in the lift, taking with them a barrel of water. Their appliances were not sufficient to pump the water to the height of the fire, and it was for that reason they took the barrel in the lift, and the deceased stood on an iron girder, witness passed him the buckets of water. Deceased stood on the girder with his back to a pillar. He was used to scaffolding work, and expressed no fear, though there was no guard between him and the floor ninety feet beneath. After working there some time the deceased attempted to get to another pillar, in order to do so he had to walk along a beam about six inches wide, and probably twelve feet long. He got midway when he over balanced himself and fell. The Coroner - Have you any idea what caused him to fall? Witness - Giddiness, I think.

You don't think he slipped? - No I don't.

The foreman Juror - Was there much smoke about?

Witness - No ,we were on the windward side.

Witness continuing, said the deceased fell ninety feet. The others immediately descended, and found the unfortunate man terribly injured. He died a few minutes later.

The Coroner - There was no compulsion about his going up the Tower?

Witness-Oh, no. We went there to assist the Tower men.

The Coroner.- There was no order given to the deceased to go there? Witness.- No.

The Coroner.- The plank did not give way or break? Witness, - No

The Coroner, in summing up, said it was an extremely sad thing that this brave fellow should have risked and lost his life in attempting to save the property. He was sure the jury sympathised deeply with the widow in her

awful bereavement. It was clearly an accident and he could not see that anyone was at all to blame in the matter. The jury returned a verdict of "Accidental death," adding that no blame attached to anybody.
Liverpool Echo 4th April 1898

The picture above shows the following members, from left to right: John Fellowes, James Lea, Robert Carson, John Dutton, James Leather (captain), Thomas Somerville and John Bleakley, with Harold Gibbons, driver. The cottage behind the carriage stood at that time opposite the water tower in Mill Lane, the occupier at one time being John Pemberton and afterwards Harry Keenan. Branches of the Brigade were formed, one at Seacombe, under Mr John Howarth, a tobacconist in Brighton Street, and another in Wallasey Village, under Abraham Halewood, one of the water inspectors. Until about 1900, the Wallasey Fire Brigade was 'voluntary', the men drawing a small retaining fee with the water dept. In 1890 it was decided that the original Liscard Fire Station in Mill Lane would be demolished and moved to Manor Road. The alarm bell, which was stationed at the water tower ever since the brigade was formed, was also moved to the new station. The central fire station consisted of an old stabling area and a yard at the top of Manor Road, Liscard. The equipment was a manual fire engine, ladders etc. with horse carts in sheds at Seacombe and Wallasey Village. When the fire took place at New Brighton Tower, one man (Shone) lost his life by falling from the top of the tower, being instantly killed. He fell to his death carrying water across a partially burned plank. The fire originated on a workers' scaffold 172ft from the ground, which in turn set fire to woodwork below. Fire originated from a riveter's furnace. The firemen clambered about the burning part of the tower with buckets served from casks of water raised by the crane. This was arduous and highly dangerous work; fanned by the breeze, the scaffolding timbers blazed furiously, and every minute saw new dangers. My great-grandfather John Dutton was a fireman who attended the Tower fire.

New Brighton
TOWER & RECREATION COMPANY LIMITED.

Official Programme
OF THE

Grand Easter Tournament
AND

AMATEUR ATHLETIC SPORTS

Under A.A.A. Laws and N.C.U. Rules (Permit for Cycling granted by Liverpool Centre)

Easter Monday, April 11th, 1898.
(WEATHER PERMITTING)

Prizes value £180.

Prizes value £180.

Entrance to Athletic Grounds—
MOLYNEUX DRIVE, ROWSON STREET.

Commencing at 2-30 p.m. prompt.

Climbing New Brighton Tower.

For the benefit of *Reviewites*, I climbed up the Tower to the crow's nest, 575 feet above Mother Earth. The experience is exciting, and, to a novice in the ways of steeplejacks, is fraught with danger. Once above the Tower buildings, which, by the way, rise 80 feet, you begin to feel the air all about you, cobwebs being swept away instanter. At a height of 400 feet the first balcony is reached. As you are fenced in by a 10 foot rail, dizziness won't lead you to terminate life's short span by throwing yourself over. Many would have been satisfied to remain here, but, with the interest of others at heart, I clambered 30 feet up a vertical ladder to balcony No. 2, and was rewarded by a still finer view of the country round.

NEW BRIGHTON TOWER THEATRE.

CALL FOR REHEARSAL,

Whit Monday, May 30th, 10·0 o'clock sharp..
Morning Performance at 2·0.
Notice.

All Artists Engaged for the Season are Requested to send in Bill Matter Fortnight Previous to commencement of each Engagement. Rehearsals Every Monday Morning at 10·0 Sharp During the Season.

Signed,   JOHN HENDERSON,
            Stage-Manager.

NEW BRIGHTON ATHLETIC GROUNDS.—Another new departure in athletics has been taken by the New Brighton Tower Company, which has arranged for a Scottish meeting, the programme including putting the stone, throwing the hammer, tossing the caber, sack race over hurdles, obstacle race, wrestling (Cumberland style), Highland dancing in costume, Highland fling, sword dance, strathspeys, and reels, and piping competition in costume. Some of the best-known dancers and pipers will compete, and, given a fine day, the attendance should be a record one.

NEW BRIGHTON TOWER RECREATION
GROUNDS AND GARDENS,
OPEN FOR SEASON WHIT-MONDAY, May 30th, 1898.
GREAT PROGRAMME of HOLIDAY ATTRACTIONS
OLDE ENGLISHE FAIRE, NOVEL ELECTRIC
RAILWAY.
TOWER GRAND THEATRE:
Performances Twice Daily, 2 and 7.
Sensational Novelties; Up-to-Date Varieties.
DANCING ALL DAY IN GREAT BALL ROOM.
Splendid Orchestra.
AMATEUR ATHLETIC SPORTS
(Under N.A. & A.A.A. Laws, and N.C.U. Rules),
SATURDAY, May 28th, and WHIT-MONDAY, May 30th.
FLAT and BICYCLE RACES.
Prizes Value £150.
Sports begin at 2-30 prompt.
REFRESHMENTS by J. LYONS & CO., London.

SPORTS AND PASTIMES.

The Cycling Tournament in aid of the Wallasey Medical Charities, held at the New Brighton Tower Grounds last Saturday, was, unfortunately, not favoured with the best of weather, and, consequently, the takings suffered thereby. Rain fell for the greater portion of the meeting, and those spectators who were not under cover had a very uncomfortable time. A most interesting programme was gone through, and some capital finishes witnessed.

The New Brighton Tower and Recreation Company opened the Tower Grand Theatre on Whit Monday, May 30th, 1898

Prices of admission were:-
        Amphitheatre 6d
        Second seats 1 shilling
        Reserved Stall 2 shillings
        Boxes I guinea.
Seating accommodation was provided for more than 2,000 people with standing facilities for another 500.

Performances were twice daily at two o clock and seven o clock, the first program.
Which was of the variety type was as follows:-
    1. Overture by Tower Theatre Band.
    2. Omega in her unique performance on the wire.
    3. Bonnie Kate Emery-Soubrette Vocalist and Dancer.
    4. The Three Apollos Graceful Athletes.
    5. Arthur St. George Descriptive Vocalist.
    6. Tillers Snowdrops (six in numbers)-
        Bewitching and youthful up to date dancers.
    7. The Kroneman Brothers-Head Balancers.
    8. The four Daniels -Musical Clowns.
    9. Onati Algerian Troupe Juggling Feats.
    10. Mdlle. Marguerite The Beautiful and accomplished
        Lion Trainer with her Seven Performing Lions and
        Singing fox Terrier.

The Tower Band was conducted by Mr. D. Dickinson, while Mr John Henderson was the stage manager.

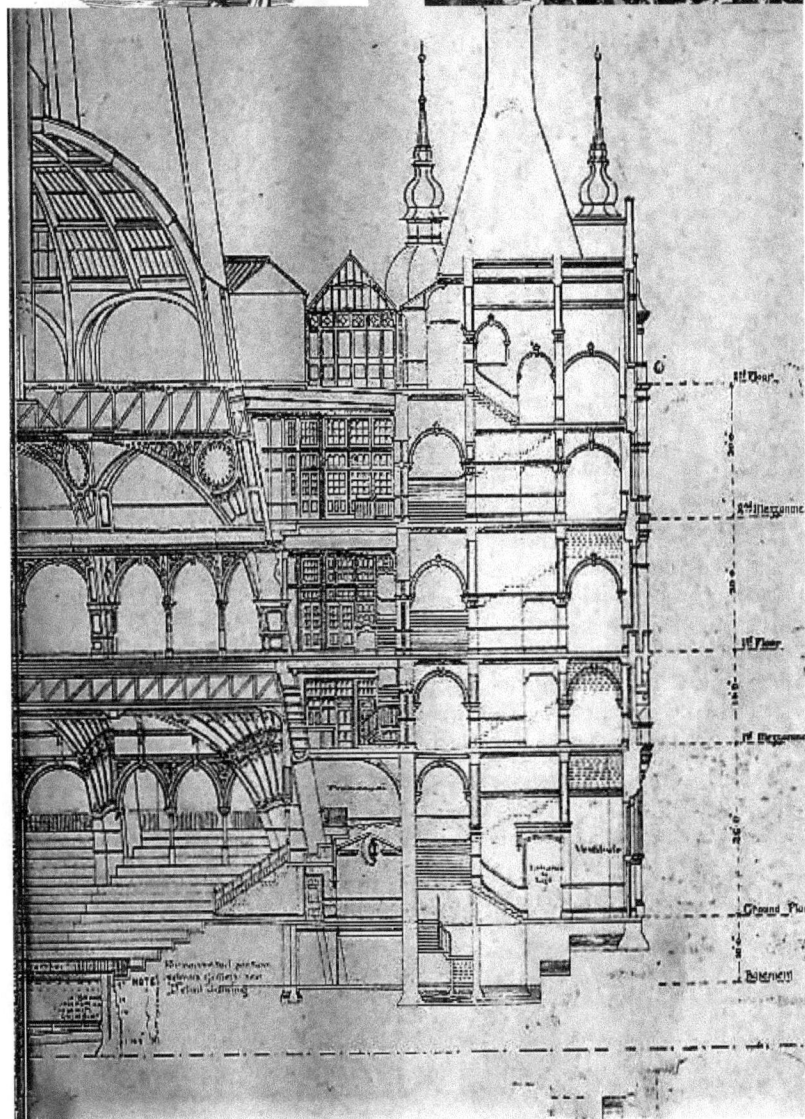

The Magnificent Tower Theatre opened on Whit Monday, 30th May 1898 with seating for 2,000, and standing room on the balcony for a further 500. The world's largest stage 45 feet wide with a depth of 72 feet, could even accommodate a full-sized circus, it opened to a fan fair of publicity. The top of the bill Mademoiselle Marguerite with her seven lions. The high light of her performance was when a member of the public was invited to enter the cage to drink champagne. Half an hour before the performance began in the enormous Theatre it was filled to overflowing, in anticipation of the new " number," which had been duly advertised.

Among the outside novelties were baby incubators, reptile charmers, the Liograph—giving a picture of Corbett-Fitzsimmons fight of 1897. Depicting a boxing match between James J. Corbett and Bob Fitzsimmons in Carson City, Nevada on St. Patrick's Day the same year. Originally running at over 100 minutes, it was the longest film that had ever been released to date; as such, it was the world's first feature film.

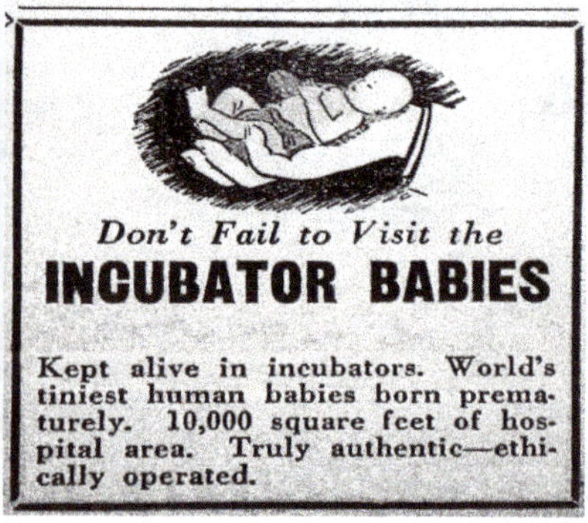

Don't Fail to Visit the

INCUBATOR BABIES

Kept alive in incubators. World's tiniest human babies born prematurely. 10,000 square feet of hospital area. Truly authentic—ethically operated.

60

"GENTLEMAN JIM"
The Story of
JAMES
J.
CORBETT

By
NAT
FLEISCHER
Editor
The Ring Magazine

•

PRICE
75 CENTS

The film no longer exists in its entirety; however, it is known from contemporary sources that the film included all fourteen rounds of the event, each round lasting three minutes. Wyatt Earp was a reporter for The New York World at the time, and published his commentaries on the fight on March 14. The film is also notable because at the time, women were essentially prohibited from viewing live boxing matches, which were seen as a male activity, but they were not prohibited from viewing this film. For those adventurous souls outside in the Tower grounds there was a water-chute, puzzle house, and electric railway. Together with Sport events all through the whit holidays.

61

Wallasey and Wirral Chronicle.

WEDNESDAY, SEPTEMBER 14th, 1898.

THE TOWER GROUNDS.

Although the holiday season is now rapidly drawing to a close, this favourite amusement resort continues to be extremely well patronised, its high-class and admirably-varied round of attractions invariably delighting visitors and residents alike. An exceptionally good programme is being submitted this week in the commodious theatre, and large as is this portion of the buildings it is more often than not crowded by a delighted audience. The truly marvellous performance of Professor Duncan's collie dogs never fails to receive the enthusiastic tokens of approbation it unquestionably deserves, whilst Spessardy's comic bears and tigers supply a couple of "turns" that have only to be seen to be appreciated. Then there are Tiller's charming troupe of dancers and vocalists ; Rose Conroy, burlesque actress and dancer ; the Three Brooklyns, grotesque musical clowns ; Zorado in his electric ladder act ; and the Musical Gerrettos. The fair ground is always well patronised, the electric railway, the water chute, &c., coming in for a great share of attention. The Tower Orchestra, under the talented conductorship of Mr. Granville Bantock, the musical director, give each afternoon a grand orchestral concert, and the Tower Hungarian Band and the Ladies' Mandoline Band perform selections at intervals in different parts of the grounds. The Sunday afternoon sacred concerts have proved very successful. The programme for next Sunday is entirely confined to Wagner's music. An attractive list of prospective engagements is announced for the remainder of the season, and it evident that the enterprising management intend to spare no expense in the efforts to efficiently cater for their many patrons.

THE MUSICAL BROOKLYN'S

SPESSARDY'S RIDING BEARS

DUNCAN'S ROYAL SCOTCH COLLIES

NEW BRIGHTON TOWER AND RECREATION GROUNDS.

The present summer will see an additional attraction at New Brighton, distant from Liverpool about four miles, in the erection and completion of the New Brighton Tower and Recreation Grounds. This tower, which is to be the highest

The Ballroom

erection of its kind in the United Kingdom. It stretches its apex 567ft. above the sea level, which is 52ft. higher than the Eiffel Tower at Blackpool. The floors are surrounded by brick-work, and form a handsome and substantial building, of which the ground-floor is a fine theatre, the next an extensive ball-room, and the third will be a rival to the hanging gardens of Baby-lon. Above this are the seven floors of steel lattice through which lifts will convey visitors to the eerie half a thousand feet up. The whole structure will be illuminated by electricity, which will play upon 1,500 variegated lights in the evening, and also distribute its rays over the twenty-five acres of ground surrounding the tower. One portion of the estate is laid out as a fair ground, where various exhibitions will encamp, the most important being the Himalayan electrical switchback circular railway, which has not yet been seen in England.

A specially constructed dancing platform, water chutes, the famous Japanese tea house, and countless other attractions will be provided. The electric display will surpass anything yet attempted in this particular direction, and will be manipulated by Mr E. Bartlett, of Oxford. The furnishing and decorating of the theatre is very superior, and although the company were granted a free dramatic licence on Wednesday, it is proposed to run variety shows for the present. This portion of the company programme is in the

The Theatre

hands of Mr W. H. Smith. Hardy, the high-rope performer, will be one of the first attractions. Visitors may choose between the Mersey Tunnel route from Liverpool, or by boat from the landing-stage. The tower and grounds open on Monday next for the season with every indication of winning popularity and success.

The Era - Saturday 28 May 1898

Hull Daily Mail - Tuesday 07 June 1898
PROSPECTUS.
10 PER CENT. PER ANNUM GUARANTEED.
From 30th June 1898 - 30th. September, 1901.
The SUBSCRIPTION LIST will CLOSE on before THURSDAY, the 9th day of June,1898.
NEW BRIGHTON TOWER AND RECREATION COMPANY, LIMITED,
Incorporated under the Companies' Acts, 1862 1890.
CAPITAL: 175.000 Six Per Cent, Cumulative Preference Shares of £1 each, £175,000
(issued July, 1896, and fully subscribed); 125,000 Ordinary Shares of £1 each
(present issue), £125,000— £300.000. Four Per Cent. First Mortgage Debentures,
£100,000. Issue, at a premium of 5s per Share, of 125,000 ORDINARY SHARES £1
EACH.
Upon which a Dividend the rate of per cent, per annum upon the amount for the
time being paid upon the Shares (exclusive of premium) is guaranteed from the
30th day of June, 1898, to the 30th day of September, 1901, by the Bank Liverpool,
Limited, with whom equivalent funds have been deposited cover the guarantee.
per Share on Application, and £1 2.s 6d per Share on Allotment
(including the premium),
DIRECTORS.
PHILIP H. CHAMBRES, Esq.. D.L., J.P., Estyn, Rhyl (Chairman).
WILFRID T. ANDERTON, Esq., J.P., Hall, near Preston. . ,
JOSEPH BRAILSFORD, Esq., Burnt Stones, Sheffield.
ALFRED S. COLLARD, Esq., Elm wood, Hooton. Cheshire.
RALPH T. NEW BOLD, Esq.. Belle, Bury.
DOMINGO DE YBARRONDO, Esq., Tower Chambers, Liverpool.
SOLICITORS.
Simpson. North, Harley, and Birkett, 1, Water-street, Liverpool.
AUDITORS.
Messrs Harmood Banner and Son, Chartered Accountants,
24, North John-street, Liverpool.
BROKERS.
Messrs Walter Pankhurst and Co.. 56, Old Broad Street,
and Stock Exchange, London. E.C.
Messrs Fernyhough and Ashe. 14, Cross-street, and Stock
Exchange, Manchester. Messrs Barber Bros, and Wortley.
Alliance-chambers, and Stock Exchange, Sheffield. Messrs Henry B. Hawaii and
Son. Queen Insurance-buildings, and Stock Exchange, Liverpool.
BANKERS.
The Bank of Liverpool, Limited, and Branches; and their London Agents— Messrs
Glyn, Mills, Currie, and Co., 67, Lombard Street. London, E.C.
The City Bank. Limited, Threadneedle Street, London, E.C., and Branches.
The Manchester and Liverpool District Banking Co., Limited, Manchester,
Liverpool, and Branches.
The Sheffield Banking Company, Limited, George Street, Sheffield.
The North and South Wales Bank, Limited, Liverpool, and Branches.
SECRETARY AND REGISTERED OFFICES.
Mr W. H. Smith, Tower-chambers, Water-street, Liverpool.

A BRIDGED PROSPECTUS.

The directors of the New Brighton Tower and Recreation Company, Limited, invite subscriptions at a premium of 5s per share for 125,000 ordinary shares of £1 each, on which a dividend at the rate of 10 per cent, per annum upon the amount for the time being paid upon the shares, exclusive of the premium, is guaranteed from the 30th day of June, 1898, to the 30th day September, 1901, by the Bank of Liverpool. Limited, with whom equivalent funds have been deposited to cover the guarantee.

A full prospectus was published in July, 1896, when the whole of the 175,000 preference shares were issued to the public and fully subscribed. This Company was formed for the purpose of acquiring the well-known and beautiful Rock Point Estate at New Brighton, and erecting thereon an Eiffel Tower, Theatre, Recreation Buildings, etc., and laying out pleasure gardens and athletic grounds. New Brighton is situated on the Cheshire side of the river Mersey, opposite to the city and docks of Liverpool, and within easy distance from the populous manufacturing and mining districts in the North and Midlands of England and Wales. The Company now owns 32 acres of freehold land. Since the formation of the Company the magnificent pile of main buildings, containing the theatre, capable of seating about 3,000 persons, the palatial ball room, winter garden, and the several restaurants, cafés, and other buildings in various parts the grounds, have all been practically completed.

The tower, the highest and most graceful structure the United Kingdom, has been completed. The upper platform of the tower, about 500 feet above the sea level, can be reached by electric lifts from the elevator hall in the short space of one minute, and affords a beautiful, varied and unique panorama of sea and country, the views seaward extending as far as the Isle of Man and the Great Orme's head. The athletic grounds, with the cycle track, admitted to be one of the finest and fastest in the world, have been opened, and have become immensely popular with both professionals and amateurs. Full advantage has been taken of the natural beauties and formation of the land in laying out the gardens. On the Old English Fair Ground a variety of amusements have been provided, including the water chute, the electrical Himalayan circular switchback railway, &c. Every endeavour has been made to secure the greatest possible variety of amusement. both indoor and out, including some surprising novelties. The greatest care and forethought have been exercised in making this a most complete and perfect indoor and outdoor place of amusement, including ample provision for the convenience and comfort of the visitors in the various large restaurants and cafés within the grounds, where an entire day of pleasure can be spent.

Arrangement have been, made on very satisfactory terms with the well-known purveyors. Messrs J. Lyons and Co.. Limited, London, for the whole of the catering on the Company's premises, also with Messrs Samuel Allsopp and Sons, Limited. This should ensure satisfaction to the visitors and a large annual revenue to the Company.

New Brighton is becoming more popular each year, and the directors of the Company have every confidence in the success of the undertaking. While the buildings were in the course of construction, the grounds were opened in a tentative way last year, and notwithstanding their unfinished and incomplete condition, they proved a great attraction to large crowds of visitors, who even then signified their approval and satisfaction.

No less than 2,738,486 passengers were landed by the ferry steamers at New Brighton Pier during the year ending 31st March, 1898, exclusive of the large number of passengers carried by the railway and tramways, and the numbers who walked from Egremont Ferry to New Brighton. The year ending 31st March,1898, shows an increase of 331,985 passengers landed at New Brighton Pier over the previous year, when the grounds were not open. From inquiries addressed to the secretary and arrangements made for excursions to the company's grounds, a very considerable increase on these figures is anticipated this season.

So great was the confidence of the vendors in the success of the undertaking, that, although they were entitled to have the whole of the ordinary shares allotted to them on the transfer of the estate and contracts, they preferred to postpone the issue until the undertaking was completed and opened to the public. Applications for shares should be made on the form enclosed with the prospectus, and sent with the deposit required to the bankers the Company. Liverpool, May, 1898.

NEW BRIGHTON GARDENS

New Brighton Tower Grounds & Lake.

NEW BRIGHTON TOWER.

The New Brighton Tower Company have just issued their guide book for the coming season, which shows that extensive arrangements have been made for pleasure seekers. The grounds cover an area of 30 acres, wherein every kind of out door amusement, will be found. Shops and side shows surround the fair ground, and in the base of the Tower is a Theatre containing some 3,000 seats, and on the floor above is a fine ball and concert room. The programme for Whit-Week is very varied and include some of the first entertainers in the country.

A LICENSING PUZZLE.
At Birkenhead Licensing Sessions an application was made for four full licenses to the New Brighton Tower, the grounds of which cover thirty-two acres, and are frequented by nearly 30,000 people a week.
The application was supported by the Rev. Charles Hylton Stewart, vicar of New Brighton, and a Roman Catholic priest of the town. The Bench granted licenses for two out of the four asked for, but with the singular restriction drink should not be served from a counter or bar, and that the houses must close at ten o'clock.
Dundee Courier - Tuesday 30 August 1898

NEW BRIGHTON TOWER MYSTERY
Police in Wallasey are still unable to state who was the young man whose mangled remains were found on Friday evening in New Brighton Tower Grounds. A macintosh and walking stick had been left on the 85 feet balcony of the structure, and this circumstance, and the fact that the body was discovered some distance from the wall of the building, induce the belief that the deceased did not fall accidentally, but committed suicide.
Manchester Courier - Monday 07 November 1898

TRAGEDY AT NEW BRIGHTON TOWER.
About eight o'clock last evening the body of a young man was discovered at the foot of the New Brighton Tower in terrible state. The lifts had ceased working, and the only place he could have come from was the hundred-foot level, as the body was some yards from the base the tower. It is thought that the fall cannot have been accidental, which view is strengthened by the fact that macintosh and umbrella were found at the hundred-foot balcony. Papers found on the body, which is that of a young man of 20, bear the name " A. E. Hurd, Brighton.
Lancashire Evening Post - Saturday 05 November 1898

RAFFLES AT CHURCH BAZAARS.
INTERESTING CORRESPONDENCE.

In a long letter to the Rev. C. Hylton Stewart, vicar of New Brighton, Mr. W. Doak protests against the introduction of draws and raffles at the forthcoming bazaar in the New Brighton Tower Grounds, and says:

You must be aware that Convocation has passed a most stringent resolution in condemnation of the practice, that the Lord Bishop of the diocese has spoken strongly against the scandal, and that the ordinary common law of the land has pronounced all such games of chance as illegal, and those who may aid and abet them as rogues and vagabonds.' Any one of these considerations ought to have some weight in the matter, but all these combined make the case against this form of gambling irresistible. There is still a further consideration to which, as a Christian minister, I desire to direct your attention-namely, the terrible extent to which betting and gambling generally prevail among the young men of the present day. You cannot close your eyes to this feature, even if you wish to do so. It is brought home to those of us who are engaged in work among this class with terrible reality, and cannot have escaped your own observation, and I venture to point out to you that you cannot with clean hands condemn a national vice, such as this undoubtedly is, so long as you bestow upon it the benediction of the Church. I must, therefore, ask you to be good enough to have any draws or raffles in connection with your bazaar withdrawn at once, and thus save me the pain of dealing with the matter in a more public way.

To this the following reply was sent:-

The Vicarage, New Brighton Church,
November 11, 1898.

Dear Sir, - I beg to acknowledge the receipt of your very interesting letter on raffles and the church building in general, and am, your obedient servant,
C. HYLTON STEWART.
W. Doak, Esq.

Mr. Doak then wrote a second letter:-

Oakfields, Holland-road, New Brighton,
November 11th, 1898.

Dear Mr. Stewart, - I am obliged for your prompt acknowledgment of my note of yesterday's date, but I regret to find that you have entirely evaded the purpose for which it was written. I must again ask you to be good enough to withdraw the raffles in connection with your bazaar, and let me have your assurance that you have done so not later than Monday next, failing which it is my intention to publish this correspondence as a preliminary step to further proceedings. In the meantime I must enter my solemn protest against children of tender years being engaged in hawking the tickets from house to house in this district.
Yours faithfully, W. DOAK.

The Rev. C. Hylton Stewart's reply was:

The Vicarage, New Brighton,
November 12. 1898.

Dear Sir. - I have to acknowledge the receipt of your letter of yesterday's date, and beg to state, in reply, that I must decline all correspondence with you on the subject.

The Chester Courant and Advertiser for North Wales - 23rd November 1898

68

THE VERISCOPE AT NEW BRIGHTON.

HEAVY DAMAGES.

At the London Sheriff's Court, yesterday, before Mr. Under-Sheriff Burchell and a special jury, a case in which the pl intiff was Mr. John Oldborough, theatrical agent, of Camden Town, and the defendants the Veriscope Company, of Henrietta-street, W.C., came on for assessment of damages.

Mr. J. J. Cooper Wyld, who represented the plaintiff, s id that early in 1898 the Veriscope Company, an organisation for giving cinematograph shows of the Corbett-Fitzsimmous fight, came to an arrangement with his clients for him to provide a hall at Liverpool suitable for their exhibitions. Mr. Oldborough succeeded in securing an agreement with the New BrightonTower Company, Liverpool, in which they agreed to provide a hall on the understanding that he would pay £125 as a deposit and £100 per week for 13 weeks. The Veriscope Company agreed to give their exhibition of the fight while the grounds were opened four times daily, t king 40 per cent of the profits. The exhibition was opened, but after a week the Veriscope Company brought their portion of the show to a close, thus leaving the hall on the plaintiff's hands. His client claimed for £1500, which included loss of profit and expenses connected with the building. The defendants were not represented and the jury assessed the damage at £1400 with costs.

THE "VERISCOPE"
The Modern Motion Picture
Machine
1915 Model

If interested in the Veriscope, ask for large folder

NATIONAL EQUIPMENT COMPANY
Motion Picture Machines and Supplies
(MOVING PICTURE DEPARTMENT OF NATIONAL EMPLOYMENT COMPANY)
417 West Michigan Street, Duluth, Minn.

THE BIG FIGHT
The championship fight between Jim Corbett and Bob Fitzsimmons, recorded by the Veriscope Company on 63mm motion-picture film, March 17, 1897, in Carson City. That event was a sensation. There were many attempts to cash in on its topicality. Veriscope's was the first feature-length film in history.

NEW BRIGHTON TOWER - ACTION BY THE ARCHITECT
At the Manchester Assizes yesterday, between Mr. Justice Bigham and a special jury, for the hearing the case of Maxwell v the New Brighton Tower and Recreation Company Limited. Mr. Shee, Q.C, Mr. Russell, Q.C & Mr. Overend Evans were council for the plaintiff and Mr. Pickford, Q.C, and Mr. Horridge the defendant company. Mr Evans explained that the action brought by Francis William Maxwell to obtain commission for services rendered, remuneration for work done, and also damages for wrongful dismissal. The defendant company denies any commission was owing to plaintiff, and that they were justified in dismissing him, also counter-claimed on various issues. With the original estimates going well over the agreed price, the Architect stated that the directors kept on changing there minds over various issues.
Aberdeen Evening Express - Saturday 04 February 1899

New Brighton Tower - Seymour street looking from Grosvenor road.
Note the High Wire - and no safety net

NEW BRIGHTON TOWER LICENSES.

At the Wallasey Police Court yesterday, before Messrs. F. Johnston, M. T. Graveson, H. Pooley, T. Joynson, and Alderman J. Smith, Mr. Hughes (Messrs. Thompson, Hughes, and Matheson) applied for the transfer of the theatrical license of the New Brighton Tower Grounds from W. H. Smith to Albert Bulmer, who had succeeded the former as secretary and manager of the company. He also asked for a music and dancing license for 14 days, to include Sundays. With respect to Sunday concerts, he asked for an extension of the hours—viz., from 3 to 6 p.m., instead of 3 to 5 as at present. — Mr. Ybarrando, a director of the Tower Company, said that people from Liverpool were unable to get to the concerts by three o'clock. Consequently the concerts were late in beginning, and could not be concluded by five o'clock.—A further application was made for a license to sell intoxicating drink at the Algerian Restaurant for Whit week. — Mr. Hughes said they wanted to supply drinks with meals, and had no intention of having a bar. They already had a license for the Japanese Restaurant and Rock Point Castle, which could only accommodate 300 and 200 respectively. Consequently on Easter Monday, when they had 40,000 people in the Tower grounds, there were many complaints about the want of accommodation.—Mr. Johnston inquired how the want of accommodation arose, and asked was there not a complaint in the newspapers as to the absence of sufficient refreshments for the people?—Mr. Ybarrando said that was partly correct. The caterers, Messrs. Lyons, had lost so much money at the Algerian Restaurant last year that they did not open it on Easter Monday. That was because people would not dine without they could have reasonable and proper refreshments.—Superintendent Macdonald opposed this application on behalf of the police. He thought the two existing licenses were sufficient.—The theatrical license was granted, also the music and dancing license, and the magistrates altered the hours on Sundays, which would be 3 30 to 5 30 p.m. The application for the drink license was refused.

THE ENGLISH CHAMPIONSHIPS.
The championship meeting of the National Cyclists' Union took place at the New Brighton Tower grounds on Saturday, 10th June.
The one mile amateur championship was won by Paul Albert, the German rider, who, at Vienna, had won the "Mile World Championship".
The time was 2min. 51secs.
The final of the mile professional championship went to:
1. S. Jenkins,
2. T. J. Gascovne,
3. J. Green,
Jack Green succeeded in capturing the quarter-mile distance from F. W. Chinn and S. Jenkins; but Jenkins won the five mile, followed in by Green and Howard. Paul Albert scored again by winning the quarter-mile amateur championship.
The Australasian 29 July 1899

NEW BRIGHTON TOWER.

The Tower Grand Theatre opened on Monday for the season with a very strong bill. The celebrated Luppu Troupe, horizontal bar experts, give a sensational turn. Sylvo, the American tramp juggler, is extremely amusing, while the quaint Mobile Quintette, with their coon songs and dances, Reede and Leene, the funniest of comedians and burlesques, Clo Lavinia, charming serio and dancer, Zetina Family, acrobatic magnets, Prof. Ted. Heaton, and the Cinematograph, form the principal items of a bill that it would be almost impossible to beat in the provinces. Next week some very strong attractions are promised. The famous Elliotts, the only troupe of 6 one-wheel bicycle riders in the world, the Seven Savonas, who play selections from all the well known composers on over 50 different musical instruments and with an act illuminated by 1,000 variegated electric lights, Cyrus and Maude, with their performing donkey, Percy Meye, the talented female impersonator, the original Otanays, sensational electric wire act, and the Luppu Troupe (retained for another week), are some of the attractions on a bill which comprises a variety performance seldom seen in the north. The beautiful grounds are daily extensively patronised and the different side shows and amusements are highly appreciated. The Water Chute and Himalaya Railway are busy the whole day, while South Sea Joe and his natives, the Cinematograph and the numerous other attractions are all liberally patronised. The confetti night every Friday evening has proved a big success, and judging by the amount so plentifully distributed, a novelty that will be thoroughly appreciated by the many patrons of the beautiful ballroom is now established.

AN ACROBAT'S TERRIBLE ACCIDENT.
Latest English files contain reference to the terrible accident to Hardy, the American Blondin, Hardy had been appearing successfully for some time at the Alexandra Palace, but just prior to the conclusion of his aerial performance on Wednesday, April 4, he met with the shocking accident which has since in all probability proved fatal. Having concluded a series of daring feats on the tight-rope, which is extended from one side of the great central hall to the other; at a height of some one hundred feet, he ascended to the roof to perform what is known as the 'long dive.'

As is usual, the band struck up a lively air when Hardy successfully leaped from the small platform, which is suspended in mid-air, and dropped into the net and rebounded to a considerable height. On again, striking the net, and by some means unexplained, it gave way, precipitating Hardy on to the orchestra stalls with great force. Dr. Webster, of Muswell Hill, and other local surgeons were called, and Hardy's injuries were pronounced serious. In addition to one of his legs being badly broken, he received terrible injuries to the head and body, and little hope was entertained of his recovery.

Two seasons ago, when the New Brighton. Tower Grounds were opened, Hardy was engaged there for practically the whole season, and excited great interest by his wonderful feats. Unlike his feats at the- Alexandra Palace, everything was done without any safe-net which of course made them all the more daring and added zest to the enjoyment of those who delighted in sensationalism. Many of the tricks were also achieved without the aid of a balancing-pole, and had an accident occurred he would have been precipitated on to the dancing platform, nearly a hundred feet below. But everything was carried out with mathematical accuracy of timing, and the only feat which could be styled blameworthy, apart from the general risk of such performances, was done on a small trapeze suspended from the main wire. The acrobat would, seat himself on the bar of the trapeze, and then fall suddenly backwards, catching with his feet in the angle formed by the junction of the bar and the suspending ropes. The great risk of that was not so much inaccuracy on the part of Hardy himself as that the sudden strain on the trapeze might cause a breakage of which an ordinary test could not forewarn him. In conversation at the time when this risk was pointed out to him, the Canadian Blondin had said' he always tested everything most carefully, and would not trust that all-important work to any person alive. Prior to visiting Britain—his New Brighton engagement being the first there- Hardy had done many wonderful acts in Canada. where be was born, and in the United States. He had crossed Niagara,and had also gone, without the aid of a balancing-pole, across one of the biggest gorges in the States, at an elevation of over 300 feet.
Auckland Star, Issue 142, 17 June 1899.

NEW BRIGHTON TOWER LICENCES

The magistrates granted the application of Mr Mathison, solicitor, for a music and dancing license for the New Brighton Tower and Grounds for twelve months. They also extended the hours on Sundays, Christmas Day, and Good Friday, from 3:30 to 5:45 p.m., instead of 5:30, as at present. With regard to the first application, the Magistrates refused to grant the ordinary form of license which would entitle the Tower to twelve extra long nights without making special application to the magistrates.

Liverpool Mercury - Thursday 01 June 1899

The Wine and Beerhouse Act 1869 reintroduced the stricter controls of the previous century. Licence conditions varied widely, according to local practice. They would specify permitted hours, which might require Sunday closing. The sale of beers, wines or spirits required a licence for the premises from the local magistrates. Further provisions regulated gaming, drunkenness, prostitution and undesirable conduct on licensed premises, enforceable by prosecution or more effectively by the landlord under threat of forfeiting his licence.

Licences were only granted, transferred or renewed at special Licensing Sessions Courts, and were limited to respectable individuals. Often these were ex-service-men or ex-policemen. Typically they might require opening throughout the permitted hours, and the provision of food or lavatories. Objections might be made by the police, rival landlords or anyone else on the grounds of infractions such as serving drunks, disorderly or dirty premises, or ignoring permitted hours.

As regards women: "Many more women are seen in public- houses; the middle-aged are the drunkards, not the young. Young people do their courting in public-houses, since both sides are rather ashamed of their homes, and like to make themselves out a class above what they are.

The young men treat the girls to a glass of wine. No harm comes of it. It is not till they get older that women take to gin and ale and become regular soakers." ...

"Public-houses are more attractive than they were; ladies' saloon bars are to be seen everywhere. Publicans tell you that it is in response to a demand, but it is difficult to distinguish between cause and effect." Such are other police opinions.

Charles Booth Life and Labour of the People

TERRIBLE ACCIDENT AT NEW BRIGHTON TOWER.

A painter named T. E. Cunyngham, aged thirty-four years, a native of Oldham, who was employed with other men to repaint the Tower, New Brighton, met with his death on Monday night in a singular manner. He was working on the top landing, and was getting on to the platform for the purpose of descending, when he missed his footing, and fell on to the next landing. There he was struck by a descending lift, and fatally injured. He was not, how- ever, knocked off the platform, and a man in the next lift coming down dragged him inside, otherwise he might have fallen at least two hundred feet. At the bottom he was examined by a doctor, who pronounced life extinct.

He had fallen only ten feet, but death was no doubt caused by the lift striking him.

The Chester Courant and Advertiser for North Wales - 13th September 1899

NEW BRIGHTON F. C. The Rumours of Dissolution. Emphatic Contradiction.
During the past few weeks the most persistent rumours have been circulated in
this district as to the probability of the dissolution of the New Brighton Tower
Football Club in the event its failing to gain a position in the First Division of the
League. These reports appear to have received additional impetus since it became
definitely settled that the Tower would have to remain content with Second
Division statue for at least another season. How the idea originated it seems
impossible to ascertain, but in order that the precise facts of the case might be
laid before the readers of the "Express" a representative of this journal this
morning sought an interview with Mr. J.C. Bulmer, the energetic and courteous
secretary of the club. When the matter was mentioned to Mr Bulmer he merely
smiled at first. "You may contradict the statement as positively as you like." he
afterwards remarked. "Our club is not going to end, and, in fact, we have every
reason to anticipate a far more successful time next season. We have already
re-engaged Allison, Leigh, Dackers, Stevenson, Hargreaves, Hammond, and
M'Guffie, and are in active negotiation with a number of other players.....
Aberdeen Evening Express - Tuesday 02 May 1899

NEW BRIGHTON TOWER CONCERT.
The concert at the Tower to-morrow afternoon promises to be very interesting, as
it will be the first appearance in this district of the celebrated Hungarian violinist,
Bela Kiraly, whose perform on the Continent have aroused such enthusiasm.
In his book on Hungarian music Liszt speaks of him as one the chief founders of
the Hungarian classical school. Mr. Bela Kiraly will be heard in Liszt's Hungarian
Rhapsody. and in Czardas by Hubay.
Miss Hetty Hertzfeld, Miss Dorothy Kilby, Miss Florence Purcell, and Mr. Hagreaves
Hudson are announced as the vocalists, while a choice selection of instrumental
music will be played by the string orchestra, conductor Mr Granville Bantock.
Aberdeen Evening Express - Saturday 13 May 1899

NEW BRIGHTON TOWER AMUSEMENTS.
Quite plethora of amusements was provided at the beautiful grounds of the New
Tower Company for Whitsuntide. Visitors and the management had their reward
in a magnificent attendance. Besides all the standing attractions of the grounds,
not forgetting the Tower itself, the fine ballroom, the water chute, the electric
railway, and menagerie, there were Egyptian dancers, Sampson the strong man,
South Sea Island troupe, electric lady, cinematograph exhibition, and a number
of other admirable side shows. The excellent military band provided plenty of
music all through the day, and there were in addition very capable orchestral
performances. The Tower Variety Theatre was opened for the first time this season,
and not a vacant seat was left in the whole of the vast and tastefully-decorated
building. The programme in the theatre was of a first-class description, including
the Stella dancing troupe, the sisters Lee Stella Star, Edgar Granville, comedian;
Wille Bros., really marvellous acrobats ; Prof Ted Heaton, in a wonderful swimming
performance, Campkin the tramp cyclist, Percy Meye, impersonator, the Macdonald dancers. and Polverini's cinematograph. At night the grounds, which are now
complete and in excellent condition, and illuminated by thousands lamps.
Aberdeen Evening Express - Tuesday 23 May 1899

NEW BRIGHTON TOWER DISPUTE ABOUT THE LIFTS. CLAIM AND COUNTER-CLAIM. Yesterday, in the Queen's Bench Division of the High Court of Justice, before Mr. Justice Day and a special jury, the action of Messrs. Easton, Anderson, and Goolden, Limited, v. The New Brighton Tower Company, Limited, came in for hearing. Mr. Bousfield, Q.C., M.P., and Mr. Gore Brown were for the plaintiffs; Mr. Carver, Q.C., and Mr. Horridge were for the defendants.

The plaintiffs are engineers, and they sought to recover £4100 for electric lifts, which they had supplied to the defendants for their New Brighton Tower; £247 for extras, and £447, the price of the pumps fitted in connection with the lifts. Defendants admitted that the lifts and pumps had been supplied, but they denied that they were liable for extras. There was a counter- claim by the defendants for damages, to the amount of £5264, consequent upon, it was alleged, - the plaintiffs' failure to complete the work according to contract time. According to Mr. Bousfield's opening, in November, 1897, the plaintiffs agreed to supply to the defendants several lifts which were to be worked at the Tower. It was stipulated by defendants that they were to be ready a week before- Easter Monday in the following year, or earlier if possible, provided the plaintiffs were not delayed by anything out of their control.

But when the lifts were ready to be fixed it was found that the structure was not in readiness to receive them, and therefore they were not able to fix them within the contract time. For that delay plaintiffs were not liable, but regarded the defendants as liable.. ...Defendants were not ready with the lift spaces until early in July. Witness was himself at the Tower works, and on May 24 he asked the defendants to remove their temporary lift, which was then still working. He made that request by letter. Witness gave details of the "extras" for which payment was claimed. In cross-examination by Mr. Carver, witness was referred to a letter written by the defendants, in which they complained that they were losing large sums of money by reason of the plaintiffs not being ready with the lifts. Witness replied that the lift shafts were not ready in the early part of July. and that the first lift was completed on July 15th. The whole of the lifts were completed on the 1st August, 1898, in readiness for the August Bank Holiday. The shops on the 80-foot level were not ready in August, and the shops on the top were not finished until September. Mr. Cyrl Rooke Prance, in the employ of the plaintiffs, gave evidence to the effect that the delay was due to the structure not being in readiness for the reception of the lifts. The brickwork of the shafts had bulges in it which caused the cage of the lift to stick, and the remedying of that defect caused a fortnight's delay.

Mr. Ybarrondo, chairman of the company, stated that the tower was all ready for Whit Monday, save for want of the lifts. People could not use the tower, and would not use the gardens. During the nine weeks they had been able to use the tower the average receipts had been about £400 a week. He had often been on the works while the tower was in course of construction, and he had never seen anything which would cause the delay which plaintiffs alleged except certain joists which had been mentioned, and which would have been attended to six months before had the plaintiffs called the attention of the defendants to the matter. - Witness, in cross-examination gave a general denial to the allegation that the delay had been caused by defendants. The further hearing was adjourned.

Liverpool Mercury - Friday 04 August 1899

NEW BRIGHTON TOWER. Mr. S. F. Cody and company are this week appearing at the New Brighton Tower Theatre. in "The Klondyke Nugget." Despite the many difficulties -that had to he faced in consequence of the fire at- St. Helens, where Mr. Cody was performing last week; and whereby he lost all big valuable properties, the initial performance last evening was successfully carried out.
Liverpool Mercury - Tuesday 17 October 1899

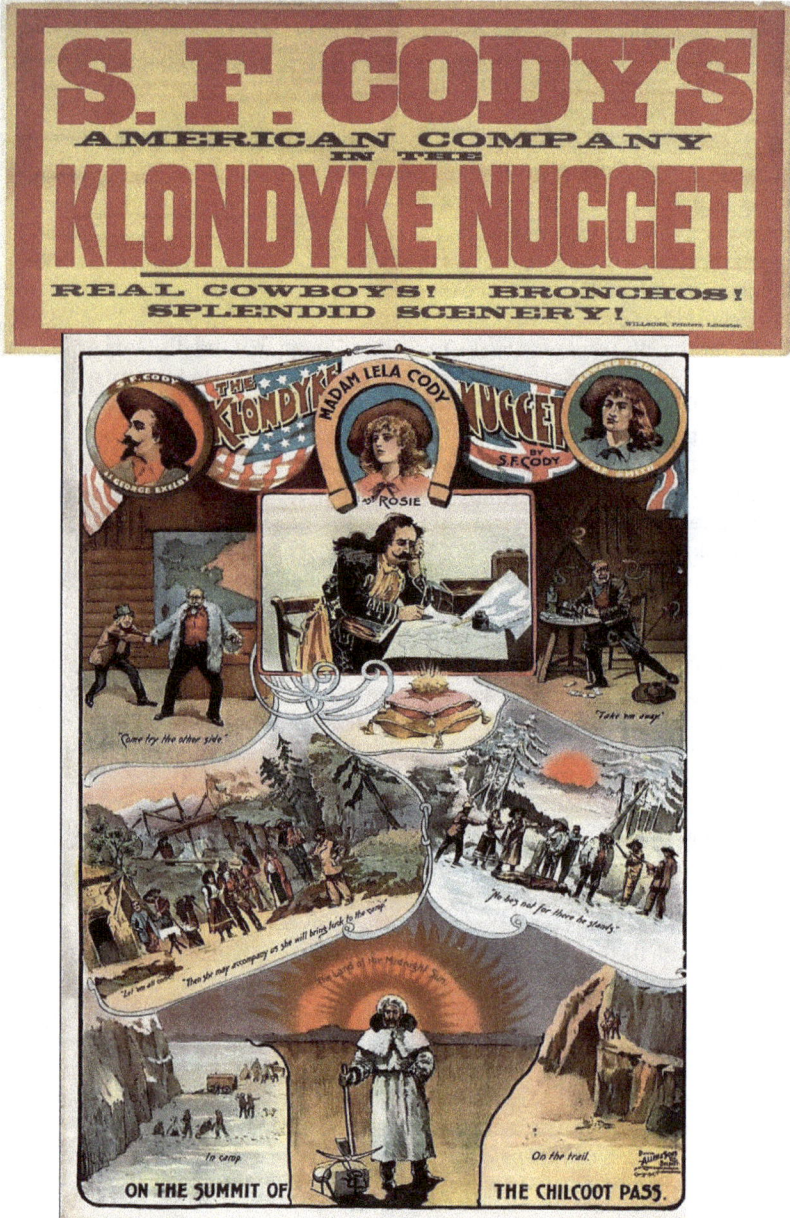

THE KLONDYKE NUGGET, written and performed by S.F. Cody appeared throughout the British Isles at the end of the 19th century. Samuel Franklin Cody (1867- 1913) was a unique figure in late Victorian Anglo-American popular entertainment. Born Samuel Franklin Cowdery, he later changed his surname to capitalize on the fame of Buffalo Bill Cody, even mimicking Buffalo Bill's clothing and facial hair style. Born in Texas, S.F. Cody trained in the Forepaugh Wild West Show, and found much of his fame in England.

He is renowned in the history of aviation as the first man to conduct a powered flight in England, and he later developed large kites that were used for artillery spotting during World War I.

Cody's life was filled with tall tales (though some of them are perhaps true), including his claim that he prospected for gold in Dawson City during the Klondike Gold Rush. That story set the groundwork for the theatrical play advertised herein, where Cody plays the role of George Exelby; Lela Cody, his

(common law) second wife, the part of Rosie; and her son, Edward LeRoy, plays Joe Smith. By 1897 the family were back in England, still racing horses against cyclists, performing chariot races and acting out scenes from the Wild West. The family fortunes took a turn for the better when, in 1898, they ventured into the world of the legitimate theatre appearing in a 'Wild West Melodrama,' an entertainment very popular with the audiences of the day, and written by Cody himself. The play 'The Klondyke Nugget' was first performed in its entirety on 5th December 1898 and this 'sensational American drama' toured the length and breadth of the country.

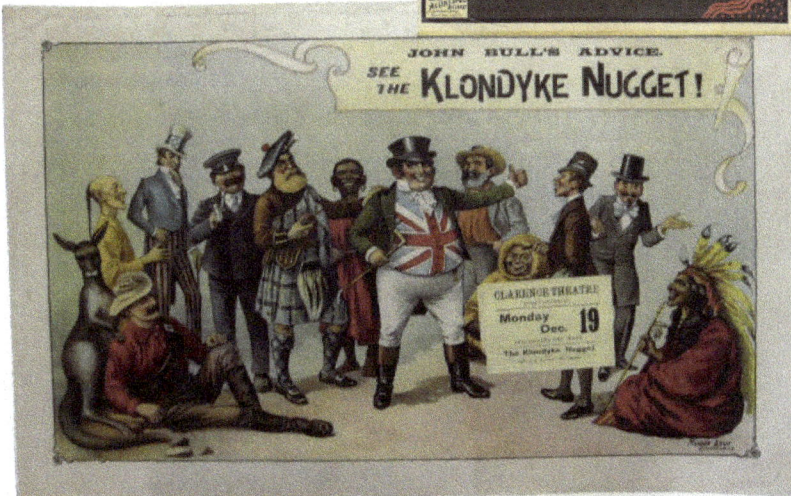

New Brighton Tower and Recreation Company Ltd.

Cycle, Horse and Variety Tournament,

Saturday, Oct. 21st, 1899,

At 2-30 p.m.

Tower Athletic Grounds,

New Brighton.

Admission 6d. and 1s.
Stands Extra.

S.F. CODY

(Roi des Cowboys), with his

Champion Cycle, Horse and . .
. . . Variety Tournament.

PROGRAMME - - ONE PENNY.

Programme.

1.—LEON CODY on Horseback against any Cyclists who present themselves at the start. 1 Mile Standing Start.

2.—S. F. CODY standing on two horses v. J. STANWORTH (North Lancashire Champion). Half-mile.

3.—Mrs. CODY on the Stallion "Vechy" against any Cyclists who present themselves at the start. Three-quarter Mile.

4.—S. F. CODY & SON (LEON). Exhibition Shooting on foot, at Toy Gas Balloons in mid-air, at a height of about 240 to 300 feet. On this occasion Mr. Cody will endeavour to break two Gas Balloons (not tied together but floating from 10 to 20 feet apart) with one bullet, whilst ascending in mid-air. The difficulty in accomplishing this feat is for Mr. Cody to get himself in line with the balloons as they cross each other—the wind being uncertain.

5.   ## "Wild Alaska."

In this Mr. S. F. CODY will give his marvellous Shooting Exhibition, Galloping on Horseback and on Foot.

Synopsis:

Emigrant train crossing the prairies—the encampment—supper—they turn in for the night—approached by Indians—the alarm—flight—pursued by Indians. Mrs. Cody and her son, Vivian, return from the hunt—Cody and son, Leon, coming from market—Cowboy sports and pastimes—Dinner—visit of old friend trapper; welcome, joins family at dinner—entrance of Nigger beggar; solicits charity, he receives food and money, and departs on his journey—dinner finished—Cody departs with his youngest son and trapper friend—Mrs. Cody and son enter cabin—Indians approach—they spy Nigger, who signals them with a flag of truce; he informs them of the money in the cabin—door is locked—entrance is achieved by way of chimney—Leon is tortured at the stake by Indians, who try to force him to divulge where valuables are hidden—Mrs. Cody pleads for mercy for her son—she is answered by thrust of Nigger's knife, which kills her—the cabin is ransacked and spoils divided between Indians and Nigger—latter steals horse and rides away—Cody approaches—pursuit of nigger—capture by lasso—brought to justice by aid of lasso and Judge Lynch—funeral of Mrs. Cody—Indians to revenge death of Nigger set fire to cabin—knife duel between Indian and Cody—Cody's Horse killed by Indian—Death of Indian—Victory of Cody.

. . Finale. . .

| Proprietor and Manager | - - | Mr. S. F. CODY. |

☞ **To-Night** at the **Grand Tower Theatre** Last appearance of Mr. S. F. CODY and his famous Company in "**The Klondike Nugget.**"

In 1900, New Brighton Tower athletic grounds boasted the UK's first visit from Sole Proprietor and director Victor Bamberger and his The Ashanti Village, in which 100 West African men, women and children re-created a village, produced and sold their wares and performed war tournaments, songs, and ritual dances.
They had arrived late, which meant that they were not set up in time for Whitsun 1900 the traditional start of the summer season.

The Ashanti Village.

The inhabitants of the **Gold Coast**, who are known under the popular name of **Ashanti**, and who are represented by the inhabitants of the Negro Village of our great Ethnographical Show, are a most wonderful tribe. Although their way of living and especially their industries, are witnesses of a permanent touch with European civilisation, yet they have preserved in their character the childish gaiety and originality of a natural people. Especially the latter qualities make the intercourse with these natives very animating to the visiting public. It has therefore been possible to arrange this show in such a perfect manner as has never been seen before either in England or on the Continent.

Everything which might have given a theatrical appearance was strictly avoided. The Village is exactly in the same style as in Ashanti, and has been built at

Trying taste of English Beer.

a very large expense. The necessary material has been chiefly imported from their own country, and several native builders have helped to erect the village and provide the necessary comfort for their countrymen, so that they will not feel the want of any of their usual comforts in this country, which is strange to them.

Visitors will be surprised by the striking originality which makes them almost forget that they are close to a large European City. Absolutely indifferent to the customs of

Ashanti Barber.—Customers while waiting, playing Games.

four young men with virtuoso and brilliant rhythm. In order to give more strength to the rhythm iron castanets and mallets are used. Under this energetic and lively rhythm the whole body of the dancers moves in perfect time.

Another attraction is the **School**, which obtains a very picturesque appearance from the lively and fresh African youths. These children win the sympathy even of those who see in the " black men " nothing else but the fact that they are savages. They regularly receive elementary lessons from their well-educated school-master *Atah-Adúqúe* All the missionaries, as well as the English Colonial Government, take great care that tribes under English Protectorate will gradually be brought to a higher standard of civilisation. For this purpose intelligent natives are trained as school-masters in government schools on the coast or at the Missions in the Interior. After having undergone a certain term of

The Children's School.

83

Whit Sunday at 3-30,
Grand Vocal & Orchestral Concert

The renowned Tower Orchestra—Conductor, Mr. Chas. Reynolds.

Vocalists:

Miss Sarah Andrews | Mr. Dan Billington
(Soprano) | (Baritone)

Solo Violin - Miss EDITH ROBINSON.

Admission to Grounds 6d., including free admission to Promenade of Theatre during Concert. Seats 6d., 1s., and 2s.

Plan of Theatre may be seen and Seats booked in advance at the Company's Offices, 7, Tower Chambers, and the Tower Office, New Brighton.

Special Boat leaves Landing Stage at 2·45, conveying Visitors direct to New Brighton for the Concert.

NEW BRIGHTON
GRAND TOWER THEATRE
Special Holiday Programme.

WHIT MONDAY at 1-30, 4 & 7-30, & during the week at 2-30 & 7-30

Important Engagement of **The THREE RICKARDS**, the Marvellous and Sensational Aerobats. Unrivalled in Double and Twisting Somersaults.
Sisters Aindow, the Premier Musical Speciality Artistes.
Two Walkers, American Eccentric Comedians and Comic Side-walk Conversationalists.
Harry Bold, the Popular Burlesque and Patter Comedian.
The WOOTONS, in their Football Match on Bicycles! A Wonderful Performance.
The Levardos, the Greatest Comic Triple Bar Act in the World!
The Hintons, the Screamingly Funny Tramp Cyclists.
First appearance here of **McCANN'S Dog Circus,** the Famous Performing Terriers with Somersaults, Tricks and Clown Dogs, and the World's Champion Leaping Dogs.

POPULAR PRICES.—Amphitheatre 3d. Unreserved Seats 6d. Reserved Stalls 1s.

On the ATHLETIC GROUNDS:
— THE —
SOUDANESE ARAB ENCAMPMENT

75 Natives and 50 Arabian Horses, Camels, Mules, &c.

The most wonderful Exhibition ever brought into England! Illustrating the Warfare, Customs, Pastimes, and Industries of the Soudanese.

Great Bedouin Dance ! ! !
Dance of Slave Girls ! ! !
The Shrieking & Howling Dervishes
Races on Camels, Arabian Horses, Mules, &c.
The Dash for Life! a marvellous exhibition of fantastic riding.

DON'T FAIL to VISIT this INTERESTING & INSTRUCTIVE EXHIBITION !

SENSATIONAL PERFORMANCES, WHIT MONDAY, at 2, 4 & 7, and during the week at 3 & 7.
6d.   Admission   6d.

£30
SPECIAL NOTICE.
distributed every week among Lady and Gentlemen Visitors in the Grounds and Buildings in Prizes of not less than £1 each.
No Competitions.—Every Visitor has a chance of being presented with a Sovereign.

A Bioscope show was a music hall and fairground attraction consisting of a travelling cinema. The heyday of the Bioscope was from the late 1890s until World War I. Bioscope shows were fronted by the largest fairground organs, and these formed the entire public face of the show . A stage was usually in front of the organ, and dancing girls would entertain the crowds between film shows. Films shown in the Bioscope were primitive, and the earliest of these were made by the showmen.

Professor Menier, "The Great Human Ostrich". His attire included "war paint", a nose ring, and outlandish exotic dress. Monsieur Antoine Menier appeared for a season at the Tower Theatre. He was still appearing with Barnum in 1902, having starred alongside Tomasso "the Human Pincushion", Mattie Price "The Magnetic Lady", Wade Cochran "the child mental wonder", the Moss-Haired Girl, and countless others.   Harry Houdini was not impressed by human ostriches. In his debunking of sideshow tricks entitled Miracle Mongers and their methods; a complete exposé of the modus operandi of fire eaters, heat resisters, poison eaters, venomous reptile defilers, sword swallower's, human ostriches, strong men, etc. (Miracle Mongers New York, E. P. Dutton & Company, 1920) he writes:
Eaters of glass, tacks, pebbles, and like objects, actually swallow these seemingly impossible things, and disgorge them after the performance is over. That the disgorging is not always successful is evidenced by the hospital records of many surgical operations on performers of this class, when quantities of solid matter are found lodged in the stomach.

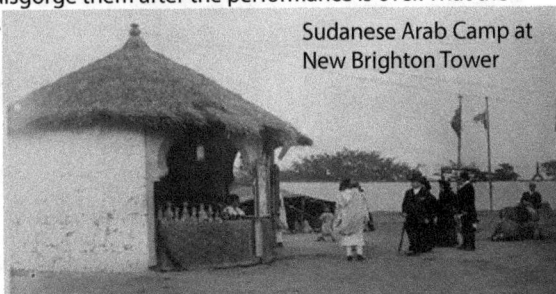

Sudanese Arab Camp at New Brighton Tower

THE BEDOUIN-ARAB ENCAMPMENT
AT NEW-BRIGHTON TOWER GROUNDS.

POST CARD — GREAT BRITAIN & IRELAND
THE ADDRESS ONLY TO BE WRITTEN ON THIS SIDE.

The Bedouin-Arab Encampment at New Brighton
Grounds, postcard sent on the 24th August 1901, early
postcards only allowed the message to go on the front.
The address and stamp on the other side.

August 1901 - New Brighton Tower Football Club

ENGLISH CUP COMPETITION - Saturday, August 31 – 1901
Considerable sensation was caused in Liverpool football circles on Saturday by
the unexpected decision of the directors of New Brighton Tower, one of the
leading Second Division clubs, to disband the organisation. The club was
admittedly founded with the idea of obtaining a First Division team as a winter
attraction for the noted Cheshire amusement resort, and their three failures in
this respect, together with the heavy financial loss that must have been sustained,
have evidently discouraged the management. Several of last season's players have
been transferred to other League clubs, or have gone South, but such well-known
men as Frank Barrett, Ben Hulse, Jack Farrell, John Holmes, Robert Petrie, and Josh
Hargreaves are still disengaged. Not only had the Tower's League fixtures been
arranged but the club had been excused participating in the early stages of the
English Cup Competition.
(Sheffield Daily Telegraph, 02-09-1901)

Like Liverpool and Chelsea , New Brighton Tower were formed to play at an
already-built stadium. The owners of the New Brighton Tower, decided there
was a need to provide winter entertainment, and had built a stadium adjacent
to the tower. What made this so unique was that at the time it had a capacity for
100,000, and thus one of the largest stadiums in Britain.
The football club was formed in 1896 to provide the entertainment, and joined
the Lancashire League at the start of the 1897–98 season. After finishing as
champions in their first season, the club applied for election to the Football
League. Although they were initially rejected, the league later decided to expand
Division Two by four clubs and New Brighton Tower were accepted. The club
signed a number of new players, including some who had played international
football, and was reasonably successful, finishing 5th (out of 18) in its first season,
and 4th in their third season. However, with the club poorly supported
(averaging gates of around 1,000), the cost of maintaining a professional football
club became too high for the Tower's owners, and the club was disbanded in the
September 1901. The consortium that had been bank rolling the club admitted
failure. On the final game of the 1900/1 season when New Brighton beat Arsenal
1-0. It proved to be the final game between the sides, and the final game ever for
New Brighton Tower, the attendance was 3,500.
They simply could not keep bankrolling the experiment so it was with some relief
that the Football League accepted their resignation with their position being
taken by Doncaster Rovers.
The ground was still used for other sports including cycling and motor bike
racing. However, the company struggled to make anything really work. They even
tried a live action cowboys and Indians show during the summer months of 1908
with over 500 performers.
In 1921, a new club was formed, New Brighton, who would also play in the
Football League from 1923 until 1951, though initially they played at Sandheys
Park until that was destroyed in World War II.
The club continued to play in the regional leagues, still using the New Tower
Ground but it was clear the future wasn't bright. Finally, they left home in 1970's
after fire and vandalism had made it unusable, and the ground lay vacant until
purchased by a developer who turned the site into houses.

A MALT LIQUORS TRANSACTION

Mr. Justice Eady to-day gave judgment in an action brought by Messrs. Allsopp against Mr. Houston, M.P. The plaintiffs, in consideration of receiving the contract for the supply of malt liquors to the New Brighton Tower Company, undertook to purchase 30,000 of Mr. Houston's shares. The licenses, however, were only obtained on condition of there being no counter trade, and plaintiffs. contending this did not satisfy the agreement, asked for a re-conveyance of the shares. Judgment was given for the defendant.
Evening Express 27th November 1901

In Victorian times, no polar explorer set off to the Baltic without Allsopp's Arctic Ale stashed in the hold of his ship.. This was a mighty brew, more than 11 per cent alcohol. Even when the temperature went down to -55 Fahrenheit the beer was unharmed by being frozen. An early example of Larger type Beer being sold in the UK *Yorkshire Evening Post Tuesday 06 September 1904*

DOG SHOW

A dog show, under Kennel Club rules, is to be held at New Brighton Tower on the 21st and 22nd inst. Entries may be made up to Saturday next by post.
Mr. A. A. Vere Beauclerk, of Tower Chambers, Liverpool, is the secretary.
Manchester Courier and Lancashire General Advertiser - Tuesday 06 August 1901

Mr. Beauclerk commenced his connection with show work in 1889, and has acted as Secretary and Manager of the Manchester Dog Show since 1896, and of shows at Brighton, Liverpool, Guildford, Tunbridge Wells, Cruft's (eight years),Birkenhead, New Brighton, Colchester, Leominster, Southport, Egremont, etc ....
He has the indispensable attributes, for a show manager, of imperturbable temper, plenty of sound common sense, invariable courtesy to all who have to do with him, and great capacity for getting through an immense amount of hard work; and it is no doubt the happy combination of these desirable qualifications in one person that has made the services of this gentleman so much in request.
Ref "Dog Shows And Doggy People", by Charles H. Lane.

New Brighton Tower.

The Highest Structure and the Finest Place of
Amusement in the Kingdom.

**35 Acres of
Beautiful
GROUNDS
AND
GARDENS.**

**MILITARY
BANDS.**

**LADIES'
ORCHESTRA.**

**The Grounds,
Menagerie,
AND
Main Buildings
are OPEN
all the year
round.**

For
Announcements
of Season
Attractions,
See Liverpool
Daily Papers.

Magnificent Display of Animals of all kinds.

WATER CHUTE, HIMALAYA RAILWAY, and hosts of other novel side shows.

TOWER LIFTS running all day, and VARIETY PERFORMANCES twice
daily in the Grand Theatre during the season.

Café Chantant with HIGH-CLASS VAUDEVILLE PERFORMANCE ; no
charge for Admission and Seats Free.

GORGEOUS ILLUMINATIONS every evening.   *CONCERTS every Sunday*
throughout the Season.   Twelve hours continuous amusement for **6d.**

Frequent Trains leave all Mersey and Wirral Railway Stations for New Brighton,
which may also be easily and quickly reached by the Wallasey Ferry Boats,
which sail every 15 minutes in the season.

91

New Brighton Tower.

SUNDAY,
July 6th, 1902 . . .
AT 3-30 P.M.

SPECIAL

DVOŘÁK = LISZT

PROGRAMME.

The Celebrated Tower Orchestra
OF 80 PERFORMERS.

Conductor - Mr. A. E. RODEWALD.

Leader - Mr. VASCO V. AKEROYD.

Accompanist - Mr. H. H. LEATHER.

*Analytical Notes kindly supplied by Mr. Ernest Newman
to Mr. A. E. Rodewald.*

[THESE NOTES ARE COPYRIGHT.]

Vocalist:

Miss SARAH ANDREW,
(SOPRANO).

PROGRAMME - - ONE PENNY.

New Brighton Tower.

Sunday, July 13th, at 3-30 p.m.

SECOND SPECIAL

Tchaikovsky Concert

SYMPHONY No. 1 (In Winter)   First Time.

PIANOFORTE CONCERTO No. 1 in B Minor.

OVERTURE "1812."

The Renowned Tower Orchestra.

Conductor - Mr. A. E. RODEWALD

Leader - Mr. VASCO V. AKEROYD.

SOLO PIANOFORTE:

Mr. JOSEF HOLBROOKE.

Entr'acte. MR JOSEF HOLBROOKE By Ernest Newman.
I shall not soon forget a certain Sunday morning about eighteen months ago, when I wandered into a rehearsal at New Brighton Tower. A weird young man, whom I afterwards discovered to be Mr Josef Holbrooke, was making the most frenzied attempts to conduct the band through a work I had never heard of before,- "The Skeleton in Armor." His notions of conducting an orchestra were as primitive as Mr. Balfour's notions of leading the House,- he was evidently a child in these things; but through the chaos that was surging round me, I occasionally caught glimpses of unmistakable inspiration. Finally, Mr. Bantock had to take the baton himself; and in the course of a few rehearsals the orchestra was able to give a very decent performance of a difficult but extremely interesting work. I had not previously heard a note of Mr. Holbrooke's music. I did not even know of his existence. But in virtue of "The Skeleton in Armor" I instantly pinned my faith to him, and was convinced that here, at any rate, was the germ of something absolutely without parallel in English music, something that instinctively set me thinking of the big names that come to us from over sea. Rare beauty of phase, individuality of method, intuitive insight into orchestral colour, all these were here: everything could well bear comparison with the work of men ten or twenty years senior, - for Mr. Holbrooke at that time was little more than twenty-one. Since then I have studied carefully almost everything Mr Holbrooke has written; and each successive experience has deepened in me the conviction that, if this young man does not leave his mark upon the history of modern music, there is no other English musician who will.
The Speaker, February 15, 1902

NEW BRIGHTON TOWER AND PLEASURE GROUNDS.

Grand Coronation

Musical Eisteddfod

To be held in the Great Theatre of the Tower,

ON SATURDAY, JUNE 14th, 1902.

PROGRAMME
of
Competitions,
Prizes,
and
Conditions.

RHAGLEN
o'r
Cystadleuon,
Gwobrau,
a'r
Amodau.

Eisteddfod Gerddorol Fawreddog

Y CORONI,

New Brighton, Ddydd Sadwrn, Mehefin 14eg, 1902.

Secretary :—

LLEW WYNNE,

Ashfield, 98, Westbourne Road,

BIRKENHEAD.

NEW BRIGHTON TOWER

GRAND CORONATION

Musical Eisteddfod

(Under the Direction of Llew Wynne,)

Saturday, 14th June, 1902.

Adjudicators—Music:

Dr. HENRY HILES, Manchester.

DAVID EVANS, Esq., Mus. Bac. (Oxon), London,

AND

HARRY EVANS, Esq., F.R.C.O., Dowlais.

Recitation:

(English) J. JAMES HEWSON, Esq.

(Welsh) ISAAC FOULKES, Ysw, a LLEW WYNNE.

Eisteddfod Accompanists:

Madame MAGGIE EVANS; Miss MILLICENT RICHARDS,
and Mr. H. H. LEATHER.

Test Room and Platform Stewards : -

Mr J. T. JONES, Mr. HUMPHREY LLOYD,
Mr. FRANK D. WILLIAMS. Mr. T. W. PLOWDEN,
and Mr. R. VAUGHAN JONES.

Preliminary Tests *(Rhagbrawfiadau).*

Preliminary Tests on the Solos will take place on the
morning of the Eisteddfod, in the Tower Building, New
Brighton, and the time will be duly announced in the
Programme of the days' proceedings.

All communications relating to this Eisteddfod must be addressed to the
Secretary :—

LLEW WYNNE,

Ashfield, 98, Westbourne Road,

BIRKENHEAD.

COMPETITIONS (Cystadleuon).

—o—

1.—Mixed Voice Choirs, 60 to 75 voices, "When winds breathe soft" *(Webbe).* First Prize, £35 and Silver Crown to the Conductor, value 15 Guineas; Second Prize, £10 and a Silver Medal to the Conductor.

Corau Cymysg, 60 i 75 o leisiau, "Yr Awel Fwyn" *(Webbe).* Gwobr 1af, £35 a Choron Arian, gwerth 15 gini, i'r Arweinydd; ail, £10 a Thlws Arian i'r Arweinydd.

2.—Male Voice Choirs, 30 to 45 voices, "The Martyrs of the Arena" *(De Rille).* First Prize, £25 and Gold Mounted Baton value Three Guineas to the Conductor; Second Prize, £5 and a Silver Medal to the Conductor.

Corau Meibion, 30 i 45 o leisiau, "The Martyrs of the Arena" *(De Rille).* Gwobr 1af, £25 ac Arwein-ffon wedi ei haddurno ag aur, gwerth 3 gini; ail, £5 a Thlws Arian i'r Arweinydd.

NEW BRIGHTON TOWER EISTEDDFOD. - MANCHESTER CHOIR SUCCESSFUL.
The second annual challenge concert and musical eisteddfod attracted a huge crowd to New Brighton Tower, on Saturday. There was a very large entry, and the greater part of the morning was taken up with preliminary tests to reduce the list. The contest took place in the Tower theatre, which was densely packed when a start was made at two o'clock. The chief evens of the afternoon was a male voice choir competition. The test piece was Crossing the Plain (Maldwyn Price), won the first prize, £25 and the Tower Silver Challenge Cup value 30 guineas. The following seven choirs entered Birkenhead Male Voice Choir, Gwalia Male Voice Choir, (Liverpool), Llangollen Male Voice Choir, Manchester Orpheus Prize Glee Society. Moelwyn Male Voice Party, St. Helens Male Voice Choir, Wigan Harmonic Male Voice Choir. The first prize was awarded to the Manchester choir (conducted by Mr. W. S. Nesbitt), and the Moelwyn Party, who were first last year, carried off the second prize (with £5 and a silver medal for the conductor). The prize quartet was Four Britons" (St Helens). Miss Violet Newbold (Huyton) carried off the prize of a guinea and a silver medal for a recital (with musical accompaniment) of The Story of a Faithful Soul," and Miss Alice Hughes, (Birkenhead) was the successful soprano soloists. The principal event of the day was a competition for mixed choirs, which was decided at the evening meeting-. Five well-known choirs entered, and the test piece was The Storm (Dr. Rogers). The St. Helens Prize Choir was awarded the victory, the spoils of which were 35 guineas and the Tower Silver Shield, value 35 guineas. The second prize went by Blaenau Festiniog Choral Union.
Llangollen Advertiser Denbighshire Merionethshire 3rd October 1902

BRASS BAND CONTEST AT NEW BRIGHTON TOWER.
Great interest was centred on the fifth annual contest in the Tower Gardens, New Brighton, Saturday, when the Tower Challenge Cup and other prizes totalling £155 were competed for by sixteen bands from all parts of England and Wales. Test piece, "Mercadaute." Adjudicator, Mr T. H. Seddon. London.
 Result: —1 - Besses' o' the' Barn, Lancashire. Challenge Cup and £30. 2.- Wingates Temperance, Lancashire; 3 - Crooke. Lancashire. 4 - Lindley, Yorkshire. 5- Irwell Springs, Lancashire. 6 - Aberaman, Glamorganshire. 7- Rochdale, Lancashire,
Edinburgh Evening News - Monday 01 June 1903

WALLASEY MEDICAL CHARITIES
Fine Performance by J.S.Benyon
New Brighton Tower Grounds, before 4,000 spectators.
Details: World's Quarter Mile (Flying Start, unpaced).—Benyon covered the distance in 26& l/5 sec, thus tying the record.
Sheffield Daily Telegraph - Monday 08 June 1903

CAKE WALK'S
The directors of the new Brighton Tower have introduced amateur "cake walks" as a weekly feature of the programme, and they are likely to prove a great attraction, as the first walk brought together upwards of 6,000 visitors.
Sunderland Daily Echo and Shipping Gazette - Monday 15 June 1903

WALKING.
A walking contest under the auspices of the New Brighton Tower authorities took place on Saturday, the distance being 23 miles. John W. Bonnett, Peterborough. was first; Henry Tierney, Southport, second and C. H. Mouleon, Southport, third.
Sunderland Daily Echo and Shipping Gazette - Monday 15 June 1903

The earliest recorded wrestling at the Tower June 1903.

WRESTLING MATCH. —At New Brighton Tower on Saturday evening catch-as-catch-can wrestling match between Harkenschmidt, the Russian Champion and Tom M'Inerney, from Liverpool. The Russian had to secure- three falls in an hour or forfeit £100. He gained the first fall 23 minutes and the second in 24 minutes, but failing the third in the time limit, M'Incerney won the stake. *Lancashire Evening Post - 03 August 1903 -*
The match was repeated on the 16th September, a mixture of Catch and Greco Roman rules. Same stakes. again McInerney survived at 2-0 with Hackenschmidt injuring his ankle and quitting.
Ref: wrestlingheritage.co.uk

Tower's first Wrestler and local boy.

NEW BRIGHTON TOWER - AN AIRSHIP BOUND FOR LIVERPOOL AND BACK

The management of the New Brighton Tower have added another interesting item to their already long list of attractions at that place of entertainment on the Cheshire side of the Mersey. The next six weeks or thereabouts, a new airship will be on view in the Athletic Grounds and occasionally, if all goes well, the huge machine will travel over the river to the city Liverpool. It had been intended that the trial flight should take place yesterday afternoon; but though the weather was bright there was stiffish blowing—estimated rate of 25 miles an hour and all thought the projected trip had to abandoned till such a time when the velocity of the wind has dropped to 14- or 15 miles an hour. The airship has been built in London during the seven months its joint owners, Mr, E. Gaudron and Mr. Charles W. Beckmann—the former clever engineer and the latter an aeronaut who, has soared high in the air "down under" —chiefly in New Zealand. In its construction there has been an attempt to incorporate the best and most practical features of previous airships, whilst an entirely new steering gear has been introduced. The balloon of cambric is 65 feet long and 18 feet deep, with a capacity of 13.000 cubic feet. The framework below the balloon is made of steel, and weighs 4271b5. There are three independent motors— one of 5-h.p. for driving the rear propeller, and two others—each for driving the amidships propellers. Either of the latter two can be stopped at will to assist the rudder in bringing the airship round to any desired angle. The motor driven at the rate of 1,500 revolutions per minute and geared to 150 in the rear propeller, which has a diameter of 30 feet. The 5-h.p. motor weighs 30 lbs., and the smaller motors 18 1bs. each. The rud-

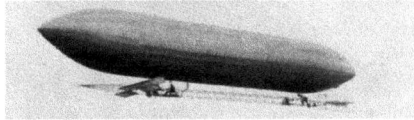

der is claimed to be constructed in a new design; it is intended to steer both the balloon and the framework. and unlike the rudders of former airships it semi-rigid. Both Mr. Gaudron and Mr. Beckmann are confident that under favourable conditions the machine will do all that is required of it—even cut through the air at the rate of 17 miles hour—and if such conditions prevail this evening Mr. Beckmann will make the attempt from the Tower grounds to cross the Mersey to Liverpool and back.

AEROSTATION, AVIATION, MANUFACTURE OF AIRSHIPS & BALLOONS

By GAUDRON, LIMITED,

Constructors of the Mammoth Balloon, Barton Airship, etc. Holders of the World's Record for over-sea journey, London to Sweden, 1907.

England's Record Distance: London to Russia 1,117 miles, 1908.

GAUDRON, LIMITED.

45, Outram Road, Alexandra Park, London, N.

Manchester Courier and Lancashire General Advertiser - Friday 24 June 1904

Professor/Captain Auguste Eugene Gaudron set various records from crossing the channel to England in a balloon. In 1901 he proposed an "aerial torpedo boat" 100 feet long (a snip @ $10,000). He designed it to carry five passengers at 30 miles an hour. It would be driven by petroleum motors, with propellers, and the lifting power was hydrogen gas, model shown opposite.

On 18 Nov. 1908, Prof. A. E. Gaudron flew in the Mammoth from Crystal Palace to Meeki Derevi in Russia a distance of 1,117 miles in 36.5 hours.

NEW FLYING SHIP. TO TRAVEL SEVENTEEN MILES AN HOUR
Seventeen miles an hour is the speed at which a new airship, built by Messrs
Auguste E. Gaudron and Charles W. Beckman, is prophesied to cleave its way
through the air. Yesterday a number of pressmen were invited to witness the
inaugural voyage of the new record-breaking craft from its canvas boathouse in
the New Brighton Tower Gardens, but as a twenty knot breeze was blowing the
experiment was indefinitely postponed. When the weather improves the
Gaudron- Beckman ship will take afternoon's cruise " over Liverpool and district.
The vessel is claimed to be an improvement on existing types, but she has
assimilated the best ideas of the pioneer airships. Instead of having one
propeller, she has three, one at each side amidships and one at the stern. Her
rudder is placed so far back as to receive the full weight of the current of air from
the large 5ft. propeller blades at the rear, causing it to act with great effort. The
balloon is cylindrical rather than cigar shaped, although the nose is pointed, and
the rear end half spherical. Each propeller is worked by a separate petrol motor,
the rear one requiring an engine of 5 h.p. and the other two of 2 1/2 h.p
The captain bridge or box conveniently situated just between the two latter, and
is thus enabled to stop or start at will either of the side paddles to assist in
steering the vessel. The rudder, which, like the screw blades, consists of oiled
canvas sheets mounted tubing, manipulated with cords. The ship really combines
both the paddle and screw systems in use on water. The framework, which is
made of bicycle tubing, is not so fragile as it looks.
The total weight of the ship, including the balloon, 4271b, which is not much
more than third of that of Mr Spencer's. The balloon itself is also much smaller.
It is 65ft. long and 18ft-. in diameter, the whole amount of hydrogen required in
sailing the ship and its skipper being 13,000.
Mr Gaudron it will remembered conducted several experiments with an
egg-shaped self-propelled balloon at the Alexandra Palace in 1898.
Sunderland Daily Echo and Shipping Gazette Friday 24 June 1904

Dolly Shepherd was a parachutist for Captain Auguste E. Gaudron, who produced
air shows at amusement parks and fairs around England. The airplane had not
been fully developed during this period, so her descents were made from gas or
hot air balloons. The only "harness" used by the parachutist was a trapeze bar to
hold onto. It was 1906 when disaster stuck, Dolly Shepherd
and Louie May decided on a double descent by parachute.
The assent went smoothly and at 3,000 feet, Dolly decided they would jump and float earthward to trill the many
spectators. But Louie could not release the pin that held the
parachute in place. Meanwhile the balloon had gained alti-
tude to about 11,000 ft. Dolly decided the only way possible
to save their lives was by using her parachute to bring them
both down to earth. The pin was pulled free and with Louie's
legs wrapped firmly around Dolly's waist and her arms
around Dolly's neck they jumped. At first the canopy failed
to open fully, but just when the descent reached a fatal
rate of speed it opened fully. The impact left Miss May with
serious inquires, but Dolly was able to walk away.

The photograph was taken in the summer of 1904, note "Dancing all Day"

PRACTICE ACCIDENT
While practising yesterday on a motor cycle for the racing to-day at New Brighton Tower. Mr Joseph Edge left the track while travelling at over 50 miles an hour, and crashed into the railings, and was badly injured about the head and arms, and had to be removed to hospital. He is, however, expected to recover.
Manchester Courier and Lancashire General Advertiser - Saturday 16 July 1904

SUICIDE AT TOWER
After climbing about 80ft. up the outside frame- work of the New Brighton Tower, John Price, a young man, slipped and fell. His head and body were terribly battered. He was of weak intellect.
Rhyl Record and Advertiser 26th November 1904

NEW BRIGHTON TOWER. AN UNFORTUNATE SPILL.
The New Brighton Tower athletic sports were last evening witnessed by about 5,000 spectators. Unfortunately the proceedings were marred by an accident in the final of the one mile bicycle handicap just before the completion of the first lap, and as the competitors were enter-ing the straight there was a spill, and out of seven riders four were brought to the ground. These were G.Boydell (Salford H.), A. W. Diddams (St. Helens C.C.), J.Highcock (St. Helens), and J.C. Beer (Rockferry) Boydell and Beer sustained but slight injuries but Diddams was reported to have broken his collar bone whilst Highcock was reported to have broken his arm.

Manchester Courier and Lancashire General Advertiser - Tuesday. 05 April 1904

DEATH OF MR J.C. BULMER

Considerable surprise and regret will be expressed in local football and athletic circles the announcement of the death of Mr. J. C. Bulmer. For many years Mr. Bulmer resided in Derby, and look a great interest in the Derby County Football Club, of which he was for some time assistant, secretary. Some eight years ago he left Derbv to take up the position of football and athletic secretary in connection with the New Brighton Tower Grounds, and created quite a sensation in the County supporters by inducing J. W. Robinson to leave Derby and throw in his lot with the new club. Mr Bulmer laboured with energy to secure admission for the professional football team, organised as New Brighton Tower to the First Division of the League, but after struggling pluckily against adverse circumstances for three seasons, the attempt was abandoned. Before the team disbanded, however, Mr. Bulmer retired from the service of the Tower Company, and became licensee of the Marine Hotel at New Brighton. Within the past week his wife died suddenly and the sad event prostrated him. His health drooped rapidly, and death ensued Thursday night. He was 44 years of age. Mr. Bulmer was active member of the Masonic Order, and was one the founders of the Egremont Lodge. He leaves two little daughters. The funeral took place this afternoon at Wallasey Cemetery.
Derby Daily Telegraph - Monday 12 December 1904

BASS EXCURSION TO NEW BRIGHTON TOWER

Free admission will be given all day to the Water Chute, Menagerie, Himalaya Railway, &c., as stated, and, in addition, there will be found numerous other side shows, at a very low price of admission,

The ATHLETIC GROUNDS, with the wonderful Cycle Track, will also be open all day for those who care to use them. On these fine grounds in the Season are given Athletic Festivals, and during the past five years all the greatest amateur and professional riders of England and the Continent have appeared at the different Tournaments promoted by the Tower Company.

The Tower grounds will be opened at 8-30 a.m., and remain open to our excursionists until 6-30 p.m., and during those hours we may again mention that FREE ADMISSION will be given to :—

Roller Skating Rink (with use of skates).
Ascent of Tower.
Water Chute.
Himalaya Railway.
Variety Performance in Theatre at 3-0 p.m.
Cloak Rooms (Ladies and Children).

All that is required to make an enjoyable holiday for those who visit New Brighton Tower is fine weather, and let us hope that we shall be favoured in this respect, for no efforts have been spared in making the best possible arrangements for our comfort and enjoyment.

The Catering is now under the Tower Company's **own management,** and visitors may be assured of obtaining the **best quality** of Refreshments of all kinds at the **lowest possible prices.**

" BASS " in Bottle—Half-pints 3d.—will be on sale at the various Bars.

ALL FOR NOTHING. BASS OF BURTON PEOPLE OUTING

Messrs. Bass, of Burton, entertained their employees and pensioners, with their families, to the number of 12,000, at Liverpool and New Brighton, yesterday. The trippers required seventeen special trains, which commenced at 4 a.m. and ran out every ten minutes until 6.50, by which time the first express had arrived at Liverpool, ninety miles away.

There is feverish bustle at the station. Special hired tramway-cars run from Burton's suburbs and deposit their freights at the station. Employees in the various departments take their trains as set out in the guide and a minute's delay in starting or arriving is unpardonable. The firm treat their trippers well, and the day's outing, including food and amusements, need not cost the employees a penny. They are even insured for £1,000 each against railway accident.

Every man is given his ticket, a day's wage, and half a sovereign to spend. At Liverpool his ticket is the open sesame to all the chief centres of attraction. The firm hires practically all the shows and facilities for travel for the day. The Burtonian can ride free all day long on the overhead railway, and at New Brighton there is hardly an attraction worth the name that has not been purchased for him. Bass's boats ply free all day, and those who desire a sea trip can run across to the Isle of Man or Llandudno. Each excursionist receives a guide-book of ninety-six pages, elaborately got up and containing over eighty fine illustrations, together with a description of the country passed through and the fullest possible instructions. The cost of such a monster trip to the firm can be but little short of £15,000. The Corporation of Liverpool have given facilities for visiting the art galleries and museums of the city, and have also offered the use of St. George's Hall in case the weather is wet. Travelling on the overhead electric railway will be free all day, and at New Brighton Tower not only all the entertainments, but the ascent of the water chute, the Himalaya railway, and even the free use of skates in the roller skating rinks, will be open to the enjoyment of the trippers.

Western Times - Saturday 16 July 1904

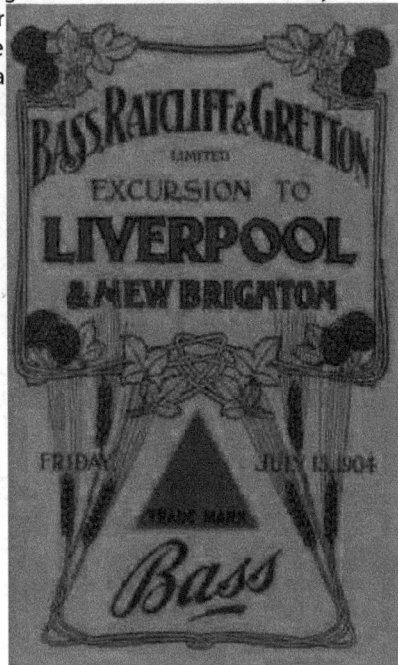

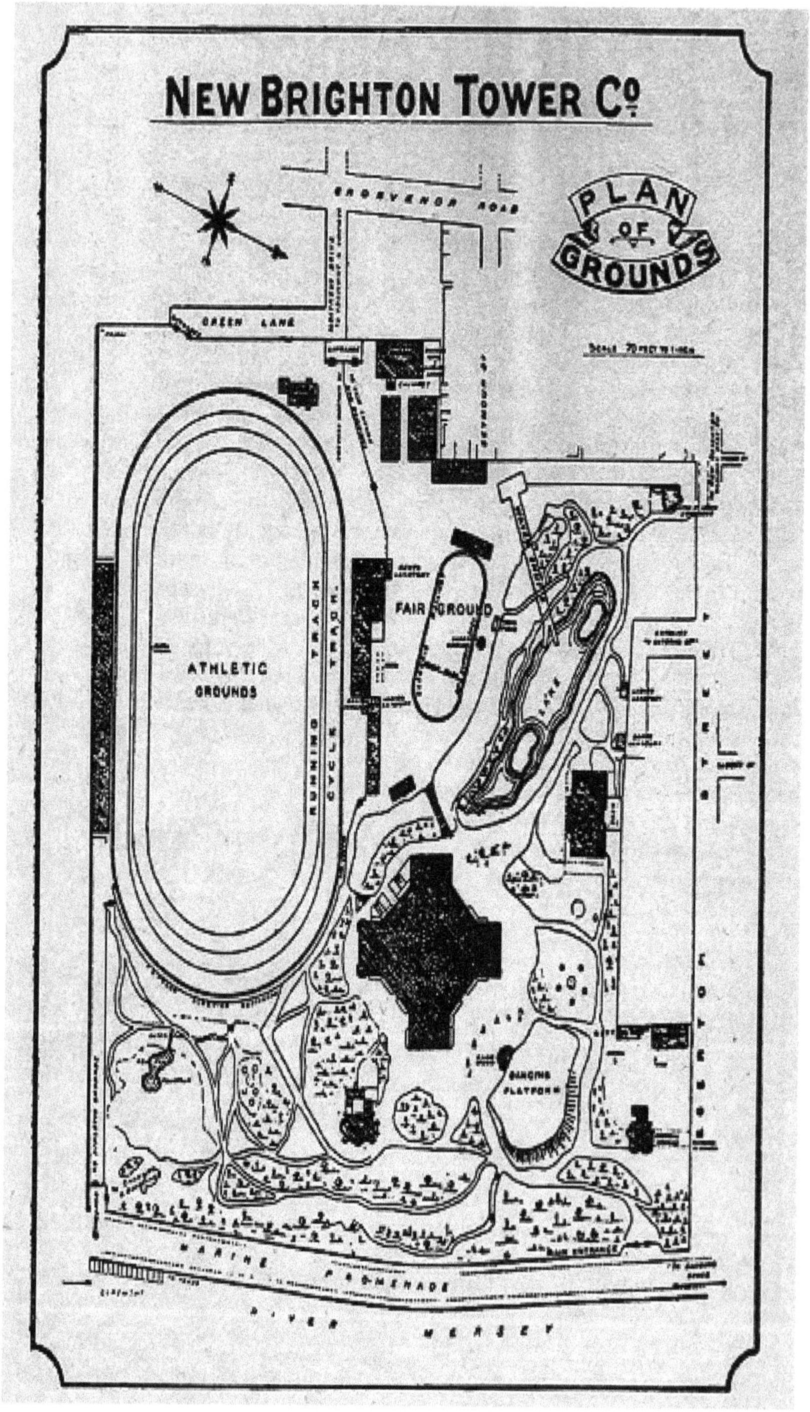
NEW BRIGHTON TOWER Co
PLAN OF GROUNDS
GROSVENOR ROAD
GREEN LANE
ATHLETIC GROUNDS
RUNNING TRACK
CYCLE TRACK
FAIR GROUND
LAKE
DANCING PLATFORM
MARINE PROMENADE
RIVER MERSEY

48

Special Programme of Entertainments.

The Grounds will be opened on the arrival of the first Steamer from the Landing Stage, Liverpool.

9.0 On the Platform facing the Sea, the **Military Band** will play:

1 March ... "Imperial Edward" ... SOUSA.
2 Overture ... "Hungarian" KELER BELLA.
3 Waltz "Mond-nach tam Rhein" VOLLSTEDT.
4 Selection ... "Mikado" ... SULLIVAN.
5 Polka ... "Le Cavalier" ... FAHRBACH.
6 Three Dances "Nell Gwynne"
EDWARD GERMAN.
7 Songe d'Amour apres le bal CZIBALKA.
8 "Invocation to Battle" (Rienzi) WAGNER.

10.0 Exhibition of all the latest **Animated Pictures** by the Royal Biograph, including latest films of Russo-Japanese War. Frequent and varied Exhibitions during the day.

10.30 Prof. Carl Travis in a high-class, unique, and fantastic Seance of Eastern Wonders, the "Mysteries of the Orient." Frequent Seances during the day.

11.0 The "Odean" String Orchestra will perform the following Programme on Platform facing the Sea.

1 March ... "El Capitan" ... SOUSA.
2 Overture "Morn, Noon & Night" SUPPE.
3 Waltz "Les Lointains" WALDTEUFEL.
4 Selection "Amorelle" GASTON SERPETTE.
5 Cake Walk "Coloured Lady's Ball"
HARRISON.
6 American Sketch "Happy Days in Dixie"
BIDGOOD.
7 Polka ... "Des Clowns" ... ALLUR.
8 Galop ... "Irrlichter" ... FAUST.

The Himalaya Railway and the Water Chute will commence running first thing in the morning and will continue all day. Visitors will be admitted on showing Ticket.

12-0 to 2-30 Pianist will play in the Ball-room for Dancing.

1.0 The **Military Band** will perform on the Dancing Platform as follows:

1 March ... "Militaire" TSCHAIKOWSKY.
2 Overture "Ruy Blas" MENDELSSOHN.
3 Waltz ... "Blanc Augen" ... PETRAS.
4 Selection "My Lady Molly" SIDNEY JONES.
5 Barn Dance "Happy Cotton Pickers"
BARNARD.
6 Polka ... "Ins Centruni" ... STASNEY.
7 Cornet Solo "Reminiscenses of Norway"
DEPPE.
8 Galop ... "Champagner" ... WIEGAND.

The lifts for ascent of the Tower (from the Elevator Hall) will run all day and admission will be granted on production of Ticket.

3.0 The Renowned **Tower Orchestra** (Conductor, Mr. Charles Reynolds) will perform the following programme for dancing in the Grand Ball-room.

1 Polka ... "Tout ou Rien" WALDTEUFEL.
2 Waltz ... "Militaire" WALDTEUFEL.
3 Barn Dance "My Lady Molly"
SIDNEY JONES.
4 Lancers "A Chinese Honeymoon"
H. TALBOT.
5 Waltz ... "Casino-Tanze' ... GUNG'L.
6 Waltz ... "Amorelle" ... BUCALOSSI.
7 Lancers ... "Cake Walk" W. WILLIAMS.
8 Barn Dance "Down South" MYDDLETON.
9 Waltz ... "Deutsche Lust" STRAUSS.
10 Lancers "The March King" LANGSDALE.
11 Waltz "Pluie de diamants" WALDTEUFEL.
12 Galop "In dulci Jubilo" ... BOHM.

The American Roller Skating Rink will be open all day and **free** use of Skates will be given on showing Ticket.

3.0 Grand Variety Performance in the Tower Theatre. Admission on production of Ticket. (First-class passengers only will be admitted to the **front seats.**)

1 OVERTURE by the Orchestra.
2 ALMA CURZON, the favourite Soubrette and Burlesque Actress.
3 STYLO, 'The King of Hoops,' manipulation extraordinary.
4 GEO. FOSTER, Eccentric Comedian.
5 THE SKANDIA TROUPE of Swedish Gymnasts. Four in number. Direct from the Empire, London.
6 THE MORRISON GIRLS. Dainty character Duettists and Dancers.
7 PERMANE'S Wonderful Educated Bears.
8 THE ROYAL KORRIES in their novel speciality Musical Entertainment.

5.0 The **Military Band** will perform the following Programme for Dancing on Platform facing the Sea.

1 Polka "Toujours Gallant" FAHRBACH.
2 Waltz ... "Nightingale" ... CZIBULKA.
3 Barn Dance "Pop Corn" ... LATH.
4 Lancers ... "Savoy" ... MOORE.
5 Waltz "Au clair de Lune" FAHRBACH.
6 Waltz "The Mill Stream" LASSERRE.
7 Barn Dance "De Gorn Coon" BIDGOOD.
8 Lancers "State Ball" LEYDEL.
9 Waltz ... ... "Naples" ... WALDTEUFEL.
10 Galop "The Narren" ... GUNG'L.

The Athletic Grounds will be open to all visitors during the day on presentation of ticket at the gates.

5-0 Animals fed in the Menagerie.

5-0 to 6-30 Dancing in the Ballroom

5-0 to 6-30 Theatre Orchestra will play at the Japanese Kiosk.

Numerous other side-shows in addition to those mentioned will be found on the Old English Fair Grounds, for admission to which a small charge will be made.

The Cloak Rooms, &c., are open to ladies and children all day.

The photograph above show the entrance to the "Himalayan Railway" located in the Old English Fairground, the Railway had been imported from the Brussels Exhibition, it was described in the guide of 1898 as follows...a great attraction to young and old. It consists of a combination of the old switchback and the modern electric railway - the rails are laid in the usual way, but in lieu of following the old fashioned horizontal line, the track ascends and descends in the peculiar fashion hitherto adopted exclusively by the Switchbacks. The passengers travel in tiny carriages which take them twice around the course, then through a tunnel, and land them safe and sound at the point of departure. The railway had been modified over the years, and was replaced in 1908 by the scenic railway.

104

BABY SHOW AT NEW BRIGHTON. AN INTERESTING SPECTACLE.
Babies to the number of 155, ranging in age from four or five to twelve months,
and hailing from the Lancashire and Cheshire sides of the Mersey, were on
Monday evening exhibited on the stage of the New Brighton Tower to the large
and admiring audience which had assembled in the spacious theatre. The
occasion was the first baby show promoted by the Tower authorities, and the
success which attended this novel venture will no doubt lead to further
competitions of a like character. Prizes, consisting of baby clothes, bassinets, etc.,
were offered, and the spectacle presented was most interesting, as the mothers,
with their young charges, waited for admission at the stage-door, and afterwards
arranged themselves on the stage in seats surrounded by scenery to represent a
drawing-room. As the competitors were admitted they were thoughtfully
presented with grotesque toys, which, judging from the freedom from squalls,
pleased greatly the little recipients.
Later, however, when the fond mothers commenced the operation of
divesting their little ones of their clothing prior to weighing some baby voices
were apparently raised in protest, but on the whole the youthful débutantes
conducted themselves admirably. As the curtain was raised on the stage full
of youngsters the audience applauded again and again, and as the weighing
proceeded and the weights were called out the keenest interest was evinced. To
obtain the correct weight a pair of scales, with a scoop at one end, was suspended
from the middle of the stage, and for baby's comfort cushions were arranged, for
which an allowance was made on the: weight side. A committee of judges,
composed of local ladies, occupied seats on one side of the stage close to the
scales; Messrs. G. Poulton and F. Ashworth assisted in the weighing, and Mr.
Albert Bulmer superintended the competition. The scene as the proceedings
progressed was alike interesting and amusing, not a little laughter being
occasioned by the comical antics of some of the babies, who were quite
unabashed despite their strange surroundings. In a few instances youngsters
managed to get to the boards and crawl towards the footlights, much to the
amusement of the audience, while in other cases the little ones shewed aversion
to or delight at seeing so many other babies around them. There were four classes
altogether, and while the smallest baby in the class for under six months weighed
14 1b. the heaviest turned the scale at 21 1b. l oz.: while the child of the greatest
avoirdupois weighed 38 1b., or more than the twins which secured the highest
award in their own particular class. The following are the awards:
Under 12 months: Jane Elizabeth Davies, age 11 months, Breck place, Poulton;
weight 38 lb. The championship was awarded to this child for being the finest,
healthiest, best looking, and best dressed of the competitors. Class 1 (under six
months): 1, Thomas Roscoe Kelly, Royston-avenue, Egremont, 21 lb. 1oz.
 2, Eva Mallett, 14, Evan-street, Liverpool, 20 lb. 8oz. Class 2 (under nine months):
1, Alfred Dawkins, Park-street, Liscard, 25 lb. 10oz.; 2, William C. Lloyd,
Hampden-street, Walton, 24 lb. 10oz. Class 3: 1, Jane Elizabeth Davies; 2, Robert
Chester, Rotherham, Altcar-avenue, Wavertree, 29 lb. 14oz. Class 4-. twins, under
six months: 1, Doris and George Vaughan, Berkeley-street, Liverpool. 32 lb. 12oz.,
combined weight: 2, Alice and James Grant, Rutland-street, Bootle, 29 lb.,
combined weight.
Cheshire Observer 29th July 1905

There were 155 babies exhibited at the New Brighton baby show on Monday. The champion baby scaled 38lb., although less than twelve months old. The contest, of course afforded much amusement. *Wallasey News July 1905*

106

NEW BRIGHTON TOWER.
W ANTED, to let, on shares or rent, several good positions on Fair Grounds, for Season. Novel and Attractive Shows. Electric light in each place.
Apply Sec., Tower, New Brighton.

The Era - Saturday 18 February 1905

WRESTLING NEW BRIGHTON TOWER
Sunday amid scenes of extraordinary enthusiasm. A wrestling match at New Brighton Tower, Saturday, attracted a large attendance, especially from Yorkshire. The contestants were Tom McInerney, of Liverpool, catch-as-catch champion of England, and Baldwin, of Leeds, champion wrestler of Yorkshire.
The Yorkshireman was beaten.
Hull Daily Mail - Monday 24 April 1905

BAND CONTESTS.
Several band contests were decided on Saturday. At New Brighton Tower the contest resulted as follow: The Goodshaw, Grand Tower 50 guinea challenge cup, and silver-mounted baton, 1; Wingates Temperance, 2; Crook, £15, 3; Gossage's, £12. 4; Irwell Springs, £10. 5; Eccles Borough, £7. 6; North Ashton, £5.
At the Lister Band Contest, at Bradford, Lindley won Lord Masham's Cup and £30. Stalybridge quickstep competition was won by Platt Bridge band.
Manchester Courier and Lancashire General Advertiser - Monday 19 June 1905

NEW MANAGER
New Brighton Tower's New Manager. Mr R. H. Davy, who for six years has had the management of the athletic meetings held at New Brighton Tower, and who has also performed the secretarial duties in connection with that place of amusement, has been appointed manager of the Tower grounds in succession to Mr Albert Bulmer. Mr Davy was at one time associated with the Blackpool Tower Company in the capacity of Assistant Secretary.
The Weekly News and Visitors' Chronicle for Colwyn...3rd November 1905

One of the most important additions to the entertainment was the installation of a roller coaster in 1905. The 'Figure of Eight' coaster was installed in the Tower Grounds close to the entrance. The figure 8 design allowed for more turns and followed on from the original out and back design, which made for a more exciting ride. The top photograph shows the entrance to the roller coaster.

At the New Brighton Tower Musical EISTEDDFOD; for the third time succession, the Manchester Orpheus Glee Society was adjudged "first" at this meeting, defeating its old rival, the Southport Vocal Union, and thereby winning outright the silver challenge cup, a gold medal, and £25.
Manchester Courier and Lancashire General Advertiser - Tuesday 02 October 1906

NEW BRIGHTON TOWER. This concern has a dismal report to present its shareholders for Christmas. With a further loss of £9,400 during the past year, the debit balance is brought up £35,900. Arrears of Preference dividends now amount to 30 per cent., or about £52,000. The best thing the shareholders can do is bestir themselves and put the company into liquidation.
Leeds Mercury - Saturday 22 December 1906

Mystery Postcard addressed to The Chaps, The office, C/O Jos Owen F.A B.A Architect, Menai Bridge. Posted July 1906, I have several postcards on the same subject, exhibition military camp? But I have not been able to identify the event.

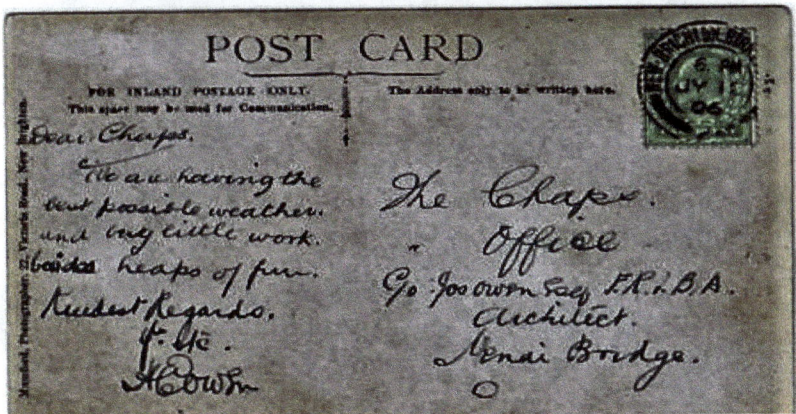

The Tiller girls appeared on numerous occasions in shows at the Tower. From the 1906 souvenir brochure the original cast which was created by John Tiller, but in the early days not all his troupes were named after its creator, the brochure includes the renowned The Superba Quartet, The Pony Ballet and The Palace Girls.

A TILLER TROUPE.

In the 1910's..the main attraction Gallopers, Chairoplanes, switchback and scenic style rides.. Top right photograph shows a switchcar ride in the Tower grounds. The Bioscope shown above was soon to be replaced by permanent cinemas.

When everyone had gas mantles at home for light, the Tower Company generated all its own electricity from a generator the largest in the land, to produce a spectacular colour light show with over 32,000 lamps. A true marvel which had engineers from all over the world visiting to inspect its awesome power.
With concealed Arc Lights that lit up the outline of the Tower, red, white and green fairy lights along the pathways, and placed in the trees. It was a truly spectacular show.

ROUND THE WORLD IN TEN MINUTES

Travel by such a rate, even in these hustling times, seems a veritable impossibility but the next approach to this idea is supplied by Hale's Tours. An American invention, it need hardly be mentioned that the thing is smart. During the height of its success across the Pond it was then introduced in London, the population of which have been held captive by it for months - and still they keep touring. Hale's company have also furnished their Pullman cars in Manchester's White City, in Brighton, Margate and many of the big towns of the North of England, as well as in Dublin and Glasgow. And now we have one of their picturesque stations, a replica of that in Oxford-street, Metropolis, situate in proximity to the main entrance to the Theatre in New Brighton Tower. It is an ornate, compact, and,

with all, complex structure. Externally attractive, it is comfortable, almost luxurious inside. Once "the journey" is started passengers find it difficult to realise they are not actually passing through the scenes so vividly depicted, for not only are the views exceptionally clear and possessing a large amount of originality, but the different effects interpolated are astonishingly and pleasing unique. The New Brighton station and its Pullman, which, under the able superintendence of Mr. W. Yates Gregory, was erected within fourteen days, will occupy its conspicuous stand for three seasons, and it is hoped and expected that the show will receive that patronage which the promoters toughly merit.
Wallasey News - 29th June 1907

Hale's Tours of the World was an entertainment which placed the audience in a replica of a railway carriage, with a film taken from the front of a moving train projected onto a screen at the front of the carriage. The conductor of the Pullman Car, actually snips the tickets on your arrival. The carriage rocked to and fro, there were train sound effects, the roar of falling waters or tossing sea waves, the pattering of rain, the rolling of thunder, and the shouts of people add reality to the excursion. and at the start of your adventure the conductor served a lecturer to explain the films. It was invented by the American George Consider Hale and the first Hale's Tours in Britain opened in London's Oxford Street in May 1906.

LIVERPOOL MAGAZINE

NEW BRIGHTON TOWER.

Foremost in the ranks of pleasure places in the North of England stands New Brighton Tower and grounds, with its mammoth programme of entertainments, sufficient to satisfy the most diverse natured holiday-makers, and do credit to its capable management. It is practically a town of enjoyment, for one can go in first thing in the morning and stay till last thing at night, and still leave plenty undone. Excellent meals are provided at popular prices in the cafes and restaurants. The attractions include an Abyssinian village, populated by 75 Abyssinians, including Emperor Menelik's bodyguard. Native workers can be seen at their occupations, and warriors display their dances. On the Fair ground all the manifold attractions of the Water-chute, Helter-skelter, Aeriel-flight, and kindred shows are to be found. A miniature railway runs from the entrance gates to the old quarry, and claims to be the smallest railway in the world. Maxim's Giant Flying Machine and Hale's Famous Tours of the World prove splendid attractions. The view from the top of the Tower—621 feet—is unequalled. Dancing goes on all day in the magnificent ballroom. Then there is the theatre, twice daily, where Mr. John Tiller's famous troupe of over 100 performers presents "Monte Carlo," which is supplemented by the Scala Girls, the Bioscope, and a first-class variety programme.

No description of the good things of the Tower would be complete without mention of the famous Sunday evening concerts. On September 1st Kreisler will appear, September 8th, Kirkby Lunn, and September 15th Marie Hall. On Saturday, September 21st, the annual Musical Eisteddfod will be held, and a list of competitions, test pieces, etc., will be forwarded on application.

HELTER-SKELTER

ON THE MAT

114

MORE ABOUT BETTING AT SPORTS.
Writing, a fortnight ago, on the subject of betting at sports. I instanced the case of hundreds of people turning away from the entrance at the Liverpool Athletic Grounds on Good Friday on seeing the N.C.U. notice prohibiting betting. Now I note that the New Brighton Tower Company, apparently fearing that recent legislation on the betting evil will seriously affect "gates," have decided not to let their track for sports during this year. If this course will be followed by sports promoters in general, we shall come to the conclusion that cycle and foot-racing have small merits of their own sporting attractions; that, indeed, their success in the past has been due to the mere excitement of speculation. It is an unpalatable suggestion, but one fears is only too true. As I pointed out in my last note on the subject, the better class of sportsmen, who have been driven away by the betting evil in the past, may return to the sport, in the hope of seeing honest and genuine racing; but their return will be by degrees, and in the meantime there is a fear lest meetings may have to be abandoned on a wholesale scale. Our contemporary, Cycling," hits off the position neatly in this week's issue. Who's going to win the handicap ?" Genuine racing, without the bookie, is surely to be preferred to the dishonesty that is, unfortunately, impossible to dissociate from the sport where the layer of odds is allowed.
Leeds Mercury - Friday 26 April 1907

THE NEW BALLET "Her Birthday" Produced at the Tower.
On Saturday evening a new ballet of a spectacular character entitled "Her Birthday" was produced by Mr John Tiller at the Tower Theatre, when a crowded audience expressed its delight by enthusiastic applause. The Ballet is most sweet and dainty,being a charming realisation of life and manners in France under Louise Quinze. With the exception of two or three pretty choruses, all is conducted in pantomime, but the gestures of the performers are most eloquent. The scene is one brightness and charm, and the painter has exercised great skill and taste. The delightful dresses are beyond description, such a magnificent combination of silks and satin and laces and velvets very rarely being seen. Exceedingly effective were some dresses in heliotropes and pale green with silver sequin trimmings and underskirts of violet. Other dresses of pale rose pink were in-crusted with large velvet roses of a deeper shade edged with silver sequins and the leaves and stems being exquisitely patterned in silver sequins. Two footmen were in magnificent costumes of white and gold. All the hats worn were simply lovely. The Mersey Mites appeared in striking dresses of tangerine silk with outer skirts of cream net and red shoes and stockings. The blend of the colours when the dances were in progress was simply enchanting. Miss May Sharples and Miss Alice Donaldson, who sustain the parts of Mdlle la Marquise and Mdlle. Julie have dresses which are simply superb and must have cost a tremendous sum. The dancing and posing of Miss Donaldson were most graceful. Several well arranged and exceedingly pretty dances are included in the ballet, through the mazes of which the performers passed with much skill.
The 'Alabama Coon' increases in popularity, and the fun goes faster than ever together of these ballets, which are both fantastic at each performance, would be enough to draw crowded houses.
26th June 1907 - Wallasey News

Easter at New Brighton Tower
Good Friday night at 8 p.m the usual Sacred Concert will be given at New Brighton Tower Theatre, with Miss Edith McCullagh, the favourite soprano, and Mr Frank Barker, the eminent tenor of the Halle Concerts, as the soloists.
Easter Sunday at 8:15 p.m, at the Grand Sacred Concerts, the soloists will be Miss Sarah Crook, the very popular mezzo-soprano of the Blackpool Concerts, and Mr Bridge Peters, the well known bass-baritone of Halle Concerts, Manchester. The instrumental parts of the programme at both concerts will be furnished by Prof. Charles Reynolds and his favourite Tower Band and Orchestra. Gates open to grounds at 10 a.m. Commencing Saturday, April 18th, and all during Easter week, at 3 and 8 p.m. each day, a great Variety Programme has been provided for the Tower patrons. An exceptionally strong bill has been made up and includes among its favourite such popular as Phil Herman, the Four Sisters Netherland, the Two Circus Boys, Mr Hesketh Meade, and Misses Madge Goodall and Marion Fletcher, besides a splendid comedy company in the brilliant playlet "The Last of the Desmonds," an episode in the life of an Irish gentleman of the 17th century. There has been a great shaking up of old things around the New Brighton Tower and Park preparatory to the opening of the regular season on May 23rd. Director Brown and Manager Ellis together with their assistants and some two hundred workmen, are engaged in making changes and improvements all over the place. The old water chute is being practically rebuilt, while the lake will be encircled by one of L.A. Thompson's Scenic Railways. Along the park enclosure fronting on the Marine Parade a great figure eight gravity road is being erected. Hale's Tours and the Big River Show will be given more prominent locations and a number of new shows will be added to the attractions of the Old English Fair Grounds. Some big work will be put on the Athletic Ground to prepare it for the Cummins Wild West and Indian Congress which will be a complete Indian Village, wherein will be shown for the first time in England the home life of these red men from North America. Immediately after Easter week the Theatre in the Tower will be done over for the big Negro Plantation Show that will open there on May 23rd. The great Tower will have some 3,000 sixteen candle power electric lights put on it and more than one hundred arc lights, and two thousand extra fairy lights, will be added to the illumination of the Grounds. The restaurants and refreshment places are being done over and freshened up.
Birkenhead Herald April 1908

New Brighton, from Tower

NEW BRIGHTON TOWER. Mr. J. Calvin Brown, managing director of the White City in Manchester, has taken over the management of the New Brighton Tower, and, in consequence, for the past two months the work of rehabilitating and improving that popular resort has been in progress, with the result that when the season begins on Saturday, May 23, there will practically be opened a new park at New Brighton. The tower, theatre, ballroom, billiard-rooms, cafés, restaurants, rifle galleries, menagerie, and other things that have attracted the public in the past will naturally be retained as drawing cards for this and all subsequent seasons, for without them the park would not be Tower Park. Hales's tours, the air-ships, the Himalaya railway, etc., are also to be arranged, but Mr. Brown has shifted all these about in a way to change the aspect of things and make the gardens more beautiful than ever. In addition to these the theatre will be occupied by Millican's Old Plantation Show, which consists of a large number of negro singers, dancers, actors and coon-shouters from the best coloured talent of America. The smaller buildings of the gardens and in the Tower proper will contain a number of small illusions, shows, etc. In the gardens and facing the promenade will be found such novelties in devices as the cycles, the helter skelter, the old light house, the beautiful areo flyte, and the fascinating gravity railroad, known as the figure 8, while encircling the lake and over the popular water chutes will be found a monster scenic railway, with a ride of nearly a mile in length. Every afternoon and evening the famous Cummins-Brown Concert Band of Cowboys will play on the Plaza and the reputation of this organisation seems to assure visitors a pleasant hour listening to them. The great attraction of the season will be on the athletic grounds, where the Cummins-Brown Wild West will give performances every afternoon and evening, of the same character as these given by Buffalo Bill.
The Chester Courant and Advertiser for North Wales 20th May 1908

In late 1910, Calvin Brown announced a plan to organise an international chain of amusement parks, with a one guinea season ticket scheme for unlimited admission to New Brighton, Earl's Court and his sites at Paris and Manchester. Probably Walt Disney copied his ideas. White City in Manchester had cost £50,000 and was an instant success, six months later, he acquired New Brighton Tower and Fun Park, and installed Albert Ellis (who had run a fairground in Blackpool) as manager

WILD WEST SHOW

One of the greatest shows ever to appear in the Tower Stadium was the
Cummins-Brown "Wild West" and Indian Congress which was staged for the
summer season, starting on 23rd May 1908, running to the autumn. The new
Manager-Director at the Tower was Mr. J. Calvin Brown, and together with Colonel
Frederick T. Cummins, was in charge of the performance on the Athletic Ground
while, in the theatre, the Millican's Minstrels and Old Plantation Show was staged.
An entertainment guide describes the act as follow: "With plantation melodies
and dances done by real Negroes brought here from the plantations of Georgia,
Louisiana and Alabama a feature brought here by Fred S. Millican under the
name of Dixie Land. Dixie Land is not the ordinary minstrel show or black-face
entertainment. Millican's Negroes are the real thing and their songs and dances
are exactly the songs and dances with which they amuse themselves in their
leisure hours, after work in the cotton fields".

The S.S. " Haverford " arrived at Liverpool on the 14th May with the contingent of
the Wild West Show including Colonel Cummins, partner of Mr. J. Calvin Brown, of
the Cummins-Brown Wild West and Indian Congress destined for New Brighton.
The party included the Sioux Indians, including Henry Standing Bear, chief
Government interpreter for the American Indians. The latter are squaws and
papooses, and have such names, such as Paul Lone Elk, Sammy Two Bulls, Philip
Iron Elk, High Eagle. Kills First. The Cowboys include Wild Bill Dillingham, Joe
Lynch, Bull McLean, Buffalo Vernon, Shoot-on Price, and so on. Miss Anna Schaffer,
"the greatest rough riding lady in the world," is also coming, and with her little
sister, Maisie Schaffer. To-morrow there is to be a parade illustrative of the
White City. It will leave the Central Station, Manchester, at 12 30, and later in the
afternoon the White City will open its gates with gala ceremonies. After several
performances in Manchester, the Show moved off by train to Liverpool.

A parade of Cowboys and Indians, Horses and a Stage Coach set off from Lime
Street in Liverpool to the Landing Stage to meet the ferry. This was all arranged
to publicise the Congress. One of the many posters on display portrayed Anna
Shaffer on her horse. It advertised "lady bronco riders, Indian Warriors, Squaws
and papoose". They claimed "Educated Wild Beasts" performing. The Wild West
Show had a six months season. It had been billed as the Greatest Show on Earth
with 500 men and horses taking part, including Cowboys and Cowgirls, U.S.
Artillery, Crack-shot Rifle Displays, U.S. Cavalry men, Cossacks, Indian Warriors,
Chariot Drivers, Acrobats and Contortionists. The horsemanship was superb with
Colonel Cummins taking part. The Redskins called him "Chief Lakota" and there
are many stories about him. American Cattle were not allowed into the country so
Wild Highland Cattle were brought from Scotland for the cowboys to lasso.

TRAGIC DEATH

Romantic tragedy at the tower - Cowboy shoots himself on wedding eve. Was the
headline in the Wallasey News of the 5th September.

At the Coroners inquest Inspector Dutton was involved in the investigation of the
death of George Price aged 22 of Oklahoma.

"He must have stood with the rifle muzzle facing him and shot himself in his
mouth" was how the affair was reported to the coroner by the Inspector.

Margaret Riley, waitress in Victoria Road, New Brighton, stated that she had
known the deceased for two months and had been keeping company with him:

they were to have been married on Thursday morning at 11 o clock. She saw him at a quarter past ten on Wednesday morning, and went with him to Birkenhead, whence they travelled to the office of the registrar in Brougham terrace, West Derby Road, Liverpool, and procured a marriage license. They made an appointment, arranging to meet at New Brighton Pier between one and half-past on the following afternoon. She turned up to time, and a girl sent by Mrs Carver came and told her that George was taken ill. She accompanied the girl and then learnt that her fiancé was dead. The verdict returned was that the deceased had committed suicide, but there was no evidence to show the state of his mind at the time he committed the act.

A large procession was arranged for the funeral at Rake Lane Cemetery. It was led by Cowboys and Cowgirls, followed by a large number of fully- dressed Indians and squaws with head-dresses, along with their "Chief", with his beautifully feathered head dress. There was also a small Cowboy Band. At the rear was the cortège on a sort of gun-carriage pulled by piebald horses. They made their way from Molyneux Drive to Rake Lane in a slow procession mourning their loved one.

High Jinks in New Brighton
Noel Smith wrote in 'Almost An Island' ....The Cowboys, when not taking part in the Show, would go down to New Brighton and shoot off their guns of a night and the police had a lot of extra work on their hands. They lassoed everything you can think of, including the pretty girls!
On account of the Indians going wild with "Fire Water", Public Houses in New Brighton were told not to serve them with liquor. They were a colourful sight as they prowled around Victoria Road and the promenade.
Another attraction at the Wild West Show was the original Dead-Wood Dick Stage coach that raced across the field, chased by the Indians and the Cowboys coming to the rescue. Then there was the pony with a gold tooth.
There was a special concert held in honour of Colonel Cummins at the Grosvenor Mansions on the corner of Molyneux Drive and many important people were invited."

CHILDREN'S CLUB AT THE TOWER.

Some members of the C.C.C. in the Old Stage Coach.

The "Courier Children's Club had attained a membership of over 8,000 children with an age range of six to eighteen ("Uncle Ned" referred to the children as his nephews and nieces), and every week they added to the number.

Prizes and events were awarded to the most energetic and enthusiastic members. Yesterday a couple of hundred of the clubs members with their mothers, had the outing that promises to become an annual event at New Brighton. First there was a run on the lift to the top of the Tower. Then a ride on the Water Chute and the scenic railway. In the Theatre a capital variety entertainment was provided by the management. Then it was off to the Wild West with a show from Colonel F.T. Cummins.

One of the incidents of the performance was the ride in the old overland stage coach of a dozen members of "Uncle Ted's" party, the quaint old vehicle being hauled at racing speed around the arena during a make-believe attack by Indians. Then a visit to the Indian Village, and a move to the Algerian cafe for tea. The directors of the new Brighton Recreation Company, Mr J. Calvin Brown (directing manager) Mr A Ellis (resident manager). Colonel F.T.Cummins and his able assistants (Messrs G. Wells, S.T. Wilbur and C.F Rhodes) Mr Frank A.Small (the picturesque and very capable press manager) Mr C. Humbernett (Catering manager) and Messrs Iles and Eslick (of the scenic railways). wished everyone farewell.

Extracts from the Evening Express Liverpool Wednesday, July 22 1908

120

WILD-WEST PARADE.—To-morrow morning, through the principal streets of New Brighton, Egremont, and Liscard, starting from the New Brighton Pier, the Cummins-Brown Wild-West, with its Cowboy band, Indians, Cowboys, Lady Riders, Sharpshooters, Old Stage Coach. &c., will make a parade. This parade is made at the request of the local people who did not see the one just before the opening of the Tower season on May 22nd. A full turnout will be made by the Wild-West forces, whose fine show in the Lower grounds is being so enthusiastically appreciated.

THE COWBOY BARONET
Sir Genile Cave Brown Cave, the cowboy baronet, appeared last night in the ring at Colonel Cummins' Wild West Show, which is appearing at New Brighton Tower Grounds. He was only on a hurried visit to Liverpool, and advantage was taken of his presence by two of his cowboy friends, who are with Colonel Cummins' band, to get him to change into the old familiar clothes. As he rode round the enclosure he received a hearty reception.
Evening Express 12th June 1908

NOT SO PROFITABLE
Extracts from a letter dated 25th September 1908.
Dear Billy Boy
This will be a short of rambling and general letter. The New Brighton Tower Park will close down on Saturday of the present week, and while the weather to-day is all that could possibly be hopped for by the most fastidious concessionaires, still the time is practically here when the public are looking for outdoor entertainments and the closing of the season does not come to early. However more often than not, the first three weeks of October are amongst the best days of the year in England, still the uncertainty makes it wise to have our affairs in order and close up for business before the first of the month.
The two big money-makers at the New Brighton Tower have been the scenic railway and the Figure 8. The Cummins Wild West Show, while playing to good business, was rather expensive for a park show, and for such a long season, the result has not been financially what was anticipated. The month of September had been particularly bad, because there were only four days of the first twenty-five on which it did not rain, and rain hard.
Colonel Cummins has been having some trouble with his horses. Some six weeks ago one of his mules, used in the stage-coach was killed by the local authorities, and on the 14th instant one of his horses suffered a like fate from the same authorities. These horses were condemned because they developed glanders liquidation.. Inoculation has recently taken place and several other horses have been condemned, but arguing this condemnation Colonel Cummins has made a vigorous protest, but it looks not enough. Several of his horses will be scarified. The results of this last inoculation which took place on Sunday evening have not yet been made known. Ten are now in quarantine for a second dose of serum. They are great suspects. These have been condemned to death, but in face of protests the authorities have not carried out the sentence. The Colonel has as yet not succeeded in arranging any place to which he will take his show for the winter, but still hopes that he will be able clean up the Dublin arrangements, so that he can put in at least a part of the cold weather in that city.
The Billboard dated 17th October 1908

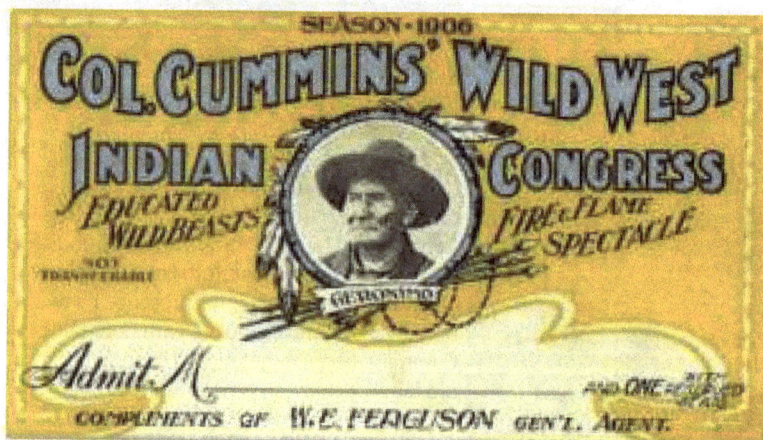

1908 - Scenic Railway

In 1908 the 'Himalaya Railway' was replaced with a scenic railway. The amusement park in the Tower Grounds promoted itself as "absolutely the First American Free Amusement Park on this side of the Atlantic". With the Scenic Railway being advertised as "Direct from Coney Island" The public fascination with American-style entertainment knows no bounds.

The 1912 guide to the tower informs the reader"... at the rear of the [Scenic] railway one may inspect the open-air Zoological Pens, whilst further on is the Shooting Gallery and the Menagerie and Lion House. The menagerie contains a most interesting and varied collection from all parts of the world, including the celebrated Lion, 'Pasha', acknowledged to be one of the finest in captivity, and, in addition, the huge favourite elephant 'Punch'.

The Scenic Railway roller coaster concept was also developed by La Marcus Thompson. The first example opened in 1887 in Atlantic City, USA. The idea behind the Scenic Railway was to create a ride where passengers could enjoy an imaginary scenic tour. They featured articulated carriages, powered cables to lift the trains up inclines, and often had their structures covered by elaborate landscapes to create the effect of mountain scenery. They were therefore the direct forerunner of the present modern-day roller coaster. One major difference, however, is that the trains did not have under friction wheels (used in modern day roller coasters to prevent them from leaving the track), therefore they required the use of a brake-man who sat between cars one and two keeping the speed in check.

The Scenic Railway was one of the main attractions at New Brighton Tower grounds which was not included in the entrance fee. Charges were 6d for adults and 3d for children. Above photograph the entrance can be seen bottom right.

NEW BRIGHTON BAND CONTEST

There were fourteen entries for the eleventh annual brass band contest, which took place at the New Brighton Tower grounds on Saturday. There were a total of seven prizes, the first consisting of the Tower Challenge cup, £30 in cash, and a silver mounted baton. The winners were: I, Irwell Springs (cup holders) 2, Goodshaw 3. Wingate Temperance; 4. Cleckheaton Victoria; 5. Shaw; 6.Perfection Soap Works; 7. Fodens. The Black Dike Band were among the unsuccessful competitors. *The Rhos Herald 12th June 1909*

Irwell Springs brass band went from strength to strength with triumphs gained at New Brighton, where they carried off for the first time the handsome challenge cup. Their performance at New Brighton can be best realised by appending the following letter which was received from a well-known Liverpool musician:

Irwell Springs Band - Crystal Palace & New Brighton Winners, 1908

"Irwell Springs notes at New Brighton ought to be printed in letters of gold, and hung up framed in every house in the Bacup District. 45 years have we been following contests, and it was the most perfect performance we have ever heard. From the first note it was a winning performance, no band that ever we have heard has such a tone as "Irwell Springs" has at present - it stands alone."

THE BEAUTY SHOW. . HUMOURS AT NEW BRIGHTON.

There was plenty of amusement of a sort at New Brighton Tower beauty competition on Saturday night. Three thousand people filled the theatre, and the boisterous certainly indulged in merry, and at times candid remarks. A girl who appeared in white costume with many red ribbons was at once greeted with a cry of "Hello here's the May horse!" whilst a show of beautiful hair led to whistling of "Get your hair out." Other ladies were advised to take the paint off. When a dozen beauties came to the front of the stage the greater part of the audience sang "Put amongst the girls."
Nottingham Evening Post - Monday 6th September 1909

ALL NIGHT ON NEW BRIGHTON TOWER
The lift attendant at New Brighton Tower on making his final ascent on Wednesday morning was surprised find a woman and her child, aged about eight years, at the summit. They gone up the night before. Prior to making his last descent at 9 30, the attendant had looked round and seen no one: and how the woman was missed he does not know. The night was cold, wet and stormy, and both had suffered considerably.
Manchester Courier & Lancashire General Advertiser - Friday 10 September 1909

NEW BRIGHTON EISTEDDFOD.
The ninth annual Challenge Musical Eisteddfod at the New Brighton Tower, for which prizes to the value of £150 are offered, will take place Saturday week. Individual competitors number about 260. and competing choirs are coming from Southport St Helens, Oldham. Colne Valley, Huddersfield, Wigan, Nelson, Burnley, Crewe, and Warrington.
Manchester Courier & Lancashire General Advertiser - Friday 10 September 1909

THE ATTACK ON LIVERPOOL. DESTROYERS OBSERVED AND BEATEN OFF.
The naval manoeuvres in the Mersey, which lasted 24 hours, ended last evening apparently in the failure of the hostile force, consisting of the cruiser Doris and two destroyers, the Lee & Fairy, to penetrate the defences of the port of Liverpool. After a futile attack on Wednesday night the warships retired, but early yesterday morning another raid was attempted. Searchlights from the battery on either shore and from the New Brighton Tower, however, soon disclosed the movement, and after a fierce bombardment the attacking party were compelled to retreat. During the forenoon yesterday one the destroyers made another attempt, but it is understood that she was captured, hauling down her colours and entering the river as a prize. The manoeuvres attracted interest on both sides the Mersey.
Nottingham Evening Post - Friday 30 July 1909

H.M.S. DORIS, 2ND CLASS CRUISER.

MALE "BEAUTIES."
There are 30 men in Liverpool and district who think so highly of their personal appearance that they entered for a male beauty competition on Saturday night at New Brighton Tower. A very large audience of at least 3,000 people assembled to see these "beauties" in all shapes and sizes, and every one was awkward. One important individual boasted a frock coat,; another appeared in a light suit with vivid waistcoat; still another came on with his overcoat buttoned, and looked as coy as a little girl; and another triumphantly entered in knickers.
Hull Daily Mail - Monday 04 October 1909

TATE'S LATEST FLY FROM NEW BRIGHTON TOWER.
Mr. Harry Tate, the latest aeroplanist," arrived Liverpool yesterday from Stockport, bringing with him the famous miniature aeroplane which six cart horses drew about London the other day. To-day, says, he will take the machine round the town and over the Mersey to New Brighton, where he intends to convey it to the top of the Tower and let go to see if it will fly." Are you going to bang on it?" he was asked. The popular comedian smiled knowingly. Well, I haven't decided yet," he said.
Thursday 02 December 1909 , Manchester Courier & Lancashire Advertiser

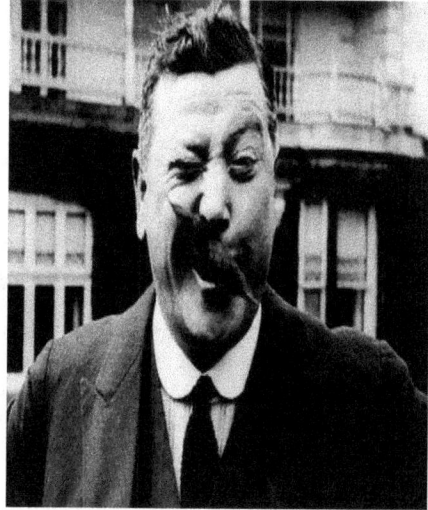

HARRY TATE
Mr. Harry Tate appeared on numerous occasions at the Tower his real name was Ronald Hutchison, he took his stage name from the firm of Henry Tate & Sons, Sugar Refiners, who once employed him. A well liked music hall performer he began as an impressionist, imitating well-known performers such as Dan Leno and George Robey.
His first big success came with his 'Motoring' sketch, in which he, a chauffeur and his idiotic son completely fail to get his car started to take the son to college. The son sat in the back making idiotic comments such as "It's amazing, pa-pa", and "Goodbye-eee" (which became Tate's best-known catchphrase and was the inspiration for the popular World War I song Goodbye-ee, goodbye-ee, Wipe the tear, baby dear, from your eye-ee,). Another of Tate's catchphrases, How's your father, has recently been put into the Oxford English Dictionary it was just another piece of nonsense to make his act even more absurd. Another claim to fame which is even more absurd, everyone knows the industry of personalised number plates is massive, but nobody really knows how the fascination began.
The earliest known personalised number plate was T 8,owned by Mr Harry Tate himself. The plate is now owned by Johnny Tate of Tate & Lyle fame, strange how things go around in circles. The pioneer of many a catchphrase 'was unfortunately killed in the Blitz in 1940, but his son Ronnie continued his act under the name of Harry Tate Jnr.

126

MISS MAUD ALLAN AT NEW BRIGHTON

While Miss Maud Allan was dancing before an audience of 5,000 at the New Brighton Tower she was interrupted by, a woman in, the gallery. At the conclusion of her performance 'Miss Allan said, that if any persons had not come for the dancing, and wished their money returned they could have it; but she asked them, to try to realize what the; dancing, was like in Greece 2,000 years ago which she-was endeavouring to portray.. She-received an ovation at the end of the Salome dance.

A few years later in 1918 the British MP Noel Pemberton Billing published an article, "The Cult of the Clitoris" which implied that Maud Allan, then appearing in her Vision of Salome, was a lesbian and German spy working in associate with German wartime conspirators. Miss Allan sued Billing for Libel based on the following counts:

1. The act of publishing a defamatory article about Maud Allan and J. T. Grein, her impresario.

2. The act, a separate offence, of including obscenities within the article.

This led to a sensational court case, at which Billing represented himself. Lord Alfred Douglas also testified in Billing's favour. Allan lost the case. The trial became entangled in obscenity charges brought forth by the state against the performance given by Allan in her dance. She was accused of practising many of the sexually charged acts depicted (or implied) in Wilde's writings herself.

At this time, the Lord Chamberlain's ban on public performances of Wilde's play was still in place in England, and thus the Salomé dance was at risk. Her brother's crimes were also dredged up to suggest there was a background of sexual insanity in her family.

The Register (Adelaide)
Thursday 14 October 1909

From the 1920s on, Allan taught dance and she lived with her secretary and lover, Verna Aldrich. She died in Los Angeles, California.

MISS MAUD ALLAN AS 'SALOME.'

GUIDE TO
NEW BRIGHTON
TOWER
BALL ROOM & LOUNGE
JAPANESE TEA HOUSE
AND
GARDENS
PRICE ONE PENNY

GUIDE

TO

NEW BRIGHTON TOWER AND AMUSEMENT PARK._____

The Highest Structure and the Finest Place
of Amusement in England.

General Manager & Secretary—R. H. DAVY.

Horrocks and Co., Ltd. Ashton-under-Lyne

For many years past New Brighton has been one of the most favoured places among excursionists from all parts of Lancashire, Yorkshire, and the Midlands, and deservedly so, for nowhere round the cost of the United Kingdom can be found another seaside resort possessing so many natural advantages as the famous Cheshire resort. Its unique position at the mouth of the noble river Mersey, with its ever varying and constant traffic of the leviathans of the shipping world, provide a sight and an instruction that is without a parallel. The splendid stretch of golden sand extends for miles, and this at the highest tide, is a source of ecstasy for the little ones, and a borne of content, rest and enjoyment for their elders. Popular as New Brighton has been for a considerable number of years past, it is as nothing compared with the extended popularity it has enjoyed since the construction of that great masterpiece, the NEW BRIGHTON TOWER, with its magnificent gardens covering an area of 35 acre. Nowhere else in the Kingdom, or in fact the world, can be found so grand a sight, or a place so replete with amusements as the NEW BRIGHTON TOWER, for from the opening each day until the close, not a weary moment need be anticipated by intending visitors. The means of access are now on the most approved scale, frequent and direct boats from Liverpool Landing Stage during the season; a splendid service of electric cars via Seacombe, and last but by no means least, the lately electrified system of the Mersey Railway Co., who run trains from Central Low Level (Liverpool),every few minutes.

The Grounds and Gardens 35 acre in extent, present most beautiful natural features, and the designers must be complimented for the manner in which they have performed their task.

There is no appearance of artificiality; everything is true to nature, and here in lies the charm. Here will be found not merely the common attraction of so many holiday resorts, but these gardens stand alone by the fact that within their boundaries every amusement that can be devised is provided for the entertainment of visitors. With such advantages, natural and otherwise, it is only natural that the Tower should be visited by many thousand every season.

The Bazaar is occupied by numerous shops for the sale of fancy articles and souvenirs. The entrances to the Theatre is from either side of the Bazaar, and is one of the finest of its kind in the world. Seating accommodation is provided for 3,000 people, and the stage is one of the largest in England, having a proscenium opening of 45 feet, and a depth of 72 feet, and is so arranged that a full-sized circus can be placed upon it, which is often done during the season. At the back of the stage there is stabling accommodation for a large number of horses, also wild animals; and all the arrangements, sanitary or other-wise, are on the latest improved plans. Variety performances are given here every afternoon and evening. The programmes include the finest London, Continental, and American talent that can be procured. On ascending the main staircases, we find Cloak Rooms, etc. and on the next floor to these is the magnificent ballroom. This is one of the finest rooms in the Kingdom, and 1,000 couples can conveniently dance at one time on the beautiful parquet floor, which has no superior. The artistic ornamentation of white and gold, is most attractive, and attention should be given to the fine paintings in panels of the civic emblems of different Lancashire towns, which ornament the pillars. The renowned Tower Orchestra plays at frequent intervals, in fact dancing is continuous from 11 a.m. to10:15p.m.daily. On the Ballroom Balcony there is seating accommodation for hundreds who care to watch the dancers. Above the Ballroom is the Elevator Hall, surrounded by fancy shops, and fitted with numerous and highly amusing automatic machines. On entering the Hall, on one side is the Shooting Jungle, and on the opposite side is the aviary, comprising a large collection of beautiful birds. From the ground floor to the Elevator Hall, auxiliary lifts are run all day free, and from the Elevator Hall the main lifts ascend to the top of the Tower. The lifts run all day, and a nominal charge is made for the ascent. From the top of this magnificent structure, which stands 621 feet above the sea level, and is in fact the highest in the Kingdom ,a view of landscape and seascape is to be obtained, that will long live in the memory of those who witness it. The noble river Mersey, with the fine line of Liverpool docks, stretches away north and south for miles, and from this great height the large ships look like pygmies. On the landward side is seen the Peninsula of Wirral, with the Welsh mountains and River Dee. A more beautiful sea view is unobtainable in any part of the globe, nor can any spot be found where so many and such beautiful steamers may be watched for so many miles wending their way to or from distant countries. It is indeed a most imposing panorama, and is appreciated to the fullest extend by all who see it.

Descending again to the gardens the first thing that strikes the eye is the ornamental lake, and immediately opposite is the Japanese Cafe where refreshments of all kinds can be obtained at reasonable prices.

The old Quarry, which faces Algerian Restaurant, with its large Rockeries planted with ferns and creepers, is another item of interest, and on a holiday it is a delightfully cool and pleasant resort; a high-class Pierrot Entertainment is given here daily. At the top of the Quarry will be seen amidst the trees, Rock Point Castle, the first-class restaurant. Ascending the steps to the Old English Fair Ground, we find first and foremost the ever popular Electric Mountain Railway, the only one of its kind in the north, and which produces a most exhilarating effect on the passengers who travel round it.

Further on is the Shooting Gallery, and the Menagerie and Lion House. The Menagerie contains a most interesting and varied collection from all parts of the world, including the magnificent pair of Cape LIONS "Prince" and "Pasha", acknowledged to be the finest pair in Europe, and in addition the great favourite elephant, "Punch". On the fair Ground and throughout the Amusement Park, in addition to those specially mentioned, will be found a numerous collection of side shows, each one being a novelty, and productive of much amusement. Another great attraction is the Water Chute running from the level of the fair ground into the ornamental lake below. It carries its passengers in specially built boats that cannot capsize, down an incline some 130 feet long, and launches them into the lake and then across to the landing place, causing a most exciting and thrilling sensation.

The boats are then drawn back into position for another party, solely by electric; in fact the whole of the machinery connected with this wonderful establishment is electric, and all the electricity is generated on the premises, the plant being of more than 2,000 horse-power. At dusk each evening the whole gardens and buildings are transformed into a veritable fairyland by means of electric light. Thousand of lamps are hung and festooned round the walks and trees, no less than 32,000 lamps being utilised for this purpose, while the inside of the buildings is one gorgeous blaze of light. The lamps are of different colours and the beautiful effect that is thus produced is extremely artistic.

THE ATTRACTIONS IN THE AMUSEMENT PARK
Details of all the shows and novelties within the Tower Grounds cannot, owing to want of space, be included, but a short description of some will be of interest to the reader.

THE SCENIC RAILWAY.
A most delightful journey of a mile midst beautiful scenery, caverns and grottos, encircling the lake will all the charming views of the Tower Grounds; an exhilarating ride which Royalty has patronised and immensely appreciated. This Scenic Railways is the very best in Great Britain, and for a real exciting and pleasurable ride with perfect safety, it will be difficult to find its equal.

THE MAXIM FLYING MACHINE.
For a flight in mid-air, its only equal is the aeroplane; all the delightful sensation of a real ride in space; a safe and bracing spin which can only be appreciated by being tried; a real novelty devised by one of the greatest inventors of all time- Sir Hiram Maxim.

LAUGHTERLAND.
"Laugh and grow fat" is an old saying. It is nevertheless a true one, as those will quickly find out who pay this amusing device a visit. Once inside you become just as your worst friend depicts you, but you are quickly put right, for you are immediately trans-formed into a dream of loveliness such as your sweetheart would image you to be. By moving a step, you see yourself expand to aldermanic proportions and look the funniest person on earth, afterwards becoming for a moment a veritable giant. This magical and mystical illusion is a specific cure for melancholia. It can only be described thus-A LAUGH; A Yell!! A SCREAM!!!

135

THE KATZENJAMMER CASTLE.
This is one of the weirdest and most mysterious novelties of the year, the Castle of the eccentric. It is full of mysterious surprises combined with fun, and a visit is worth a great deal for one leaves the Castle full of wonder and amazement; the shrieks of laughter from its crowds of patrons testify to its efficiency as a laughter maker.

ELECTRIC MOUNTAIN RAILWAY.
The innovation of all gravity rides; the many thousands who have patronised this pleasurable ride can tell of its exhilarations. It is an exciting and rollicking journey which must be tried to appreciate its merits.

THE GREAT WATER CHUTE.
"Shooting the chutes" is not a new form of Amusement but still retain its hold on the public a fancy as a "thriller" second to none. The Boats run at intervals of about two minutes. The above list does not by any means exhaust the host of attractions that New Brighton Tower offers to pleasure seekers.

THE FIGURE EIGHT RAILWAY.
Of all the riding devices this is one of the most fascinating and enjoyable. The novelty of the ride makes it far ahead of most others of its kind.

The delight which is afforded by the excellent Tower Military Orchestra, which gives a promenade Concert each evening, under the above charming circumstances, is long remembered. We might write pages and pages in expatiating on the extraordinary profusion of sights and novelties of the New Brighton Tower- its attraction are innumerable- its amusements limitless, and the surprised visitor find it is impossible to see everything in one day.

136

Consequent upon the erection and popularity of this noble structure, New Brighton has it self reaped enormous benefits from the influx of visitors who pour in daily during the season, and from what was practically a small village has now sprung a young town with fine residential property, as well a plenty of comfortable apartment at a most reasonable charge which defy competition with similar seaside resorts, so that day or weekend visitors, or those desirous of staying longer, will find no difficulty in obtaining all they require.

This Guide would scarcely be complete unless mention were made of the magnificent Sunday Evening Concert, which are given during the Season. The Instrumentalists, comprise the finest soloists of the Richter, Halle, Philharmonic and other noted orchestras, and the concerts given weekly have earned the just reputation of being the finest in the provinces.

NEW Brighton is easily reached from all parts of England and Wales.
The Cheshire Lines, Great Central, Great Western and London and North-Western Joint, Mersey, Wirral(via Liverpool Landing Stage or Mersey Tunnel),Railways have direct access into New Brighton Station, whilst the Cheshire Lines, Great Central, Great Western, Lancashire and Yorkshire, London and North Western London and North-Western and Great Western Joint, and Midland Railways all issue excursion tickets to New Brighton via Liverpool and the Wallasey Ferries; also (with the exception of the Great Western, London and North-Western, and London and North-Western and Great Western Joint Lines) via Wirral Railway.
The Ferry Steamers run all the year round from the Landing Stage to New Brighton frequently, and on holidays and other busy days the departure are increased to suit the requirements.
The Mersey Railway (Central and James Street Station) in connection with the Wirral Railway, also run very frequent trains (every ten minutes from Central Low Level Station on holidays).There is, therefore, no difficulty in reaching the grounds either in fine or wet weather.

WHAT PEOPLE SAY OF NEW BRIGHTON TOWER.
The "DAILY MAIL" says:- LIVERPOOL'S LOSS AND GAIN.
Liverpool is losing and gaining as a place of holiday pilgrimage- losing in so far as docks and ships and warehouse exteriors are not so very novel sights in this much-tripping age, and gaining because such places as the New Brighton Tower and Gardens supply attractions which the idle day of a great mercantile city conspicuously lacks.

The "DAILY TELEGRAPH (LONDON) says:-
Now-a days, the public is a very master, and the watering-place which has nothing besides natural physical advantages to offer, will not attract to itself the experienced tripper. Southport, Blackpool, and Douglas have educated this individual up to such a point that they will have nothing but the best in the shape of concert-halls, ball-rooms, marine drives, or illuminated gardens. Recognising this fact, the New Brighton Tower and Recreation Company has embarked upon an enterprise which has involved an outlay of not less than £400,000,and the result of which is that in future this pleasant watering-place on the West Coast

should be able to hold its own against all competitors. Some thirty-five acres of land have come under the company's sway, and this extensive area has been laid out in such a fashion that it will be a matter for surprise if each individual visitor does not find something to his taste.

The "CITY NEWS"(Manchester)- Speaking of the New Brighton Tower says:- At the height of 80 feet is the Elevator Hall, from which ascent to the 440 feet level of the Tower is made by lifts. The view from this elevation- neatly twice the height of the Manchester Tower Hall Tower - is without parallel in this country, or indeed in the world. Ten thousand persons ascended by the lifts to this gallery on Easter Monday.

WIGAN"EXAMINER" -New Brighton Tower- The Whitsuntide preparation are on a scale never before attempted even in this beautiful place of recreation. In view of the immense crowds which invade the grounds at Easter, the catering accommodation has been considerably increased. On Whit Monday the whole of the Entertainments will be in full swing.

The" PRESTON HERALD" says:- Despite the inclement weather during the holidays, the New Brighton Tower as been exceptionally will patronised. Thousands of visitors have visited these beautiful gardens, and the management have made every possible provision for their reception. The fine menagerie has been crowded daily, and no doubt, does comprise a splendid collection of animals.

July 1910 Weekly Courier Picnic

MOTOR CYCLE CHARGES INTO CROWD. Several people were seriously injured in a terrible motor-cycle accident on the New Brighton Tower athletic grounds on Saturday. During the first heat of a two mile motor team race, T. Henshaw, Liverpool representative, was turning the western corner of the track at a speed estimated at fifty miles an hour when his machine suddenly swerved up the embankment, dashed through a rope at the top and into the crowd of spectators. In addition to Mr. Henshaw, who received broken leg and injuries to the face, five persons were injured.
Diss Express - Friday 15 September 1911

FLIGHT OVER LIVERPOOL.
Mr. Henry Melly made a complete circuit of Liverpool and its suburbs on his Bleriot monoplane on Tuesday. Accompanied, he left his hangar at Waterloo at 7.30, and, passing over the racecourse, flew over Mossley Hill Church at a height 1000ft. crossing the Mersey, he circled the New Brighton Tower, covering in all thirty miles.
Ballymena Observer - 02 June 1911

GUARDS' BANDS BARRED.
The Wallasey (Cheshire) magistrates recently refused an application for a licence for two sacred concerts at New Brighton Tower, on the ground that a Guards' Band was not, in their opinion, a suitable band to give sacred concerts. The decision has caused indignation among the members of all the Guards' bands. Lieut. J. Mackenzie Rogan, of the Coldstream Guards, points out that his band is giving sacred concerts for the National Sunday League nearly every Sunday throughout the winter months, and says the magistrates' decision can only be due to a general objection to bands altogether. "If military bands cannot play sacred music, how is it," he asks, "that the best sacred songs are scored for them? Our repertory includes The Messiah,'the "Stabat Mater,"and the 'Hallelujah Chorus.'"
The Southern Cross Times Wednesday 29 March 1911 p 3 Article

LIONESS AT LARGE.
The management of the New Brighton Tower are somewhat concerned over a fine young lioness which, since being recaptured after escaping into the grounds on her arrival, has refused to take food. The keepers were just completing the delicate task of placing a number animals in their permanent home when the lioness escaped and led the whole staff a rare dance for over half an hour before she could be recaptured.
The travelling cage had been brought on a trolley close up to the permanent cage, when the trolley moved slightly. The lioness bounded out, and in a most frisky way careered round the grounds with the staff at her heels, no one seeming very anxious for the first place. What seemed an almost hopeless chase was brought to an end by driving the animal into a corridor, the doors being bolted behind her. The cage was then brought up, and keepers entering the corridor at the other end drove the lioness back to captivity.
Derry Journal - Wednesday 07 June 1911

Quote from New Brighton & District Official Guide June 1911.
Places of Entertainment and Amusement
The lake is surrounded by shady walks, and into this lake the water chute runs
from the level of the Fair Grounds. The great scenic railway also winds several
times round the lake. The water-chute boats are specially designed for the
purpose, and cannot capsize. They come down an incline of some 130 feet in
length, and plunge very gracefully into the lake, being afterwards propelled by
an efficient boatman across the water to a small landing-stage, causing a most
exciting and trilling sensation not only to the occupants of the boats but to the
spectators who congregate to witness this exciting sport.
The old quarry, which is called the "Happy Valley" is a charming shady spot, and
nestling in one corner is found the Parisian Tea Garden where visitors may partake
of light refreshments whilst listening to the Pierrots who perform at intervals
during the day and evening. The large grounds contain every kind of attraction
and amusement that can be desired for entertainment of the visitor. There is, in
addition, to the Scenic Railway, a figure 8 gravity ride, a Flying Machine, a Joy
Wheel, a Katzenjammer Castle and many other novel and exciting shows,
including a lion house and menagerie, also "Punch" the favourite elephant. The
cycling track which surrounds this park is the finest in England. Prominent amongst the attractions is the bazaar, which is occupied by numerous shops for the sale of fancy articles.....

THE NEW BRIGHTON
Amateur Operatic Society
IN
LA FILLE DE
MADAME ANGOT,

Tower Theatre,
March 14th to 18th, 1911.

New Brighton Amateur Operatic Society - 11 February 1911
The opera which the New Brighton Operatic Society will produce in March is probably the most tuneful production ever attempted by local societies. It is many years since it has been played in the Liverpool district, and opera lovers will doubtless welcome the decision of the New Brighton Society in producing this old but in many respects matchless opera. The action of the opera takes place in Paris, during the period of the Directory established after the Revolution of 1793, when Barras was at the head of the Government. The Society have arranged for the supply of the scenery and dresses from the same sources as in the production of "Amasis," so that a spectacular point of view opera will be in every respect equal to the very successful efforts which they made last December. The principal parts will be as follows:-

"La Fille de Madame Angot."

A COMIC OPERA IN THREE ACTS.

Adapted from the French of M.M. Clairville, Siraudin and Koning, by HENRY J. BYRON. The Music by CHARLES LECOCQ.

Dramatis Personæ.

Mdlle. Lange	(Actress, and favourite of Barras)	Mdme. Lillian Carter
Amaranthe	⎧	Mdme. Bessie Burnett
Javotte	(Market Women)	Miss Annie Forsyth
Therese	⎩	Miss Clarie Bolshaw
Hersilie	(Maid to Mdlle. Lange)	Mrs. Lily Hegan
Babette	(Maid to Clairette)	Miss Dorothy Welsh
Clairette Angot	(Daughter of Madame Angot and Betrothed to Pomponnet)	Mrs. Robert Walker
Larivaudière	(Friend of Barras, and conspiring against the Republic)	Mr. A. L. Roberts
Pomponnet	(Barber of the Market and Hairdresser of Mdlle. Lange)	Mr. Jack Henderson
Ange Pitou	(A Poet, in love with Clairette)	Mr. Harold G. Humphreys
Louchard	(Police Officer at the orders of Larivaudière)	Mr. John D. S. Batie
Trenitz	(Dandy of the Period)	Mr. Perim MacGregor
Cadet	⎧	Mr. R. R. Burnett
Guillaume	(Market Men)	Mr. P. H. Brunskill
Buteaux	⎩	Mr. Frank Nelson
Officer of Hussars		Mr. C. E. R. Dibdin

Chorus of Market Men, Conspirators, Hussars, Citizens, Market Women, Ladies, &c.

Act I.—Market Place on the Environs of Paris.
Act II.—Mdlle. Lange's Salon.
Act III.—The Calypso Gardens, Belleville, Paris.

33

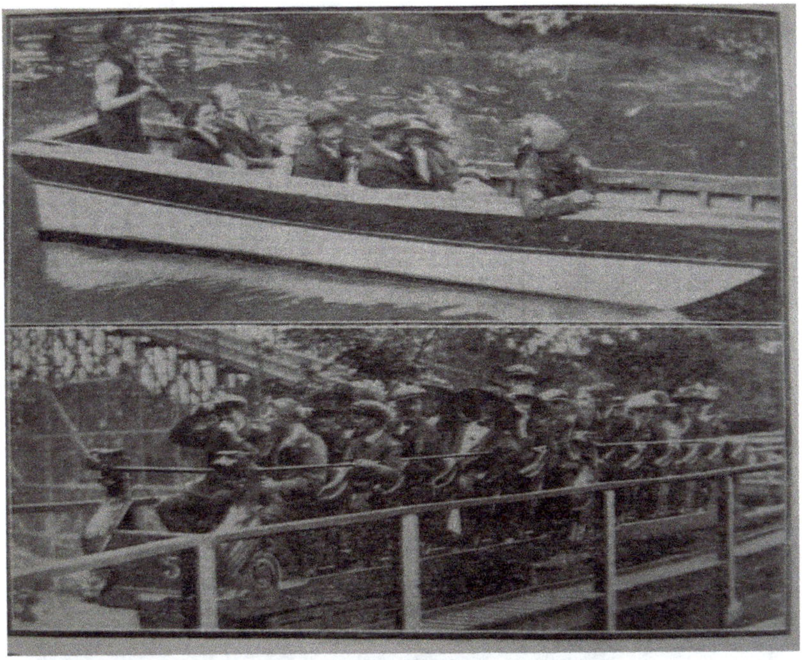

GREAT BREWERY EXCURSION TO NEW BRIGHTON
The employers of Messrs. Bass's, who made their annual trip to Liverpool and New Brighton yesterday, enjoying themselves in the Tower gardens. The picture shows (above) a party returning from a trip down the water-chute ; (below) on the switchback. Daly Mail 20 July 1912

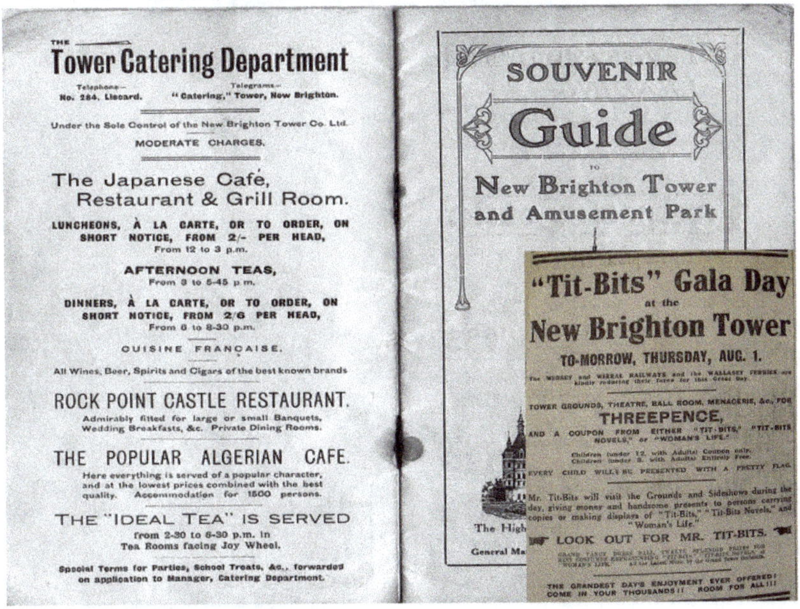

THE
Tower Catering Department

Telephone— No. 284, Liscard. Telegrams— "Catering," Tower, New Brighton.

Under the Sole Control of the New Brighton Tower Co. Ltd.

MODERATE CHARGES.

The Japanese Café, Restaurant & Grill Room.

LUNCHEONS, À LA CARTE, OR TO ORDER, ON SHORT NOTICE, FROM 2/- PER HEAD, From 12 to 3 p.m.

AFTERNOON TEAS, From 3 to 5-45 p.m.

DINNERS, À LA CARTE, OR TO ORDER, ON SHORT NOTICE, FROM 2/6 PER HEAD, From 6 to 8-30 p.m.

CUISINE FRANÇAISE.

All Wines, Beer, Spirits and Cigars of the best known brands

ROCK POINT CASTLE RESTAURANT.

Admirably fitted for large or small Banquets, Wedding Breakfasts, &c. Private Dining Rooms.

THE POPULAR ALGERIAN CAFE.

Here everything is served of a popular character, and at the lowest prices combined with the best quality. Accommodation for 1500 persons.

THE "IDEAL TEA" IS SERVED

from 2-30 to 6-30 p.m. in Tea Rooms facing Joy Wheel.

Special Terms for Parties, School Treats, &c., forwarded on application to Manager, Catering Department.

SOUVENIR
Guide
TO
New Brighton Tower
and Amusement Park

"Tit-Bits" Gala Day
at the
New Brighton Tower
TO-MORROW, THURSDAY, AUG. 1.

TOWER GROUNDS, THEATRE, BALL ROOM, MENAGERIE, &c., FOR
THREEPENCE,
AND A COUPON FROM EITHER "TIT-BITS," "TIT-BITS NOVELS," or "WOMAN'S LIFE."

EVERY CHILD WILL BE PRESENTED WITH A PRETTY FLAG.

Mr. Tit-Bits will visit the Grounds and Sideshows during the day, giving money and handsome presents to persons carrying copies or making displays of "Tit-Bits," "Tit-Bits Novels," and "Woman's Life."

LOOK OUT FOR MR. TIT-BITS.

THE GRANDEST DAY'S ENJOYMENT EVER OFFERED! COME IN YOUR THOUSANDS!! ROOM FOR ALL!!!

THE NEW BRIGHTON

... AMATEUR ...

OPERATIC SOCIETY.

FROM THE SHADOW OF THE TOWER.

(By "NEW BRIGHTONIAN.")

"NELL GWYNNE."

"Nell Gwynne" is one of the most charming light operas ever written, and is a great favourite with amateur operatic societies. The New Brighton Society, however, although it has a long record of light operas produced, has presented "Nell Gwynne" for the first time in its history this week. With its talented members the society has been able to place before New Brighton audiences really excellent interpretation of Planquette's delightful creation. Admirable though the disposal of the various parts was, I cannot help feeling that by the absence of several well-known personalities and the somewhat thinness of the chorus as compared with other productions, the cast was not quite so strong as it has been on previous occasions. It is true that Mrs. Robert Walker made a welcome re-appearance, and she is one of the "stars" of the society. Her presence was undoubtedly a source of inspiration, and once again the society is to be congratulated upon having the services of so accomplished an actress.

"NELL GWYNNE,"
TOWER THEATRE,
MARCH 19th to 23rd 1912.

144

TOWER THEATRE, NEW BRIGHTON.

Five Nights, March 19th to 23rd, 1912.

The New Brighton Amateur Operatic Society in the romantic light Opera

(by arrangement with Metzler & Co., London)

"NELL GWYNNE,"

by Planquette, composer of "Rip Van Winkle,"

"Paul Jones," etc.

CAST:

Nell Gwynne	(of the King's Theatre)	Mrs. ROBERT WALKER
Clare	(Ward of the King)	Miss ANNIE COXEN
Jessanine	(Niece of Weasel)	Miss DOROTHY WELSH
Marjory	(Parish-waif, servant to Weasel)	Miss NAN FORSYTH
Buckingham	(in disgrace at Court; landlord	Mr. J. D. S. BATIE
Rochester	and waiter at Dragon Inn	Mr. H. G. HUMPHREYS
The Beadle	(the local authority)	Mr. JACK HENDERSON
Weasel	(the Village Pawnbroker)	Mr. GEO. E. F. REID
Falcon	(a strolling player)	Mr. A. MARTINI
Talbot	(cousin to Clare)	Mr. CHAS. E. MULLINEUX
Perigrine	(Buckingham's footboy)	Mr. J. M. G. DUGUID
King Charles II.		Mr. ROBERT WALKER

Stage Manager   -   Mr. R. W. LOMAX.

Musical Director   -   Mr. C. K. JAMES.

POPULAR PRICES.

IN AID OF LOCAL CHARITIES.

J. A. LLOYD, Hon. Sec.,
22, Seafield Drive, New Brighton.

"Chronicle," Seacombe.

NELL GWYNNE N.B.A.O.S.

Last evening this society produced Planquette's tuneful opera "Nell Gwynne" at the
Tower Theatre, New Brighton. Mrs. Robert
Walker made a charming Nell; Miss Annie
Coxen sang gracefully as Clare, and Miss Nan
Forsyth as the parish waif was generally ad-
mired. Mr. George E. F. Read was never
better cast than as the village pawnbroker,
and the beadle of Mr. Jack Henderson was
always excellent. Praise is also due to Mr.
John D. S. Batie, Mr. Harold G. Humphreys,
Mr. Adrei Martini, and Mr. Charles E. Mul-
lineux for their respective performances. The
chorus effects were very good, and if the opera
dragged considerably last night this will no
doubt be remedied at subsequent performances.

146

New Brighton Tower.

The Highest Structure and the Finest Place of
Amusement in the Kingdom.

35 Acres of
Beautiful
GROUNDS
AND
GARDENS.

———

MILITARY
BANDS.

———

LADIES'
ORCHESTRA.

The Grounds,
Menagerie,
AND
Main Buildings
are OPEN
all the year
round.

For
Announcements
of Season
Attractions,
See Liverpool
Daily Papers.

Magnificent Display of Animals of all kinds.

WATER CHUTE, HIMALAYA RAILWAY, and hosts of other novel side shows.

TOWER LIFTS running all day, and VARIETY PERFORMANCES twice
daily in the Grand Theatre during the season.

Café Chantant with HIGH-CLASS VAUDEVILLE PERFORMANCE; no
charge for Admission and Seats Free.

GORGEOUS ILLUMINATIONS every evening.   CONCERTS every Sunday
throughout the Season.   Twelve hours continuous amusement for **6d.**

Frequent Trains leave all Mersey and Wirral Railway Stations for New Brighton,
which may also be easily and quickly reached by the Wallasey Ferry Boats,
which sail every 15 minutes in the season.

THE 1913 TOWER GUIDE

The different guides reproduced within these pages are a good indication of the trends and changes in the entertainment. This particular guide of 1913 introduces "A Cafe-Chantant," conducted on Parisian lines, open free to visitors.

Each Sunday classical concerts with daily performances at 3 and 8, were held in the ballroom, and performed by a 100 piece orchestra. The admission to the grounds remained the same at sixpence. With the Tower and grounds now open all year round.

The pleasure and recreation grounds, were used for travelling shows, located between the athletic ground and the lake. On the athletics ground and cycle track, a full program of athletic and cycling events continued throughout the year. New Brighton Tower Football Club was formed in 1897, in order to attract people in the winter. The start of the season would sometimes include a circus, a cinematograph show and even Japanese performers.

Whitsuntide 1899 saw the arrival of three Venetian Gondolas, complete with their native gondoliers, they arrived to convey visitors around the lake.

An ever changing spectrum of events helped to maintain the resorts popularity.

The 'Himalaya Railway', arrived in 1898, and behind this was the menagerie and Lion House. In 1908 the 'Himalaya Railway' was replaced with a scenic railway.

In 1905 the 'Figure of Eight' roller coaster was installed near the entrance of the grounds, this would remain in operation until the grounds closed. We even had a visit from the Wild West in October 1899 the S F Cody Cycle, Horse and Variety Tournament. Performed on the Athletics ground, but not to be confused with Buffalo Bill Cody.

From Animated Picture Shows using photographs, to the Vistascope, Bioscope and upwards and onwards to the cinematograph. With the Chronophone singing and dancing picture show. The Tower had all the latest developments to produce the magic of the moving screen.

The popularity of films meant the decline in live entertainment.

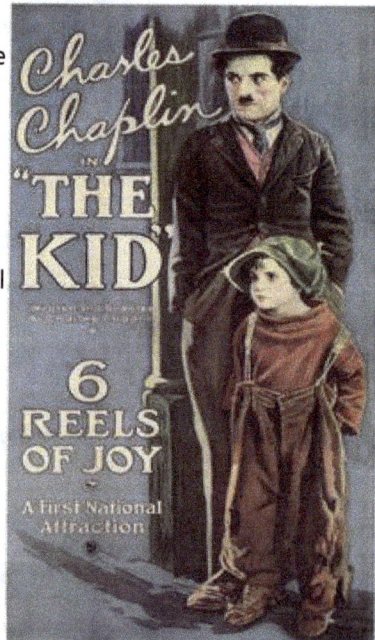

Charles Chaplin in "THE KID" 6 REELS OF JOY A First National Attraction

BRASS BAND CONTEST.
FODEN'S MOTOR WORKS WIN CHALLENGE CUP AT NEW BRIGHTON
Upwards of thirty bands from Lancashire, Yorkshire, and Cheshire took part in the fifteenth annual brass band contest at New Brighton Tower Saturday. Last year's winner of the Challenge Cup, Shaws, of Oldham, failed to obtain a prize. The test piece was Balfe's "Bohemian Girl" selection, and Mr. J. O. Shepherd,of Liverpool, was the adjudicator. The winners were as follow:

> 1 (Challenge Cup), Foden's Motor Works.
> 2, Hebden Bridge.
> 3, Crossfieid's.
> 4, Wingates Temperance.
> 5, Black Dyke Mills.
> 6, Irwell Springs.

Manchester Courier - Monday 19 May 1913

CYCLING AND ATHLETICS.
CYCLE RECORD AT NEW BRIGHTON
A large crowd of spectators patronised the New Brighton Tower Grounds yesterday, a feature of the sports being an attack on the ten mile motor paced cycle record by Leon Meredith. Detail Leon Meredith v. the Ten Miles Record of 17m 15 & 1-5th sec. Meredith covered the distance 16m. 20 sec & 1-5th sec. beating the record by 55 seconds.
Yorkshire Post and Leeds Intelligencer - Tuesday 25 March 1913

A LION'S BROKEN HEART
A pathetic story of a magnificent lion's death from a broken heart comes from Wallasey. Some time ago the lion and his mate formed a great attraction at the New Brighton Tower menagerie, both animals being splendid specimens of their tribe. The lioness contracted an illness and died, and the grief of the lion the following morning was very pronounced.
For hours it paced to and fro in the cage keeping guard over its dead mate and refusing to allow attendants to enter the cage to remove the body. Every few seconds it stopped to lick the body, and after the carcase had been removed the lion appeared to take no interest in its surroundings. It was found impossible to rouse it in any way, and gradually it refused to take any food. Only after considerable coaxing could it be prevailed upon to partake of a bowl of milk or a young rabbit. It gradually wasted away, and at last death has taken place. An examination has failed to reveal any sign of disease (says the "Daily Chronicle") and death is attributed to a broken heart following the loss of its mate. Both animals were together in captivity for a number of years.
Sheffield Evening Telegraph - Friday 06 June 1913

149

WALLASEY MAYORAL BALL. The Mayor and Mayoress of Wallasey
(Mr. and Mrs. T. V. Burrows) entertained fifteen hundred guests at a
ball at New Brighton Tower last evening. The handsome ballroom is
admirably adapted for a large reception, and so great was the number of
those present, there was no unpleasant, crowding to interfere with the
enjoyment of the dancers. The effect of the coloured lights and drapery
that encircled the hall was an excellent framework for the brilliant scene,
and alcoves round the sides were invitingly arranged with settees and
lounges for the guests. The host and hostess were assisted at the reception
by two daughters, Miss Burrows and Miss Rhoda Burrows. The Mayoress
was presented with a bouquet of scarlet carnations by Mrs. Thomas on
behalf the stewards. The unqualified success of the function owed much
to the hearty goodwill with which the stewards tackled their duties.
Liverpool Echo - Friday 16 January 1914

JUVENILE FANCY DRESS BALL. Given by the Mayor and Mayoress of
Wallasey at New Brighton Tower on the 13th January 1914.

- NEW BRIGHTON TOWER, -

Saturday, 19th Sept., 1914, AFTERNOON AT 2. EVENING AT 7.

Fourteenth Annual Challenge

MUSICAL ∴ EISTEDDFOD
AND TOURNAMENT OF SONG.

Entries comprise upwards of 1,200 Competitors.

7 MIXED VOICE CHOIRS—Accrington, Colne Valley, Hanley and District, Gledholt (Huddersfield), Liverpool, Providence (Upper Hanley), and Nottingham.

12 MALE VOICE CHOIRS — Accrington, Blackheath, Brierfield, Holme Valley, Liverpool, Llanrwst and Trefriw, Manchester, Nelson, Runcorn, St. Helens Todmorden and Wavertree.

6 CHILDREN'S CHOIRS—Birkenhead (2), Bootle, Ellesmere Port, Llanfihangel and Stretford.

3 ACTION SONG PARTIES and a host of Soloists and Reciters.

Admission to each meeting, 2/6, 1/6 and 1/- (including admission to Tower Grounds). Reserved Stalls (2/-) can be booked at Crane & Sons, Church Street Liverpool, or Tower Offices, New Brighton.

Excursion Trains from all parts. See Railway Companies' and other Announcements.

At the New Brighton Tower Eisteddfod on Friday, Mr. Llew Powell, of Rhydymwyn, was adjudged the winner of the class for baritone solo.
Flintshire Observer 24th September 1914

John Maskelyne and George Cooke took over the Egyptian Hall Theatre in Piccadilly in 1873. Hugely popular, they billed themselves as "Royal Illusionists and Anti-Spiritualists", They invented many illusions still performed today. Maskelyne was adept at working out the principles of illusions, one of his best-known being levitation They blended comedy, illusion and conjuring, changing their act frequently to ensure that audiences were never bored.

151

NEW BRIGHTON TOWER. A good variety show is to be seen, at New Brighton Tower. Thursday, Friday, and Saturday Maskelyne and Devout company will appear.,
Liverpool Echo - Monday 17 August 1914

NEW BRIGHTON TOWER. The ordinary general meeting of the shareholders of the New Brighton Tower and Recreation Company Limited, was held at the Exchange Station Hotel, Liverpool, yesterday, the chairman of the directors (Mr. George H. Appleton) presiding. It reported that after the outbreak of war the receipts fell off considerably, and consequently the improvement shown last year had not been maintained. The report and account were approved and adopted, and Mr. J. D. Flood, the retiring director, re-elected.
Messrs. Harmood Banner and Son were reappointed auditors.
Liverpool Daily Post - Tuesday 08 December 1914

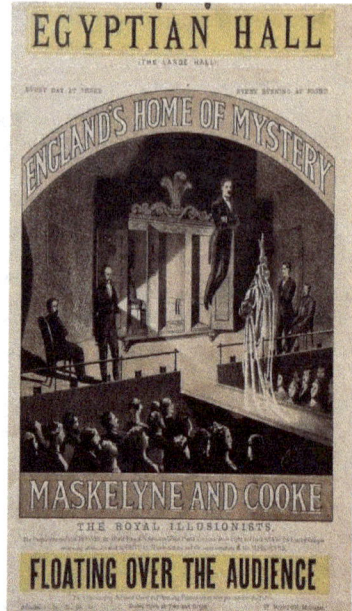

NEW BRIGHTON TOWER. Not for the first time were Madame de Boufflers and her choir the acceptable contributors of the Sunday evening concert at the New Brighton Tower, and last night she conducted a rendering of Rossini's "Stabat Mater." The principals were Madame Annie Goodwin, Miss Maud Holmes, Mr. Arthur Jones, and Mr. Ralph Smith. The Tower Orchestra furnished the accompaniments. The orchestra also gave some familiar Gonnod and Weber items under the direction of Mr. Thomas Rimmer, while the two choirs were heard in attractive chorus pieces, the ladies singing Boito's "Song and the Sirens" and Offenbach's "Night of Stars, Night Love."
Liverpool Echo - Monday 29 June 1914

NEW BRIGHTON TOWER. There is another entire change of programme for this week the variety theatre, the artistes engaged including Wee Walter Dearden, the phenomenal child artiste; Billy Willis, comedian; and the Andino Trio in clever musical pot-pourri. The picture include a drama entitled "The Man of Destiny," depicting incidents in the life of Napoleon Buonaparte; " Broncho Billy's Elopement"; and "The Right Man." There is to be a Hungarian Waltz competition in the ballroom this evening.
Liverpool Echo - Tuesday 14 July 1914

LUSITANIA TOWER CONCERT PROCEEDS TO THE WIDOWS & ORPHANS
The sinking of Lusitania was one of the most horrific incidents at
sea during the First World War (1914-18). In early 1915 the German
Government declared that all Allied ships would be in danger of attack in
British waters. Lusitania sailed from New York on 1 May 1915 with 1,266
passengers and a crew of 696, total of 1,962 people.
On 7 May 1915 at 2.10pm, the liner was near Kinsale in Southern Ireland
when she was torpedoed by the German submarine U-20. She sank in
under twenty minutes with the loss of 1191 lives.
The sinking of this unarmed passenger ship caused international
outrage. There were riots in Liverpool and London, as well as other cities
around the world. The German government claimed that Lusitania was
a legitimate target due to the war supplies she was carrying.. However,
British and American enquiries later declared the sinking to have been
unlawful. This event devastated the tight-knit dockland communities in
north Liverpool, where most of Lusitania's
crew lived. 405 crew members died,
including many Liverpool Irish seamen.
This warning had been printed adjacent to an
advertisement for Lusitania's return voyage.

TOWER, NEW BRIGHTON
General Manager and Secretary - R. H. DAVY.

Part of the Receipts will be given to the Widows and Orphans of the
poor men who lost their lives on the LUSITANIA.

MAY 23rd, at 8.15.
By arrangement with Mr. Linam, Powell., London.

YSAYE
THE WORLD-FAMOUS VIOLINIST
Who lost all his treasures in the War, and has three sons fighting at the front.
REPRESENTING BELGIUM.

FIRST APPEARANCE IN LIVERPOOL OF
M.

VALLIER
THE FAMOUS BASS.
Of the Scala, Milan: Grand Opera, New York; Brussels and Paris.
REPRESENTING FRANCE.

and Mr. WILLIAM

MURDOCH
THE DISTINGUISHED PIANIST,
REPRESENTING BRITAIN.
At the Piano - Mr. CHARLTON KEITH
CHAPPELL GRAND PIANOFORTE

Boxes 31s. 6d. and 21s.   Reserved Seats—Orchestra Stalls 4s.,
Stalls 3s.   Unreserved Seats 2s. and 1s.
Seats may be booked at the TOWER OFFICE (Tel. Liscard 276) or Messrs. CRANE & SONS,
Church Street, Liverpool.

OCEAN STEAMSHIPS.
CUNARD

EUROPE via LIVERPOOL.
LUSITANIA
Fastest and Largest Steamer
now in Atlantic Service Sails
SATURDAY, MAY 1, 10 A.M.
Transylvania, Fri.,   May 7, 5 P.M.
Orduna, - J Tues., May 18, 10 A.M.
Tuscania, - Fri., May 21, 5 P.M.
LUSITANIA, Sat., May 29, 10 A.M.
Transylvania, Fri., June 4, 5 P.M.

Gibraltar—Genoa—Naples—Piraeus
S.S. Carpathia, Thur., May 13, Noon

NOTICE!
TRAVELLERS intending to
embark on the Atlantic voyage
are reminded that a state of
war exists between Germany
and her allies and Great Britain
and her allies; that the zone of
war includes the waters adjacent to the British Isles; that,
in accordance with formal notice given by the Imperial German Government, vessels flying
the flag of Great Britain, or of
any of her allies, are liable to
destruction in those waters and
that travellers sailing in the
war zone on ships of Great
Britain or her allies do so at
their own risk.

IMPERIAL GERMAN EMBASSY
WASHINGTON, D. C., APRIL 22, 1915.

R. M. S. Lusitania at Landing Stage, Liverpool.

153

Vesta Tilley topped the bill on numerous occasions at The Tower. She appeared in the biggest and best music halls all over the land. Tilley's popularity reached its all-time high point during World War I, when she and her husband ran a military recruitment campaign. In the guise of characters like 'Tommy in the Trench' and 'Jack Tar Home from Sea', Tilley performed songs like "The Army of Today's All Right" and 'Jolly Good Luck to the Girl who Loves a Soldier'. This is how she got the nickname 'Britain's best recruiting sergeant' – young men were sometimes asked to join the army on stage during her show.

She was at times a little controversial. Famously, for example, she sang a song "I've Got a Bit of a Blighty One", about a soldier who was delighted to have been wounded because it allowed him to return home to England and get away from those deadly battlefields.

"When I think about my dugout / Where I dare not stick my mug out / I'm glad I've got a bit of a blighty one!"

Tilley performed in hospitals and sold War Bonds.

Vesta aimed to create convincing male characters. Her most famous character was the man about town – smart, middle class, well dressed and polite. This was the character in her hit song 'Burlington Bertie'. It tells the story of a 'swell' who stays out all night partying and doesn't get up till 10:30 in the morning. She was very popular with female audiences who saw her as a symbol of independence (she earned over £500 a week). She also poked fun at men and their vanities and mannerisms. When Vesta Tilley is on the bill at the Tower you had best book far in advance, or you may tip-toe disconsolately at the back of the 'standing room', and catch but only a stray glimpse of the goddess through the bobbing leafage of ladies' hats. Ref: Nancy Bruseker

NEW BRIGHTON TOWER A large assembly, including many short leave men in khaki, and blue, enjoyed "a long night" in the ballroom of the New Brighton Tower, a late boat being run to Liverpool for the convenience these visitors.
Liverpool Daily Post - Tuesday 28 December 1915

NEW BRIGHTON TOWER Vesta Tilley is paying a flying visit to the Tower to-night, and her appearance here is being eagerly anticipated by her admirers. " The people's idol " will be supported by capital company of artistes, including Look Louis Nikola, who is to give a demonstration of original magical problems.
Liverpool Echo - Wednesday 04 August 1915

New Brighton Tower. Large numbers of visitors are being attracted to the Tower. In the ballroom dancing is enjoyed to the strains of a full band, while in the theatre a fine selection of films is shown on the Towerscope, variety turns being provided by the Two Welfares, comedians Lucie Prinella, vocalist and dancer; and Will Durkin, Scottish comedian.
Liverpool Echo - Tuesday 08 June 1915

NEW BRIGHTON TOWER The Tower retains for another week Mdlle. Leila Leilina, the charming member of the Russian Imperial Ballet, who made an adventurous escape from Germany. Arthur Diamond is an active knockabout juggler, while other turns are contributed by Harry Bunt, and the Taffies. A Chaplin film makes a diverting addition to the programme.
Liverpool Echo - Tuesday 07 September 1915

NEW BRIGHTON TOWER Great scenes at the Tower yesterday with the majority of visitors to New Brighton appearing to find their way to this popular place of resort with its manifold attractions- With such favourable weather conditions the outside shows did remarkably well, and the water chute, the joy wheel, the figure 8. the flying machine, the railway, and the menagerie were especially well patronised. There was dancing all day in the big ballroom to the strains of a full band: the Aigburth Subscription Prize Band played selections on the outside platform: while in the theatre there were two performances in the afternoon and one in the evening by a company of high-class vaudeville artistes. including Zabas and El Chicq. in an Arab speciality; the Six Sisters Volka, acrobats and dancers. Bert Rayburn, comedian: Chant and Chant, comedy duo: Doris Welsby, juvenile comedienne and dancer; Burton and Company, vocal comedy cross-patter act; and the Sisters Brooklands. vocalists. A capital selection of films was also shown on the bioscope.
Liverpool Daily Post - Tuesday 06 April 1915

Robert Harold Davy

NEW BRIGHTON TOWER.

Madame Clara Butt, the deservedly popular contralto, made her first appearance in New Brighton, last night, when, thanks to the enterprise of Mr. R. H. Davy, the secretary and manager of the Tower, she appeared at the first Sunday concert of the season, the spacious theatre being filled, the necessary advance of prices notwithstanding. The great singer was accorded an enthusiastic reception, and unstinted applause was showered upon her after each of her appearances, encore after encore being vociferously demanded and willingly conceded in accordance with what has for so long been the custom at all popular concerts. Madame Butt sang both old and new songs, the former including Elgar's "Land of Hope and Glory," Liddle's "Abide with me," Sullivan's "God shall wipe away all tears," and Mendelssohn's "O rest in the Lord," Mr. Harold Croxton accompanying on the pianoforte and Mr. Arthur E. Godfrey supplying effective organ obbligati. Two of the new songs, it might be mentioned, were compositions of the pianist. An altogether admirable concert party supporting the star of the occasion were Miss Esta d'Argo, a brilliant and world-famous soprano; Mr. Percy Heming, the popular baritone; and Mr. W. H. Squire, who ranks among the foremost 'cellists of the day. The whole programme was thoroughly enjoyed by a quite exceptionally appreciative audience.

Liverpool Daily Post Monday 5th April 1915

JOLLITY AT THE TOWER.

Exuberant Holiday-Makers.

The "Bunny Hug" in a Cafe.

Police Prosecution Fails.

Scenes which occurred in the Algerian Cafe, in the New Brighton Grounds last Bank Holiday were described to the Wallasey magistrates on Wednesday when Mr Robert Harold Davy, manager and secretary of the Tower Company, was summoned, as licensee, for permitting riotous conduct to take place on the premises. He pleaded not guilty.

Mr G. Livsey (Deputy Town Clerk) appeared to prosecute on behalf of the police. Accusations of loud singing, some patrons involved in a bunny hug. It was another example of the intolerance of the authorities towards the Tower and holiday makers enjoying themselves.

Wallasey News 4th September 1915

LIVELY CAFE SCENES.

RENEWAL OF A NEW BRIGHTON LICENCE REFUSED.
The renewal of the licence of the Algerian Cafe, at
New Brighton Tower, was refused at the Wallasey
Licensing Sessions, to-day, by a majority of the
magistrates, over whom Alderman T. Raffles Bulley
presided. The application for renewal was opposed
by the Chief Constable (Mr. P. L. Barry), for whom Mr.
W. Proctor {instructed by the Town-clerk) appeared,
while Mr. Greaves Lord (instructed by Mr. Sidney Dod)
represented the Tower Company. Evidence was given
regarding scenes in the cafe during a recent Bank
Holiday. Detective-inspector Pearson said that on the
evening of Whit Monday, 1914, he saw a couple singing,

Ir Percy L Barry – Chief Constable

dancing, and making a considerable noise in cafe. One
man threw a bottle and broke some glasses. The ages of the customers,
male and female, from eighteen to twenty-five, in his opinion the place
was not being conducted properly. He saw no one in charge but after a
few minutes he saw a man who was in charge and drew his attention to
the matter. This man said, "Jim, see the crowd I have to deal with; what
can I do?" The man who threw the bottle was pointed out by witness and
ejected. Other evidence having been given in support of the police case
Mr. Greaves Lord urged that the bench was not dealing with an ordinary
licensed house on ordinary days, nor with a class of the community
engaged in ordinary, every-day life. Some Bank Holiday crowds were, Mr.
Lord continued, very difficult to handle, but there had never been any
suggestion that they had not been properly dealt with until now. When
the licences were originally granted there was a condition that, there
should be no bar or counter for drinking purposes when people were
standing up.
It was thought that this would assist in the management of the place, but
this had not proved to be the case. The customers often had to wait to
be served, and this frequently led people banging on the table to attract
attention. The licensee was prepared to carry out any wish expressed by
the bench.

MAGISTRATES' DECISION.
The Chairman announced that the renewal of the Algerian Cafe licence
was refused almost unanimously on the ground that the place had been
ill-conducted. Mr. Greaves Lord intimated that there would be an appeal
against this decision. The licences of the Rock Point Restaurant and
the Japanese Cafe were renewed, but an application for the removal of
the restrictions prohibiting the consumption of drink except when the
customers were seated at tables was refused.
Liverpool Echo - Tuesday 07 March 1916

157

NEW BRIGHTON TOWER There were two concerts in the Tower
Theatre yesterday to inaugurate the opening of this popular place of
entertainment for the week end and for Easter week. At the afternoon
concert an enjoyable programme was contributed by the Tower
Orchestra and Miss Adie Forde and Miss Kathleen Poole, while in the
evening the gifted boy pianist, Solomon, took part, being supported
by Miss Gladys Moger. a charming singer, and Miss Gladys Clark, clever
violinist. The thirteen year-old pianist, who has been acclaimed one of
the marvel of the century, gave a brilliant performance of Beethoven's
Moonlight Sonata." Mendelssohn's Rondo Capriocioso." and three of the
best known studies of Chopin.
Liverpool Daily Post - Saturday 22 April 1916

TOWER SCENE.
ASSISTANT MANAGER KNOCKED DOWNSTAIRS.
After a prolonged hearing of highly contradictory evidence the
magistrates sitting at Wallasey, today. Major Nesbitt and Mr. J. T. Chester
fined two young clerks in Government employ £5 each for an assault
upon Mr. Goffin, assistant manager of the New Brighton Tower.
The defendants were William Henry Thomas (21), Bute-crescent, Cardiff,
and Frank Groome Howes (18), of Pydfit-place, Cardiff, both described
as clerks in Government employ, and both attested men, and they were
charged on remand with unlawfully inflicting grievous bodily harm on
Robert Edward Goffin, assistant manager of the New Brighton Tower Co.,
by throwing him down a flight stairs.
The defence was that the two defendants were struggling in fun for the
possession of a stick, and that Mr. Goffin's hat was accidentally knocked
off. The defendants wished to apologise, whereupon Mr. Goffin sprang
upon Thomas, and in doing so overbalanced himself and fell downstairs.
Complainant denied the accuracy of this version of the affair.
Liverpool Echo - Wednesday 21 June 1916

AT NEW BRIGHTON TOWER
The vaudeville artistes to appear in the New Brighton Tower Theatre next
week are Savonne (the youngest magician in the world), Nellie Dean
(a dainty and versatile comedienne), and Coleman, Davies, and Eunice
Udall (in comedy entitled "The Grumblers").
Liverpool Echo - Friday 14 July 1916

NEW BRIGHTON TOWER, The vaudeville turns in the Tower Theatre this
week are contributed by Winifred Ray, dainty comedienne: Neely and
Ford, comedy duo: and Hobart, the Charlie Chaplin juggler. The pictures
are interesting and well-varied as usual.
Liverpool Daily Post Tuesday 22 August 1916

NEW BRIGHTON TOWER. There was a very large audience in the New Brighton Tower last night to hear Mark the well-known pianist he was heard to the greatest advantage in a programme including Beethovon. Liezt, Chopin, and Debussy, and concluding with the well-known Schubert-Tansig Military March. Miss Annabel M'Donald was the vocalist, and gave a number of songs in a particularly pleasing manner.
Liverpool Echo - Monday 04 September 1916

NEW BRIGHTON TOWER. The variety artistes appearing in the Tower Theatre this week are Edna Watson, skilful and pleasing dancer; Johnnie Dwyer, character comedian; and Hosk and Hosken, comedy duo. Some interesting pictures are shown.
Liverpool Daily Post - Tuesday 05 September 1916

NEW BRIGHTON TOWER. An enjoyable vocal and orchestral concert was given in the Tower Theatre last night, the interest of the occasion being enhanced by the participation of Miss Annie Coxen, the popular local contralto, whoso fine voice was heard to much advantage, especially in Liddle's "Abide with me," The orchestra, conducted by Mr. T. Rimmer, played, among other selections, the "Raymond" overture (Ambroise Thomas), the well-known dances from " Henry VIII." (Edward German), and the polonaise from Liddle's "Abide with me the concert concluding with Cowen's stirring march "Fall In." An attractive programme of varieties and pictures will be given to-night and during the week.
Liverpool Echo - Monday 11 September 1916

RUSSIAN RED CROSS.
WALLASEY'S SPECIAL EFFORT TO HELP THE FUNDS.
There have been many " Flag Days" in Wallasey, as elsewhere, but it is felt that there have been none more important than that to be celebrated on Saturday next, when the Mayor (Alderman Sidney Dawson), with a loyal band of workers, will make a special effort on behalf of the Russian Red Cross Funds.
During the afternoon the new motor-ambulances provided for the conveyance of wounded to the new Town Hall hospital and the local Red Cross hospitals will be formally inspected in the Central Park, Liscard.
A further effort in aid of the Russian Red Cross Fund is to be made by theatrical and cinema managers in the district, who have formed themselves into a committee, with Mr. R. H. Davy, manager of the New Brighton Tower, chairman. A matinee performance is to be given by the Kinema Minstrels at the Scala Theatre, Seacombe, next Wednesday; while a vaudeville performance is being arranged for the following Wednesday at the Winter Gardens, New Brighton.
Liverpool Echo - Wednesday 18 October 1916

PICTURES AT THE TOWER
Have you noticed that New Brighton Tower have forsaken the variety
turns and put instead some of the best of pictures? It is a good idea,
for the Tower Theatre is a big place, and star pictures such as now form
the programme should draw well, especially an "extra" to the ballroom,
gardens, sideshows, &c.
Liverpool Echo - Friday 29 June 1917

NEW BRIGHTON TOWER. Under the very favourable climatic conditions
of the past week this highly popular resort has been doing excellent
business. The scenic features of the enclosure are of themselves
highly attractive, and these added to the other phases comprehensive
programme, including the mammoth water chute, the menagerie,
the mysterious castle the figure gravity ride, the joy wheel, the flying
machine, animated pictures, dancing to orchestral music make an irresistible ensemble.
Liverpool Daily Post - Tuesday 24 July 1917

The Companies Acts, 1908 and 1913.

Notice of Meeting of Creditors.

In the Matter of the NEW BRIGHTON TOWER AND RECREATION COMPANY Limited.

(In Voluntary Liquidation.)

PURSUANT to section 188 of the Companies (Consolidation) Act, 1908, a Meeting of the creditors of the above named Company will be held at the office of me, the undersigned, 60, Castle-street, Liverpool, on Tuesday, the 20th day of February, 1917, at 11 o'clock in the forenoon, for the purposes provided for in the said section.—Dated this 10th day of February, 1917.

SIDNEY W. DOD, Solicitor for Mr. Robert Harold Davy, the Liquidator.

NEW BRIGHTON TOWER. The ballroom at New Brighton Tower proves
extremely popular. Also cinema exhibitions of the latest screen successes
are given twice daily in the Tower theatre, with a mid-week change. All
the sideshows and riding devices are continued, including the exciting
mile journey on the scenic railway.
Liverpool Daily Post - Monday 10 September 1917

160

THEFT FROM NEW BRIGHTON TOWER

Joseph Francis King (12), 35, Flamanke street, Birkenhead, was charged at Wallasey, to-day, with stealing a revolver from the New Brighton Tower, on or about September 3, and Reginald Glover, cycle dealer, of Price street, Birkenhead, was charged with receiving it.

Both pleaded guilty. King was met in Birkenhead by a youth in the employ of Glover, who gave the latter 1 shilling to buy the revolver. Glover had not seen the article. Mr. John Joyce (chairman) said the case against Glover was serious. He had encouraged boys to steal. He would have to pay a fine of £5. If he came there again he would punished without the option of fine. The boy's mother was ordered to pay 5 shillings, and the boy to receive six strokes of the birch.

Liverpool Echo - Monday 24 September 1917

WALLASEY VOLUNTEERS.

An inspection took place at New Brighton Tower last evening of the 11th (Wallasey) Battalion Cheshire Volunteer Regiment, by Brevet Lieutenant-Colonel F. H. Burnell- Nugent, D.S.O. (Rifle Brigade), the supervising officer of Volunteers, Western Command There was a good muster of all ranks, the parade number reaching 458, and the transport about fifty cars and motor-cycles.

The smart appearance of the men elicited the appreciative comments of the spectators, and the exercises, which included bayonet work, bombing, extended order drill, company drill, entrenching, musketry, signalling, and ambulance were gone through with marked efficiency.

Liverpool Echo - Thursday 26 July 1917

161

NEW BRIGHTON TOWER.
GREAT PROGRAMME MARKS THE NEW REOPENING DATE.
The New Brighton Tower season opens this year with truly magnificent programme On Good Friday:

> Madame Ciara Butt,
> Madame Stralia,
> Miss Marie Hal,
> And Lady Tree.

This will be the opening concert, on Good Friday evening, 8.15, although there will be a minor concert in the afternoon.
On Saturday all the Tower amusements, including the ballroom, will be in full swing. On Easter Sunday Miss Carrie Tubb and party provide another good programme, while on Easter Monday there will the full run of amusements, including special films in the theatre.
Liverpool Echo - Tuesday 19 March 1918

NEW BRIGHTON TOWER. IS IT DOOMED?
It is just possible that with the coming of peace New Brighton Tower, the purchase of which by the Ministry of Munitions has been under negotiation for some time, may yet be saved as a landmark. The object of the Government department in acquiring the structure was to make good use of the steel, and for its transference were completed, requiring only formal approval. With the end of the war. however, it is not unlikely that its possession by the Ministry is no longer necessary. This, of course, remains be seen. The Tower (620 feet high) is higher than the more famous tower at Blackpool, but not so high as Eifel. As a tower it has always been considered of most graceful proportions, and set amidst the trees of the grounds, and overlooking the river and the sea, it has always been an attractive and the first object of interest to all who enter Liverpool—the gateway of the Western world.
Liverpool Daily Post - Wednesday 11 December 1918

WELCOMING THE AMERICANS.
A JOY-DAY FOR 600 AT THE NEW BRIGHTON TOWER.
On the invitation of Mr. R. H. Davy, manager of the Tower, New Brighton, between five and six hundred American soldiers and sailors will visit that popular resort on Saturday. Elaborate arrangements have been made for their enjoyment, and they will be at liberty to make full use of all the numerous side attractions. Tea will be served to them in the Algerian Restaurant, at the conclusion of the afternoon baseball match to be held on the Tower Athletic ground (let gratis for the occasion) between American and Canadian teams, and to which the visitors have been invited. The entire gross proceeds of the match will be devoted to the funds of the Seacombe canteen for wounded soldiers.

In the evening the visitors will be present at a " go-as-you-please" contest in the theatre. A special boat has been provided take the party over the river.
Liverpool Echo - Wednesday 14 August 1918

" GO-AS-YOU-PLEASE."
The chief point about Go-As-You-Please contests is that as rule you Don't. The idea is that in most of the streets we live in there is somebody dead sure he or she is a better singer or player than the bulk of the people filling the bills of the various musical halls and theatres. Perhaps you have been bored stiff by Little Willie's recitation in the best parlour? Or may be you know several of those people who will sing. Well, the go-as-you-please contest offers an opportunity for revenge. Encourage the entertainers to go in for one, and go to see it. You will be amused and amazed. The audience, right of custom, considers itself free to applaud itself hoarse or howl with derision. It is delighted to indulge its faculty for quick judgment by cutting off your golden hopes (the prize is in cash) even your silvery notes are warbling through only the first line; or, if opinions differ, the "for" section promptly tells the "against" crowd to " shut up and give 'er a chance." It is very human, occasionally perfectly sound in judgment, but always an exhibition of sentiment. The prizes are awarded according to the heartiness of the applause.
Just now there are typical examples the New Brighton Tower Saturday night shows, attended by thousand of merrymakers.
One evening there were two soldiers competing, one with excellent voice, admirably managed, and with good expression; the other not a "finished " singer but a trifle lame, obviously sincere, meaning every word of the little sentimental homily the rather hectic words conveyed. No. 2 got the prize.
You will see feminine competitors, without the least charm, not a bit tuneful, but possessing a self-confident determination, and a going-to-do-it spirit that would win any war, sticking it for four or five minutes, despite howls, catcalls, jeers, laughter, and ironical cheering! Others will come timidly on, tremble over the first line, and almost give way to the inevitable titter, then win through and get applauded to the echo.
Mr. Coffin, manages his mixed crowd with tact, and when he does black out one of the "impossibles," throwing the irrepressible artist into utter darkness, he is always right. He knows just when the audience is fed up. There is one suggestion to make —songs limited to two verses. Artists not bad enough to hiss or youngsters too young be shamelessly bullied, will persist, despite "hints" from their judges. There is one suggestion to make —songs limited to two verses. And the audience is always pleased with itself, whatever it may think of you.
Liverpool Echo - Wednesday 28 August 1918

A MERSEY LANDMARK.

New Brighton Tower, the familiar landmark to ocean travellers entering and leaving the Mersey, as well as to people who have spent holidays on the Cheshire coast, is to be pulled down before Whitsuntide.

Its height of 582 feet from the ground level is rather more than that of the Blackpool Tower.

The ballroom, theatre, and other amusement-places beneath are be left untouched.

Lancashire Evening Post - Wednesday 15 January 1919

NEW BRIGHTON TOWER FORECLOSURE.

New Brighton Tower and Recreation Compact (Limited), owning the principal pleasure resort in the Merseyside watering-place, appeared before the Lancashire Chancery, Liverpool, yesterday, in a motion to secure immediate foreclosure absolute against them. The petitioners were the British and South American Steam Navigation Company, mortgagors.

Mr. Whitty, on behalf of the liquidator of the Tower Company, contented to order asked for.

Stating that the plaintiffs had advanced on mortgage twice as much as the property was worth, and shareholders regarded it as impossible to raise the money to discharge the mortgage. An order for immediate foreclosure was thereupon granted.

In the Matter of the Companies (Consolidation) Act, 1908, and in the Matter of the NEW BRIGHTON TOWER & RECREATION COMPANY Limited.

NOTICE is hereby given, that pursuant to section 195 of the Companies (Consolidation) Act, 1908, a General Meeting of the above named Company will be held at the registered offices of the Company, The Tower Grounds, New Brighton, on Monday, the 5th day of May, 1919, at 3 o'clock in the afternoon, for the purpose of having the Liquidator's accounts showing the manner in which the winding-up has been conducted and the property of the Company disposed of laid before such Meeting, and of hearing any explanation that may be given by the Liquidator; and also of determining, by Extraordinary Resolution, the manner in which the books, accounts and documents of the Company, and the Liquidator thereof, shall be disposed of.—Dated this 28th day of March, 1919.

R. H. DAVY, Liquidator.

E 2

Yorkshire Post and Leeds Intelligencer - Wednesday 29 January 1919

BLAZE NEW BRIGHTON TOWER. In the early hours yesterday morning a fire was discovered in the grandstand at the Athletic Grounds of the New Brighton Tower Company. The fires spread rapidly, and the efforts of the local fire brigade were unavailing, the place being totally destroyed. The adjoining buildings, including the menagerie, were saved.

A football match between some Boy Scouts had been played the previous evening, and it is thought a match carelessly thrown away was the cause of the conflagration. The damage, which is estimated at several thousand pounds, is covered by insurance.

Yorkshire Post and Leeds Intelligencer - Friday 16 May 1919

BOXING FARCE

Nothing better than a farce the only description that can be given to a 15 round boxing contest at New Brighton Tower last night, between Fred Fulton of America, and Custave Marthuin of France. Marthuin was obviously untrained, and Fulton made short work of him, simply sparring through the first round, and putting his opponent out with a right hook early in the second.

Yorkshire Evening Post - Thursday 06 November 1919   Fred Fulton

TOWER AND GARDENS.

"NEW BRIGHTON'S HAPPY VALLEY."
with Riding Devices, Seal Pond, Monkey House, Aviaries, etc., from 2 p.m.
CINEMA THRICE DAILY. 3, 5.30 and 8.
Continuous DANCING, 2.30 to 10.30.

SPECIAL BANK HOLIDAY ARRANGEMENTS.
11 a.m., GARDENS OPEN.

FULL BRASS BANDS & ORCHESTRAS ALL DAY
DANCING FROM NOON.
Continuous Cinema in Theatre from 2 p.m.
Adm. (in. tax) Gardens, Theatre and Ballroom
Balcony 9d., Ballroom (dancers) 6d. extra (pay
at Ballroom).

SUNDAYS, GARDENS, etc., from 2 p.m.
BIRKENHEAD BOROUGH SILVER PRIZE BAND
at 8.15. Adm. (inc. tax) 5d.

Seals at the Tower.

Latest arrivals at New Brighton Tower include a number of fine seals. The animals are in splendid condition, and will add greatly to the attractiveness of the Quarry, to the pond in which they have been relegated, and which also includes an aviary containing many rare and beautiful birds and cages of lively and mischievous monkeys. A fine new bandstand has been erected in the Quarry, which should be an exceedingly popular part of the Tower grounds.

THE TOWER

JOHN RIDDING
GRAND OPERA CO.

Principal Artistes :—

Miss Josephine Healy,   Miss Lilian Coomber,
Miss Margaret Pemberton.   Miss Beatrice Hill,
Miss May Florence,   Messrs. Aubrey Standing,
Philip Hill,   Percy Martin,   Jay Ryan, and
JOHN RIDDING.

Full Orchestra and Chorus.

TO-NIGHT, (Sat.), "BOHEMIAN GIRL."
Adm. (inc. tax): 9d., 1/3, & Res. Stalls, 2/4.

GARDENS, etc., from 2 p.m., DAILY.
CINEMA at 3, 5.30 and 8 p.m.
DANCING from 2.30.
Adm. (inc. tax) Gardens, Cinema, and Ballroom
Balcony 9d., Ballroom Floor (dancers), 6d. extra.

BALLROOM, WEDNESDAY EVENING NEXT,
THIRD GRAND
FANCY DRESS & CONFETTI CARNIVAL
Augmented Orchestra. Costume Prizes value £6 6s.
Adm. Dancers to Ballroom Floor (this night
only) 1s.   Spectators Gallery Free.
Exhibition of the latest Dances including
"LA FRILLE."

A HANDSOME STRUCTURE

The Tower itself was really one the handsomest ever erected in this country, and the Manchester architects, Maxwell and Tuke, were as proud of it as the Derby engineers who built it. Its width at the base was 143 feet, and the weight of the steelwork on the Tower was 1,760 tons, and of the buildings 650 tons. Its erection was marked by a sad accident, which a couple of Derby men were killed, and later there was a serious fire, which, however, left the steel-work practically intact.

Now that it is coming to an end people on both sides of the Mersey are very outspoken in their regret at the disappearance of so notable a landmark, for nothing that is left is anything like as attractive and as striking.

The New Brighton Tower has other memories for another section of the Derby public. Some 20 years ago it was decided to run a football club in connection with the enterprise, and Mr. James Bulmer, who had been associated with the Secretary's department of Derby County, became secretary and manager of the new organisation. He did his work all too well from the point of view of his old employers, for amongst his captures was J. W. Robinson, Derby County's brilliant goalkeeper. We question whether the sensation created by the news that Robinson had deserted his old club has ever been surpassed in the entire history of Derby football. Mr. Bulmer, who died some years ago, never set Mersey alight with his new

J. W. Robinson,
Southampton.

Ogden's *Cigarettes.*

club. He certainly got together some famous players, but never managed to infuse into them the spirit of a team, and it is the spirit in these matters that counts. After somewhat undistinguished career in Second League football, the club found it expedient to confine their energies to competitions of a less ambitions class.

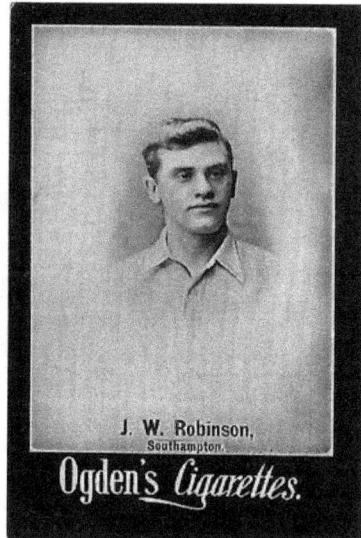

Derby Daily Telegraph - Saturday 23 August 1919

DISMANTLING OF NEW BRIGHTON TOWER
The reasons for the dismantling of the Tower structure are complex and are not just the lack of maintenance. We have to look at the background to this sorry affair. Starting with the decision to manufacture the structure from mild steel and not cast Iron, unlike Blackpool Tower. The mild steel would require regular painting to prevent it from rusting. The sea side air only speeding up the process.
Members of the council adopted polices and restrictive practice that prevented the business from generating worthwhile profits, the refusal of bar licences beyond 10 p.m, and in some cases the refusal altogether only hampered the management. Their reluctance to adapt progressive pricing policies on combination travel tickets connected to the ferries. Interference and unfair treatment of music licensing only added to the Towers financial problems.
The only obvious conclusion that one can arrive at, that this was an intentional ploy adopted by the council to limit the number of day trippers arriving at the resort.
With a lack of investment and the outbreak of the First World War the public were not allowed to travel in the lifts to the top of the Tower for military reasons. During the war the government made unsuccessful attempts to buy the tower for its metal.
The cost of renovation was more than the company could afford. Earlier in the year the New Brighton Tower and Recreation Compact (Limited) had been placed into liquidation with an immediate foreclosure granted. It was inevitable that the structure would rust away and become unsafe.
Messrs, Hughes, Bolckow, and Co., Limited a well-known ship breaking company based out of Blyth in Northumberland, were given the task of dismantling the Tower
The scrap mild steel did have a value, the price of scrap had dramatically increased after the war, so this could have been yet another consideration of the management in the demise of the Tower.
The top portion of the structure commenced to be dismantled on 7th May 1919 with the flag-pole removed and was completed in June 1921. The brick portion comprising the Ballroom and Theatre remained, together with the spires. During the Second World War the basement was used as a communal air-raid shelter.
It was not until the Wallasey Act of 1927 that the policy of the council was to change. with the new promenade extension, the pools, and road modernization, purchase of the pier and new developments. All a bit too late for the highest structure in the United Kingdom. But at long last the authorities had started to take an interest in the development of the resort. In the future battles were to be fought between the residents and business owners.

167

An explanation of the slow progress made in dismantling New Brighton Tower is that the workmen are compelled to cease operations at one o'clock every day. This is necessitated because of the Tower grounds being open to the public, from 2 p.m., and the management are anxious that visitors should run no risk of injury from falling debris. * * * 31.7.1919

New Brighton Tower is slowly but surely disappearing, and the many hundreds of inland people who annually visit the Merseyside resort will, while obtaining their last gaze at the steel structure, notice that several prominent parts have disappeared. The covering of he dome has gone, and the flagpole has been removed. Demolition is proceeding apace, and by the summer the tower will present a vastly different appearance to visitors. 30.5.1919

Stacking up the pieces for transport to Newcastle.

FROM PLEASURE TO BUSINESS. — The New Brighton Tower, claimed to be the highest structure in Great Britain, is being removed to Newcastle for shipbuilding purposes. The dismantling of the tower is proving a difficult task, as the wind often holds up work.—(*Sunday Pictorial* exclusive)

Removal of flag-pole photograph dated 7th May 1919. Progress was slow in dismantling New Brighton Tower, they had to stop work at 1 p.m. The grounds being open to the public at 2 p.m.

The contractors entered into an agreement of defraying costs by the sale of the steel. The Tower cost £120,000 to construct and nothing to demolish. The dome was also removed a while later.

On 25th June a select party assembled at the Rock Point Cafe upon an invitation from Mr Sherat (M.D of Hughes, Bolkow) for a celebration dinner. Mr Sherat wanted to celebrate the successful completion of a hazardous task with NO injury to a single person.

Bill boards displayed outside the Tower advertise silent films. The term 'silent film' is a misnomer; silent films were never silent. With full symphonic orchestras to accompany their movies. You will note on one of the advertisements the use of two orchestras, it must have been quite an experience. I have posted a couple of ads from the Wallasey News dated January 1920 showing the films being shown on the Tower.

Cowboy films were a popular topic, and featured regularly at the Tower. "Light of the Western Stars" was a 1918 American silent western film starring Dustin Farnum and Winifred Kingston.

A discontented cow puncher Gene Stewart (Farnum) makes a bet that he will marry the next woman who comes to town. Majesty Hammond (Kingston), the sister of a successful ranch owner, arrives that night and Gene in a drunken state threatens old Padre Marcos (Swickard) with death unless he marries them. She buys the ranch of a Mexican desperado and needs Gene to run it for her, but he has gone with a gang of Mexicans and is too drunk to be appealed to by anyone but Majesty. She finally persuades him to return, Majesty gets a reprieve for Gene and a warrant for Carlos, and saves Gene from death just in time.

A popular actress of this era was Mabel Normand and by a coincidence she was born in New Brighton, Staten Island, New York on the 9th November 1892. She played a key role in starting Chaplin's film career and acted as his leading lady and mentor in a string of films in 1914. Her earlier Keystone films portrayed her as a bathing beauty but Normand quickly demonstrated a flair for comedy and became a major star of Sennett's short films. Normand appeared with Charles Chaplin and Roscoe "Fatty" Arbuckle in many short films as well as men who would later become icons such as Oliver Hardy, Stan Laurel, and Boris Karloff.

DUSTIN FARNUM IN THE LIGHT OF WESTERN STARS

In the history of women's football, The Dick, Kerr Ladies are the most successful team in the world. They were formed at a munitions factory in Preston during the First World War. The team was named after its two Scottish founders, William Bruce Dick and John Kerr who set up Dick, Kerr & Co Ltd around 1900 to manufacture trams and light railway rolling stock. During a period of low-production at the factory in October 1917, women workers joined the apprentices in the factory yard for informal football matches during their tea and lunch breaks. After beating the men of the factory in an informal game, the women formed a team, under the management of office worker, Alfred Frankland. They can also boast the biggest crowd ever recorded for a women's club team game. On Boxing Day 1920, 53,000 spectators packed into Goodison Park, Everton
The popularity of the team led the Football Association (FA) to ban women's football at its member's grounds on 5 December 1921. The FA ban would stay in place for fifty years - finally being rescinded in 1971
A short silent film produced by British Pathe title reads - Dick Kerr's Ladies International Team play Ellesmere Port Cement Works Team before big crowd at New Brighton, Merseyside.

The crowds are cheering on the local hero Mr. G.E.Tottey's Garage, West Kirby who held many world motorcycle records during his career, he is seen here travelling at 50 mph on the 5th June 1922.

The Tower Athletic Grounds was a multi-purpose stadium The field was encircled by an athletics track surrounded by a banked cycle track, which hosted the World Cycling championships on the 28th July 1922. It was the biggest sporting and motorcycling track in the North of England.

A short silent film produced by British Pathe entitled: "WORLD'S CYCLING CHAMPIONSHIPS - Wonderful racing and many records broken."

The theatre continued to swing back and forth between films and live entertainment. Week commencing September 21st 1925 Gracie Fields appeared at the Tower Theatre in 'By Request', a review written and produced by Archie Pitt her husband., and it was being presented for the first time on any stage. In the same year Dougie Wakefield appeared in 'Too Many Cooks'.

In 1926 'Variety Artists and Pictures' were advertising nightly, whilst two stage attractions for Easter 1927 were Jack Hylton's Famous Band on Good Friday, and Dame Clara Butt and Party on Easter Sunday. These were complemented by cinema performances from 3.00 to 10.30 pm.

In the 1920's, for a period, the theatre stage was used to accommodate two badminton courts. .With films projected onto the safety curtain at the front of the stage, thus leaving the stage itself free for badminton players. From 1928 films were no longer on the programme and its main use was to stage wrestling matches and occasional concerts.

By the late 1930's the entertainment was mainly films being shown with the occasional spectacular stage presentation.

Wallasey   **Cheshire.**

NEW BRIGHTON AND WALLASEY VILLAGE
SEASIDE, HEALTH AND PLEASURE RESORTS.

Official Holiday Guide

ILLUSTRATED AND   DESCRIPTIVE.

New and Revised Edition, 1926.   Issued by the Corporation of Wallasey.

THE TOWER

NEW BRIGHTON.

Open all the Year round.

THE LARGEST PERMANENT PLEASURE RESORT IN THE WORLD,

General Manager and Licensee :
ROBT. E. GOFFIN.

Shelter accommodation for 50,000

OUR LICENSED CAFES are the most modern and best equipped in the district. Seating capacity for over 3,000

During the Summer Season from 2 p.m.

Dancing in the Magnificent Ballroom.

RECREATION, SPORTS AND GAMES ON THE TOWER ATHLETIC GROUNDS.

REVUES, CONCERTS and FEATURES FILMS in the PALATIAL THEATRE.

Grand Tower Syncopated Orchestras.

See Press announcements for current attractions and Special Holiday Programmes.

Unlimited Free Garage for Motoring Patrons.

:: THIRTY ACRES OF :: ORNAMENTAL GARDENS.

New Side Shows and sensational Riding Devices.   Waxworks.

An extraordinary profusion of Free Sights and Novelties

Popular Admission Charges.

DINNERS	Handsome
LUNCHEONS	Restaurants.
TEAS	Excellent Service.

Write for special terms for large parties.
Telephone—Wallasey 275 and 284.

The New Brighton Palais de Danse was the name given to the event held at the Ballroom located in the New Brighton Tower.

The Ballroom was one of the largest in the world, with a sprung floor with a dance band stage. The orchestra had as many as 60 players. Big bands played at the Tower, including Bert Yates, Bill Gregson and Victor Sylvester. Vesta Tilley has packed it from floor to ceiling, the same as the late Mde Dame Clara Butt at the big Sunday Concerts. Other well known artists appeared at the Ballroom including Mae West in November 1945. Well over 1,000 couples could dance without undue crowding. It was decorated in white and gold, with the emblems of various Lancashire towns. The Ballroom had a balcony, with seats to watch the dancers below. Behind this was an open space, where couples used to learn the dance without interfering with the more proficient ones.

The interior of the ballroom was completely destroyed by fire in 1956, but it was restored in its original style and reopened two years later.

TOWER BALLROOM
New Brighton.

Wallasey's Wonderful Palais de Danse.

DANCING.
Wednesday and Thursday 1s.
Friday and Saturday 1/6. Balcony 6d.

AFTERNOON TEA DANCES at 2.45.
Admission 1s. Tea served free.
SCARISBRICK ORCHESTRA,
undoubtedly the finest dance combination in the north.

FRIDAY NEXT, MAY 20th, at 7.30.
THE RESIDENTS' GALA AND MIDNIGHT CARNIVAL.

TWO BANDS. Latest Novelties.
Streamers, etc.
GRAND CABARET INTERLUDE,
with new items by
"DORIS" AND "JACK."
Admission 2s. Balcony 6d.
Special late buses. Tables reserved free.
Tel. 276 and 284 Wallasey.

THURSDAY, MAY 26th—
REVIVAL OF OLD FASHION DANCES AND MIDNIGHT CARNIVAL.
EXHIBITION OF OLD FAVOURITES
by Miss Evelyn and Professor Dossor.
Admission 1/6. Balcony 6d.

Mersey Building Co Ltd, from Allerton in Liverpool were employed on the project to convert the original lake into a boating pool. Using Ferrocrete when the mortar is applied over a layer of metal mesh. Photograph below shows the finished product, and top left the original lake.

Tower Boating Pool, New Brighton

The boating pool was constructed sometime before 1929. The programme opposite being the first printed literature with a mention of boating on the lake. The original lake had been enlarged with two small islands added during the turn of the century.

⊥

From 29 July to 12 August 1929, the third World Scout Jamboree was held at Arrowe Park, in Birkenhead. With about 30,000 Scouts and over 300,000 visitors attending. The New Brighton Tower Jamboree Caterers offered a reduced menu, in aid of the event.

Start of the 1930's
This was to be a real decade of contrasts, the promenade extension
opened with long hot summers and big plans, it closed with black-out
curtains and air-raid sirens.
In 1932 they opened the Derby Pool., to be followed a year later with the
largest open air pool in Europe New Brighton Bathing Pool. Swimming
was a big attraction in this era. Hundreds of people joined a walk through
the newly-completed Mersey Tunnel. At the Tower ballroom the younger
generation danced away the hours to the music of Dave Collins and his
Playboys, and later Archie Craig. With the sensational voice of Wynne
Harrison, an 18-year-old from Liverpool, who became the heart throb of
the girls, but without the screaming that was to happen a lot later.
Notices declaring that there were "No Vacancies" a common sight in shop
windows and outside factories, with long queues outside the Labour
Exchange in Secombe, with very little money around things were difficult.
The Tower Company started the new decade in the financial doldrums,
trying to cut costs with rate appeals, and even a proposal to sell the
business to the council.
The introduction of Dirt Track Racing/Speedway all helped to stem the
tide. In the last couple of years of the decade things started to improve
"Happy Days Are Here Again" sang the crooners on the radio.
War was declared on the 3rd September 1939. The outbreak of war led to
large-scale evacuation of women and children from Wallasey and other
large cities.

From my research it would appear that The Wall of Death was introduced into the UK in 1929 courtesy of some American Riders. Until the early 1970s they enjoyed a period of immense popularity and all of the major fairs would have had at least one Wall of Death. Many different stunts were tried - it was quite common for a lion to be taken on the wall in a side car. The Austin Seven motor car was also adapted for riding on the wall. New Brighton Tower grounds must have been one of the first with this spectacular amusement with records dating back to 1930, with different riders and owners over this period I have tried to include as many as possible within these pages.

The motor cyclists have to travel at a speed of 80 miles an hour around the circular and vertical walls. Sometimes blindfolded, and standing up. Then the most dangerous trick is the dive down the wall in a perpendicular manner. The grand finale is the pursuit race, in which both cyclists take part. The one travels around the top and the other at the bottom, and at one moment in time they change position. The noise was deafening but his just added to the excitement. The final show in the Tower Grounds occurred in the 1965 session with the Wall being dismantled and re-assembled at a fun fair on the south coast.

Photographs above are of Billy Bellhouse
"Cyclone Billy"
Billy appeared at New Brighton for the 1931 season and returned on numerous occasions.
Danny Carter tending Billy Bellhouse following his accident in June 1935 whilst performing in Spain. He was never to appear on the Wall of Death again and opened a fish and chip shop in Sheffield the following year.

Bill Miller & Fred Heyward Tower

Ronnie Hayhurst & Kitty O'Neil

WIZARDS on the WALL

TOWER GARDENS,
—— New Brighton ——

YOU MUST SEE
Fearless Fred Farrow
and
Cyclone Billy Bellhouse
THE ENGLISH WIZARDS.
Riding and Stunting on High Power Motor Cycles
on an Upright Wall.

A SUPER THRILL
THE AUSTRALIAN PURSUIT RACE.
Two Riders on the Wall at the same time
Racing at Terrific Speeds.

CONTINUOUS DEMONSTRATIONS
(Including Sundays)

ADMISSION NOW REDUCED TO
ADULTS 6d. CHILDREN 3d.

184

The New Brighton Tower Company instructed Edmund Kirby & Sons architects and surveyors to appeal against the 1933-34 rate assessments. Of special interest to the reader are the enterprises operating within the Tower Grounds and the rents and profit sharing arrangements.

ALL COMMUNICATIONS TO BE ADDRESSED TO THE COMPANY AND NOT TO INDIVIDUALS.

TELEGRAMS, TOWER, NEW BRIGHTON.

TELEPHONES,
GENERAL OFFICE, WALLASEY 276.
CATERING DEPT, ,, 294.

New Brighton Amusements Ltd

THE TOWER,
NEW BRIGHTON,
CHESHIRE.

25th August, 1933.

Messrs. Edmund Kirby & Sons.
5, Cook Street,
Liverpool.

Dear Sirs,

TOWER. NEW BRIGHTON.
and
WALLASEY CORPORATION.

We have pleasure in handing you herewith list of the Amusement Devices shewing rents, sharing terms, etc. and plan shewing the general arrangement as set out in the Amusement Park.

We also enclose drawing shewing the proposition for the roof garden.

Yours faithfully,
NEW BRIGHTON AMUSEMENTS, LTD.

PLAN REFERRED TO

	Rent		
Palmist	£ 70	..	..
Three Rock Stalls	£ 57	10	..
Guess Weighing Machine	£ 12	10	..
Side Stall & shooter	£ 32	10	..
Willow Café	£ 75	..	..
Gold Wire Stall	£ 20	..	..
Kicker & Side Stall	£ 28	..	..
Fairy Coaster	£ 40	..	..
Three Round 'uns	£ 75	..	..
One Round 'un	£ 15	..	..
Quarry Gardens	£ 200	..	..
Camera pitch	£ 30	..	..
Lake £250 + 33% of takings over £800 Total Takings £1,356	£ 435	12	
Side Staff	£ 45	..	..
Promenade Kiosk	£ 100	..	..
Miniature Circus	£ 30	..	..
Juvenile Horses,18-ft. Round 'Un 20-ft. Round 'Un, Cocoanut Sheet.	£ 55	..	..
Three a breast Gallopers, Cake Walk Chair-o-planes, Ocean Wave, Mystic Tank, Juvenile Horses, Juvenile Chairs, and Swings	£ 175	..	..
Concert Party Pitch	£ 1.	15	9 per week
Punch and Judy Pitch	£ 1.	2.	10 per week

1933 New Brighton

186

Most of the rides and sideshows were owned by individuals who paid the company rent.

	£	s	d
The Ghost Train	673.	15.	1.
The Kiddies Whip	94.	10.	9.
Scenic Railway	660.	3.	6.
Auto-Scooter	840.	12.	4.
Skid Ride	798.	4.	11.
Bomb Dropper	297.	11.	3.
Automatics	933.	10.	6.
Essien's Canaret Show	152.	16.	7.
Figure 8.	1,684.	11.	9.
Waxworks	385.	4.	7.
Theatre	59.	-.	-.
Ballroom	2232.		
Egerton Steet Garage	50.	-.	-.
Lodge Egerton Street	54.	-.	-.
1 Green Avenue	39.	-.	-.
Parking Rents	12.	-.	-.
Athletic Grounds.	114.	6.	-.
Hoarding	39.	-.	-.
Stalls, Roundabouts, etc. As per Sheet	£1,313.	8.	
Boating Lake – Rent	£250.		
+ £185.12.4.	£435.	12.	4.
Grand Total	£10,869.	11.	2.

Edmund Kirby & Sons architects and surveyors appear to have been involved in the possible sale of New Brighton Tower & Grounds to the Council. The reply below from the Town Clerk, implies that the original offer was too high, and they would consider a "bargain" price.

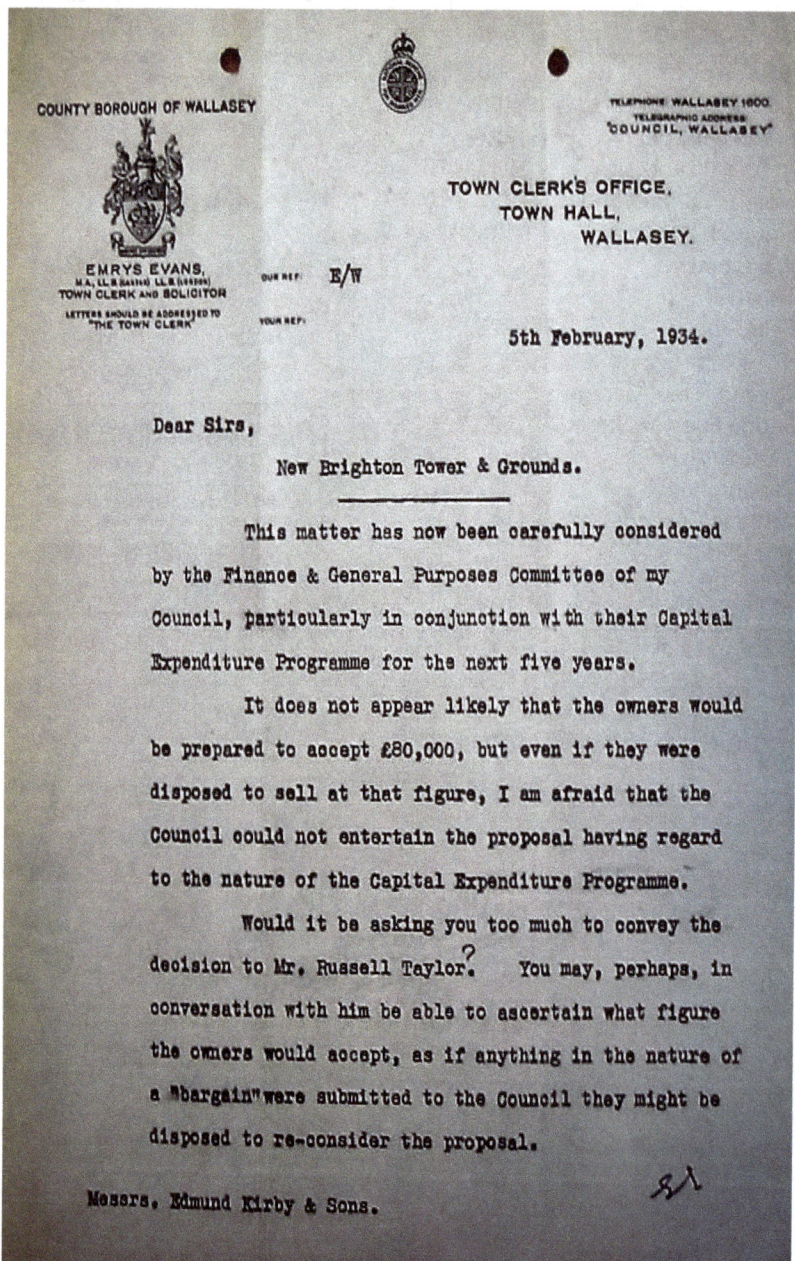

COUNTY BOROUGH OF WALLASEY

TELEPHONE WALLASEY 1800.
TELEGRAPHIC ADDRESS
"COUNCIL, WALLASEY"

EMRYS EVANS,
M.A., LL.B (BARRIS) LL.B (LONDON)
TOWN CLERK AND SOLICITOR
LETTERS SHOULD BE ADDRESSED TO
"THE TOWN CLERK"

OUR REF: E/W

YOUR REF:

TOWN CLERK'S OFFICE,
TOWN HALL,
WALLASEY.

5th February, 1934.

Dear Sirs,

New Brighton Tower & Grounds.

This matter has now been carefully considered by the Finance & General Purposes Committee of my Council, particularly in conjunction with their Capital Expenditure Programme for the next five years.

It does not appear likely that the owners would be prepared to accept £80,000, but even if they were disposed to sell at that figure, I am afraid that the Council could not entertain the proposal having regard to the nature of the Capital Expenditure Programme.

Would it be asking you too much to convey the decision to Mr. Russell Taylor? You may, perhaps, in conversation with him be able to ascertain what figure the owners would accept, as if anything in the nature of a "bargain" were submitted to the Council they might be disposed to re-consider the proposal.

Messrs. Edmund Kirby & Sons.

Dirt Track as Speedway was originally thought up in Australia on December 15 1923 as an amusement at the Hunter River Society Agricultural & Horticultural Midsummer Electric Light Carnival. Soon the sport spread to England. The Motor Cycling Magazine reported the first Dirt track meeting to be held on May 7 1927 at Camberley, Surrey.

Liverpool 1937 Team Tom Price, Len Eyre, Stanley Hart, Oliver Hart, Ernie Price. On the bikes Charlie Oats, Eric Blain, Alan Butler.

The multi-purpose facility was very popular with the public with New Brighton FC occupying the centre of the ground around which was the athletics track and that in turn was encompassed by a cycle track which hosted the World Cycling Championships in 1922.

Speedway came to the venue at New Brighton comparatively late on, not being staged until 1933 when a suitable track was laid on top of the now disused athletics track. The promotion was the Wirral Heath Motorcycle Club who ran the meetings under a restricted permit.

A couple of paragraphs from the "Homes of British Speedway" are of interest and read as follows: -

"One of the programmes from 1934 stated: 'Motorcyclists wishing to compete must give all particulars of their name etc. to the secretary at least fifteen minutes before the start of the meeting. All competitors must pay an admission fee of 1 shilling to the stadium only - there is no entrance fee to race." And the second :-

"In autumn of 1948, Cheshire County Council gave approval in principle to an application by the New Brighton Tower Amusement Co. to reopen the speedway track at the stadium, despite strong protests from local residents over noise. However, the company was refused a licence to run speedway in 1949. By the late 1960's, the speedway track had been covered in tarmac for use as a stock car circuit. In 1973, a further proposal to reintroduce speedway to the venue came to nothing."

THRILLS AT NEW BRIGHTON DIRT TRACK.

Lap Record Broken.

The third meeting at the New Brighton Dirt Track, at the Tower Grounds, on Saturday, started off well with the standing start lap record being broken within the first minute or so.

Tommy Price, of the Mersey M.C., gave the crowd a splendid exhibition of riding, and cheers greeted the announcement that he had beaten the existing record. His time was 1 min. 33 secs.

Mick Petty made a game effort to beat Price's record but failed by the narrow margin of 2-5 secs.

Sprouts Griffo, who enjoys wide popularity with the crowd, won the Multi-Cylinder Push Start Race in fine style.

The big thrill of the evening came with the team races between Mersey M.C. and Hell's Angels (representing Wirral Heath M.C.).

Taken in four heats, these races produced some exciting neck-to-neck riding, the cornering at times being brilliant.

Hell's Angels, in spite of a splendid performance, lost to Mersey M.C. by 11 points to 12.

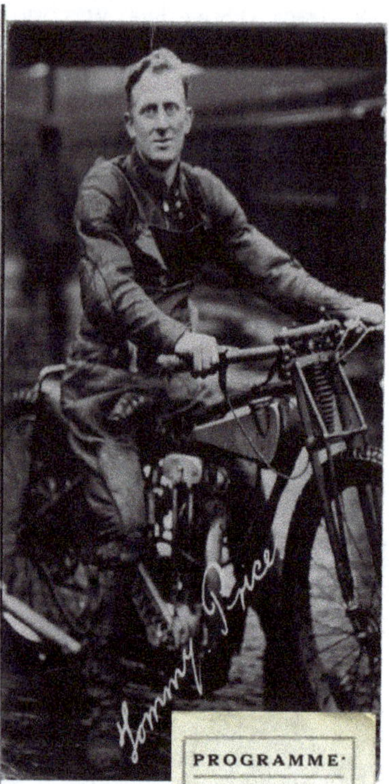

Tommy Price

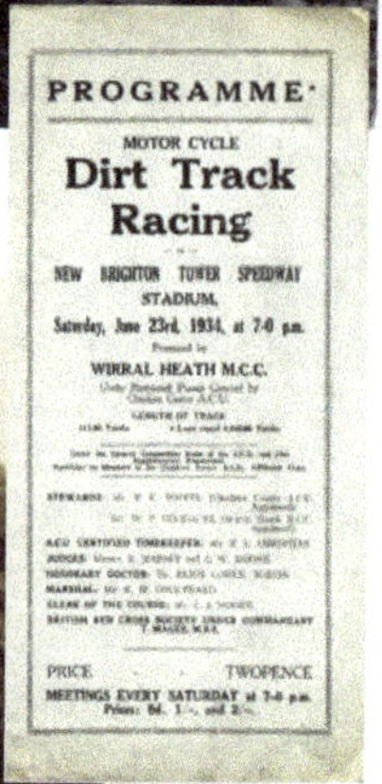

PROGRAMME

MOTOR CYCLE

Dirt Track Racing

NEW BRIGHTON TOWER SPEEDWAY STADIUM,

Saturday, June 23rd, 1934, at 7-0 p.m.

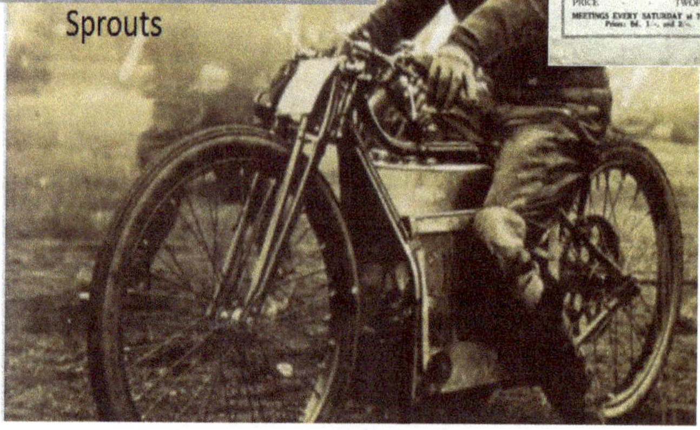

Sprouts

190

The spires on New Brighton Tower were removed between 1932 and 1934 according to the aerial photographs produced by "Britain from above"
With the central dome containing the Elevator Hall, and a miniature village being removed late 1935. It was a sad fact that the management of the Tower, found it more cost effective to remove these features than trying to maintain them. The Tower Guide of 1936 shows these features clearly missing.

The following information originates from a scrapbook compiled by Joanna the wife of Charles William Binks.

The couple married on Tuesday the 26th May 1942, at the Memorial Church, Manor Road. Miss Joanna Florence Marian Strafford, was the daughter of Mr and Mrs George William Strafford, of Upton, Wirral.

Mr Strafford had been a director of New Brighton Amusements (1939) Ltd, along with O.V. Asser, L.T. Delaney, C.A.E. Lawes, H.A.G. Sorrell, with J.W. Evans being the Managing Director.

The bridegroom was serving with H.M. Forces and is well known in Wallasey theatrical circles through his association with the New Brighton Tower, where he was Theatre and Ballroom manager for twelve years, in recent times he was the licensee of the New Brighton Hotel until he left to join the colours.

The bride was also associated with New Brighton Tower, being secretary to her father, Mr G. W. Strafford, up to the time of his retirement.

Following on from the success at the Tower Ballroom, C.W. Binks made the announcement that commencing from Sunday, January 14th, 1940, the Playboys along with Guest Vocalists and Star Variety Artistes, would be appearing at the Coliseum Wallasey village. Conducting the band will be Pat Davey an exceptionally talented young lady who can play both Accordion and Electric Guitar, along with a very pleasing voice. I quote from the flyer issued at the time.

AT THE TOWER.

WHITSUN ATTRACTIONS.

The Tower offers a host of attractions for the Whitsuntide holidays.

The Amusement Park, re-set out and gaily painted, contains all the latest riding devices, thrillers, novelty entertainments, side-shows, etc. There is fun and pleasure for children of all ages—from toddlers to youngsters of 90.

For dancers there is the magnificent and spacious Ballroom where The Playboys, a band of talented musicians and artists presented by C. W. Binks, provide programmes of outstanding merit. It is a Band that can entertain you even if you are not a dancer. They are playing for dancing to-night (Saturday), on Whit Sunday they appear on the stage at the Gaumont Palace, Wallasey, and on Whit Monday there are two sessions in the Ballroom (afternoon and evening). Wednesday the usual mid-week dance.

Phone : Wallasey 276.

DBDA

C. W. Binks.

Tower Ballroom & Theatre,   Also Presenting
New Brighton, Ches.   BANDS OF DISTINCTION.

YORKSHIRE EVENING NEWS JUNE 13TH 1940

★ New Brighton's Super Entertainment Resort ★

THE

TOWER

VARIETIES OF ATTRACTIONS

THE NEW

— PLEASURE PARK —

RIDING DEVICES	THRILLERS	SIDE SHOWS
BOATING LAKE	GLIDERDROME	SPEEDWAY

Rock Point & Japanese Cafes (Licensed)

HOT LUNCHEONS — TEAS — LIGHT REFRESHMENTS
PARTIES A SPECIALITY
BEERS ON DRAUGHT   WINES AND SPIRITS

— WAXWORKS —

MODERNISED — ENLARGED. NEW CHAMBER of HORRORS,
INCLUDING THE GESTAPO OUTRAGES — AND THE LATEST
ADDED ATTRACTION — WONDERLAND.

— BALLROOM —

THE PREMIER OF THE NORTH
DANCING NIGHTLY (during the Season)
TO THE POPULAR BALLROOM, STAGE AND BROADCAST BAND—
THE PLAYBOYS

"THE PLAYBOYS" ON THE AIR.
"The Playboys," under the baton of
Mr. C. W. Binks, will leave the New
Brighton Tower for a few hours on Monday next for the B.B.C. studio to give
a broadcast from 5-30—6 p.m. on the
H.M. Forces programme. Then they will
make a dash back to New Brighton to
take the stage for the benefit of people
who wish "to dance their troubles away"
in the most delightful ballroom in the
North of England. So, success, Mr.
Binks! WOL NEWS 27/7/40

193

THE
TOWER

SUPER
ENTERTAINMENT
RESORT

VARIETIES
OF
ATTRACTIONS

THE NEW

—PLEASURE PARK—

The largest collection of up-to-date
RIDING DEVICES — THRILLERS — SIDE SHOWS
GLIDERDROME.
BOATING LAKE. — SPEEDWAY.

—ROCK POINT and JAPANESE CAFES (Licensed)—

Picturesquely situated in the Grounds.
HOT LUNCHEONS — TEAS — LIGHT REFRESHMENTS.
Parties a Speciality.
Beers on Draught. — Wines and Spirits.

MODERNISED—ENLARGED

—The WAXWORKS and MUSEUM—

with the New CHAMBER OF HORRORS,
including the GESTAPO OUTRAGES.

The latest added Attraction
THE MODERN ELECTRICAL WONDERLAND

Mickey Mouse and his Gang—The Seven Dwarfs—The Mad Musicians
Cinderella—Babes in the Wood—Parade of the Tin Soldiers,
and many other Favourites. *YOU MUST BRING THE KIDDIES.*

—BALLROOM—

The premier of the North.
Dancing every WEDNESDAY—1/-, 7.30 to 11. SATURDAY—1/6.
WHIT MONDAY—2 Sessions, 2.30—5.30, 1/-; 7—11, 2/-.
The popular PLAYBOYS, with Norman Sinclair and Pat Davey.

194

GUIDE

—— TO THE ——

TOWER

AND

GROUNDS

NEW BRIGHTON

ALSO

CATALOGUE

FOR

WAXWORKS

AND

MUSEUM

AND

Other Attractions in New Brighton

FIRST EDITION JUNE 1936.   REPRODUCED JUNE 2010

Proprietors - - - - - New Brighton Amusements Ltd.

Licensee - - - - - - - - - - - W. B. Dunn

Theatre and Ballroom Manager
} - - - C. W. Binks
Publicity and Advertising - - -

Ballroom M.C. - - - - - - - - - - - H. Beatty

Catering - - - P. Manghin, Miss Burgess, Miss Woods

Ground Engineer - - - - - - - - C. D. Davies

5

197

6

198

Foreword.

The object of this Guide is to enable visitors to enjoy every minute of their visit to the Tower, by describing all the various entertainments and attractions that can be seen, also as a Catalogue to the exhibits in the Waxworks and Museum.

We also hope that it will be kept as a souvenir of a happy and enjoyable time spent in New Brighton.

For many years New Brighton has been a popular seaside resort for the people of Lancashire, Yorkshire and the Midlands, but during the last few years it has risen to one of the foremost positions as a holiday centre, attracting visitors from far and near, and now stands as a rival to any.

The enterprise shewn by the Corporation in their endeavour to place New Brighton firmly on the holiday map, through their magnificent Promenade, the World's Super Bathing Pool and Marine Boating Lake have met with great success and been well supported by the efforts of the individual Amusement Caterers.

We, the New Brighton Amusements Ltd., have, during these last two winters, spent close on £50,000 in modernising and bringing the Tower on a line with any other Amusement centre, and offer this season many new attractions which are fully described in other parts of this Guide.

The famous **Ten Temponics**—The brilliant show dance band play every night in the Tower Ballroom.

7

199

Amusement Park

The Amusement Park is one of the largest permanent ones in the country and during the winter it has been re-set out and again enlarged.

A short description of some of the Shows and Novelties will, we feel sure, be of interest to the reader.

FIGURE 8.

Still one of the most popular Riding Devices in any Amusement Park, one never tires of its encircling journey, a whirl of excitement with safety.

DRAGON SCENIC RAILWAY

Also another switchback ride always popular.

SKID RIDE

For those who crave more excitement and thrills this device stands alone.

MOTOR DODGEM

This commands great popularity, the fact of having your own Car under your own control is in itself a thrill, and as they say on the Ride, there is more fun in dodging than bumping.

GHOST TRAIN

New thrills and novelties have been added so that a ride on the Ghost Train always produces a scream.

OVER THE TOP

A thrilling experience—if you can manage it.

MOTOR SPEEDWAY

One of the favourite rides of the budding motorist.

CATERPILLAR RIDE

Another switchback ride, but its thrills are entirely different.   Try it!

BEN HUR RIDE

Exciting and thrilling.

MONT BLANC

This is from the Paris Exhibition, nuff said.

On the following page is given a list of Tenants and their various attractions.

9

10

GHOST TRAIN LTD., BLACKPOOL.
GHOST TRAIN
New novelties and thrills. Listen to the screams.

BRITISH AMUSEMENTS, LTD., BRIGHOUSE.
Proprietors of the
AUTO SCOOTER
Fun in every minute of the ride—Your own car under
your own control.

GREEN BROS., PRESTON
Proprietors of the
DRAGON SCENIC RAILWAY,
CATERPILLAR RIDE and MONO RAIL
The most popular rides—thrills without spills.

HIBBLE and MELLORS, NOTTINGHAM.
MONT BLANC
The ride that's different

HOLME, G. E., LIVERPOOL
GOLD WIRE SPECIALIST—
Fancy Goods and Novelties.
Kiosk near main entrance, promenade.
For your little gift to take back from New Brighton—
Call and see me.

LAWES, C. A. E., LONDON.
SKID RIDE—BOMBER
The ride for those wanting thrills. Amusement and
Skill. Good Prizes.

MAXWELL, J. and T., CATFORD.
Proprietors of the
SPEED, ROWING BOATS and CANOES.
The Boating Lake—The children's paradise—Let
your kiddies enjoy themselves in safety, depth of the
water only 20 inches.

11

12

13

204

Book Via

MERSEY RAILWAY

SPECIAL
CHEAP RETURN TICKETS

Liverpool Central (LOW LEVEL)

and James Street

TO

Wallasey & New Brighton.

WEEKDAYS —BY ANY TRAIN AFTER 10·0 A.M.

SUNDAYS
BANK HOLIDAYS } BY ALL TRAINS.

9d.   1/2

THIRD   FIRST

THESE TICKETS ARE ALSO ISSUED FROM WALLASEY & NEW BRIGHTON TO LIVERPOOL.

NOTE.—SPECIAL SINGLE FARE—NEW BRIGHTON TO LIVERPOOL (CENTRAL L.L. or JAMES ST.) AFTER 4·0 P.M. WEEKDAYS - - **6**D.

EVENING EXCURSIONS★

EACH WEEK-DAY INCLUDING BANK HOLIDAYS
BY ANY TRAIN AFTER 6 P.M

6d.

THIRD

CHILDREN UNDER 14 YEARS HALF FARE.

*Also issued from HAMILTON SQUARE, BIRKENHEAD CENTRAL, GREEN LANE and ROCK FERRY.

14

Waxworks

In the Tower Buildings is one of the largest Waxwork exhibitions outside of London. Though one of the oldest entertainments the Waxworks always proves one of the most popular attractions to both young and old.

Ask anyone who has visited London what places they went to, and out of all the numerous places of interest and sights to be seen, you will find from the majority, Madame Tussaud's mentioned, it is really astounding the appeal, or should we say fascination, that the Waxworks has for the public.

Among the newly added tableaux to the Tower collection are many portraying the old-time tortures and punishments, after you have viewed these you will no doubt thank your lucky stars that you did not live in the "goode olde days," our present modern tortures such as Income Tax, Tea Tax and other Taxations are certainly more preferable.

—

1.—A tableau of Charles Peace on one of his burglary adventures. Born 1832 at Darnley, started his notorious career at Manchester as a Portico robber. In 1876 shot P.C. Cook, who attempted to capture him when burgling at Whalley Range. He disappeared for years and was in fact living in Evelina Road, Peckham, as Mr. Thompson, a gentleman of independent means, at night carrying out numerous burglaries. He was eventually arrested on Blackheath, although it was not then known who he was. Hanged at Leeds for the murder of Dyson in February 1879.

2.—Tableau of King Edward VII., Queen Victoria and Lord Balfour in the gardens at Windsor.

3.—Our Amy (Mrs. Mollison) being congratulated by John Citizen (the Daily Express cartoonist "Strube," Little Man), on her record flight.

4.—Archbishop of Canterbury, Lloyd George and Ramsay MacDonald.

5.—Robbie Burns and Souter Johnny in a tavern scene.

6.—Our late Sailor King (George V.).

7.—The late Edgar Wallace, the crime Novel specialist.

8.—Ghandi.

8a.—Adolphe Hitler.

9.—The late King (George V.) and Queen Mary in their Jubilee regalia.

10.—Tableau of the Sleeping Beauty.

11.—Edward the Black Prince, son of Edward III. of England, the victor of Crecy and Poietiers, died June 8th, 1376.

15

206

12.—Richard I. (Coeur de Lion) taken prisoner by the Duke of Austria, kept in captivity in the Tyrol, discovered by the minstrel Blondel (as shown in the tableau), ransomed for £100,000.

13.—"The Maid," Jeanne d'Arc, commanded an army of Charles VII of France. Captured and burnt at the stake by the English at Rouen, May 30th, 1431.

14.—Tableau depicting the execution of Mary Queen of Scots at Fotheringay Castle, February 8th, 1587.

15.—Sir Francis Drake, Pirate and Buccaneer, Lt. of the Fleet when the Spanish Armada was defeated.

16.—Christopher Columbus.

17.—The knighting of Sir Walter Raleigh by Queen Elizabeth.

Collection of amusing and novelty Automatic Machines

ONE LONG LAUGH—THE CRAZY MIRRORS

CHAMBER OF HORRORS

1. The Gibbet.

The scene before us is at Gibbet Hall, Hindhead, Surrey, where the murderers of a sailor expiated their crime. The sailor was tramping from Portsmouth, upon him was a purse of gold, his leave pay, when he encountered three villains who attacked him, cut his throat and stripped the body. The corpse was discovered by a labourer who remembered seeing the sailor, and the three men who had endeavoured to sell the victim's clothes. They were arrested, tried at Kingston, and condemned to death.

2.—The Drunkard's Cloak.

The victim as shewn in this scene, was led through the town to the view of all beholders and as an example to all other drunkards. It should be noted that what is peculiar to this particular torture is that the prisoner is unable to feed himself, and the only food he or she obtained is that which was actually given by another person.

3.—Scold's Bridle, also known as Gossip's Bridle and Brank.

Used for women only, the shrew or chiding and scolding woman. The one shown depicts a woman who has slandered her neighbours and friends.

4.—The Pillory and Stocks.

This scene is opposite an old country Inn, where the unlucky ones are pelted with rotten eggs, this was a common sight in almost every town and village.

The Pillory is where the condemned malefactors for in-

16

numerable minor offences were fastened, in full view of the public as shewn in the tableau.

5.—The Rack.

In the scene before us GUY FAWKES is being racked—He plotted to blow up James I. and his Parliament on the 5th November, 1650. Caught redhanded he was asked what was the purpose of so many barrels of gunpowder, he replied, "To blow the Scotsmen back to Scotland." He stubbornly refused to divulge the names of his accomplices, was tortured on the rack and eventually confessed.

6.—Branding.

The tableau before us shows James Naylor, a Quaker, who claimed to be the Messiah. The punishment inflicted being that of "Branding"—being guilty of horrid blasphemy and that he was a grand impostor, his tongue should be bored through with a red-hot iron, and that he should be stigmatised on the forehead with a letter "B." Branding was totally abolished in England in 1879.

7.—Pressing to Death (Peine forte de dure).

This barbarous torture originated in England about 1406. The last reported case, from Ireland, was in 1740. It was instituted to make a prisoner plead guilty, in which case all his property went to the Crown. The scene depicts Thomas Spiggott, a highwayman, who suffered this torture in January 1721, beneath the Old Bailey. The third figure is an official waiting for the moment when the prisoner may decide to plead.

8.—The Boots.

Another old-time torture, the prisoner having one of his feet in a large Iron Boot filled with cold water, whilst the other in another Iron Boot in which molted metal was poured.

From the expression on the prisoner's face it can be taken that it was hardly a "party game."

9.—Group of Notorious Characters.

Tableau of Rouse on the Scaffold, also present the Chaplain, Warder and Executioner.

10.—William Fish (Blackburn murderer).
11.—David Davies (Dartmoor Shepherd).
12.—Dougal (Moat Farm murderer).
13.—Miss Le Neve
14.—George Smith (Brides in the Bath murderer).
15.—John Schnieder (Bakehouse murderer).
16.—Mrs. Thompson.
17.—John Jackson (Strangeways Prison murderer).
18.—Mrs. Berry (Oldham murderess).
19.—Dr. Crippen.

Ballroom

The Tower Ballroom is known the world over, and for close on 40 years has held the title of "Premier in the North," we feel confident that after this season it will win the name of "Premier of the Country." Now for the reason of this statement—During the winter the Ballroom closed for the work of taking up the old floor and laying a new one. A new stage was built, the spacious promenade round the dancing floor was re-laid, new lighting, new furnishings and a super dance band engaged for the season. From the entrance right up to the balcony and the entire ballroom re-decorated in a most elaborate design, the general comments and press reports can be summed up in one word, wonderful, so that we do not think that our earlier remark was too complimentary.

The spacious floor which can dance 2000 is the delight of the experienced dancer who can stride out to their heart's content, also to the beginners who do not feel that they are in anyone's way while they are learning.

During the season dancing takes place every night, in the autumn and winter public dancing is every Wednesday and Saturday, special and extra nights are advertised through the press.

The ballroom is available for Private or Semi-Private Dances and is, of course, ideal for Staff or Club Dances.

Dancing every night in the Tower Ballroom to the
Ten Temponics—The super dance band.

21

209

Museum.

Tableaux of interesting and historical events.

ENTRANCE—

1.—African Spears.
2.—Two Indian Battle Axes.
3.—Japanese Water Colour.
4.—Collection of Persian, Indian and Malay Swords and
Daggers.
5.—Military Single Sticks and Masks.
6.—Indian Musical Instrument.
7.—Collection of Engravings of Old Japan.

1.—On the left as we enter we have a tableau depicting
early Canada. Indians, Trapper and Soldier. All costumes are genuine of the period.
2.—Sir Wm. Wallace (Hero of Scotland).
3.—Two models of Cargo Steamers.
4.—French Armour time of Battle of Waterloo.
5.—Florentiene Italian Engraved Armour.
6.—Collection of Springfield Rifles and three-cornered
Bayonets (American Civil War period).
7.—Two French Bayonets (Franco-Prussian War).
8.—Mammoth Jaw Bone.
9.—Turtle Shells.
10.—General Lord Baden Powell. Chief of the Boy Scout
movement which he founded 1908   Born 1859.   Distinguished himself in the South African War by holding
Mafeking for 7 months against the Boers.

18

210

11.—''Lord Nelson,'' dated 1770, presented to Montsioa, father of Wessels, the Kaffir Chief—buried for 20 years —unearthed and used all through the Siege of Mafeking (Africa).

12.—Charles Gordon, C.B., Major General Royal Engineers. Killed at Khartoum, 26th January 1885.

13.—Field Marshal Earl Kitchener. Born 1850. Saw considerable service in the South African War. On the outbreak of the Great War in 1914 was appointed Secretary of State for War—organised an army (known by his name). He was drowned in 1916 on the ''Hampshire,'' of the Orkney Islands whilst proceeding to Russia.

14.—Japanese Wood Carved Masks.

15.—Japanese Buddhas.

16.—Japanese Dragon, placed outside their houses to ward away evil.

17.—Japanese Priest's Shell Horn.

18.—Japanese Guitar.

19.—As we go over the bridge we have a tableau on the left of Japanese Warriors in full Fighting Armour, this was worn up to 60 years ago.

20.—Original Wall section of Japanese House, showing wood framework before covering with paper.

21.—Japanese Silk, Hand Painted Kakémono (or Wall Picture).

22.—Japanese carved Screen, silk panel.

23.—Japanese Clogs.

24.—Old Japanese Bronzes.

25.—Japanese Drum.

26.—Japanese Guitar.

27.—Japanese Wood Pillow.

28.—Two Japanese Carved Coffee Tables.

29.—Japanese Lacquered Trays.

30.—Pair of Japanese Cast Bronze Vases.

31.—Japanese Lacquered Wood Saddle and Metal Stirrups, Horse Trappings.

32.—Two Japanese Tapestries.

33.—Two Carved Screens.

34.—Japanese Fencing Masks and Body Armour.

35.—Japanese Lacquered Helmet.

36.—Two Oriental Buddhas (carved guilt wood).

37.—Two Bronze Deer (Japanese handicraft).

38.—Carved Wood Spill Vase.

39.—Japanese Blow Pipes and Darts.

40.—Japanese Carved Metal Lacquered Screen.

41.—Two 3 pronged Spears (Chinese Boxer Rebellion).

42.—Japanese Naturalist Specimens.

43.—Collection of Indian Beadwork.

44.—Specimen of Japanese Colour Painting from Wooden Blocks by Hand.

45.—Illustrations of Japanese Handicraft and Customs.

46.—Collection of Japanese Silks.

CENTRAL TABLEAUX

1.—Field Marshal Earl Roberts, V.C., known by all as "Bobs." Born 1832, died 1914. Buried in St. Paul's Cathedral. Won V.C. at Delhi. This tableau depicts him at the Fort of Adi Musjid in Khaibar Pass.

2.—Duke of Wellington. Born 1769. Known as the Iron Duke," was one of England's greatest Generals. He overthrew the power of Napoleon Bonaparte at the Battle of Waterloo. Died 1852.

3.—Napoleon Bonaparte. Born 1769. From being born in poor circumstances he became the Emperor of France. His ambition to conquer the world led to his downfall when he was defeated at Waterloo in 1815. Died in 1821 in exile at St. Helena.

4.—Tableau depicting Clive of India at the Battle of Plassey

Catering

⁜

One of the most important sides of any Amusement Centre is the catering department; hungry people cannot enjoy themselves. Here in the Tower Grounds there are no less than six Cafe Restaurants, three being licensed.

We will first describe our newest innovation, the Roof Garden Cafe, situated at the top of the Tower Building. This has only been opened this season and is one of the most modern of its kind and commands one of the finest views in the country. Below, one of the great commercial highways of the Nation, the majestic River Mersey, vessels of all description from sailing boats, coasters, to the graceful and luxurious liners departing and returning from all parts of the world.

One can follow with the naked eye these boats many miles out to sea, a wonderful panorama, to the right the Lancashire Coast can be traced northward till it is lost in the distance which hides Southport, to the left the Cheshire Coast and out to the distant Welsh Mountains, and if the atmosphere be clear the Little and Great Ormes' heads can be seen in the dim distance marking the extremities of the Bay of Llandudno.

You must hear the brilliant show dance band playing every night in the Tower Ballroom.

23

213

The Sunsets viewed from New Brighton are gorgeous, and have been famous from the days of that great artist J. M. W. Turner. No other seaside resort can compete with New Brighton in the above respects.

Delightful afternoon teas and light refreshments are served, and the Lift to the Cafe is Free.

Rock Point Cafe (licensed), is picturesquely situated in the Grounds overlooking the promenade. It has been completely renovated and decorated throughout, and new steps have been built leading right up from the promenade to the entrance. Luncheons, Teas, etc., are obtainable here, and there are private rooms for Parties. Arrangements must be made beforehand with regard to the latter.

Japanese Cafe (licensed), is to be found at the lakeside, this has also been re-decorated. Luncheons and Teas, etc., may be obtained here.

At the Algerian Cafe (licensed), and the Woodlands, seating accommodation can be found for 2000 at one sitting. Parties are a speciality, and there is free parking for Patrons (Car and Motor Coaches).

For full particulars regarding Menus, etc., apply to the

NEW BRIGHTON AMUSEMENTS LTD.,

(Catering Dept.),

THE TOWER, NEW BRIGHTON,

Telephone Wallasey 276.

24

214

Of Interest

The present Roof Garden was known originally as Elevator Hall. It was all built in, a Miniature Village with Shops and Stalls all round. Up here also was the Monkey House and Aviary. From this level the lifts used to start their ascent to the top of the Tower . . . All this had to be demolished before the Roof Garden could be started, this meant a new roof for the building.

It had to be remembered that an even surface was required for use as a Promenade and waterproofed in the most efficient manner possible. Many forms of waterproofing were considered and it was decided to use Patent Vulcanite Roofing.

The work was carried out by . . .

Messrs. VULCANITE LTD.,

of TRIDENT WORKS, WIGAN,

who are the Original Patentees of Vulcanite Flat Roofing, and who have been carrying out this class of work for almost half-a-century.

Patent Vulcanite Roofing was adopted, because in addition to being perfectly watertight, it is practically imperishable and will last indefinitely without deterioration. It has many advantages over other types of flat roofing, for it is not effected by expansion and contraction, nor will any settlement of the building cause it to crack.

The Tower is another of the many important buildings throughout the British Isles which have been successfully waterproofed with the Patent Vulcanite Roofing.

The New Rock Point Cafe has also been covered with Patent Vulcanite Roofing which has been finished in a pleasing shade of red.

25

Public Enemy No. 1, Al Capone, made his fortune through the laws of Prohibition that remained in place from 1920 to 1933. Al's 1928 Cadillac Model 341 own Sedan was at the forefront of America luxury.

It also was at the forefront of armoured car history, being one of the first built. Said to weigh 3,000 pounds with bulletproof windows, it had other special features such as specially designed windows for exchanging fire with pursuers and radio to help his henchmen evade the law.

The U.S. Treasury Department impounded and kept Capone's Caddy after he was arrested in 1931 on tax evasion.

In 1933, the real 1928 Capone Cadillac was sold and shipped to England and didn't return until 1958. It went to the new owner who ran an amusement park overseas. After U.S pressure to stop glorifying gangsters, the owner soon tired of he car and sold the Cadillac to dance hall owner Tony Stuart.

Al Capone's Car Sold At Auction

MANCHESTER, England (P) — Anyone want to buy Al Capone's car

Tony Stuart, a British dance hall proprietor bought it at an auction today for $510.

The car is a 1928 Cadillac with bullet-proof windows, an armor-plated body and a black window turret through which a machine gun can be fired.

Stuart bought it from the Belle Vue Zoological Gardens. The car was brought here just before the war for an exhibition.

"I bought it as a museum piece," Stuart said. "I am not going to keep it. but intend to advertise it in an American newspaper. I hope some American will buy it."

Al Capone's Car To Go in Sideshow

Chicago, May 9 (P)—An armored brougham Al Capone reputedly used is destined to go back into service —in England, in a sideshow, detectives learned today.

A Sensational Attraction!

Al (Scarface) Capone's
20,000 Dollar Bullet
Proof Gangster Car ..

Exhibiting at the Tower Amusement Park,
New Brighton.
Presented under the exclusive direction of J. J. Caddick

Ken Hoods Wall of Death New Brighton with Len Cotton in white 1937

 Postcards from the period are still sought after by collectors. Originally they would form part of the Wall riders publicity material, sometimes the cards are signed. Such was the popularity of the Wall of Death it would be impossible to list all the riders at any given time. They became celebrities, including Ken Hood, Jack Cody and the Perry husband and wife act. Some of the riders operated their own travelling Walls.
New Brighton Tower featured a Wall of Death almost continuously up until 1965. Women riders rapidly became a feature of the show, Kitty O'Neil being one of the first at New Brighton in 1930. With more and more daring stunts being devised it was a competitive business with each show trying to out do the other, along with showmanship to pull the public in.

These low quality photographs have been taken from a home movie produced in 1938 entitled "Concert Party", and is available to watch on YouTube: https://www.youtube.com/watch?v=3cLRyavFTkI
Some of the attractions featured in the move include the Skid Ride, Over the Top, Motor Speedway, Caterpillar Ride, A high Dive Stunt, and not forgetting Mysteria the X-ray Girl.
The Caterpillar is a circular ride with a continuous string of cars completely covering an undulating track. Once up to maximum speed, a canopy would cover the cars, giving the ride the appearance of a caterpillar. As this part of the ride would be in darkness, Caterpillars were particularly popular with young couples.
The New Brighton caterpillar was built in 1929 by Henry Iles he had purchased the European rights to patents taken out in the U.S.A. Several rides had been constructed and one was moved to the Tower grounds by the Green Brothers in1935, having been located in Great Yarmouth. It went on to have different owners including C.J Hill in 1939. There is conflicting information on the history of the Caterpillar ride. It is now in the ownership of Henry Chipperfield and David Littleboy, and is being restored.
Once a very popular ride found at many amusement parks, there are only a few left operating around the world.

Mysteria the X Ray Girl was a gipsy woman who claims to possess a special vision that allows her to look inside human beings and tell the future. It was titled "A trip to the unknown in full view of the audience".

TONIGHT : THE TOWER
NEW BRIGHTON. 1939
(Jan. 18th) AT 7.30 (Jan. 18th)
FIRST TIME IN ENGLAND!
WORLD'S COLOURED CHAMPIONSHIP.
10 Rounds, 2/3 Falls, K.O. or Points.
ROBERT ADAMS
17st. HOLDER. Coloured Champion of
South America. v.
PHILIP SIKI
17st. CHALLENGER. Coloured Champion
of the West Indies.
Referee: TAFFY JONES, Liverpool.
A GRAND AMERICAN TOURNAMENT FOR
"THE MERSEY STAKES"
Open to Heavy-weights between 15½ stones
and 20 stones
Entries Received:
RAY ST. BERNARD
20 stones (England)
BULLDOG BILL GARNON.
17 stones Champion of Wales.
BENITO BORATTI
16 stones (Italy)
DONALD DUBARRY
15st. 8lbs. (South Africa).
1/-, 2/6, 3/6 (Ringside).
Phone: WALLASEY 276.

WRESTLING
THE TOWER
NEW BRIGHTON 22/11/39
TOMORROW (Wednesday),
7.30 p.m.
SPECIAL ATTRACTION
FOR THE FIRST TIME IN NEW BRIGHTON
TEAM WRESTLING
GENTLEMEN: Whipper Billy
Watson (Capt.), Vic Hesselle,
Bob McNab, Joe Reid
RIOT SQUAD: Jumping Joe
Devalto (Capt.), Jack Hunter,
Wild Tarzan, Joss Simms
THIS IS THE LATEST AND MOST
THRILLING FORM OF WRESTLING.
Book Early to avoid disappointment (Wall. 276)
Popular Prices: 1/- 2/- 3/- 4/-

Karl Pojello (left) and The Ghoul, wrestling rivals tonight.

TONIGHT : THE TO
1939 NEW BRIGHTON.
(Feb. 5th) AT 7.30
THE ANGEL
21 stones. 5ft. 9ins. (Ural Mountains)
v.
THE GHOUL
25 stones. 7ft. 3ins. Canadian
Lumberjack.
THE PERSONAL APPEARANCE of
ENGLAND'S KNOCK-OUT KING
NORMAN THE BUTCHER
6ft., 15 stones, v.
PHILIP SIKI
6ft. 2ins. 16st. (Trinidad)
Coloured Champion of West Indies.
JOHN NELSON
(Manchester) 146lbs., v.
TOMMY THE DEMON
(Liverpool) 146lbs.
BOSUN "EGG" WATERS
(Portsmouth) 14½st. Navy Champion
MARTIN CONROY
14½ stones.
1/-, 2/6, 3/6 (Ringside)
Phone: WALLASEY 276.

The Ghoul was said to be a Canadian Lumberjack, at seven feet tall the match was billed for a £100 side stake and Pojello (The Angel) was to concede 10 stones in weight and was five feet nine inches tall.
Seldom did Pojello get beaten on British soil.
He was here to teach and exhibit his polished skills and showmanship.
And it was strange rules in 1939 that even though Pojello got an equalizing submission with a Japanese double leg-lock, the victor was judged to be the Ghoul on points.   *Ref: wrestlingheritage.co.uk*

As far as the war went, it looks to have had little effect on New Brighton Wrestling in the years 1941-1943. But long before the war ended wrestling was doing great guns by 1944 it was one of the most popular sports at the Tower. Many Lancashire venues, kept going throughout. Belle Vue was showing wrestling twice a week all through the war, supported by Blackpool and Morecambe.

THE TOWER, New Brighton
WEDNESDAY NEXT 15/3/39
(March 15th)   AT 7.30   (March 16th)
GOLIATH
25 stones, 7ft. 1in., (Ireland). v.
THE GHOUL
25 stones, 7ft. 2ins. (Canada).
MARIO   BILL
MAGISTI   v.   BRENNAN
(Italy).   (America).
European Heavyweight Championship.
KARL REGINSKY
Holder (Germany) 15 stones. v.
JOE DEVALTO
Challenger (Italy) 15 stones.
THE AMAZING   BASHER
AMERSHAM v. CUNNINGHAM
(America).   (South Africa).
PAUL LORTIE
Famous Star known to all Liverpool fans.
Remember his great battles? v.
MIKE DeMETRE
A Great Wrestler.
1/-, 2/6, 3/6, 5/- (Ringside).
'Phone, WALLASEY 278.

TOWER THEATRE—— WRESTLING
21/11/45
TOMORROW (WEDNESDAY) at 7.15 p.m
GRAND TEAM MATCH—
A Challenge from the Unknown Star
JACK & BULLY PYE
v.
UNKNOWN STAR & FARMER MIKE JONES
All four in the ring together The first
contest including two Pyes and two
Americans. A real thriller.
BILL OGDEN v. TOMMY FOX
JOHNNY CLARKE v. TONY RUSSELL
JACK BEAUMONT v. LEW ROSEBY

EUROPEAN CHAMPIONSHIP
KARL POJELLO
and ARMSTRONG
THE LATEST & GREATEST SENSATION
THE AMBLING APE-MAN!!
ANGEL
BULLDOG CLAYTON
CM CASHFORD v BABE SPARKES
1 26 36 5/

THE TOWER, New Brighton.
TWENTIETH CENTURY CATCH-AS-CATCH-CAN WRESTLING
Note the Date ! Wednesday, November 2nd at 7-30
COLOSSAL ATTRACTION
HORROR NIGHT !
The most amazing and astounding night of thrills and sensations ! The
most original breathtaking roof-raising Programme, and the most daring
ever presented to the British public. The whole strictly copyright to the
Twentieth Century Wrestling Association.
KARLOFF
MANOOGNAN
16st. 6lbs. The Ugliest man in the World. Armenian Champion. Conqueror
of Steve Casey. Claims to be World Champion. V. BULLDOG
GARNON
16st. 6lbs. World's Toughest Welshman. Loathes and detests Manoognan
like H——. This match is a "Wow."
The GHOUL
25 stones, 7ft. 3ins. The most sinister figure in Wrestling, and only man
to conquer Karl Reginsky (outside Sherry). V.
Rex GABLE
16 stones, 6ft. 4ins. The finest figure of a man the World has seen in ten
years. An Australian Adonis.
The ANGEL
20 stones. A Throwback, half-man and half-ape. Barred at Belle Vue. No
words can describe this ghastly creature whose head is as big as a horse's. V.
Ray BERNARD
20 stones. Jewish Star. The roughest Jewish Heavy-weight ever born.
Boy, oh boy ! can this Colossus rough 'em up ? What a man too !
KARL
REGINSKY
15 stones. Toughest man in the World. Years of special training have
rendered him impervious to pain...Even Sherry failed to hurt him in
Thirteen furious rounds. V.
Vick HESSLE
14st. The Gem. This marvellous Heavy-weight is quite the finest, most
spectacular young boy we have ever matched. Watch him move Reginsky !
POPULAR PRICES : 1/- 2/6 3/6 5/-
BOOK AT THE TOWER.   PHONE WALLASEY

221

The emergence of wrestling in the Tower dates back to 1903 as a spectator sport it demanded many participants. With a ready supply of veterans from a previous age, and some really exciting amateurs and a sprinting of overseas participants the scene was set for some real entertainment though the 1930's and during the gloomy war years. Promoters were in the most part local businessmen, all a bit chaotic, with some boxing promoters adding wrestling to their bill. It was not until 1936 with the formation of the British Wrestling Board of Control with a promise not to fix the contests that some order was established. Promoters advertising all-in wrestling with nothing barred would be liable to prosecution. But it didn't stop the Tower advertising a "Horror Night" in 1939.

With strict Sunday Observance laws in place one promoter was fined for promoting wrestling shows on a Sunday.

With the war fast approaching and the gloom and doom of the time what could provide a greater escape from reality than a night at the wrestling. With such stars as Black Butcher Johnson, The Bone Crusher, The Strangler and not to forget the most Terrible Turk in the world Douglas the Turk. Masked men were increasingly popular with stars such as the Red Devil, Brown Masked Marvel and the Green Asp. All the spectators hoping that the unmasking would happen in the unlikely event of their defeat. One of the most popular wrestlers on the Tower being The Ghoul billed as "A monstrous mammoth, nameless and homeless. Without a soul or nationality" the promoter could guarantee a full house. Using a vast arsenal of skills he very rarely lost every part of his opponents body was a target for submission, These men were pro wrestling before the time when matches were fixed - when the blood, sweat and tears were for real. Even when the matches were fixed they still required great wrestling skill since the fans were meant to believe what they were seeing.

(Dirty?) Jack Pye - The Doncaster Panther
One of Jacks' favourite tricks was to grab a metal bucket from the seconds
in one of the corners. He would then jam it over his opponent's head and
bash it until it was so bent and buckled that his rival couldn't remove it.
This would of course have the crowd
venting their indignation at Jack with
a crescendo of catcalls and jeers. With
almost near Riots going on after they
would bait the crowd over and over.

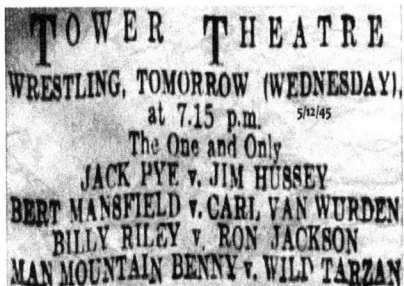

TOWER THEATRE
WRESTLING, TOMORROW (WEDNESDAY),
at 7.15 p.m. 5/12/45
The One and Only
JACK PYE v. JIM HUSSEY
BERT MANSFIELD v. CARL VAN WURDEN
BILLY RILEY v. RON JACKSON
MAN MOUNTAIN BENNY v. WILD TARZAN

Ray St Bernard war a muscular giant amongst heavyweights the 23 stone
wrestled some of the greats such as The Angel, Strangler Lewis and Jack
Sherry. The sight of this massive man was
enough to strike fear into lesser opponents.
A frequent bill topper at the Tower, Ray St
Bernard's finest moment probably came
when he was just twenty-five years old
when he tackled former World Heavyweight
Champion, Dick Shikat, in 1939 at the Tower
Ballroom, New Brighton. The contest was
a titanic struggle between two of the pre
war greats, and it lasted over fifty minutes
before Shikat gained the upper hand and
took the bout.

William "Billy" John Potts, was a Canadian
professional wrestler best known by his ring
name "Whipper" Billy Watson, and was a two-
time world heavyweight wrestling champion.
He was sidelined for six months with a fractured
shoulder and numerous broken ribs. It was on
this tour that William Potts became Billy Watson.
Watson would deliver a high back body drop, a
manoeuvre that became his signature move. In
over 40 years he stayed at the top of his sport.

223

WHITSUNTIDE ATTRACTIONS - A walk around the grounds - 1939
The New Brighton Tower fairground scheme is estimated to cost £27,000,
with delays due to the shortage of steel. The new attractions include
bang-a-deer guns, automatic rifles, scales, and games.
A new sensational ride is on its way from the manufacturers, Messrs.
Orton, Sons and Spooner of Burton-on-Trent. It is on the gravity principle,
and has two-seater cars. This ride resembles the figure of eight, with
thrilling dips but with no friction boards.
Miss Marsden of the Quarry Gardens Cafe mentioned that a lot of animals
had been arriving for the new Pets' Corner. But suggested Mr George
Lauri at the Rock Point Cafe may be able to furnish more details. He
confirmed the completion of his plans for a show appealing especially to
children. All the exhibits are small and amusing. There are baby monkeys,
and many young animals.
 Mr Richard Hall manager of the Tower Waxworks with Mrs Kelly his
assistant, had been doing good business with the crowds wanting to see
the exhibits. A Mr Myer was in charge at the "Doughty Darts"
With the Crooked House. Topsy-turvy corridors, distorting mirrors a
popular attraction with the inquisitive visitors.
The Kamlya Ghost train operated by Mr Thomas Clark had many new and
ingenious additions to help scare the occupants, with the exterior having
a new lick of paint.
The Wall of Death was run by Mr Johny Campell, and his beautiful wife
Zoe, formerly a Russian college student. It was at this time that the wall
had been modified to accommodate a car as well as motor cycles, with
new stunts being devised to entertain the crowds of holiday makers.
A new addition to the district was introduced by Mr Jesse Parkinson of
the Lilliputian Marionette show . The "little people" laugh and dance there
way into the hearts of the audience. With the Playboys and Archie Craig
billed on the Tower Ballroom.
Included in the list of attractions is the large automatic arcade, the
coaster ride, the speedway with attendants in smart new white uniforms.
Maxwells boats with festoons of fairy lights, the Japanese Cafe; the
Octopus: the jockey scales; Madame Smith, palmist; Doughty's mat
slide Helter Skelter; the big wheel; the Caterpillar; and the interesting
photographic stand of Mr H Felton.
Mr Albert Codman's Punch and Judy show remains a firm favourite with
the children.
Clarissa, the hair setting lotion had a small audience of ladies watching
the demonstration.
A newcomer to the Tower grounds is a member of the Mahatma Magical
Circle, Mr Christopher Armfield, who opened a stall for the sale and
demonstration of conjuring tricks.
Reference The Worlds Fair Saturday June 1939.

These photographs were taken in May 1939 when preparations for the

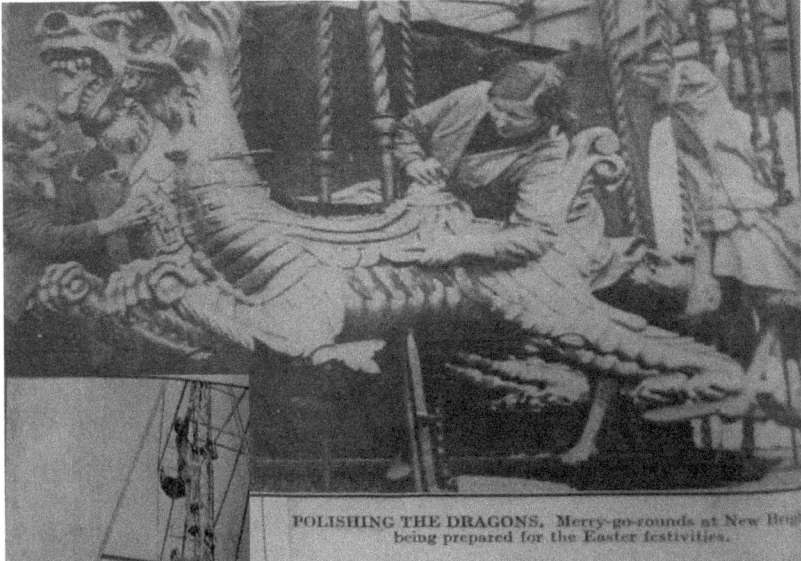

POLISHING THE DRAGONS. Merry-go-rounds at New Brighton being prepared for the Easter festivities.

Dragons being polished on the merry-go-round
The Big Wheel getting a lick of paint.

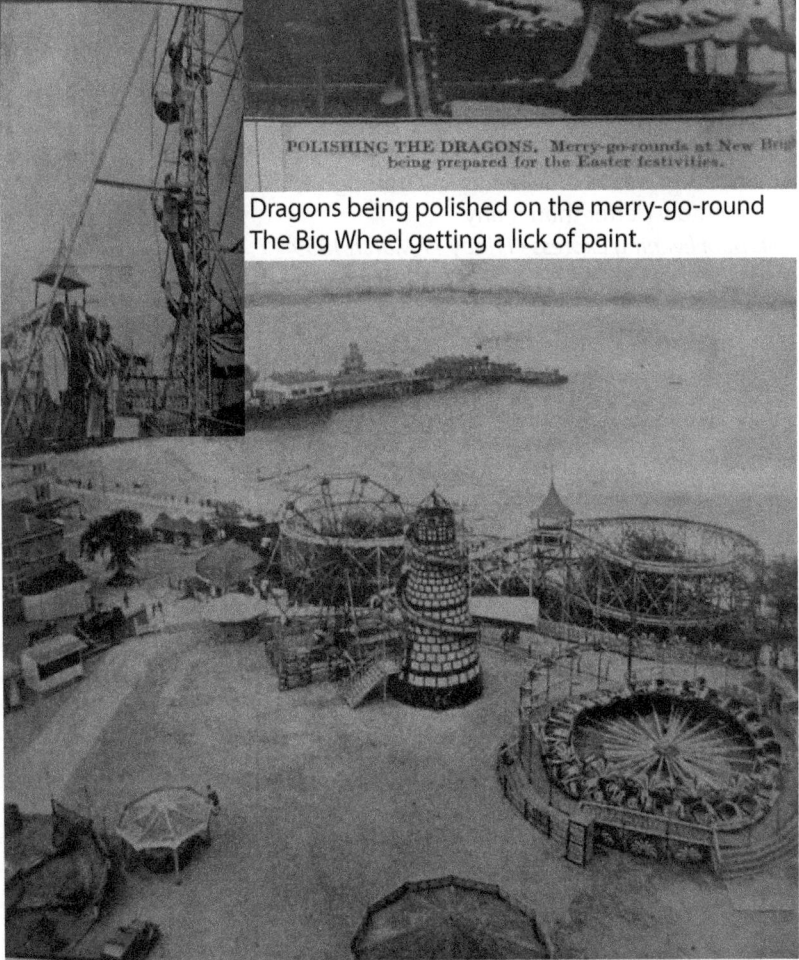

PRAISE FOR WALLASEY

A tribute to the excellent progress Wallasey had made in regard to Air-raid Precautions was paid by Wing-Commander E. J. Hodsoll, Inspector- General of the Air-Raid Precautions Department when he addressed a mass meeting of 2,000 A.R.P. volunteers at New Brighton Tower Theatre last night. The Mayor of Wallasey (Councillor Frank Pullen) presided. Wing-Commander Hodsoll stated he had seen that afternoon the preparations that Wallasey was making, and he could only describe their organisations as splendid ...There were people who said they would join A.R.P. services if the necessity arose, but such people would then be a nuisance, because they would not have been trained. In the new form of defence it was essential that each component part must be ready to take the place and duty appointed.

"We are getting ready as quickly as we can, not because we think a crisis will come, but because we are quite certain that the more ready we are, the less likely is a crisis to come," said the speaker.

The Chief Constable (Mr. J. Ormerod) said he would like to see first-aid introduced as part of the curriculum in every school.. Major Broadhurst, A.R.P. Regional Inspector, appealed for volunteers. He said the Wallasey organisation was as efficient as any borough within his knowledge, and considerably better than many.

Liverpool Evening Express - Friday 17 March 1939

Sir,

New Brighton Tower.

In connection with the use of the basement of the Tower as a public shelter, the Emergency Committee have given further consideration to the matter. The position is that the shelter has been used so much that there has been an overflow and the Managing Director of the Tower has very kindly allowed persons for whom accommodation could not be found in the public shelter itself to use the theatre for dormitory purposes. This has resulted in considerable extra cost for cleaning, lighting, etc., and, in addition, a great deal of damage has been caused to the theatre by members of the public, many of whom do not appear to have any regard for property or common decency. The Emergency Committee have, therefore, decided that, subject to your approval, a further payment not exceeding £1 per week be made for the use of accommodation allocated to public shelter purposes and, in addition, an officer from the Regional Commissioner's office has been invited to visit the Tower for the purpose of seeing whether or not the Regional Commissioner should be recommended to make new arrangements with regard to the whole of the premises.

I should be much obliged if you could kindly arrange to go into this matter further with a view to considering whether or not you can recommend an additional payment of £1 in respect of the facilities provided for the public generally.

I am, Sir,
Your obedient Servant,

NEW BRIGHTON TOWER AIR RAID SHELTER

With Extraction Fans required,electric meters and compensation for the use of the building the Tower Managment raised many objections and complaints concerning the requisition by the Government of the Tower basement for use as an air raid shelter.

All shelters were placed into groups depending on their location. In Group 1 there was the Borough's largest and believed to be the strongest, public shelter and therefore very popular - the basement of the Tower Building. As this had been originally constructed as the foundation for, and to carry the strain of the former observation tower- the belief in its strength was probably justified. But that belief meant an influx of people in excess of the number deemed suitable in the interests of comfort and hygiene.

The New Brighton basement shelter was scheduled to hold a maximum of 200 people, but the shelter was liable to serious overcrowding, and the Tower requested a ruling by the Chief Engineer concerning the question of ventilation. With the Managing Director of the New Brighton Amusements Ltd lodging a complaint with the Town Clerk that the ventilation was unsatisfactory.

Wallasey suffered severely during Christmas week 1940 with many casualties, 119 killed and 91 seriously injured. On December 20th, the first raid lasted nearly 10 hours. During these raids, the Luftwaffe came over in waves. During the month of March 1941, there were 174 people killed and 158 seriously injured in the Borough, with over 10,000 people made homeless.

From a letter dated 15th January 1942, the Shelter Supervisor reported several accidents where persons have fallen down the outside flight of steps giving access to the shelter.

A letter from The Tower dated 7th June 1941 made a complaint about people sleeping in the Theatre.

On the 15th January 1942, a letter from the Town Clerk was to remind the Tower management that a store, private room, consulting room and isolation room, was requisitioned on the 18th June 1941 for the purpose of a Medical Aid Post for use in connection with the Public Shelter. Requisitioning was confirmed on the 28th July 1941, on behalf of the Minister of Home Security (A.R.P and Public Shelter Department).

On the 15th February 1945 to the relief of the Tower Management, a letter was received concerning the de-requisition.

Ref; Letters and information held in Wirral Archives

TRICK CYCLE TRAGEDY Man Killed In "Wall Of Death*' Mishap
WOMAN AND GIRL INJURED

A startling and unusual tragedy occurred in the New Brighton Tower pleasure grounds on Saturday evening, when a spectator of the sensational Wall of Death display was killed, and a young woman trick cyclist and a girl spectator injured and taken to hospital.

An exhibition of trick motor-cycling was being given in the Wall of Death enclosure with a number of spectators standing on the surrounding platform, about 18 ft. from the ground, when the incident happened. The woman rider, Mrs. Zoe Campbell, who was performing with her husband, Mr. John Colin Campbell, had circled the cylinder several times, and her husband was about to start a pursuit race when her machine appeared suddenly to get out of control. It raced along, flew across the safety cable fixed about foot above the wall, and was hurtled over the heads of the onlookers, crashing through the wooden enclosure and plunging to the ground outside with the rider still in the saddle.

The startled spectators were scattered in all directions, the motor-cycle flying over their heads. One of them, however, who was directly in line with it was unfortunately struck by the machine and received such serious injuries that he died almost immediately.

It was ascertained from a driver's licence in his possession that he was Mr Leonard Sidney Sutton, aged 24, of Bell Road, Coventry.

He had brought a motor-coach load of men for a day's outing to New Brighton and when the tragedy occurred the passengers were assembling in the motor coach ready for departure. Another driver was obtained later and the coach taken to Coventry. Yesterday morning Mr. Sutton, senior, visited the Wallasey mortuary and identified the body of his son. The unfortunate woman driver, Mrs. Campbell, aged 21 years of age, and a 15-years-old girl, Annie Holton, who was on a visit to New Brighton from Hollinwood, and was lodging in Tollemache Street, were taken to the Victoria Central Hospital.

Mrs. Campbell had sustained a broken leg and head abrasions and was suffering from shock. Miss Holton was also detained suffering from abrasions and shock. The injured cyclist, it transpired, is a Russian. She was three years ago studying as an analytical chemist at Leningrad University, when Mr. Campbell, a Glasgow man, four years her senior, who has done trick cycling in various countries, made her acquaintance. She was an expert motor-cyclist and their friendship culminated in marriage. They have been in England eight months and have been performing at New Brighton Tower since Easter. They were staying in lodgings in Greenbank Avenue.

Interviewed yesterday, Mr. Campbell said that his wife and he had been performing together in various parts of the world and had given numerous exhibitions of the Wall of Death at New Brighton Tower. Describing the tragic occurrence, Mr. Campbell said: "My wife was circling round and round the wall and I was preparing to follow her for the pursuit race from the bottom of the wall when I heard the engine of her machine racing. I therefore kept off the wall in order to give her all the room possible. I could not see what happened, but when I looked her machine had gone over the wall and over the heads of the spectators on the platform. I cannot understand how the cycle cleared the safety cable." The facts of the tragedy have been reported to the Wallasey coroner, Mr. R. T. Highet, who has arranged to hold the inquest at 4.30 this afternoon. Mrs. Campbell has not been informed of the fatal result of the occurrence in which she was the central figure.

Jack Roche Campbell, Johnny Bates & Bill Miller, New Brighton.

Liverpool Daily Post - Monday 05 June 1939

229

EXAMINED EVERY DAY

Joseph James Caddick, amusement caterer, 5 Sandrock Road, Wallasey, said he had been proprietor of the "Wall of Death for three years and there had been no previous accident, nor had he heard of any similar accident elsewhere. Mr. and Mrs. Campbell had been riding New Brighton Tower since Easter and as far as he could judge they were both competent riders. John Colin Campbell said that the cycle ridden by his wife, which was his property, was in very good condition. He was responsible for the inspection of the "Wall of Death" structure, at the top of which was a steel cable to prevent the machine going over. He had to give a certificate of examination to Mr. Caddick each day, and he had done so on the day of the accident. He had never heard of a machine going over the top; whenever an accident occurred the rider fell down the well. Police-Sergeant Petherbridge, coroner's officer, said that examining the machine ridden by Mrs. Campbell he found a defect which was, in his opinion, the cause of the accident. The outer cable housing the throttle control cable had been secured by a clip held by a single small bolt, this bolt was loose, and had allowed the cable to fall away, with the result that when the throttle was opened by means of the twist grip handlebar control, it would not close again even though the handlebar control was turned back to the zero position.

Coroner's Comment The Coroner, Mr. R. T, Highet, told the jury that unless structure was unsafe the authorities had no right of control, but could only make suggestions. The Chief Constable, Mr. J. Ormerod, remarked that he thought it high time that some of these instruments of amusement from which persons derived their livelihood should be inspected by responsible Government department with view to protecting the public. Mr. Roberts said his clients would welcome any inspection.

Liverpool Daily Post - Wednesday 14 June 1939

Barrage balloons became a familiar sight over Merseyside, preventing bombers from attacking below 5,000 feet. However, despite the blackout being enforced, German planes were able to find Liverpool, checking their position by radio beams and the lights of neutral Dublin. A large hydrogen-filled balloon can be seen on the photographs. The RAF also started decoy oil fires in the Dee estuary and at Bidston marshes, in an attempt to draw German bombers away from their main targets.

The first German bombs landed on Merseyside on 9 August 1940 at Prenton, Birkenhead. In the following sixteen months, German bombs killed 2716 people in Liverpool, 442 people in Birkenhead, 409 people in Bootle and 332 people in Wallasey.

New Brighton Tower never got a direct hit during the War, which is amazing considering its size and location. The only incident being an unexploded bomb in the grounds.

By the middle of 1940, there were 1,400 balloons in the skies above Great Britain, by 1944 the number had risen to nearly 3,000.

Ballroom dance competitions were a regular feature at the Tower all through the forties. In competition ballroom, dancers are judged by poise, the hold, posture, musicality and expression, timing, body alignment and shape, floor craft, foot and leg action, and presentation. Judging was subjective in nature, and controversy and complaints by competitors over judging placements are not uncommon. The scorekeepers tally the total number recalls accumulated by each couple through each round until the finals, when the Skating system is used to place each couple by ordinals, typically 1–6, though the number of couples in the final may vary. Sometimes, up to 7 couples may be present on the floor during the finals.

Harry Parry played with several dance bands, including Percival Mackey's, then led his own six-piece unit. He was engaged at the St. Regis Hotel in 1940 when he was selected by the BBC to lead the band for their Radio Rhythm Club show. One of the first DJs on BBC Radio he presented Radio Rhythm Club, Housewives Choice, and was an early celebrity on Desert Island Discs and for a brief period formed the resident band on the popular BBC's Crackerjack children's programme. He toured the UK, Europe & India entertaining the troops during WW2. He then recorded over 100 titles for Parlophone Records with his sextet.

HARRY PARRY AT NEW BRIGHTON

Harry Parry and his Radio Rhythm Club sextet will visit New Brighton Tower next Wednesday.

On New Year's Eve there will be a dance, ending at one o'clock on New Year's Day, to which admission will be by ticket only. Tickets bought before New Year's Eve cost 4s. (2s. 6d. for members of the Forces), and afterwards 6s. and 3s. 6d. respectively.

KIDDIES' FUND

A dance in support of the Wallasey Kiddies' Christmas Fund was held at New Brighton Tower under the patronage of the Mayor and Mayoress (Alderman and Mrs. P. G. Davies) and was well attended. The committee intend to entertain on December 28 at least 150 children from all parts of Wallasey who suffered particularly from the blitzes.

AMATEUR DANCING CHAMPIONS AT NEW BRIGHTON

EVENING EXPRESS

Sheffield partners, Mr. Bob Stanley and Miss E. E. Peat, won the 1942 amateur dancing contest and the Tower Challenge Cup at New Brighton Tower last night for the third year in succession. Our picture shows (left to right) the Mayoress of Wallasey (Mrs. Davies), who handed over the trophies; Miss Peat, Mr. Bert Beattie (Tower Ballroom manager), Mr. Stanley and the Mayor of Wallasey (Alderman P. G. Davies).

234

the JOY OF DANCING at the Tower

DANCERS from all over the country will tell you that the magnificent TOWER Ballroom is one of the finest in the British Isles. The sprung floor can accommodate 3,500 Dancers.

Visiting Bands have included GERALDO, JOE LOSS, OSCAR RABIN, TED HEATH, HARRY DAVIDSON, THE SQUADRONNAIRES, and other well known Broadcasters. The TOWER Challenge Cup Contest, held in July, and open to amateur couples, offers a prize which is one of the most coveted trophies in Amateur Dancing Circles.

You will find that a visit to this Ballroom is one which afterwards will live in your memory.

18/12/43

The TOWER
NEW BRIGHTON

TO-NIGHT (SATURDAY)—
GRAND GALA DANCE.
7—11 p.m.   Adm. 3/-.   Forces 2/-.

MONDAY—
REQUEST NIGHT.
7—11 p.m.   Adm. 1/6.   Forces 1/-.

WEDNESDAY—
DEMONSTRATION NIGHT,
THE CHAMPIONS OF CHAMPIONS
(Ella Spowart and John Herbert).
7—11-30 p.m.   Adm. 2/-.   Forces 1/-.

FRIDAY—
GRAND XMAS EVE DANCE.
7—11-45 p.m.   Adm. 3/-.   Forces 2/-.

SATURDAY—
XMAS DAY DANCE.
7—11 p.m.   Adm. 3/6.   Forces 2/-.

PLAYING AT ALL SESSIONS—

THE TOWER RHYTHMICS under the direction of **BERT YATES**.

Have you bought your tickets yet for **NEW YEAR'S EVE DANCE?**

The Premier Event of the Year

TOWER CHALLENGE CUP FINALS
Valued 100 GUINEAS.   Open to all Amateur Dancers

WEDNESDAY, JULY 28th, 1943

TOWER BALLROOM, NEW BRIGHTON

Couples residing within 15 miles of the Tower Ballroom must enter a Preliminary Heat either Monday, July 19th, or Wednesday, July 21st. Outside couples enter finals direct.

ADJUDICATORS:

JAMES HOLLAND and ELSA WELLS   CYRIL FARMER and JOAN DAVIES

ARTHUR NORTON and PAT EATON   HAROLD TOOTILL and JOAN WALL

Chairman: J. E. EVANS, of Stockport   Contest starts at 8.30 prompt. Presentation 11 p.m.

DANCING 7 until 11.45 p.m.   Tickets 3/6 (limited); Forces 2/-

All Enquiries re Forms, etc., to BERT BEATTY (Manager)

TOWER BALLROOM DANCES
The Tower Ballroom is no longer a Summer Season Rendezvous. Not withstanding the blackout and restricted travel services, enthusiastic dancers throng the Ballroom every-time there is a dance, which is usually four nights per week. Monday is Residents Night; Wednesday, Demonstration Night; Friday Charity Night and Saturday Gala Night... Most of the big B.B.C Bands whilst on tour have played in the Ballroom and leading demonstrators throughout the country have also been featured. The holiday dances broke all records New Year's Eve drew a crowd of over 2,500, while on New Year's Night over 1,800 patrons enjoyed dancing to Felix Mendelssohn's Hawaiian Serenader's.
A New Silver Trophy has been introduced known as "The Mersey Challenge Cup." This was danced for on January 19th. Henry Jacques and Vicey Burke adjudicating, but the result will have to wait until next month. On Friday, February 4th, another big Competition Night has been arranged, this being the second Annual Dancing Tournament in aid of the "Daily Dispatch and Evening Chronicle" War Comforts Fund. There are two contests, one for Amateurs and the other for Novices.
In the amateur Section competitors are required to dance the Waltz, Foxtrot, Quickstep and Tango, while the Novices will dance the Waltz only. Solid Silver Challenge Cups are some of the prizes. James Holland and Elsa Wells will be giving one of their brilliant demonstrations on the same evening.
The photograph above shows Alan Jolliffe and Nan Roberts. Winners of the Mersey Trophy at the Tower Ballroom. Organised by the popular Manager, Bert Beattie.
The Modern Dance and the Dancer - March, 1944

HOW THEY TOOK THE NEWS
Holidaymakers at New Brighton left boarding houses to gather in front of the Pier-head for community singing. There were similar gatherings in front of the Town Hall and at Seacombe Ferry. In front of the Capitol cinema, Liscard, an effigy of the Jap Emperor was hung from a jibbet and set on fire, surrounded by hundreds of children cheering wildly.
Wallasey magistrates this morning granted permission for New Brighton Tower Ballroom and another dance hall at Moreton to remain open until I a.m. tomorrow and Friday.
Liverpool Evening Express - Wednesday 15 August 1945

TRACK PLAN REFUSED Proposals to establish a greyhound racing track on New Brighton Tower grounds were turned down by Wallasey Watch Committee last night. The chairman Councillor J. H. Wensley, said the application was refused on the grounds that the proposal was against the amenities of the district, and that it would be detrimental to young persons receiving instruction in the district.
Liverpool Evening Express - Thursday 17 May 1945

1945 - Rock Point Restaurant

VICTORY CONCERT Mayor's Tribute;
Guest of Honour at the Town Hall Lieut. Fraser. Two thousand people
filled the New Brighton Tower Theatre Saturday night for the choral
and orchestral concert given as the climax of the Wallasey Victory
celebrations, with shrieking sirens and the firing of guns. The celebrations
finished by welcoming the young V.C. of whom Wallasey is so justly
proud." The stage was occupied with the 300 members of the Wallasey
Civil Defence Choir and Orchestra, and their conductor, Mr. Stainton
B. Taylor, took his place in the centre of the stage, flag bearers filed in
from both sides and placed their flags at the back of the stage, with the

Union Jack, and the American and Soviet flags
in the centre. Another thrill came when the
Mayor (Alderman W. B. Millward) brought to
the rostrum and formally introduced Wallasey's
midget submarine V.C., Lieutenant Ian E. Fraser,
who is to be invested by the King at Buckingham
Palace, to-morrow, with the V.C., and also the
D.S.C., previously awarded to this twenty-four-
years old hero. The audience rose en masse and
cheered vociferously. Lieut. Fraser modestly
bowed his acknowledgements.

At the end of the war this exhibition appeared in the Tower grounds, with many gruesome photographs of the Concentration Camps at Buchenwald and Belsen. The New Brighton Tower Company had arranged for all the proceeds from the admittance charge of 6d to go to local charities.

The 11th Armoured Division as it drove into Germany, occupied the Bergen-Belsen concentration camp on April 15, 1945, following an agreement with the retreating Germans to surrender the camp peacefully. And then all the horrors of the Nazi persecutions came to light.

TOWER THEATRE, NEW BRIGHTON.

FREE STYLE WRESTLING.

TONIGHT (WEDNESDAY), 29/11/45

at 7.15 p.m.

BY REQUEST: Jack Pye v. Chick Knight, Wild Tarzan v. Dick Wills, Jack Stockwell v. Johnny Clarke (Doncaster), Val Cerino v. Joe Batten, Ted Beresford v. Carl Pellakinsky.

Prices, 1/6 to 6/ including tax.

LIVERPOOL YOUTH SHOT

A youth's visit to New Brighton Tower Fun Fair resulted in a shooting tragedy. The victim was Ronald Randal Hannah, aged 17, an apprentice engineer, of Grenfell Road, Liverpool.

Accompanied by two companions, Vincent Lydiate and Geoffrey Whitehouse, he visited the fun fair on Sunday night. They went to the shooting gallery, and each paid for six rounds at a shilling. They stood together while firing. Whitehouse in the centre.

Thinking he had fired his six rounds, Whitehouse swung his rifle to the left in order to examine it. Hannah was standing at the left and in the act of firing when Whitehouse's rifle went off, and the bullet passed through Hannah's head, killing him instantly.

NEW BRIGHTON TOWER
The list of applications will open and close on Thursday Nov 21, for an offer for sale by Messrs Ian Anderson & Nairn of 850,000 Ord. shares of 1s each at 2s 4d per share . The Co.mpany has acquired the freehold Tower buildings and amusement, athletic, and sport grounds on the Cheshire side of the River Mersey at New Brighton, near Liverpool .
The Scotsman - Monday 18 November 1946

RUSH FOR SHARES
Butlin Interest in Mersey Venture
So great has been the rush for New Brighton Tower 1s. shares offered at 2s 4d per share that applications amounted to the huge total of 33,777,843 shares for the 700,000 shares available, after allowing for firm applications of 150,000 writes the City Editor of a national newspaper.
This means that for approximately £100,000 in shares £3,800,000 were subscribed by investors, in other words, the offer was 47 times over-subscribed.
 It was therefore, decided to resort to balloting. Applications for up to 10,000 received 300 shares and for over 10,000, receive 400 shares.
Attractions of the offer were enhanced by the fact that Butlin's, Ltd., have taken an interest in the company. Butlin's Ltd., and Mr. W. E. Butlin have

also agreed to take 240,000 shares each at 2s. Butlin's Ltd., and Mr. W. E. Butlin have also agreed to subscribe when called upon by the company for a further 250,000 shares at 2s 4d.
Lincolnshire Standard and Boston Guardian - Saturday 30 November 1946

MR. W. E. BUTLIN, managing director of Butlin's, Ltd., pictured with Miss Gracie Fields at one of Butlin's Fairs.
   Subscription lists open and close today for the issue at par of £150,000 Five-and-a-Half per Cent. First Mortgage Debenture stock and 250,000 £1 Six per Cent. Cumulative Participating Redeemable Preference shares in the company.

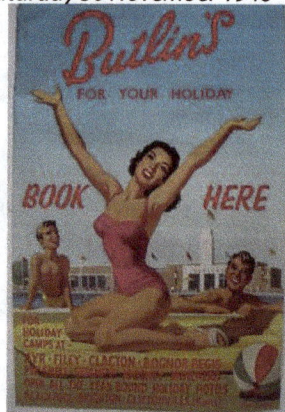

NINTH ANNUAL

Tower Challenge Cup Contest

Under the Patronage of

THE MAYOR AND MAYORESS OF WALLASEY

(Alderman J. L. Gill, J.P., and Mrs. Gill).

Rules:

Judging will be based on "All Round" efficiency in the Waltz, Foxtrot, Tango, Quickstep.

No Entrance Fee for Contests. All Competitors to pay General Admission to the Ballroom and defray own travelling expenses.

The Contest is open to all couples who are Amateurs under the Rules of the Official Board of Ballroom Dancing.

Winners to hold "Tower" Challenge Cup for twelve months.

Adjudicators.

1. Mr. WALLY FRYER, M.I.D.M.A., London.
2. Miss VIOLET BARNES, M.I.D.M.A., London.
3. Mr. PERRY LLOYD, F.exI.S.T.D. (B.B.), I.S.T.D. (B.B.), Shrewsbury.
4. Miss CONSTANCE GRANT, F.I.S.T.D., F.I.D.M.A., N.A.T.D., Sheffield.
5. Mr. ALBERT COWAN, E.S.T.D., I.S.T.D., Manchester.

Scrutineers:

Mr. TIM SHAW.   Mr. ARTHUR CARR.

Music by

BERT YATES AND HIS TOWER RHYTHMICS.

Competitors In Action   1947 Grand Finals.

TOWER ATTRACTIONS

The Saturday gala dance rounds off a successful week's dancing programme, and many holiday folk are to be seen mingling with the patrons in the ballroom as the season continues. Every facility is offered for their comfort and enjoyment in this social centre, which has no equal on the Merseyside old time dancing on Tuesday which is a weekly event and firmly fixed in the programme. The exhibition given by Wally Smith and his partner of the "Florentine Waltz" last Tuesday met with immediate success. Much enjoyment is derived during the old time dances when the patrons really do seem to extract the last ounce of pleasure out of their evening. Next week's programme in the ballroom continue with dances every night commencing with the popular night on Monday for the Moderns followed by old Time dancing on Tuesday. Wednesday is the usual Dancing time and Thursday is once again guest night. On this night patrons are invited to bring a guest to the ballroom free of charge. Many patrons have already taken advantage of this special concession. Friday resident night with its many spot prizes is now becoming a social event of the week and has its own regular following.

However, visitors are always welcome on these occasions. The next broadcasting band to visit the Tower will be Teddy Foster and his band on Wednesday July 2nd. This outstanding combination with its radio fame is a big attraction.

Tower Cup Night.

Tickets are now on sale for the social event of the year, the Tower Cup Night, which is to be held on Wednesday, July 23rd. Many requests for tickets are coming in from various parts of the country even at this early date, and local patron's will be well advised to obtain their tickets in advance.

Tower Restaurant

The latest enterprise of the New Brighton Tower Co Ltd is the new Rock Point Restaurant, facing the Tower Promenade.

It has a commanding view of the river and is beautifully furnished throughout. The Tower Restaurant will soon become a popular rendezvous and can be recommended to club secretaries who wish to organise dinner dances for their members during the winter season. It is in fact already being supplied on application to the management. In the meantime, the restaurant is open daily for morning coffee, lunches, teas and dinners under the personal supervision of first class chefs.

Amusement Park.

Continues to be open each day, including Sunday, with all the fun of the fair,and the latest rides and thrills to cater for the many visitors. to the New Brighton.

Wrestling

A heavyweight thriller tops the wrestling bill at the Tower for Wednesday, when Bert Assiratti the British and European heavyweight champion, meets the greatest rough-house exponent in the game, Man Mountain Benny. Some splendid wrestling will be seen in the following bouts, Lew Roseby versus Gene Reska, Ray Raymond versus Danny Flynn, and Joe Batten versus Bob Silcock.

Boxing

There a great demand for seats for the opening nights boxing tournament next Friday, and a full house is confidently expected.

1947 - Top: Fancy Dress Ball. Bottom: Martins Bank Staff Dance

PERSONALITY GIRL

Chosen Preston's Personality Girl for the second year in succession in the town final at Worsley's Ballroom in February, Miss Brenda Hankins was third in the 1947 North of England Personality Girl contest, held last night by the Printers' Pension Corporation in New Brighton Tower Ballroom. She is the only daughter of Mr. and Mrs. G. T. Hankins, of 32 Howick Cross-lane, Penwortham. Miss Dorothy Bellhouse the Blackpool finalist, was fourth.

Lancashire Evening Post - Saturday 07 June 1947

BOXING - NORMAN TENNANT WELL ON TOP

Norman Tennant, the Dundee fly-weight, scored a points victory over Eddie Douglas, of Liverpool, at New Brighton Tower last night.
It was Tennant's bustling tactics which carried the day, for Douglas was the better tactician, but was taken out of his stride by the Dundee lad, who swept in punches which completely baffled the Liverpool man. Tennant was always the busier workman. He swept in half a dozen blows to one of his rival's, and on that score was a clear points winner.

Dundee Courier - Saturday 12 July 1947

KANE K.O's BELGIAN

Peter Kane (Golhorne) knocked out Albert Braedt, former bantam-weight champion Belgium, in the third round of scheduled ten-rounder at New Brighton Tower last night.

Dundee Courier - Saturday 28 June 1947

246

THE FAIRY GLEN MINIATURE RAILWAYF 1947 -1965

Very little is known about the earliest pleasure railways which operated on the Tower Promenade at New Brighton, another miniature railway did operate around the boating lake for a while. Its seems that there were two different railways successively on the site in the late1930s/early 1940s. It is certain that both lines were very short. The 18' gauge story continued in about 1947/48,when Tommy Mann bought the remaining equipment from Jacywick Miniature Railway situated on the Jaywick Sands Estate about two miles from Clacton-on-Sea. The Sentinel and the three saloon coaches were now turned into a very different use, Commander Parsons at Jaywick had been both an enthusiastic and a competent engineer, but Tommy Mann was an out and out showman.

He ran the Marine Lake on the Promenade at New Brighton, and set about installing his new railway in the Tower Pleasure Gardens, in time to open for the 1948 season. With many of the other rides also owned by Tommy his empire started to take shape. The first change was in the Sentinel, Tommy wanted it to produce steam to attract the children, so had it rebuilt by a firm called Charnley Davidson, who affixed a plate. The result was a long fat chain driven 0-4 OT- unique to say the least. Yet more strange was the vertical boiler in the dummy coal bunker, the wide hollow boiler and the oil tank inside what should have been the smoke box. Power itself was from the same Stanley steam car engine, slung between the frames. After the Fairy Glen Miniature Railway opened, the Sentinel, which was later named Tim Bobbin was its sole motive power for 3 seasons. The railway itself was also distinctive, having a total run of no

247

more than 200 yards.

This was not out of choice, but enforced by the narrow confines of the site. After travelling straight, adjacent to the Promenade, the main feature of the railway was a severely curved return loop cut deep into an old quarry the fairy Glen. The first section was covered over to make a tunnel and to add to the interest an illuminated model fair performed on a ledge inside, where the train paused during each journey. Although the Sentinel did good service, Tommy decided to obtain another locomotive, and late in 1950 he contacted the firm of David Curwen Ltd.

However the 18'gauge locomotive was a lot bigger than any of their previous 10 1/4' gauge designs, it had also to cope with the extremely tight curves, as sharp as 40 feet radius. The result a 3 ½ tons, 19 feet long with a boiler height of 5ft 3in locomotive, delivered on the 3rd May 1951, with a new station being built further back towards the "figure 8", with new flower beds and a signal box it was all ready for the season.

This was to be the peak of the railways success with two trains, being able to operate in peak periods. During its 17 years life it gave enjoyment to many thousands of children along with their parents. The railway closed in the 1965 season.

Ref: Uncle Tommy's Kiddies Railway - Simon Townsend

Above: *Tommy Mann's Railway pictured at* **New Brighton.** *Opened in 1948, this 18in. gauge miniature railway operated here until 1965*[UKTR]

LEGEND :-
A, TUNNEL. C, RAILS LEFT FROM ATTEMPTED
B, MODEL FAIR   RUN LENGTHENING SCHEME.
EXHIBIT. D, SIGNAL BOX.
E, TEA GARDEN. F, OLD TERMINUS.
G, NEW COVERED TERMINUS.

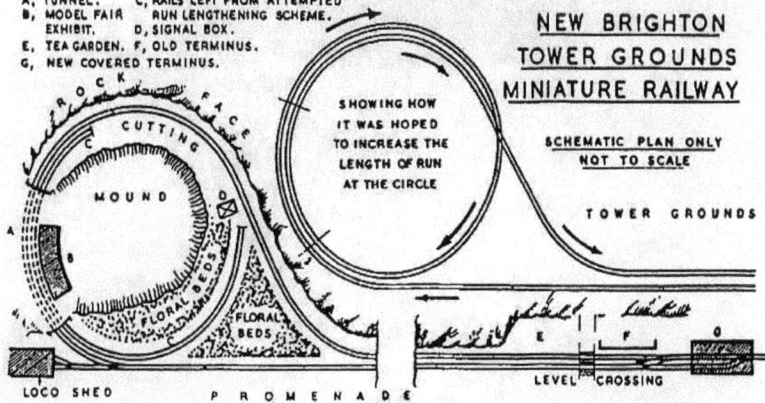

NEW BRIGHTON
TOWER GROUNDS
MINIATURE RAILWAY

SHOWING HOW
IT WAS HOPED
TO INCREASE THE
LENGTH OF RUN
AT THE CIRCLE

SCHEMATIC PLAN ONLY
NOT TO SCALE

TOWER GROUNDS

Tommy Mann was a successful businessman associated with many ventures in New Brighton all through the 40s and 50s. He had the miniature railway and the children's amusement park situated in the Tower Grounds. He sold his business to his brother Charlie in 1952 then took over the Marine Lake and also had an interest in the Fort Perch Rock which he and his partner purchased at Auction from the Crown cira. 1956. In 1960 the family moved to Southport and took over the Marine Lake.

In the 1950s Tommy was a member of the Wallasey Council. He did however hold the office of chairman of the Council in Shaw were he once lived. Tommy passed away in Southport in 1971.

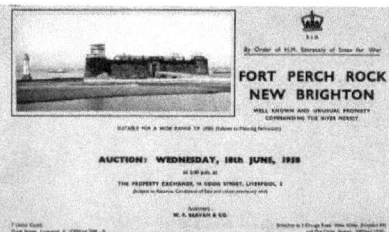

FORT PERCH ROCK
NEW BRIGHTON

AUCTION: WEDNESDAY, 18th JUNE, 1958

Councillor Tommy Mann's civic reception

The Mayor and Mayoress of Wallasey (Alderman J. L. Gill and Mrs. Gill) at the civic reception at Shaw given by Councillor Tommy Mann, chairman of the Crompton Urban District Council and owner of the Kiddies' Playground Miniature Railway at the Tower. Mr. J. W. Evans, manager of New Brighton Tower, is on the extreme left.   Photo: Elsam, Mann & Cooper Ltd., L'pool.

Let me take you on a journey back in time. Standing in front of the Wall of Death. Ahead is the Caterpillar, owner Ernie Brennan. Behind it to the left the Dive Bomber. To the right the Dodgem Cars, owner Freddy Heywood. Looking left a small stall can't remember its function then we have Ken in the Waxworks.

Higher up Cyril Man with the first pub to sell Tetley ale. Looking right name forgotten big sloping ride with circular cars and very loud music, owner Ernie Brennan. Next to it the Helter-skelter, run by Peter who also worked on the river Gig Boats.

Then the steps to the ground level, the other side of the steps was The Big Wheel. Then the Kentucky Derby. Owner Cyril Fletcher who also had a very popular Radio Show. Next to it a stall I think a mystic, next Freddy Heywood with small stall showing the Worlds Biggest Rat. Then Freddy again with the Ghost Train, alongside was Johnny Parker believed to be the first to sell potato crisps. Then Bobby and Mrs Ryders family stalls. Lakeside Café over the road the Lake the steps and the Sleeping Beauty, then the entrance to The Ballroom. In the centre was the Waltza. Last but not the least was the Gallopers and Stanley Creighton, Stanley the great fixer of all things in the Fairground.

Think I'd forgotten Ivor he who everyone called when there was any trouble. The guys on the Wall of death Bill Miller the owner, Jack Campbell Roach. Nobby Dare (Clark). Later Peter Catchpool and Ronny Swift who came to drive the Austin Seven but never did. Tommy Mann with the kids miniature train and the Figure of Eight were down below as was Johnson and Humpage, George and Fred who owned the Walkie Photo sites. Phil who worked the entrance to the tower ground made more money than the Prime Minister. Then there was me and my mate (Forgive me I forget his name) we worked the Slipway to the Fort and the Pier. Keith Medley and Bob Bird worked higher up the prom and also the outdoor Baths. Ahh happy days.

Photo below: Brennans Moon Rocket

The above photograph was taken in 1948. The photograph below a bit later with the speedway on the left, and the Octopus bottom right before they installed the Gallopers with the little red train top right. On the boating lake was moored a metal boat in the centre fitted with coloured lights. Later they made a whale from chicken wire and cement. At the time of this photo there was a train running partially around the lake.

Professional football came to Wallasey in 1921, when physician Dr Tom Martlew launched New Brighton FC . With entry into the Lancashire Combination following the demise of South Liverpool FC, whose place New Brighton took over.

This was the second attempt to host a League club with New Brighton Tower F.C having foundered 20 years earlier. In 1925 New Brighton achieved their best ever position, finishing third in Division Three (North). New Brighton were known as "The Rakers" after their ground, in Rake Lane but Football League matches were played at the Tower Grounds, home of the former New Brighton Tower: they moved permanently into this ground after the Second World War because Rake Lane had been destroyed by air raids, and then taken over by the council to build houses to replace those lost in the war.

 In 1947 they made it into the history books when due to a player shortage the 52-year-old manager Neil McBain turned out in goal to become the oldest player ever to appear in a Football League match. In 1951 they failed re-election and were replaced by Workington FC. The club returned to the Lancashire Combination until 1965 when they moved to the Cheshire County League. In 1983 they were wound up.

New Brighton 1948-49

OFFICIAL PROGRAMME

PRICE 3D

HULL CITY A·F·C
v.
NEW BRIGHTON
BOOTHFERRY PARK, SATURDAY, 30th OCTOBER, 1948
KICK-OFF 3-15

The Carnival Queen, Miss Norah Wilson, is pictured above with prizewinners at Wednesday's Wallasey Charity Carnival Committee annual fancy dress ball held at the Tower Ballroom. (Left to right: Mrs. Greenstead, R. Greenstead, the Carnival Queen, Carole Bellis, Sybil Shone, Mrs. Bristow, and Mr. F. Neilson.

William Dutton won best decorated turnout in aid of Victoria Hospital Memorial Scheme.

The Wirral Show, started life in 1977 as a revival of the Wallasey Carnival. It went on to become one of the UK's biggest free-to-enter attractions, drawing many thousands of visitors each year to New Brighton Dips, it started as a community project of the Rotary Club of Wallasey who decided to mark the Queen's Silver Jubilee by reviving the Carnival with a procession of decorated floats through the town. The parade finished on New Brighton promenade where a number of stalls had been erected. In the following years, the number of floats decreased while the number of stalls increased, which then became the main attraction.

Over the years, Wirral Show audiences enjoyed attractions like military and aerobatic displays, music, a vintage and classic car cavalcade and stunt teams. With many famous stunt acts such as the Lings Motocross team and a huge variety of aircraft displays ranging from the Battle of Britain Memorial Flight to the giant of the skies, the A380 Airbus and the Red Arrows. Above photographs of previous attractions at the Carnival.

TOWER THEATRE ③D
N E W   B R I G H T O N

Managing Director - - - - -	**J. W. EVANS**
Theatre Manager and Licensee - -	**H. G. BEATTY**

WRYTON PROMOTIONS LTD.,

Newcourt Hotel, Manchester, 13

in conjunction with

NEW BRIGHTON TOWER COMPANY LIMITED

Present

. . on . .

Wednesday, 28th December 1949

>—●+●—<

BOOKING AND BOX OFFICE ARRANGEMENTS.

Telephone: 276.

Theatre Box Office opens Monday to Friday
9-30 a.m. to 5-30 p.m.

Seats Bookable in Advance: 3/-; 4/-; 5/- (no Booking Fee).
Why not have a Permanent Seat ?
Back Seats (not Bookable) 2/3; Balcony (Standing) 1/6.

Refreshments at popular prices obtainable from Snack Bar
in the Corridor.

TOWER THEATRE

NEW BRIGHTON

Entertainments for Everyone—
EVERY SUNDAY

Afternoon 3—6 p.m. Continuous Performances	Evenings at 7-30 p.m. Doors open 7-0 p.m.

VARIETY Concerts : "SWING Concerts"

Presenting
Capt. Syd Howes and his Forest-Bred Lions

★

" Variety on Strings "
Presented by
MARTIN MARIONETTES TRAVELLING THEATRE

★

HARRY DUNCAN
Comedian Conjurer

★

NOTE THE PRICE—
☞ **6d. All Classes**
Wet or Fine—Seats for 2000

Presenting
Johnny Gordon and his Band

You've heard his Music on the Pier —Now see his Stage Presentation

Featuring
The Norman Hunt Bop Group,
The Dixie Group,
Martin Davis, Gordon Rose,
Freddy Potter,
and Doris Henderson—the
New Discovery

★

2000 Seats at
2/6 & 1/6 (Inc. Tax)
payable at the door

Commencing Saturday, 29th July, 1950
Until Further Notice

Grand 'Standard' Fireworks Display

In the TOWER ATHLETIC GROUNDS

(NEW BRIGHTON FOOTBALL CLUB GROUND)
At 9-0 p.m. prompt   Gates open 8-15 p.m.
Admission all Classes **9d** (Including Tax)

Printed by Wallasey Printers Ltd., Church Road, Wallasey

★DODGEMS EVERYONE ENJOYS THEM Make sure you try the
FUN ! THRILLS ! SPEED & SKID !! DODGEMS !
★ ★ ★ ★
TRAVEL on the WEIRDEST JOURNEY OF YOUR LIFE !!
★THE GHOST TRAIN SHRIEKS — LAUGHS SURPRISE—SUSPENSE !
★ ★ ★ ★
You Must Visit Our GREAT SHOW
★THE WAXWORKS Crammed with Interesting and Exciting Tableaux
GREAT STORIES OF LOVE, CRIME AND ADVENTURE TOLD IN BRILLIANT WAX ARTISTRY and a great CHAMBER OF HORRORS— one inclusive charge only
★ ★ ★ ★
★ GIANT AMUSEMENT ARCADE
(Left of Tower Building Entrance)
★ THE LATEST IT'S NEW ROLLO HAVE A FINE TIME WINNING GRAND PRIZES !
OVER 150 FUN AND PRIZE MACHINES
Shooting Ranges ! —— Automatic Rifles ! —— Radio Rifles !
Also in the Grounds : Skid — Electric Speedway — Skee Rolls — Mirror Maze — Crooked House — Autodrome
AMUSEMENT EQUIPMENT COMPANY

THE TOWER New Brighton
Proudly Announces the Opening of the New
ZOO
Admission 6d.
With the Greatest Collection of Animals, including Lions Leopards, Bears, Wallabys, Llamas, Monkeys, Baboons and many others. Also Kiddies' Pet Corner.
AND
CARTOON CINEMA
45 MINUTES SHOWING OF THE LATEST CARTOON FILMS, POPEYES ANITOONS PUPPETOONS Etc.
Admission 6d.
— OPEN DAILY —
from 21st MAY, 1950
Also CAPTAIN S. HOWES' SENSATIONAL STAGE PRESENTATION
★ PERFORMING LIONS' ACT ★
DAILY at 2 p.m., 4 p.m. and 6 p.m.
SUNDAYS 3.30 p.m. and 4.45 p.m.

The first mention of a Menagerie/Zoo was from the Liverpool Mercury dated April 1st 1899.

"A new attraction on the Fair Grounds will be a large menagerie, which arrived in the Mersey last night by steamer from Havra. The wild animals will be conveyed across the river from Liverpool landing stage during this forenoon by the Wallasey luggage boats, and will be on exhibition later in the day". With open-air Zoological Pens and a Lion House appearing in the 1912 guide, the menagerie was well established.

I remember the Zoo in the late 1960's located at the side of the Tower with cages made from old tram Cars. The animals were held in poor conditions but in fairness most didn't know any better in those days.

DANCERS NEW WIN
Following successes at the London old-time dance festival and at
Folkestone. Mr. and Mrs. H. Croasdale. 521. Brunshaw road, Burnley, on
Tuesday night won the Tower trophy at New Brighton Tower ballroom, in
the open three-dance competition.
Saturday 12 July 1952, Burnley Express, Lancashire

MISS LITLEWOODS
Miss Kathleen M'Dowell, a leather-goods saleswoman, of Beechmount
Parade, Belfast, has been selected as "Miss Littlewoods" for next year. The
judges were Terence Morgan and Joan Rice, the film actor and actress and
the judging took place New Brighton Tower ballroom.
Northern Whig - Saturday 06 December 1952

Many of the girls that worked for Littlewoods working in the catalogue
sales department would enter the New Brighton Tower competitions.
Mr John Moores was a man that valued his workforce. To celebrate 25
years in business he took the whole factory on the 8th June 1951 to
Blackpool all expenses paid with 12 coaches, a good time was had by all.

Photograph by Jack Sidderley - New Brighton v Darwen September 1953

A cartoon of Johny Vincent one of the heroes from the 1956/57 FA Cup run. With a list bottom right of all the teams knocked out by The Rakers, which ended with a 9-0 defeat to Burnley.
From the National Football Collection.

WELL-KNOWN RIDERS AT HORSE SHOW

Many well-known riders braved cold wind and heavy rain on Saturday to compete in the revived New Brighton Horse show. Organised by the Wallasey Conservative Association in the Tower Athlete ground the show for which there were 250 entries, was a success from the competitors point of view, and many requests have been made by riders, including the Olympic Gold Medallist, Wilf White, for a repeat. Bad weather, however kept the spectators' away, and the financial loss that resulted from the poor attendance was not very encouraging.
Wallasey News 22nd May 1954

IN THE TOWER THEATRE

Every Saturday and Sunday, with continuous performance from 2 p.m the Tower management present in the theatre, a popular summer feature "Sylvia and her little People" an all star marionette show, plus a number comedy films.

It's a real family show and one the children will love to see.

Admission to any seat in the theatre is 6d.

Following numerous requests from local residents, the Tuesday night variety concerts will again be presented this year in the theatre ,with many local amateur acts appearing in the show. On stage will be featured Bill Gregson and his full Orchestra, with Vince Newton, Bill Bolland, Alan Wright, Tommy Jones ,and vocalists Eric Bentley and Pearl Scott. An additional attraction will be the 1954 Amateur Talent Contest, to include vocal acts, tap and ballet dancing and comedy acts. Full Particulars for entry, etc are obtainable on application to the manager. The show commences each Tuesday at 7:30 p.m. and the admission is adults 2/-, and children and old age pensioners 1/-, to any seat in the theatre.

FIRE AT THE TOWER
Ballroom saved in tower blaze Firemen last night saved one of the largest ballrooms in the North of England when fire broke out in the third storey of New Brighton Tower. Using breathing apparatus the firemen fought their way through the smoke filled ballroom to tackle the blaze with extinguishers. Others, guided by searchlights, used a 60ft escape ladder to tackle the fire from outside. A store room, its contents and the adjoining cafe were severely damaged.
Yorkshire Post and Leeds Intelligencer - Friday 21 January 1955

The fire took hold on the 20th January the alarm was raised at 7.25pm this was the second major fire to hit the Tower. The fire was first spotted by the Ballroom Manager Mr Cyril Isherwood and along with John Williams a night watchman, they tackled the blaze with a fire extinguisher until the Wallasey Fire Brigade arrived. It required three appliances to tackle the furious fire which at its peak the flames reached over 20 feet. The Chief Fire officer , Joseph Holt commented "If the fire had not been discovered when it was, the whole Ballroom would have been involved and the flames might have spread up the building, as well as below, if they had reached a lift shaft nearby. This would have acted as a flue".
If the Manager had not seen a flicker of light in the cafe, and gone to investigate, this could have been the end of the Tower before we had all the fun in the 60's with the Big Groups, the Beatles, Rolling Stones etc appearing in the Mecca of the North, New Brighton Tower.
In the Tower Theatre there were always buckets of sand hung on the walls so that an outbreak of fire could be quickly dealt with.
Ref; Helmets, Handcuffs and Hoses, Part Two. The Wallasey Fire Brigade by Noel E Smith

HOLIDAY TOWN PARADE

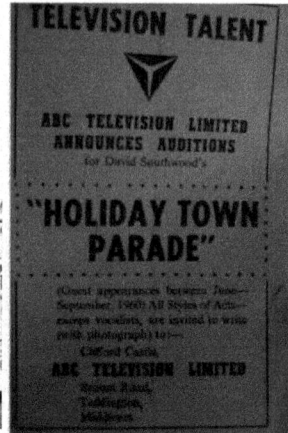

"Make a date, don't be late for Holiday Town Parade"

Holiday Town Parade was a regular summer attraction, with audiences of up to 20 million. With a Beauty Contest, a Fashion Contest and an Adonis Contest.

It started in ABC's first year of broadcasting in 1956, and was hosted by McDonald Hobley. At the New Brighton heat, a strap of a bathing costume snapped, this was a live event, so a fast response from the producer sent the camera and commentary in a different direction.

Winner of he Holiday Town Parade of the 1956 series was Marion Lewis who came from the Isle of Man, with the chief judge Errol Flynn.

Other venues for the show in this first season were Morecambe (first programme on July 14th), Llandudno, Rhyl, Southport, New Brighton and Blackpool. The 1957 series began on June 15th at the same venues as 1956, coming from Central Pier Ballroom Morecambe. Future venues included Floral Hall Southport (June 22nd 1957), Tower Theatre New Brighton (June 29th).

The 4th Series July 11th 1959 Tower Ballroom New Brighton guest Vic Oliver, and the 5th Series from the Tower Ballroom New Brighton 16th July 1950.

The 6th series in 1961 started on June 24th at Morecambe's central pier then the Tower Ballroom New Brighton on the 15th July guest Vic Oliver. The resident band being Joe Loss. From the 6th series a new idea was born "Out and About" meeting local characters and holidaymakers.

The final series in 1962 when the prize fund was actually lowered to £4,000 and the Adonis section dropped, was hosted by Keith Fordyce, fresh from Thank Your Lucky Stars. With the new compère arrived a line of dancing girls to replace the formation dancers.

The very last final was held at the Norbreck Castle in Blackpool on the 22nd September and was judged by Norman Hartnell and Richard Todd.

264

The opening sequence was unforgettable, our immaculately dressed man in full evening dress, wore a full sized marching bass drum on his chest which he proceeded to thump as he announced - "Make a date, don't be late with Holiday Town Parade". The Adonis Competition designed for the ladies featured a body building slot, in which the former Mr Universe, Arnold Dyson was the chief judge.

TV SHOW FROM NEW BRIGHTON TOWER NEXT SATURDAY
New brighton has retained its place in the A.B.C - TV Holiday Town Parade series of programmes, although the number of resorts has had to be reduced and David Southwood will televise next Saturday's Parade on the national network from the Tower Ballroom at 6pm. The news was informed yesterday that no more tickets are available. The programme will include. as usual, heats of the £5,000 Bathing Beauty, Fashion Queen and Adonis contest with a number of star guest artistes.
Six contestants to appear in each heat are to be selected from preliminary heats to be held in New Brighton Bathing Pool at 3 p.m. next Friday or, if wet, in the Tower Ballroom. The T.V.unit stays in Wallasey over the weekend to televise morning service from St.Hilary's Parish Church on the Sunday, July 17.
Article from the Wallasey News July 1960

ABC schedule for Saturday 11th July 1959

1.40 **News** from ITN
1.45 **Motor Racing** -*from Silverstone* (and at 4.15)
2.45 **Racing from Sandown Park**
5.00 **Flash Gordon** - *Tree Men of Mars*
5.15 **The Adventures of Robin Hood** - *The Ghost that Failed*
5.45 **News** from ITN
6.00 **Holiday Town Parade** - *from New Brighton, guest Vic Oliver*
7.00 **Cheyenne** - *Iron Trail*
8.00 **Saturday Spectacular** - *The Jo Stafford Show*
9.00 **News** from ITN
9.05 **The Invisible Man** - *Picnic with Death*
9.35 **Great Movies of Our Time** - - *Four's a Crowd starring Errol Flynn*
11.15 **Drive In** - *admag with Dave Morrell*
11.30 **The Francis Linel Show** - *with Georgina Brown* (ABC)
11.45 **The Epilogue** - *Rev Donald Tyler, Director of Religious Education, Diocese of Birmingham*

NEW BRIGHTON TOWER CO. LTD.

TETLEYS ALES	Managing Director .... J. W. EVANS	**AFTER THE SHOW**
ON DRAUGHT IN OUR	Ballroom and Theatre Manager .... S. THREADGOLD	MAKE YOUR RENDEZVOUS
NEW WOODLANDS BAR	Licensee .... H. C. GURNEY	THE
(LICENSED AS ALGERIAN RESTAURANT)		*LAKESIDE BAR*

OPEN TILL 10 p.m.

★

The Season's Closing Programme

YOUR MAIN EVENT

FRED WOOLEY
(Salford)

SPECIAL CHALLENGE CONTEST

JACK DEMPSEY
(Wigan)

versus

COUNT BARTELLI

versus

HARRY HALL
(Bolton)

versus

BERT ROYAL
(Bolton)

ERNIE RILEY

Light Heavyweight Champion of Britain)

★

★

REX HARRISON	versus	**TOMMY TUCKER**
(Doncaster)		(Blackpool)

OUR	**DANCING TIME**	(a) The public may leave at the end of the performance by any exits and exit doors open at that time to open. Note.—The Theatre can be emptied very quickly if the audience leave in an orderly manner.
ROCK POINT BAR	IN THE	(b) All gangways, passages, staircases and exits must be kept entirely free from any obstructions.
GUARANTEES TO QUENCH	**TOWER BALLROOM**	(c) Persons shall not be permitted to stand or sit in any of the intervening gangways or stand in any unseated place in the auditorium, unless standing in such place has been specially allowed by the Watch Committee. A Notice is exhibited in that part of the auditorium in which standing has been sanctioned.
Even YOUR thirst		
AND ITS	EVERY TUESDAY, WEDNESDAY,	
OPEN TILL 10 p.m.	FRIDAY and SATURDAY	

Bill Gregson and his Radio Orchestra

Patrons are requested to note that all Cars must be parked on Public Car Park only. No parking allowed on Amusement Grounds.

NEW BRIGHTON
TOWER
★ THEATRE ★   17

BOOKING AND BOX OFFICE OPEN DAILY
(EXCEPT SUNDAY)
9-30 a.m.—5-0 p.m.
Phone : NEW BRIGHTON 6176

★

WRYTON PROMOTIONS LTD.
133a HIGH STREET, MANCHESTER, 13
in conjunction with
NEW BRIGHTON TOWER CO. LTD
present

ALL	STAR
FREE	STYLE

★   ★

WRESTLING
EACH   WEEK

PROGRAMME - - 3d.
for
Saturday, 1st September, 1956.
at 7-15 p.m.

ENSURE ★ COMFORT!
★   BOOK YOUR SEAT
WELL IN ADVANCE
ALL TELEPHONE BOOKINGS MUST BE COLLECTED
BY 6-55 p.m. ON THE NIGHT

DANCING TIME
IN THE
TOWER BALLROOM
★

DANCING EVERY
TUESDAY, WEDNESDAY, FRIDAY and SATURDAY
BILL GREGSON and his RADIO ORCHESTRA

EVERY TUESDAY IS OLDE TYME
" SEQUENAIRES " ORCHESTRA—Admission 2/-

★

FREE-STYLE RULES OF WRESTLING.

A WRESTLER LOSES A FALL, WHEN . . . . .
 1.—His shoulders are pressed flat on the mat for three consecutive seconds.
 2.—He admits submission in calling " enough."

A WRESTLER IS DEFEATED, WHEN . . .
 1.—He loses two falls.
 2.—He is disqualified.
 3.—He fails to arise or re-enter the ring before the count of ten.

A WRESTLER MAY BE DISQUALIFIED, WHEN . . . . .
 1.—He hits repeatedly with a closed fist.
 2.—He kicks deliberately with a pointed toe.
 3.—He attempts to strangle his opponent.
 4.—He attempts to gouge, bite, scratch, pull his opponent's hair, or ignores the referee's warning.

FOREARM BLOWS ARE PERMITTED.

The Referee has sole charge of the Contest and his decision is final.
Contests are governed by International Rules of Wrestling.

Catchpole's Mont Blanc Tower Gounds 1956

Machine Gallopers

Go-Kart tracks began appearing everywhere in the late 1950s. The McCulloch MC-10 being the first real Go-Kart from a two stroke modified chainsaw motor to actual motorcycle engines.

FIVE HURT IN "WALL OF DEATH" BOOTH

Five people were injured when part of a "wall of death" booth fell during a performance at New Brighton tower fairground, Cheshire, yesterday. A 10ft.-wide section, on which the five people were standing in a crowd of 50 watching a trick motor cyclist, suddenly broke away, sending them crashing 15ft. to the ground.

Mr. Joseph Atherton, aged 50, who broke an ankle said: "It was a terrifying experience. The floor just fell under us and about a dozen people went crashing ·to the ground." The booth was closed for the day.

Some of the Post War riders regularly appearing at the Tower Wall.

Bill(Ron) Miller	1945- 50	
Jack Roche	1947- 53	
Peter Catchpoole	1948 -	(Photo below)
Norman McGonigal	1957- 61	
Ursula Cole-Brown	1957 -61	(Photo above)
Tony Carr	1957 -65	

Other riders include Jack Roche, Johny Bates, and Ken Maxfield.

Peter Catchpoole became a Wall of Death entrepreneur. He went into partnership with Ken Fox who is owner of one of only two surviving wall of death shows in the UK. They built a new 'wall' in the shipbuilding hall in Cammell Laird's in 1995 it was completed in just 20 weeks. It then went on a world tour. The Wall itself is 20ft high and 32ft diameter and made completely of Oregon Pine. The partnership lasted until Peter Catchpoole died in 2002.

OBITUARY BILL MILLER

Wall of Death rider known to thousands of visitors to New Brighton in the late 1940s Mr William (Ron) Miller has died at his home in Sidney Avenue, Wallasey. He was 60. Born at Whitley Bay, Mr Miller worked with travelling shows in Germany, Holland and Russia. He came to New Brighton after the war and set up his own "Wall of Death" platform in the Tower grounds. He rode it each summer season until 1950, when he took over the Tower's boating lake and other attractions. For a number of years he held the licences of the Pink Elephant and Tudor Club at New Brighton. In resent years he helped run an amusement arcade in Birkenhead. Mr Miller leaves a widow and two daughters.

1959 - Space Age Ball

ALAN G. WHARTON
PRESENTS THE NORTH'S MOST SPECTACULAR

SPACE AGE BALL

JAZZ :: ROCK :: CHA CHA :: BALLROOM DANCING
AT
TOWER BALLROOM, NEW BRIGHTON
Friday, 20th March, 7-30 p.m. to 1 a.m.

Personal appearance of Britain's Top Golden Disc Star

RUSS HAMILTON
(MILLION RECORDS with "WE WILL MAKE LOVE")

PLUS TELEVISION'S FABULOUS

WALL CITY JAZZMEN

BOB EVANS and His Five Shillings ★ KEN CARLOS and His Famous Cha Cha Band

BILL GREGSON AND HIS ORCHESTRA
THE NORTH'S TOP BROADCASTING DANCE ORCHESTRA

Novelties ● Spot Prizes ● Mammoth Draw

1000 CIGARETTES GIVEN AWAY FREE
1000 CASCADING PRIZE LADEN BALLOONS FALL AT MIDNIGHT

LICENSED BARS — LATE TRANSPORT: Liverpool, Birkenhead, Wallasey

Tickets at the Door 7/6
Student Nurses' Forces (in uniform) 5/- till 10 p.m.
Tickets in advance 6/- from

LIVERPOOL: Lewis Ltd., Rushworth & Draper Ltd., Cranes Ltd.
WALLASEY: Stothers Ltd., Lincad & Moreton; Tower Ballroom
BIRKENHEAD: Rushworth & Draper Ltd., Grange Road

IN AID OF WALLASEY SPASTICS ASSOCIATION

RUSS HAMILTON
TOMORROW RAINBOW

271

Recollections of Alan Clay his memories of the sixties:

On entering the grounds via the upper Egerton street entrance. I lived off Egerton Street and you could hear the music from the rides quite clearly. On your right was the Tower lodge which was the home of old Mr Bedson and his daughter. I believe he used to be a fisherman but was quite old even then. I'm afraid he had to put up with a lot from us kids, plus his house used to get flooded when they emptied the lake each year.

On the left of the entrance there used to be a stall selling hats, toys etc, in later years it became a tattooist's for a while. Going up the drive on your right was the tower lake. I worked on this as a 13-15 year old. In the early days there was a metal "boat" in the middle which was lit up at night. At times it would become "live" and you could get a shock from it. This was replaced by a "whale" made of mesh which was rendered and painted grey. I only fell in the lake once when the seat of the boat I was standing on collapsed on me and I fell backwards. This gave me a fright because I was disorientated for a minute or so. We used to bail the boats out using various implements and one time we had an electric pump which could also give you a nasty shock. A couple of times when starting the boat engines, petrol that had leaked into the engine compartment would ignite and give you singed eyebrows. I don't know how we survived sometimes?

We had a little fiddle but everyone who worked on the fairground had something going! In cahoots with the cashier we would hand the odd ticket back to her and she would pretend to tear it off and hand to a customer. We shared the proceeds of two shillings fifty, fifty.

Opposite the lake were the toilets which you entered by going down a ramp at the side of the Lakeside bar and restaurant. There was also a donkey track.

The Lakeside or Japanese cafe and bar was next along the driveway. It housed a large restaurant with the bar at the front. It was used by trippers and fairground workers. Locals knew it as the "Jap". There were frequent fights in the bar but as it was also frequented by some Wallasey hard men, there was usually only one outcome.

Opposite the Jap were a couple of small stalls and an arcade. Candy floss and toffee apples were the main goods on sale. Both cost sixpence.

Going around the corner to the right was the Waltzer owned by Leo Clarke. He drove a big red Jaguar just like inspector Morse the TV detective. He always had a big cigar in his mouth. Standing on the side watching the Walzer was a local pastime, especially with most girls wearing miniskirts, who were more interested in gripping the safety rail rather than protecting their modesty much to the delight of us young lads. It was also one of our main rides for searching for cash that had been thrown out of pockets. Of course this was mainly done early mornings before the fair opened, there was always some cash to find even when the staff had searched the night before after it had closed. Going further to the right towards the steps leading to the coach park, at one time they had the chairoplane ride. I think this only lasted a couple of years? There was also a stall selling tea and pies etc.

Across from the stall was the entrance to the old zoo which backed on to the tower building. It was a really poor zoo and looking back was a disgrace and no way to keep any animals. When it closed, we used to go into it and realised that some of the cages were made from old tram cars complete with the old lights and

272

they still had the bell pushes inside.

Going back towards the Waltzer with the tower building to your right, you came to the enchanted caves. This was a water ride that seemed to go under the building but was probably just on the front of it? Very gentle and not scary and the love birds seemed to like it for some reason!!!

Opposite this was the Gallopers although in earlier years we called them the bobby horses. They were operated and maintained by a man named Stan Creighton. He always seemed to be covered in grease and probably was because you had to keep the working parts well lubricated. We had a nickname for him but not really PC these days! The gallopers had an electric organ which was probably a steam organ originally. It played by large folded card with holes punched in feeding through the organ. We knew every tune on it by heart. I hear that music now and it takes me right back! I worked on this for a while and you became quite adept at jumping on and off without hurting yourself.

Next to the gallopers nearly opposite the main entrance to the tower building was a small hot dog stand operated by a man named Wilf. He seemed to have been there for years and probably was! My claim to fame is that Susan Hayward gave me her hot dog when she put too much sauce on it. She was filming "I thank a fool" at the time. This was in 1962. Next to the hot dog stall was the Dodgems. Looking back at the film, everything looks very dated. Years later in the declining years and the dodgems had closed down, they put asbestos sheets on the floor and tried opening a roller skating rink on it. It didn't last! I ripped my school trousers there and got a good hiding from my mother, happy days!

Continuing along the front of the tower building you came to the caterpillar ride, again quite popular with the lovers especially when the cover came over. Opposite this was a large arcade. Some of the machines in this one were quite dated and you could always find a few pennies if you needed to. Next to this was the waxworks and the chamber of horrors. Turning the corner to the right after the waxworks, there was a large building which was open on three sides when working. You bought a sealed ticket and they had a large machine shaped like a football. When they had sold enough tickets, they pressed a button or something and the names of football teams spun around until it stopped on one. If you had that team you won but I haven't a clue what the prizes were? The floor all around this building used to be covered in used losing tickets.

Across from that building was another donkey track. Both tracks in the tower were operated by Clarkes as were some on the shore. Stables were in Tollemache Street, Grosvenor road and Seymour Street. Next to the donkey track at various times you had the Wall of Death or the Dive Bomber.

The Wall of Death was another place to search for cash because the customers used to throw their change down in appreciation of the show and some of it wedged between the boards. I got bashed by my brother once for not bringing a knife to prize the odd sixpence out. I think that was known a nobbins to the riders? The dive bomber that replaced it snapped an arm on at least three occasions to my knowledge. No serious injuries as far as I remember but pretty frightening. I think half the problem was caused by allowing young lads like us to operate these things but that was the way of the world then!

Next to the dive bomber was the moon rocket. Not much to say about that really although I do remember there was a little man sitting on a rocket which went in the opposite direction to the ride and he looked half demented.

Alongside that was the Helter-skelter. Sounds good and looks good but a hell of a climb up those stairs just to slide down again. Always felt a bit rickety to me climbing up there! I think the lady who operated that was called Nan? She took the cash and gave you a mat to slide down on. Next were the steps to the lower part of which I will come to later.

Across the steps was the big wheel. This was mainly operated by a man called Tom who always had greased hair which was probably brycreem or similar. We called him sly Tom simply because he had a turn in his eye and we were a bit afraid of him as youngsters. In later years we got on very well with him and he was a nice guy. He might not have had the looks but he could charm the girls and many is the time we saw him escorting one up the tower hill for some hanky panky.

Next to the big wheel was the Kentucky Derby. I can't remember how many horses there were but probably about twelve or so? Each person had a horse and had to roll a ball up a chute to try and get it in a hole. Every time you got the ball in the hole, your horse moved along. The winning horse owner got a prize.

Next to that were various stalls such as the hall of mirrors with its distorting mirrors that had everyone laughing at their reflections. Another arcade and then stalls such as feed the ducks, darts and air rifle range. Opposite the stalls was another ride which I knew as the Swirl but some call it the Skid. I seem to remember it looked very dangerous with its cogs in the middle and they had no guards on them. This was later replaced by the Miami Twist which I believe was operated by the Brennans. There were more stalls after that selling do-nuts and drinks and later popcorn. Watching do-nuts and popcorn being made was quite fascinating to us when they first came to New Brighton. Just past that was the Ghost train, probably looked scarier than it was from the outside. Once again the lovers liked it! In later years, it was closed season I think and a few of us were chatting up the girls and sitting on the wall of the ghost train. Generally messing about until we decided to move on, about ten minutes

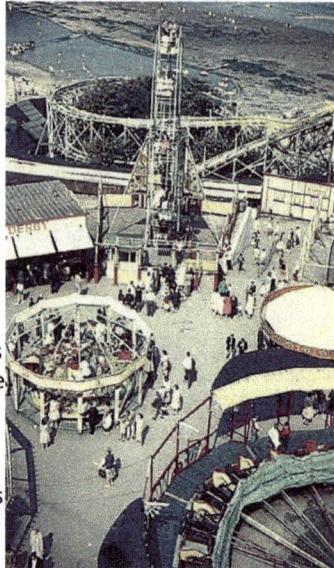

later there was a violent explosion and the Ghost train went up in flames. We were interviewed by the police at the time but were not suspected of any wrong doing. Things had a habit of going up in flames around this time but it wasn't caused by us or at least knowingly caused by us. We did all smoke at the time but you still have to explain the explosion?

Opposite the ghost train was the Peter Pan railway for children, nothing to say about that really. Very gentle and sedate although there was a bell on the front of each car the kids could ring. Quite noisy I suppose although it just mingled with the other noises at the time.

Next to the ghost train if memory serves there was a rifle range with point .22 rifles. Next to that was the fun house which I don't remember much about the inside although the big thing about it was the grid as you came out into the open air which blew air upwards. Lots of girls got caught out showing their stockings which most wore in the early days before tights. This attracted a lot of males obviously! Further along were numerous stalls, darts and one run by Nan Brennan in which you threw wooden balls at crockery. Not sure what the crockery was made of or where they got it from but I doubt you could eat your dinner off it or drink your tea out of the cups? Very flimsy and obviously made to be smashed.

Opposite those stalls were little round ones with various games. Darts again and Hoopla. The hoopla was all sweets with the top prizes in the middle such as a box of liquorice allsorts (wow) which no one ever seemed to win. Minor prizes were threepenny toffee bars. One night some local kids got in and nicked the lot. Most of it was what we now call well past its sell by date but it was still eaten or so I was told!

Between those stalls and the Jap (we've come full circle) was a small red train that seemed to have been there forever when I was a kid and later. Just went around in a circle but was nice for the kids.

Lower part of the grounds starting from the steps alongside the ghost train. At the bottom of the steps, the first ride you came to was the Rock and Roll. Each car had the name of one of the current pop stars of the day on it. At one time the Dive bomber was on this site. I remember one of the arms collapsing whilst it was in this location. Behind that near to Egerton Street was at one time the Rotor. Before the chairlift was built, the Octopus ride occupied the site of the chairlift entrance. This was later taken by Steam Yachts for a couple of years. They really ran on steam and I can remember the fire being stoked in the middle. I can remember someone being thrown from this ride and an ambulance being called. I don't think it was fatal? In 1960 the Chairlift was built and occupied the site until the demise of the tower grounds.

Continuing on to the left, there was the Speedway ride which was on the slope leading to the promenade. A small cafe occupied the corner of the slope and Egerton Street. Crossing over the slope there was a large Walls Ice Cream stall. This opened on two sides, one in the tower and one on the promenade.

It used to be very busy in the fifties and early sixties. Tucked away in the corner of this stall a bit further along the prom was the jockey weighing scales. I think it was two pence (old money) to have yourself weighed by sitting on a chair and large brass weights were put on the other end and your weight was written down on a card. My aunt and uncle owned this and I believe the scales and weights are still in the family somewhere?

Going back up the slope on the left hand side you came to a stall selling pop, crisps and novelties. I think there was a small child's roundabout alongside that before you came to the Figure Eight later Big Dipper ride. A bit further up was a small stall with a "pond" where children fished for plastic ducks and fish with numbers on the bottom. A prize every time was their motto but the prizes were rather poor quality. Kept the kids happy though!

Next to this stall was Mr and Mrs Brown's Palmistry booth. Mr Brown was a very imposing black man and was always immaculately dressed. His wife was white and also always immaculate. At this time, you never saw a black person and he was a rarity. I never once heard or saw any racist remarks towards these very nice people.

Further up was an arcade which I think was owned by Leo Clarke? There were other stalls along this stretch although I can't remember much about them. It was the same on the other side as you walked back towards the slope until you came to the end where there was the large .22 Rifle Range which appears in many photo's looking up from the prom. Turning left back towards the ghost train steps you came to a very large Fish and Chip bar which at the time was owned and run by the Pastouna family. One of the sons Andrew later became a DJ on the British Forces radio in Germany which we used to listen to a lot when I was in the army. Then came various stalls, bingo, ball in the bucket etc. and we are back at the steps. The steps alongside the Big Wheel. Straight ahead was a photo set up. Think this was operated by the Clarkes as well? Very old fashioned cameras and you could put your head through various boards which when photographed was supposed to be hilarious, simple pleasures for the trippers. Turning right you could take the steps to Tommy Manns (later Charlie Manns) kiddie's playground. To the right was the skating rink. At one time they set up a high dive there and Mr Leyland used to dive off this very high platform into a small tank. He was known as Dare Devil Curly and was registered as virtually blind. Mr Leyland was injured quite badly by something that had been thrown in the tank unbeknownst to anyone. You then came to the Rock Point Castle bar and Restaurant. My mother used to waitress there some times.

276

CHAIR LIFT

In 1960 the County Borough of Wallasey celebrated its 50th Anniversary. Charter House the eleven story block of flats opened in Church Street Wallasey. New Brighton was still full of holidaymakers, and cheap foreign flights had not been invented. So with no competition all the fun of the fair, a zoo; skating; two open-air swimming pools; Miss New Brighton Bathing Beauty competition; cinemas; theatres; and entertainments on the pier the resort was in full swing. At the start of the 1960 season a chair lift was installed operating from the roof of the Tower building down to the fairground below. The twenty plus open air cabins/buckets attached to a steel rope would swing in the wind which was a bit un-nerving for the passengers who would stand in the small carriages. In windy weather it had to cease operations. Following the fire in 1969 it was sold to a company in Ireland.

I remember taking a ride on the "Roller Coaster/Figure of 8 and the whole thing shook violently. It was made of timber and held together with wire rope. It had been portable at one time, and did not appear to be a permanent feature. It certainly was getting past its sell by date.

An article in the Wallasey News dated Saturday the 30th September 1961, the paper announced the arrival of M.G.M at New Brighton Tower next Friday night. With the Tower's "Merry-Go-Land" grounds being opened for a special all-night film shooting session.

With the stars of the film Susan Hayward and Diane Cilento playing some of the scenes against the backdrop of the fun fair, and also sampling some of the rides.

With many of the local people who have already been selected being used as extras for the nights shooting, it should prove to be a memorable occasion. The filming is due to start at 6pm and will go on all night.

FILM EXTRAS FOR THE DAY

Photograph below entitled "Caught by the camera" as they queued to sign on as extras on Saturday afternoon for the M.G.M production of "I Thank a Fool" In the front are Susan Btyan (left) and Melanie Sullivan, both sixteen-year-olds. One of the extras, Dilys Robertson of 26 Egremont promenade, writes:- "I was one of the lucky Wallasey people chosen as an extra. This not only gave me a glimpse behind the scenes but the privilege of appearing along side film star Susan Hayward.

"We all found it a tiring but an exciting day, every scene being taken three to four times before director Robert Stevens was satisfied.

"I appeared in seven scenes, a jiving sequence outside the Tower, a scene at the Ghost Train with Miss Hayward searching for Diano Cilento, a large crowd sequence involving the 'Moon Rocket' and 'Caterpillar' and four other general scenes.

"We all enjoyed our close-ups of Susan Hayward, Diane Cilento and Kieron Moore.

The story line of the film: After mercifully killing her terminally ill lover, Dr. Christine Allison (Susan Hayward) loses her medical license and spends two years in prison. Once she has completed her sentence, the lawyer who prosecuted Christine, Stephen Dane (Peter Finch), hires her to care for his emotionally unstable wife, Liane (Diane Cilento). Christine takes the job, but when Liane's allegedly dead father (Cyril Cusack) reappears, Christine sets out to reveal the family's dark secrets.

The decade was particularly revolutionary in terms of popular music, as it saw the formation and evolution of rock. At the start of the roaring sixties the Tower was conservative in its choice of bands. It missed out on the 50s without booking any real stars like Buddy Holly or Bill Haley who had all toured the UK, and even played in Liverpool. With many of the up and coming stars Cliff Richard, Marty Wild and Billy Fury doing the rounds in the late 50s it had been a lost opportunity. But all that was to change during the start of 1961 a programme of dances in the Tower Ballroom on a Thursday and Saturday night set the changes in motion. With "The Tony Osbourne Band" and "The Swinging Blue Genes" appearing live on the Saturday Palais Night Show. Admission 4/- Before 8:30 p.m 3/-.Then a disco on the Thursday called "Off the Record Night" dancing to Top of the Pops. Admission 1/9. This was to be the standard programme for most weeks, except for Bank Holidays and when a special attraction was booked. Thursday the 27th April had the Fabulous Lance Fortune a Pye recording star as top of the bill, admission 3/-
Followed on the 27th May with"The Big All Star Night" with Ricky Valance (Tell Laura I Love Her) fame topped the bill with The Lucky Strikes and Tony Osbourne in support. Admission 3/-
Valance was the first artist from Wales to have a number one single, the 1960 hit 'Tell Laura I Love Her', sold over a million copies in 1960.

Nero And The Gladiators during the second Gene Vincent - Eddie Cochran Tour, in Spring 1960. Top row from L to R: Rodney "Rocki" Slade (Bass), Don Adams (Lead Guitar). Bottom row L to R: Mike O'Neill (Vocals) and Tommy Brown (Drums)

Photo courtesy Don Adams

The Echolets Fontana Recording stars featuring Dane Lawrence appeared on the 24th June along with the resident Band. Admission had now increased to 5/-

An advert in the Wallasey News dated the 1st July informed the reader that the Tower Ballroom was Under New Management To-Night Saturday Ladies Gift Night - two groups appearing Tony Osborne & Blue Genes. The Echolets proved popular and returned on Thursday 13th July with Dee and the Dinamites admission 3/-.

Tony Osbourne was a talented trumpeter and pianist but he made his mark as a gifted arranger on many successful singles and albums during the 1950s and '60s.

He was a consummate professional able to cope with prima donna antics from the likes of Shirley Bassey, Eartha Kitt and Dorothy Squires.

In 1957, Osborne wrote the arrangement for Gracie Fields' hit recording of "Around The World", which was produced by Norman Newell.

"The engineer thought that there was some problem with the microphones," said Osborne, "as we kept hearing this click on Gracie's mic.

We changed it over and it was still there. Eventually, we realised it was Gracie's false teeth.

Norman said, 'Would you mind telling her?' I said, 'No, I just write the music and conduct. You're the producer: you do the hard stuff.

'In 1960, the American star Connie Francis recorded in England and Osborne wrote and conducted the arrangement for her

282

million-selling "Mama", which was sung in Italian.

"I never thought of that as a hit single," said Osborne, "but Pete Murray got behind it and everybody loved it.

" Among his arrangements were "Sisters" for the Beverley Sisters, "Out Of Town" for Max Bygraves, "Love Is" for Alma Cogan, "Little Donkey" for Nina and Frederick, and "Say It With Flowers" with Dorothy Squires and Russ Conway.

Osborne often worked with Shirley Bassey, writing songs for her ("Gone" and "You") and arranging her very dramatic hit single,

"I (Who Have Nothing)" in 1963. "I wrote that in 5/4 which enabled us to put a big tympani beat in it.

Shirley wouldn't have known if it was 5/4 or 10/4 but it didn't matter as she was somebody who could feel an arrangement and knew when to come in.

KART MEETING AT TOWER ON MONDAY

Wallasey Motor Club has a Kart Meeting at the Tower Stadium on Easter Monday, the first of the 1961 season.

Members and friends are asked to meet at the Tower Ground at 10 a.m. on Sunday to tidy up the track and set up the course.

As many helpers as possible are required on Monday and should report to the chief marshall by 10 a.m.

The meeting should finish by 6 p.m.

Following on from a meeting this week with representatives of the New Brighton & Wallasey Ratepayers Association, residents of the New Brighton area have agreed to hold back further anti-nuisance petitions to the Council about go-karting at the Tower Stadium. They will wait a month to see if matters improve. The complaining residents mainly in Dalmorton Road and Vaughan Road have been assured that everything possible will continue to be done to eliminate excessive noise.

Wallasey News 10th June 1961

283

TOWER BALLROOM
NEW BRIGHTON

MERRY - GO - LAND
NORTHERN ENTERTAINMENTS
Present

BEAT NIGHT
(10th EDITION)

A Dangerous and alarming state of
CHAOS
created by the Human Monster with
two ft. long hair and horns

SCREAMING LORD SUTCH
WITH HIS WILD HORDE
THE SAVAGES

WATCH — JIVE — LISTEN
but if nervous
KEEP WELL CLEAR

THURSDAY, JUNE 15th
7.30 p.m. — 11.30 p.m.   Admission 3/6

ROCK POINT RESTAURANT
NEW BRIGHTON : TOWER GROUNDS
UNDER NEW MANAGEMENT
Dinners, Weddings, Hot-pots, Buffets,
Dances specially catered for.
Open each SATURDAY EVENING
for DRINKS with MUSICAL ENTERTAINMENT

Sam Leach promoted "Operation Big Beat" at the Tower Ballroom, New Brighton, on November 10th 1961, a miserable foggy night. Headlining on that first extraordinary night were The Beatles alongside Gerry and the Pacemakers, Kingsize Taylor and the Dominoes, Rory Storm and the Hurricanes and The Remo Four. Around 4,000 fans all paying 5/- a ticket packed into the Tower Ballroom for the first in a series of Sam Leach's " Operation Big Beat" shows.

The show started at 7.30pm and the Beatles appeared at 8pm. They had been booked to appear at Knotty Ash Village Hall on the same evening, so had to make the trip through the tunnel and back again for there second spot on the Tower at 11.30pm.Neil Aspinall a mate of Pete Best drove the group in an old second-hand van he had recently bought.

Tickets for the event had been sold weeks in advance at NEMS Whitechapel store, which was managed by Brian Epstein. This only helped to reinforce his opinion that the Beatles were a popular and up and coming band. With late night transport laid on for the fans this all proved to be a very successful start of Sams involvement with the Tower.

As the night wore on the two licensed bars had done a roaring trade, the Birkenhead teddy boys just had to get involved in fights. One of the thugs at the downstairs bar threw a table at Paul McCartney missing him by inches and smashing the mirror behind the bar. The Tower's general manager Tommy McArdle was not very happy with the situation. And insisted that Sam hired bouncers to protect the place and the groups in the future.

The Tower had placed its indelible mark on the history of Pop Music it was the only British venue The Beatles played at more often than the Cavern Club.

Brian Epstein first discovered the Beatles in November 1961 during a lunchtime Cavern Club performance. But it was a visit to New Brighton

Tower with Bob Wooler that was a turning point. Paul and George sang into one microphone, while John sang the lead of "Baby It's You" with passion and meaning in the other.

From Bobs recollections at the time.

"Brian was transfixed - I was talking with him but he wasn't listening, he was on cloud nine. It was both the message of the song and the person that attracted him.

It made a lasting impression and he wanted to manage the boys especially John. They just had to be his first signing.

There was no stopping Sam with this level of support from the fans and with the money rolling in, he went on to promote even more events on the Tower. Operation Big Beat II on the 24th November, was his next successful venture. In fact on a gamble he had booked the Tower for similar shows every Friday to the end of the year. With ticket prices increased to 6/- and longer opening times until 2am and 3 bars with an extended licences to 12.45, it was money for old rope. The Beatles had just played at the Casbah Coffee Club, in West Derby, which was owned by Pete Best's mother Mona, it had been Pete Best's 20th birthday on the 24th November 1961 so after the show and a short celebration, it was a quick dash of to the Tower for their next gig.

An added treat for the fans was the appearance of Emile Ford, He got up on stage and sang with Rory Storm & the Hurricanes while American singer Davy Jones joined the Beatles on stage and sang two numbers with them.

Following on from the previous trouble, Sam had to recruit the services of Eddie Palmer alias "The Toxteth Terror" by hiring bouncers in large numbers he could overcome the Birkenhead treat. This did do the trick and even thought some thugs managed to evade security, they did not kick off. Friday 29th June the Beatles were top of the bill in another of Sams ambitious promotions Operation big Beat III.

"Operation Big Beat I" (last Friday, Nov. 10th) was such a phenomenal success, that by public demand we now present

"OPERATION BIG BEAT II"

at the TOWER BALLROOM,
NEW BRIGHTON

on FRIDAY, 24th NOVEMBER 1961
7-30 p.m. to 2-00 a.m.

THE "BIGGEST BEAT" LINE UP EVER
The Beatles - Rory Storm and The Hurricanes
Gerry and The Pacemakers - The Remo Four
Earl Preston and the Tempest Tornadoes
Faron and The Flamingos

Three Licensed Bars (until 12-45 p.m.)   Buffet

TICKET 6/-

TRANSPORT ARRANGEMENTS:

An article in the Wallasey News commented on the announcement that the New Brighton Tower Company had allotted 750,000 1s shares for cash at par to rank with the existing Ordinary shares. This caused speculation in Wallasey yesterday as to whether the move was concerned with future development at New Brighton. The issued Ordinary capital, previously £112,500 is raised by this issue to the full authorised amount of £150,000. No dividend was paid for the year to February 28th last.

A financial commentator in the Financial Times yesterday stated that the current market price was around 1s to 1s 3d, and the net book asset value was 1s 2d. He added that the addition to the equity represented by the shares allocated was one third precisely and – as far, at least-approval for the issue from shareholders had not been sought.

A statement on behalf of the Tower Company last evening: New Brighton Tower Company announces that it has acquired "Photomatics" for £83,826 in cash.

Of this amount £52,500 has been paid and the balance of £31,326 will be paid in three equal annual instalments commencing on the 1st August, 1963.

To assist in the financing of this deal the New Brighton Tower Company has issued the balance of the Ordinary 1s shares – 750,000 one shilling shares for cash at par. A circular will be sent to shareholders shortly.

We understand that "Photomatics" is concerned with amusement machine equipment.

Wallasey News 2nd September 1961

The next Tower promotion took place on 8 December 1961 and featured South African singer Danny Williams whose current hit 'Moon River' was No. 4 in the British charts, but went on to become No1 in January 1962. Once again the top of the bill was Davy Jones, backed by the Beatles. On 15 December five bands were featured on a five-and-a-half hour show. The Beatles topped the bill. The event also saw the appearance of Cass & the Cassanovas. When Brian Casser left the group the remaining three members continued as the Big Three.

The Beatles played at New Brighton Tower Ballroom on 27 occasions. In 1961 they appeared six times 10th & 24th November, 1st, 8th, 15th & 26th December Boxing Day.

288

The Beatles' 11th show at the Tower Ballroom on the 16th February 1962 was billed as a "Panto Ball", and followed the previous night's "Pre-Panto Ball", both of which featured The Beatles on the bill. They returned the following week after playing a 30 minute slot at Birkenhead Technical College, between two spots performed at the Tower. Earlier in the day they had also performed at a lunch time session at the Cavern Club. This was the norm for most groups at the time, appearing in different venues on the same day, to make a living.

On the 14th June 1963 this was to be the last of 27 live shows by The Beatles at the Tower Ballroom in New Brighton. On this evening it was one of Brian Epstein's Mersey Beat Showcase concerts, in which The Beatles headlined a bill made up of acts managed by Epstein's NEMS Enterprises.

At 11.45 after the show, Paul McCartney was stopped by police for driving over the speed limit on Seabank Road in Wallasey, Merseyside. On 26 August 1963 he received a fine and a one-year driving ban.

The Beatles played at the Tower Ballroom on 27 occasions. The other dates were 10 and 24 November; 1, 8, 15and 26 December 1961; 12, 19 and 26 January; 15 and 23 February; 2 March; 6 April; 21 and 29 June; 13, 21 and 27 July; 17 August; 14 and 21 September; 12 October; 23 November; 1 and 7 December 1962; and 14 June 1963.

The Rock and roll legend Jerry Lee Lewis backing band The Echoes were without a drummer and as Rory Storm & The Hurricanes had not long returned from a stint in Hamburg, Ringo Starr sat in as the drummer on this gig!

An original Order Of Appearance typed list appeared in Auction relating to the Jerry Lee Lewis concert that took place at the Tower Ballroom, New Brighton on 17th May 1962. The list details the order in which the groups and artists would appear and it also states the length of each performance. Jerry Lee Lewis was the headline act at the show. The list additionally details an unusual solo performance by Rory Storm on viola. Bob Wooler noted in black ballpoint pen that the group The Strangers had cancelled their performance. He has also indicated the amount that would be paid to each of the acts that were due to perform on the evening.

The order of appearance list is from the collection of the Cavern Club compère Bob Wooler. Bob was a pivotal figure in the Merseyside music scene of the early sixties. He introduced The Beatles countless times during their 292 appearances at The Cavern and was a great ambassador for the group. The lot is accompanied by a letter of authenticity on Tracks Ltd. letterhead confirming that this item is from the collection of Bob Wooler.

290

The very same week that the Beatles "Love Me Do " appeared in the charts, Brian Epstein, the band's manager had promoted a spectacular show at the Tower Ballroom. It featured 12 acts, and was headlined by the US rock 'n' roll legend Little Richard, Part of his strategy was to bring in big stars like Little Richard and put the Beatles on as the second biggest act. Tower manager Tommy McArdle had helped Brians NEMS

company to make this, the Beatles' 23rd show at the Tower Ballroom a massive success. . Among the bands was Lee Curtis and the All-Stars, whose new drummer was Pete Best; the former Beatles drummer and by all accounts they had an awkward encounter backstage. Little Richard was one of the all-time rock and roll greats," John Lennon once said. "The first time I heard him, a friend of mine had been to Holland and brought back a 78 with 'Long Tall Sally' on one side, and 'Slippin' And Slidin'' on the other. It blew our heads – we'd never heard anybody sing like that in our lives and all those Saxes playing like crazy. "Little Richard was born Richard Penniman and was one of the original rock-and-roll artists who had the greatest influence on The Beatles. He was the third eldest of the 12 children of Leva Mae (née Stewart) and Charles "Bud" Penniman. His father was a church deacon who sold bootlegged moonshine on the side and owned a nightclub, the Tip In Inn. Little Richard enjoyed the Pentecostal churches the most, because of their charismatic worship and live music. Little Richard's most celebrated work dates from the mid-1950s, when his dynamic music and charismatic showmanship laid the foundation for rock and roll. Little Richard influenced numerous singers and musicians including the Beatles; his music helped shape rhythm and blues for generations to come, and his performances and headline making thrust his career right into the mix of American popular music. His first hit was a risqué song he had improvised from his days on the club circuit called "Tutti Frutti".The song's a cappella introduction was based on a drum rhythm Little Richard had devised. The record producer Blackwell felt the song had hit potential and hired songwriter Dorothy LaBostrie to replace some of Little Richard's sexual lyrics with less controversial words. Recorded in three takes in September 1955, "Tutti Frutti" was released as a single in November, and the rest is history.

THE BIG THREE

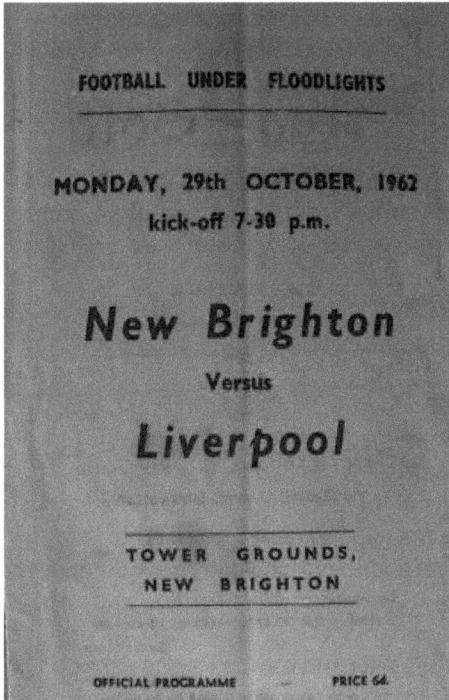

1921-22 Joined Lancashire Combination
1923-24 Joined Football League Division Three North
1939-40 Football League programme abandoned due to outbreak of war
1951   Not re-elected to Football League
1951-52 Rejoined Lancashire Combination
1956-57 Lancashire Combination runner-up
1958-59 Lancashire Combination Champions
1959-60 Missed runner-up spot on goal average
1965-66 Joined Cheshire County League
1979   Relegated to Division 2
1981   Left Cheshire County League

Programme cover from the game on the 29th October 1962 to commemorate the first match to be played under the new floodlights at the Tower Grounds New Brighton. Liverpool sent a strong team and went on to win the game with goals from: St John 2, Callaghan, Wallace and Melia. New Brighton featured special guest appearances by Tom Finney, Nat Lofthouse and Big Billy Liddell and replied by scoring 2 goals.
Final score New Brighton 2 – 5 Liverpool . The attendance was 8,500
Liverpool side, Lawrence in goal, Full Backs Ferns and Moran,
Half backs: Milne, Yeats, Stevenson,
Forwards: Callaghan, Hunt, Lewis, Melia, and Wallace.

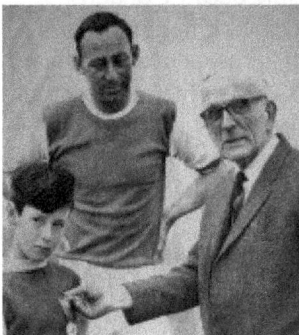

Ted Dutton my uncle veteran secretary of New Brighton A.F.C who retires from office at the end of the season, was presented with a fine tankard by the Rakers number one supporter and team mascot Robert Wooley before last Thursday's floodlit cup-tie. Also in the picture is player-manager Roy Lorenson who thanked Ted for his services on behalf of the team.

Damage estimated at thousands of pound was caused last Saturday night the 17th August when fire swept through part of New Brighton Tower completely gutting the Tower Social Club and causing damage to the theatre and ballroom the finest in the north of England other parts of the building were also seriously affected by heat and smoke. When the outbreak was discovered shortly after 7:30 p.m. by Mr Alex McIntyre General Foreman at the tower early arrivals for the usual Saturday night dance were asked to leave the premises and police cleared the adjacent fairground of thousands of holidaymakers.

"This made our job much easier". said Mr Frank Fradley, Wallasey's Deputy Chief Fire Officer, we did not want thousands of people milling around getting in the way of operations.

Twenty six appliances and 160 firemen from Wallasey, Birkenhead, Cheshire, Liverpool and Lancashire brigades fought for four hours to bring the blaze under control and prevent the flames from spreading to the huge ballroom and other parts of the building. The fire spread rapidly through the central ceiling of the theatre and flames leapt up to the ballroom floor above The clubroom and theatre balcony were completely burnt out, but firemen working in relays and using breathing apparatus, managed to prevent further serious damage.

After seeing the smoke seeping through ventilators of the social club while on his rounds, Mr McIntyre raised the alarm. On entering the theatre he found the club premises and balcony blazing fiercely with flames leaping up to the false ceiling.

Blazing pieces of timber and red-hot slabs of concrete crashed from the balcony into the auditorium, setting the seating alight. Mr Frank Fradley, who was in charge of fire-fighting operations, told the "News" afterwards, "At one stage it was touch and go whether the entire building would become involved but everyone did a magnificent job"

Lowered Theatre's Safety Curtain

Important company records were rescued from the office section of the building by Bill Roberts, managing director of the Tower Company, and Mr McIntyre. They found one staircase impassable because of dense smoke but managed to gain access to the office by a different route.

After raising the alarm, Mr McIntyre, aged 38 of Barnwell Avenue, Liscard, groped his way through thick smoke to lower the theatre's safety curtain and guided firemen through the smoke-filled passages of the 70-year-old building. He was overcome by smoke but later went back into the building with Mr Roberts to retrieve the company documents.

"Mr. McIntyre did a really wonderful job", said Mr Fradley, "We were hampered all the time by smoke and the peculiar construction of the building, but he acted as our guide. It was a concerted effort by everyone that helped save the Tower building from being a complete write off"

NEMS ENTERPRISES PRESENT AT THE
NEW BRIGHTON TOWER

FRI. JULY 26 NORTHERN SOUNDS 1963

BILLY J. KRAMER AND THE DAKOTAS • FREDDY AND THE DREAMERS

THE UNDERTAKERS
*
EARL PRESTON AND THE T.T's
*
JOHNNY SANDON AND THE REMO FOUR

THE FOUR MOSTS
*
MARK PETERS AND THE SILHOUETTES
*
PETER MacLAINE & THE CLAN
*
SONNY WEBB & THE CASCADES
and
FREDDY STARR AND THE MIDNIGHTERS

also The BIG THREE

11 Fabulous Groups!

TICKETS 6/- IN ADVANCE   ON NIGHT 7/-

A BOB WOOLER PRODUCTION ★ 7·30 to 1 a.m.

NEMS ENTERPRISES PRESENTS AT
NEW BRIGHTON TOWER ★ STARS IN YOUR EYES
FOR ONE NIGHT ONLY
FRI. JUNE 28

JET HARRIS and **TONY MEEHAN**
BILLY J. KRAMER with THE DAKOTAS
THE BIG THREE
FREDDY STARR AND THE MIDNIGHTERS
TOMMY QUICKLY AND THE CHALLENGERS
★ A BOB WOOLER PRODUCTION
PLUS FOUR MOSTS

TICKETS
6/- IN ADVANCE   7/- AT DOOR ON NIGHT
7·30-11·30

THE BIG THREE

ROCK POINT
TOWER GROUNDS, NEW BRIGHTON.

FULLY LICENSED.   NEW Brighton 6390

ENJOY YOURSELVES AT OUR
POPULAR CLUB NIGHTS

SAT.—MUSIC AND ENTERTAINMENT .... 7.30 — 10.30
SUN.—DANCING, TOMBOLA, etc. .... 8.00 — 11.15
WED.—AFTERNOON TOMBOLA. .... Eyes down 3.0 p.m.
THURS.—JIVE AND TWIST NIGHT .... 8.00 — 11.15
FRI.—BUFFET DANCE .... 8.00 — 11.15
★ PLEASE NOTE.—For our Tombola Sessions you must have been a member
for 24 hours and over 18 years of age before being allowed to play.
MEMBERSHIP FORMS NOW AVAILABLE.

NOW BOOKING FOR WEDDINGS, PARTIES, ETC.

The Beat Festival was held in New Brighton F.C Ground. Mr Bob Wooler was the host of the show and introduced some of the groups. Including The Searchers, Mersey Beats, Concords and Coasters. Held on the 14th May 1964. I attended the Festival with my mate Robert Bailey.

The top groups are being booked for New Brighton. Little Richard, The Animals, Brian Poole and the Tremelos, The Nashville Teens, Manfred Mann. Possible Elvis Presley. Maybe Dusty Springfield and the Dave Clarke Five. Specially chartered ferryboats will being the fans from the Liverpool side of the river.

Television cameras may relay the big programmed promotions planned at the Tower Ballroom by Mersey Sounds limited of Liverpool.

A spokesman for the promoters of what will be the most ambitious series of pop session yet held in the town Mr Peter Catchpoole told the News this week! The aim is to put New Brighton right on the forefront of the pop scene and to give fans in the North the chance of seeing the really big names.

Mr Sam Leach of Mersey sounds has drawn up of programme of shows by the leading Stars. He brought the Beatles and Gerry and the Pacemaker together on the same bill here two years ago. Now the plan is to stage beat shows of similar importance.

Next Friday August 28 Manfred Mann set the series going. A ferryboat with a local group The Outkasts on board will bring hundreds of fans

NEW BRIGHTON TOWER COMPANY
LIMITED

DIRECTORS
(Chairman)
L. DAVIES, M.Inst., E.E.
(Managing)
W. B. GREGSON
J. S. ELLISON, M.A., F.C.A.
J. E. BINSTOCK

The TOWER
NEW BRIGHTON

Telephone
Central Office
NEW BRIGHTON

20th July, 1964.

LD/IK.

Mr. Bob Wooller,
The Cavern,
Liverpool.

Dear Mr. Wooller,

Further to your call at my office with the representative of "Raelbrook Shirts", I confirm the date of Monday, 10th August, for the "Rolling Stones". The price of the hire for the hall is £135 for the night, plus 6d. a head over 2,000; you are supplying 12 stewards over and above the four main stewards which are included in the price.

I trust that you will write and confirm this booking by return and wish you every success in your venture. If there is any further information we can give you, we shall be delighted.

Yours faithfully,

L. Davies
Managing Director

over from Liverpool. Boats will be chartered for all the coming shows
Tower visitors already booked are Long John Baldry the Merseybeats
The Denezins, Brian Poole and the Tremelos (on October 2) Little Richard
(October 16th), The Mojos (November 6th),George Fame and the Blue
Flames (November 20th) The Animals (November 27th) and the Nashville
Teens (December 4th)
Negotiations are in hand for the possible return of the Rolling Stones ,
and visits sometime in the future from Elvis Presley, Dusty Springfield
and the Dave Clarke Five.
Wallasey News August 1964

The PLAYGROUND OF THE NORTH
Enjoy Yourself!

TOWER NEW BRIGHTON

NEW BRIGHTON TOWER CO. LTD.

AMUSEMENT PARK NOW OPEN
until 10.30 nightly — Bright Lights Galore !

TO-NIGHT !   TO-NIGHT !   TO-NIGHT !
New Brighton Tower Co. Ltd. presents All Star International

WRESTLING

Doors open 7 p.m.   Commence 8 p.m.

SENSATIONAL HEAVYWEIGHT CONTEST

KING KONG
Hollywood, U.S.A. The monster of the mat, 6' 6", 23 stone
VERSUS

HENRI DOLAN
FRANCE. Sensational mat star.

| PAT CURRY (CANADA) Tough Lumberjack | STOKER BROOKS (ROYAL NAVY) |
| IRON MAN McKENZIE (SCOTLAND) | PEDRO THE GIPSY (No Fixed Abode) |

TERRIFIC MAIN SUPPORTING CONTEST

PIET VON SLABBERT
Light/heavyweight Champion of South Africa.
VERSUS

DUNCAN McROBERT
Scotland. A certain future champion.

BODY 3/6 & 5/-.   RINGSIDE 7/6
Book at the Tower Booking Office ('phone 6175) and at Ushers Travel
Service, Wallasey and Birkenhead.
YOU MAY NOW OBTAIN A PERMANENT BOOKING ON YOUR
FAVOURITE RINGSIDE SEAT.—Contact the Manager for details.

TOWER BALLROOM
PRESENTS

ROLLING STONES
Plus 12 Top Groups in Rael Brook Contest Final on Monday
August 10th, 1964. 7.30 to 11.30 p.m. TICKETS 8/6

TOWER AMUSEMENTS   ●   BALLROOM
CATERING AND LICENSING BARS FOR YOUR ENJOYMENT.
YOU'RE ALWAYS WELCOME AT THE TOWER.

The PLAYGROUND OF THE NORTH
Enjoy Yourself!

TOWER NEW BRIGHTON

Follow the Stars of Sport and Entertainment
to the Tower !
TO-NIGHT IS SATURDAY'S ALL-STAR

WRESTLING

Doors open 7 p.m.   Commence 8 p.m.

Sensational Top-of-the-Bill Heavyweight Contest

THE GHOUL
? ? ? The diabolical masked monster of the mat
VERSUS

TARZAN OF AFRICA
From the jungles of the great Continent.

| RAY CHARLES (WALES) | CON MURPHY (IRELAND) |
| FRED WOOLLEY (MANCHESTER) | DENNIS TRACEY (LIVERPOOL) |

International Main Supporting Contest

BILLY GRAHAM
The Popular Scottish Boy
VERSUS

ROBERT SHERRY
(Bolton)

REFEREE — DANNY FLYNN
Licensed by the Wrestling Board of Control

BODY 3/6 & 5/-.   RINGSIDE 7/6
Book at the Tower Booking Office ('phone 6175) and at Ushers Travel
Service, Wallasey and Birkenhead.
YOU MAY NOW OBTAIN A PERMANENT BOOKING ON YOUR
FAVOURITE RINGSIDE SEAT.—Contact the Manager for details.

FRIDAY, AUGUST 28th, 1964.
DO-WAH-DIDDY-DIDDY (Current No. 1 on the Charts)
5 4 3 2 1

MANFRED MANN
Plus
ROCKIN' HENRY AND THE HAYSEEDS
DANNY SEYTON AND THE SABERS
and Seven Top Recording Groups.
7.30 to 10 p.m.   Late Transport.

ADVANCE TICKETS 7/6
Available from The Tower and usual Agencies
PRESENTED BY MERSEY SOUNDS LTD.
The Management reserve the right to refuse admission.
PERSONS WEARING JEANS WILL NOT BE ADMITTED.

TOWER AMUSEMENTS   ●   BALLROOM
CATERING AND LICENSING BARS FOR YOUR ENJOYMENT.
YOU'RE ALWAYS WELCOME AT THE TOWER

What a night it was – Sea of screamers in Tower Ballroom
The 4,000 plus frenzied teenagers were kept in check by thirty-odd beefy "bouncers" who rescued the fainting and protected the long-haired beat group. Valerie Evans the Wallasey News Reporter who attended the gig remarked that "Not once during the 40 minute performance did she hear the voice of Mike Jaggar or the strains of the lead guitar.
The compare and promoter was Bob Wooler of the Cavern Club and on the bill were twelve finalists in a beat contest. Elaborate plans had been made to get the Rolling Stones into the venue by means of a chair-lift, but it was finally decided that it would be too dangerous if fans got out of hand. The crowd got out of hand anyway. The group waited five hours to go on stage before Jimmy Savile, one of the contest judges introduced the group to the delight of the fans. The first five minutes produced an avalanche of fainting girls. Then followed by various punch ups that keep the roving stewards busy pouncing into the sea of screamers. A first-aid room in one of the Tower's soft drinks bars was manned by St. Johns Ambulance volunteers. Bill Wyman records in his autobiography "Fighting began when we struck up the music; it was Mods versus Rockers, with the Tower Ballroom's spotlights picking out the fights! The battle lasted forty-five minutes and fifty youths had been ejected from the hall, two with knives. We had orders to carry on as normal, and so we played a set of fourteen songs and there was no arrests."
The group also had time to visit two fans who had been involved in an accident on there way to see the Stones in concert. With a visit to Ward E3 at Clatterbridge Hospital, Julia Skelly and Jean Farnie had a surprise visit from the group.
Ref: Wallasey News August 15th 1964 & "Stone Alone" Bill Wyman

1964

The Programme of Wrestling started on the 19th May 1964 with the top of the bill Lord Bertie Topham, the wrestling millionaire with his Valet Captain Smythe Smythe. The contest also featured Wild Angus Campbell the black-bearded Highlander over 6ft and 20 stone. With ringside seats going for 7/6.

At the same time the Tower Grounds carried advertisements "Come to the Fair" Open Weekends until 10:30 p.m. with three licensed bars, and all the thrills of the rides.

In the Tower Ballroom "Top of the Pop Parade" was a regular feature each Monday and Thursday, admission 2/-

A new feature on Friday the 12th of June the "Swingin Beat Parade". Followed on July 17th by the Tower presents "Mersey Sounds No 1" featuring: The Nightwalkers,The Tributes, The Executioners, and the Kiwis with compare Gerry Norton.

Then "Its a Mod Ball" on the 24th July. The next special being on July 31st "Rock Around the Clock" featuring Vince Earl and the Talismen, The Nightwalkers, The Elements and Subterranes.

With Wrestling starting King Kong (The Mask), Martin Robson. This was followed by "The Big Beat Show" featuring eight bands on Bank Holiday Monday.

Manfred Mann had been booked and was advertised to appear on the 28th August. along with seven top recording groups. Advance tickets cost 7/6, late transport had been laid on. The promoters Mersey Sounds Limited were expecting a large crowd, and with Do-Wah-Diddy-Diddy in the charts at No 1, and a late bar it was hoped to be a resounding success. Then the bomb shell, late on Thursday night just before the group was going to appear at the Tower. Following an examination by a London throat specialist of lead singer Paul Jones. The doctor found he was suffering from tonsillitis, and was told that he must not sing for several days. It meant a busy day for the organisers who were making arrangements for the amateur group "The Pretty Things" to deputise for Manfred Mann.

Over 4,000 tickets for the show had already been sold, those who were disappointed could have their money refunded. The group announced that after their American Tour, they would try and arrange another date, and the tickets will be valid.

Then on Friday the 18th of September New Age promotions presents for the first time on Merseyside "The P.J. Proby Show" with his backing group the Diamonds.

In September a new promotion each Wednesday "Record Sessions and Group Auditions".

On Friday 30th October Alexis Korner's with Blues Inc. plus the Outcasts, The Rockefellas and the Adds, admission 6/-

The Mandred Mann Show came to town on Friday the 6th November, tickets 7/6 or pay at the door 8/6, advertised as an original N.B. Tower/Malcolm Rose Production.

The Big Pop Show on the 4th December with seven groups appearing. With a mass rally planned for the 30th November in protest at the proposed closure of New Brighton Ferry.

Wrestling continued up the 19h December with "The Tower Challenge Cup" the Welterweight Championship of Great Britain.

Party Night in the Rock Point Castle on Boxing Night and Carnival Night at New Year.

P.J Proby on the Tower

The Band would play a couple of numbers to get the crowd excited then following on from the James Brown type intro Proby would come out, and he was really good on stage. The band were the best with people like Big Jim Sullivan, Bobby Graham he was a famous Jimmy Page type session genius who played [drums] on many a hit record – a tremendous sounding band.

Now the idea was that Proby would never ever finish the set. He never wanted to do the full 90 minutes. So if a riot developed it was a fast exit to the nearest hostelry. With provocative gestures and other tricks like splitting his trousers the girls would rush the stage. This all led to bans on Proby appearances by the ABC theatre chain, its TV namesake and BBC TV. He had a clause in his contracts which said, "If you can't control the crowd then you have to pay us in full and let us go home." They nearly always had a riot every time they played.

It got to the point where the musicians were cracking up, because by the fourth chorus of the second song they always had a riot. Girls later threw underwear at the band, but in beginning it was the group that threw the underwear at the girls! All to create mayhem and it worked.

Proby had UK top 20 hits in 1964 and 1965 including "Hold Me" (UK No.3), "Together" (UK No.8, featuring guitarists Big Jim Sullivan and Jimmy Page), "Somewhere" (UK No.6) and "Maria" (UK No.8); the latter two songs were both lifted from the musical West Side Story.

Ref: Kim Fowley: Sins & Secrets of the Silver Sixties, https://en.wikipedia.org

P. J. PROBY is coming . . . .
Friday, 18th September, at
TOWER BALLROOM   New Brighton

P. J. PROBY
THE DIAMONDS
DAVID JOHN and the MOOD
THE SUNLINERS

Tickets 8/6
from NEMS and RUSHWORTHS
9/6 on the night

7-30 — 11-30 p.m.
Late transport applied for
A NEW AGE Promotion

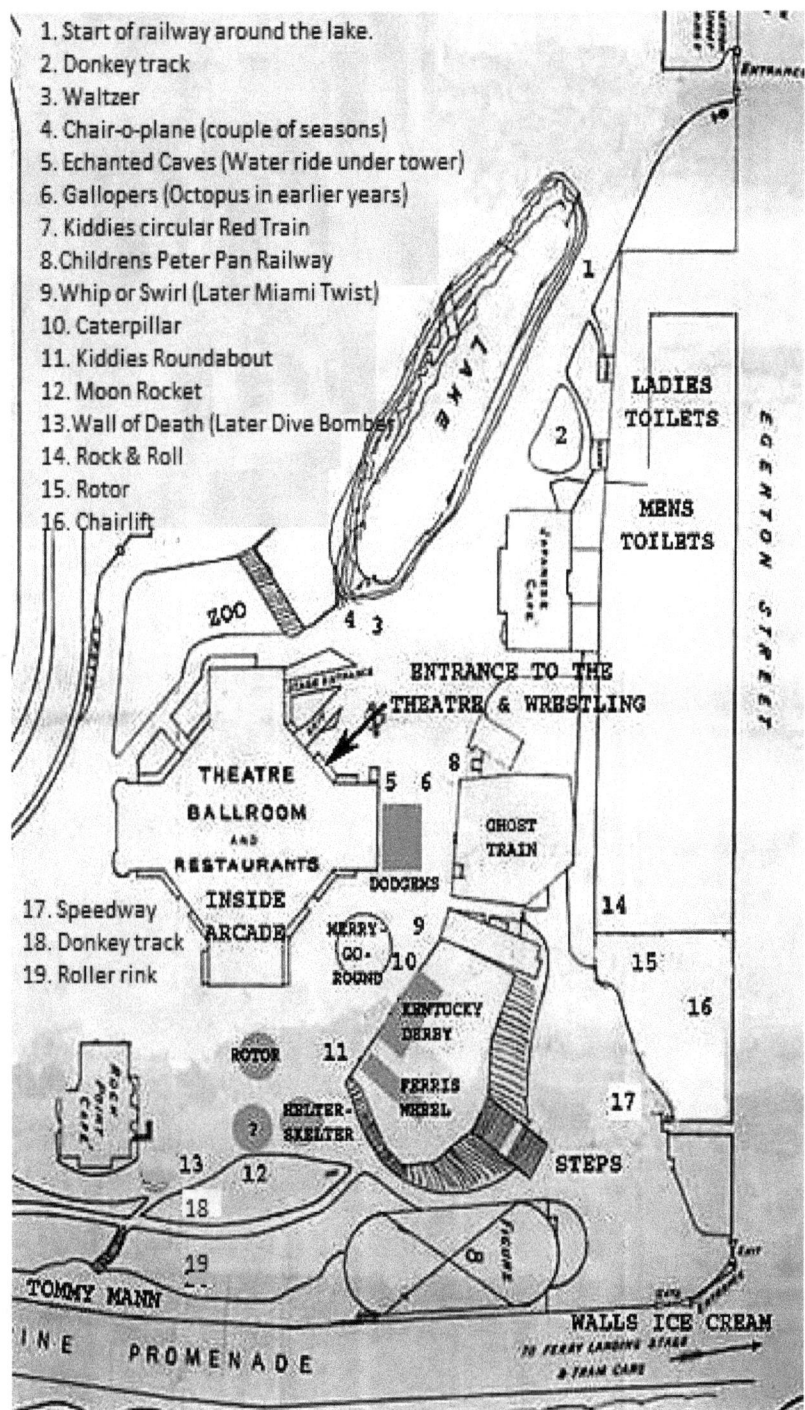

1. Start of railway around the lake.
2. Donkey track
3. Waltzer
4. Chair-o-plane (couple of seasons)
5. Echanted Caves (Water ride under tower)
6. Gallopers (Octopus in earlier years)
7. Kiddies circular Red Train
8. Childrens Peter Pan Railway
9. Whip or Swirl (Later Miami Twist)
10. Caterpillar
11. Kiddies Roundabout
12. Moon Rocket
13. Wall of Death (Later Dive Bomber)
14. Rock & Roll
15. Rotor
16. Chairlift

17. Speedway
18. Donkey track
19. Roller rink

LAKE

LADIES TOILETS

MENS TOILETS

EGERTON STREET

ENTRANCE

ZOO

ENTRANCE TO THE THEATRE & WRESTLING

THEATRE BALLROOM AND RESTAURANTS INSIDE ARCADE

DODGEMS

MERRY-GO-ROUND

GHOST TRAIN

ROTOR

HELTER-SKELTER

KENTUCKY DERBY

FERRIS WHEEL

STEPS

TOMMY MANN

PROMENADE

WALLS ICE CREAM

WAXWORKS AMUSEMENT

Tower bear mauls woman

Whilst visiting the Zoo in New Brighton Tower Grounds on Thursday evening, Miss Mary Gorman, aged 49, of St. Domingo Grove, Liverpool, had her arm mauled by a Himalayan bear.

It is thought she was attempting to feed the animal through the bars of its cage.

Miss Gorman was taken to Victoria Central Hospital, where yesterday her condition was described as "fairly comfortable".

305

Dare Devil Curly real name William Leyland was a high diver. It is
an extreme occupation, whereby the artist attempts to dive from
the greatest height into the shallowest depth of water. It is typically
associated with travelling circuses. Dare Devil Curley was a one man
show he appeared up and down the country defying the laws of nature.
Sometimes balancing on a chair and then tipping over backwards into
the tank. Other times the tank was set on fire. Diving from a height of
60-80 ft this was truly amazing, and crowds would gather to view the
spectacle. He learned his trade from the one legged diver who would
collect pennies from passengers who would toss them into the water at
New Brighton Pier. After so many dives his eye sight started to fail, and
he was even more dependant on his wife. While being interviewed at
New Brighton baths in 1964 by Granada television, he dived from the
top board to illustrate his prowess. In preparation for his return to New
Brighton Tower for the Whit Monday spectacular dive from a platform
80ft in the air into a 6ft wide tank of shallow water. The location being
the roller skating rink the authorities made him reduce the high to 60ft
because of the high wind. During this dive he fractured his scapula and
humorous and also hit his head. It was a little later that they discovered
vandals had thrown bricks and an old bicycle frame into the tank. William
was to die 6 months later from complications caused by his injuries, at the
young age of 52.

William diving off the top board at New Brighton baths, afterwards being
handed his white stick by his wife. He was totally blind during the later
part of his life. He had performed in all the major circuses including Billy
Smart, Bertram Mills and Copperfields.

Sensational!   Free Attraction!

DARE DEVIL CURLY

appearing at

Simon's Amusement Park
COUNCIL FIELD   .   LLANDUDNO

7 and 9 Monday to Friday

3, 7 and 9 Saturday

★

See his
Death-defying
Dive from an
80 foot tower
into five feet
of water

Sensational
Fire Dive
at evening
Performances

Wrestling continued but on a limited scale and only through the month of August. On the 27th August Manfred Mann was featured on the Tower, and was the final big name act to appear. To lower costs all the local advertisements had been reduced in size with only local groups appearing on the Saturday nights, the Thursday "Top of the parade" event had been cancelled.

This was the start of the demise of entertainment on the Tower.

With cheap overseas holidays advertised in the local papers, this was the beginning of the end.

The Rakers Return & Rockpoint featured throughout the year.

308

The fastest Kart Racing ever seen on the New Brighton Tower Stadium Track was recorded at the meeting on Bank Holiday, organised by the Chester motor Club when speeds of 80 m.p.h were reached.
Twice the lap record was broken early in the same race. A.K.Hesketh of Blackpool (26.9 seconds) was first to achieve a record, and then Roger Keele from Tring, did it in 26.5 seconds in the finish Hesketh beat Keele in a photo finish. Hesketh also won the principle 15-lap Broster Trophy event.
Wallasey News 12th June 1965
Following on from a letter from a Dalmorton Road resident protesting about the noise from kart-racing at New Brighton football club's ground. The chairman of Wallasey Council's Health Committee, writes to the Editor of the News this week :-
New Brighton A.F.C wish to obtain some income from the use of their large grounds in the summer months, and they let the area around the pitch to Chester Motor Club for Kart Racing on a few occasions each summer.
Three years ago to appease some of the residents in the neighbourhood, the Council effected an agreement with the kart-racing promoters to restrict their activities at the Tower to six half-days per annum (from 12 noon to 6am) and to fit efficient silencers to all machines taking part An official from the Health Dept. attends all meetings to see that this is adhered to......
Saturday June 12th 1965
A drivers comments:- An ex cycle track (location for the world cycling championships in the 20s!) with high concrete banked bends - 33 degrees at one end and 20 degrees at the other ! Pretty awesome to see and drive. Located at RAKERS FOOTBALL GROUND in Molyneux Drive.

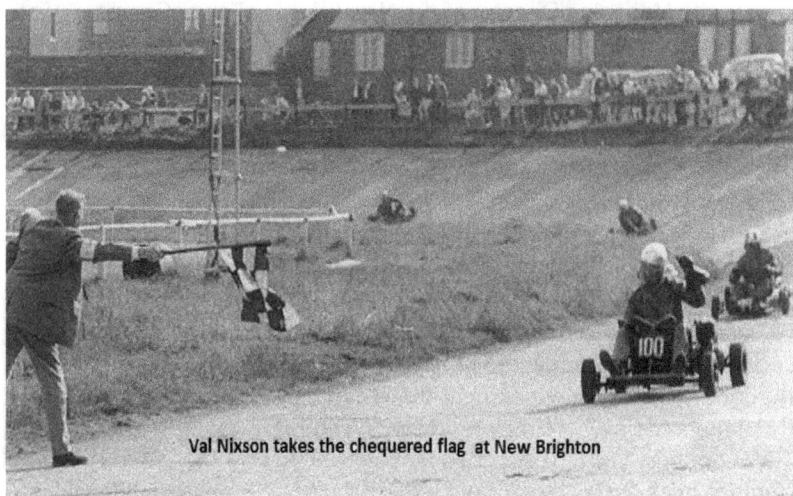

Val Nixson takes the chequered flag at New Brighton

The wheeling and dealing of the directors of the New Brighton Tower Company took on the form of smoke and mirrors. In late 1964 the New Brighton Tower Co. had acquired 50.1 per cent of the £100 company running the casino concern of the Victoria Sporting Club probably the most famous casino in the United Kingdom. After less than a year this shareholding was sold by New Brighton Tower for £212,500. The sale to "private parties" took on an air of mystery. The company took up 1,001 1s. shares in Victoria Sporting Club (out of a total of 2,000) . Since then the holding has multiplied 4,250 times. New Brighton Tower also placed £160,000 of loan stock into starting the venture, and this was in the process of being repaid. This together with a 50-50 interest with Mecca in the Golden Nugget, another gambling club.

All this was to come to a head, amid frequent uproar during the first meeting in 22 months of the New Brighton Tower Company, held in London on the 4th April 1966.One man was carried out of the hall still sitting in his chair, while another was threatened with removal. The chairman challenged two more men to sue him for slander for his remarks about a circular. The trouble centred on the sale by the company of the controlling interest in the Victoria Sporting Club. An accountant, who claimed he was holding about 750,000 shareholders' votes by proxy, warned that it might be necessary for the shareholders to ask the Board of Trade to appoint an inspector. Following on from the passing of accounts and the re-election of the chairman and two of the directors, the meeting ended in acrimony and dissatisfaction by many of the shareholders present.

Mr. Binstock a Solicitor and Director of the new Brighton Tower Company Limited. Master minded the next purchase/merger of Ardmore International Film Studios Limited. located in Bray, County Wicklow. Mr Davies, the Managing Director of the New Brighton Tower Company, was placed in control at the Studios, which triggered litigation by Mr Powell and Dr McNally and his associates. The position had been promised to Mr Powell. A Board meeting of the Directors on 20th March 1967 stated that the Plaintiff should be removed from being a Director but this Resolution was adjourned. In1967 under the ownership of Judah Binstock and George Wynberg the Victoria was sold to Norwich Enterprises, a group owned by a consortium of businessmen, including Binstock..

Mr Binstock, a former London solicitor, set himself up in Marbella in 1977. Two years before he left London, a Department of Trade inquiry into his companies stated that he and his colleagues "appeared to have given more thought to their own enrichment than to that of the shareholders whom they represent, "A report in The Economist in 1979 described Mr Binstock as a "fugitive financier".

Jadah Binstock

310

Part two of the saga begins in 1971 when an obscure Manx Company called Ardfern purchased the burnt out New Brighton Tower site for £96,000 and sold it to Northern Developments for £500,000.
Northern Developments a public company had withdrawn an earlier offer of £160,000. Ardfern's nominated director later told HM Inspectors that the Manx company was controlled by Harry Waterman of H. King & Co (Liverpool) Interestingly in the same year H King was a modestly profitable company running a bottling operation. The company was run by none other than Waterman, the baron of Liverpools clubland, with Mr Binstock in the background. His original connection with New Brighton Tower had been through the leasing of bars on the site.
The inspectors John Corbett and Robert Turnbull were clearly unhappy about Ardfern's highly profitable deal. But they had to rest with censuring Judah Binstock in absentia for feathering his own nest. Binstock had already resigned from New Brighton Tower in 1968.
He moved off into newer pastures and was ensconced as a Paris property speculator making money for the ICI Pension Fund (and himself) via another offshore company in Liechtenstein. The inspectors informed Binstock that he must return to Britain to answer questions.
All the rats had certainly jumped ship Harry Waterman had decided to live in Dublin. Harry Isaacson sold his control of the company to Binstock in 1972. With a web of offshore companies, property deals and a complex saga of nominee directors New Brighton Tower did not stand a chance, even before it burnt down. Wirral Borough council did eventually own part of the site 10.62 acres which went up for Auction in 1981.
Binstock has his official residence in Paris, where he went to live, but in the 70s and 80s his main business activities were in Marbella, he was reported to be one of the largest landowners in Marbella, successfully buying up rural land and persuading the town hall to reclassify it as land which can be built on.
Ref: The Sunday Times, 7th Dec. 1965, April 5th 1966, & 18th April 1976

New Brighton Tower Directors on the board of the Golden Nugget.
From left, Leslie Davis, George Wunberg and William B. Gregson.

Wrestling and all forms of entertainment ceased from the very start of the year. It was the being of the end for this magnificent Tower building. The council continued to try and decide the future of the resort.
A motion by Alderman Philip Banister that immediate action should be taken on the urgent problem of New Brighton with a view to its development primarily as a residential area, was unanimously rejected at a meeting of the Town Council on Tuesday.
Victoria Road was in an extremely bad state and was crying out for improvement with sixteen properties at present vacant and the old Trocadero cinema, which the council bought in 1963 at a cost of £12,000, is still boarded up.
The meeting was informed by Councillor Bill Wells, the Labour Leader, "that a fresh look was needed. New Brighton will never complete with Blackpool or Southport, and as for the pier it should have been pulled down years ago. He added that New Brighton could be the playground for the one and a half million people on Merseyside. There should be a fresh look at the resort with a meeting of boarding-houses and hotel keepers and traders to discuss its future".
Wallasey News 30th April 1966.
These problems are only compounded by local politics with various fractions on the council who wanted the resort to be residential, while others wanted a seaside resort. It was difficult for the typically high proportion of family owned businesses to adapt to the fast changes in the tourist trade. The future looked quite grim with no plan to move forward.
THE GHOST TRAIN & Fun House destroyed by fire.
On 17th September 1966 an explosion occurred in the Ghost Train which set fire to the structure and quickly spread to the Fun house. Mr Stanley Creighton the manager of the ghost train arrived and guided the firemen to the electric supply. The fire lasted until 10pm with the wood and plastic structure helping to produce clouds of black smoke. It took 30 firemen under the supervision of Mr Frank Fradley deputy chief fire officer to quell the blaze.

The purchase of the 22-acre site would probably be completed within the next six weeks, Mr John Duff, the 35 year old Irishman told the "Wallasey News" The £10 million scheme to transform New Brighton was still progressing. Anxiety about the future of the scheme grew this week after Mr Leon Davies, chairman of the company owning New Brighton Tower Company, said contracts for the sale of the site had been prepared, but not taken up. The purchase of the land for £125,000 was with our solicitors. A delay in the purchase of the New Brighton A.F.C. football ground has caused the club some financial embarrassment, but Mr Duff said this deal, too, would shortly be completed. The club was selling for a five figure fee. The plan was to turn the soccer ground into a sports stadium rivalling Wembley.

Mr Bill Baker the chairman, said this week that on the strength of the plan, they had engaged professional footballers this season when they could have managed, on their gates with amateurs.

As a result the club, with weekly takings at the gates of £15 and a playing bill of £100 a week, is losing £85 a week on players alone.

Wallasey News 25th October 1968

The beginning of the end for the Rakers came on the 29th January 1969 with the cancellation of the proposed 10 million scheme to transform New Brighton Tower grounds into a giant sports centre.

Ted Dutton had battled on to try and save the deal, but as reported in the Wallasey News "Some members of the board are beginning to lose faith in the whole thing," said secretary Mr Ted Dutton, "But I am very optimistic." Councillor Baker said the club was fighting for its very existence. "We intend to keep going and will honour our obligations to the player's contracts this season. But next season we will have a largely amateur side." Ted Dutton refuses to look on the black side. "There is room for a wonderful development here. If we get these things advanced there is every chance we will get into a higher grade of soccer. I have made application for re-election to the Football League every year since 1961.

Tower Football Ground refreshment Kiosk at the Banks end Bend

On Saturday 5 April 1969 The New Brighton Tower caught fire. The first
call received by the Fire Brigade was at 05:08. At around 8.30pm the
previous evening the manager and his staff had made a routine check on
the building and all was in order, they did not check the stage area.
The roof of the Tower had been open to the public on Friday 4th April
for the first time that year with access by means of the Chair Lift. Police
Constable Edward Brimage was on patrol in Victoria Road when he
smelt smoke and set about looking for the fire, by the time he reached
Egerton Street, they discovered that the Tower was on fire in the stage
area of the West tower. It was then that the Fire Brigade was called.
The first appliance to arrive was driven by Dave Liston, followed by a
second, driven by Walter Peach, the Station Officer. He went to look at
the situation and he then climbed the steps to the car park at the higher
ground. No sooner had he reached the top when a huge section of the
building collapsed. Had he stayed down he would have been killed by the
fall of bricks.
By this time large bellows of smoke was pouring out of the windows. The
Officer in charge radioed for more assistance and additional pumps. The
Assistant Division Officer now arrived and took command at 5.20pm with
20 pumps. The collapse of the wall exposed the Ballroom and theatre to
the open air and allowing the flames to reach other parts of the building.
Things were made worse by the fact that the Tower Boating Lake had
been drained and the Fire Brigade had difficulty in obtaining water from
the Marine Lake some distance away.
The Chief Fire Officer, Mr E.E Buschenfeld, was now in command and
through the lack of water it was obvious that the Ballroom would be
a complete loss. Parts of the roof began to fall in. There were some
compressed oxygen and dissolved acetylene cylinders in the offices
of the fifth floor which were exposed but luckily no one was hurt with
the two blasts. Firemen had managed to get into the building from the
south but the staircases were impassable due to the debris from the
collapsed roof. The Liverpool Fire Brigade were called in with their heavy
water unit. Soon after seven o'clock there were 25 Pumps at the scene
and further relays were deployed. Further sections of the roof fell in and
relief crews were called in from Birkenhead, Liverpool, Cheshire County
and Lancashire County with over 150 Firemen being at the scene with 20
pumps and four Turntable Ladders.
Mr Buschenfeld sent for five more Pumps and surveying the situation and
the seriousness of the fire, thinking of his men, he shouted to them, "I
don't want any heroes, let it burn." Lives of Firemen were more important
than bricks and mortar. The promenade was one mass of Hoes-Pipes and
by 9 o'clock fresh crews had to take over, but within half an hour the fire
was under control with crews working on. It was the end of the Tower. In
all 119 Firemen and 37 Officers had fought the fire.

The equipment had used up to 313 gallons of petrol, 71 gallons of diesel fuel and 36 pints of engine fuel. By Wednesday the heap of rubble inside had cooled down sufficiently for an examination to be made but this was not possible on account of the condition of the remaining walls. Some of the blackened red- bricks started to crumble and steps were taken to have it taken down as soon as possible. Mr Leon Davies, the managing director of the New Brighton Tower, was concerned that youngsters who could venture near the site could be injured or killed. Soon after the fire, demolition work started for fear of children who might try to play in the area with the fairground and grounds being closed off. What caused the fire is uncertain. The Deputy Fire Chief, Mr Alec Dean, said: "A thorough investigation of the cause of this fire was made by the fire department in consultation with the Home Office forensic department and the Cheshire County Police. After the elimination of the possible causes it seems that this fire was due to unauthorised entry to the building and subsequent vandalism or accident in the ignition of the stage area caused by vandals. There could have been no other cause. Electricity and gas had been cut off so these were eliminated and there was no other source. There was a lack of direct evidence to pinpoint vandals but it is the only source that was left ."

The Police had investigated the matter but nobody would come forward with direct evidence. The official verdict was 'Unknown'. By the Wednesday, the heap of rubble had cooled down sufficiently but on account of the dangerous condition of the ruined walls

Ref: Helmets, Handcuffs and Hoses by Noel E Smith.

315

Death rattle of a 140ft giant

The last remaining sentinel of the once majestic Tower was reduced to a heap at 4:33 p.m yesterday. An Enormous crashing sound which produced dust-clouds that mushroomed into the sky marked the end of the East Tower. It had was battered into submission by a tug of war with a giant 30-ton crane. Demolition experts Spencer Brothers of Chester spent hours trying to rip through the lift shaft, with steel hawsers which snapped on several occasions, when the steel finally gave way the 140ft tower crumbled in a shower of bricks and dust. The massive demolition operation has been going on for 12 weeks. Three of the eight solid steel supports remain. The base of one of the supports weights over 13 tons on its own. Each support is embedded in up to 20ft of concrete, it takes hours of burning with oxyacetylene equipment.

Spencer Brothers will be able to sell about a thousand tons of steel as well as their demolition fee. Most of the rubble will be used as an in fill to level off the site and fill in the large cellars. It was estimated by Mr Tommy Harford from Saltney the foreman that another six weeks will be needed to complete the job, before any development can take place.

Liverpool Echo Tuesday 30th September 1969

The above photograph shows the remains of the Zoo after the fire. The side of the tower building had a "zoo" which cost 2/- to enter and was just the length of the tower building with animals in cages. It was a short walk past a few bedraggled specimens. The first two cages were made from a crashed Crosville bus, followed by a couple of railway carriages thrown in for good measure. Previously the "zoo" had been on higher ground between the tower and the quarry right on the edge of the grounds. Close to the entrance was a open pen with wolves in it.

Wallasey Liberals want to turn New Brighton Tower Grounds into a place like Hoylake but the businessmen who own hotels and restaurants have a dream of it being like Blackpool.

Dr David Caldwell, the Liberal leader of the Council, suggested that the development of a first class group of dwellings on the site would restore prosperity to New Brighton.

Hurdy-gurdy fish and chip riffraff, as Dr Caldwell calls them, might be discouraged from visiting this tonier New Brighton.

Wallasey News 14th March 1969.

The resort's decline had been catastrophic, with the changes in tidal flow of the Mersey removing the sandy beach, public awareness of the pollution on the increase. A marked decline in day-trippers, and the advent of cheap foreign travel all made New Brighton a less attractive destination. The resort had become a political football between the rival groups on the local council, with Conservative policies encouraging the holiday industry and the Liberal advocacy of a switch to residential development. And labour oscillating between the two camps seeking political brownie points. Schemes came and went just like the tide that removed the sand from the resort. Photographs below show Victoria Road in a dismal condition all boarded up.

319

The circuit consisted of a concrete oval cycle track, with banked bends and a football pitch in the centre. The cycle track was eventually converted into the stock car track, by shortening the oval at the waterfront end. A new banked bend was constructed, and the crescent-shaped space between the old and new bends became the pit area.

The first race meeting was held on Easter Monday 12th April 1971.

Steve Parry http://newbrightonstockcars.co.uk/

Banger Racing

Bangers are production cars that are raced with modifications. With safety doors and roll over bars added, and windscreens removed etc. The racing is full contact and very aggressive with 'wrecking' usually playing a more important role than 'racing'. Top drivers included 513 Stan Woods, 508 Alan Latham, 516 Ian Fraser and Invaders team captain Tommy Upton.

From the Left in dark jacket Mr Tom Morris, Mayor of Wallasey. Alan Smith, Gerry Marsden, Deric Parr (Driver)

Hot Rods

Hot Rods where vehicles based on road cars, and deliberate contact was not allowed. With a purpose built space frame chassis and a Kevlar body which mimics a production car. With highly tuned cars such as Minis and Ford Anglias. Top drivers included Roger Tattersall and Pete Helms.

Stock Car

These were purpose-built single-seaters, similar to BRISCA F2 cars. They were originally up to 1200cc, but from the start of the 1975 season this increased to 1500cc. Top drivers included 310 Pat Byrne, 113 Alan Smith, and 204 Geoff Buck.

STOCK CAR ROAR FINALLY DIES

Stock car racing will never return to New Brighton's Tower Stadium. Wirral Borough Council took possession a few days ago and told Trackstar Promotions it had no right to use the stadium for stock car racing again. Trackstar immediately cancelled the meeting planned for this Sunday a spokesman said his company was planning to negotiate with the council for permission to continue until the end of the season in September. Trackstar director. Mr. Mick Smith, said he was still looking for a site on the Wirral as well as a new stadium at Crewe which would be ready for use this autumn. "I do not want to disappoint all the people who are looking forward to the season at New Brighton. Since the council has not finally made up its mind about the Tower site it might consider the 13,000 letters of support for the races it has received and allow stock car meetings to continue until at least the end of the season." he said.

Director of legal and Administrative Services, Mr Gerald Chappell, said the stadium was bought with vacant possession and that the vendor ended the stock car racing agreement on the last day of March.

"We have asked Trackstar Promotions to identify the equipment which they own in the stadium and we will then give them facilities to remove it." he said.

Although New Brighton Football and Athletic Club have no plans to take the stock car racing to their new ground in Hoylake, Mr Smith said he would be glad to keep the sport on the Wirral where he said there was a great deal of support for the stock cars.

Liverpool Echo March 1976

STOCK CAR RACING

*CHAMPION DRIVERS

*THRILLS AND SPILLS!!

COME & SEE

THIS MEETING
Hot-Rod Racing,
Banger Team Racing
Ladies Racing
SUNDAY, 22nd
JUNE, 3 p.m.

NEW BRIGHTON A.F.C. STADIUM

Tower Grounds, Molyneux Drive. Adults 60p,
Children 25p. Licensed Bars & Refreshments.

plus BANGER RACING

NEW BRIGHTON
TOWER GROUNDS, MOLINEUX DRIVE

AUTO SPEED-WEEKEND

STOCK CAR
HOT ROD « «
2½ Hours of
Thrills & Spills
Family
Entertainment
AND BANGER
RACING

SUNDAY   MONDAY
MAY 26TH & 27TH AT 3 P.M.

RACING FORTNIGHTLY
COVERED   CAR PARKING
ACCOMODATION REFRESHMENTS

auto RACING 5
Micky Pittman
5
with
TRACKSTAR

NEW BRIGHTON meeting no 3
& HINCKLEY meeting no 2
Sunday March 28th 1976 3pm
STOCK CARS - HOT RODS - BANGERS
Official Programme 10 pence

The spectator area at Bank Bend showing Louise's house.

Small stand at Dalmorton Straight. Below Starter's rostrum

Top photograph a view across
Bank Bend, with the houses
of Dalmorton Road in the
background.
Middle photo taken from
Dalmorton, to the left of the stand
are the remains of the clubhouse.
Bottom photograph: The Turnstiles
at the Molyneux Drive end.
Photographs curtsey of Martin G.
Bartley

The Rakers Return went through most of the 60's and early 70's unscathed. Changing its name to the Tower Restaurant and Theatre Club, it hoped to complete with Joe Barnes "The Haig" and the "Melody Inn". With many well known stars treading the boards, it proved a popular venue. Until the inevitable happened and it burnt down, like so many other places of entertainment in New Brighton.

DON'T FAIL TO VISIT . . .

TOWER RESTAURANT & THEATRE **CLUB**

NEW BRIGHTON A.F.C. FOOTBALL GROUND

Telephones 051-639 5982/7839

- All Star Cabaret from 8-30 p.m.
- Dancing to Tower Trio
- Excellent Cuisine
- Luxurious Tiered Seating
- Open Sunday, Wednesday, Thursday, Friday, Saturday — 2 a.m. licence
- Membership available
- Unlimited Car Parking space
- The ideal setting for all types of parties, receptions and functions
- Wirral's most luxurious Theatre Club

Miss Kathy Kirby appears the Winter Season at Star Cabaret

"RAKERS' RETURN"

New Brighton A.F.C.'s New Luxury Members' Social Club.

Tower Ground, Molyneux Drive. NEW 5982.

★ Live Entertainment at its very best ★

To-night — **SATURDAY SOCIAL** With JOE AND GEORGE, Top Musical Act.

To-morrow — **SUNDAY SOCIAL** With BOB OSTIN, T.V.'s Comedy Novelty Act.

EVERY WEDNESDAY — TOMBOLA, at 8 p.m.

Every Friday — SOCIAL Featuring Bert Johnston on the Hammond Organ.

TO-MORROW 12 noon—2 p.m. and every Sunday— "SHOP WINDOW" SHOW featuring top local artistes.   Members' Free.

Book now for our next big Variety Social featuring Irish Radio and Television star HARRY BAILEY AND FULL SUPPORTING BILL Tuesday, 13th October.   TICKETS 4-

FOOTBALL MATCHES TO-DAY — RAKERS RES. v. NEWTON.   Kick-off 3 p.m.

"RAKERS' RETURN"

New Brighton A.F.C's Luxury Social Club

TOWER FOOTBALL GROUND, NEW 5982.

Under new jurisdiction. Full Variety Shows Saturdays and Sundays. TONIGHT—MOUNT ROYAL GROUP.

SATURDAY, August 16th— JUNIOR JOHNSON (dynamic comedy, vocal/guitar) CURLEY CARTER (top Blackpool comedian). ANNE VIVIAN (glamorous vocal entertainer).

SUNDAY, August 17th— MICKY MORAN (outstanding musical/vocalist) The girl to keep you alive. SID DOOLEY (guitar / vocalist). FRIDAY, August 22nd—DRAG NIGHT.

FORTHCOMING ATTRACTIONS Friday, August 29th—THE MOREOK SHOW. First time on Merseyside. Fabulous entertainment. Friday, September 5th—BACHELOR NIGHT. Friday, September 12th—THE KRIS CHRIGHTEN PROFESSIONAL OLDE TYME MUSIC HALL CAST. FOOTBALL—NEW BRIGHTON v. SANDBACH R.—E.O. 3.0 p.m.

"RAKERS RETURN"

NEW BRIGHTON A.F.C.'s LUXURY SOCIAL CLUB

TOWER FOOTBALL GROUND MOLYNEUX DRIVE — NEW BRIGHTON

Tel. NEW BRIGHTON 5982

LIVE ENTERTAINMENT AT IT'S VERY BEST !

LICENSED MEMBERS' BAR AND SNACK BAR NIGHTLY SOCIALS WITH STAR VARIETY ARTISTES Also TOMBOLA

MAGNIFICENT HAMMOND THEATRE ORGAN

Accommodation for 400 Large Free Car Park Alongside Club

SPECIAL ARRANGEMENTS FOR COACH PARTIES AND VISITING CLUBS

Sun Terrace and Children's Playground

TEMPORARY MEMBERSHIP AVAILABLE TO HOLIDAY VISITORS Write Secretary for details

Please mention this Guide when replying to Advertisers

325

VAIN BID TO SAVE CLUB
Firemen battled for almost two hours to save the Tower Theatre Club at New Brighton football ground. Almost all the timber-built club including the cabaret room, was destroyed. The buildings and fixtures were valued at over £22,000. First indication of a fire was when the club's burglar alarm went off in the Police Station at Manor Road. Poor water supplies hampered fireman, with a total of eight pumps being brought in to set up a water relay. A Fire Brigade spokesman said the cause of the fire was not known. *Liverpool Echo 10th September 1974*

CLUB CLAIM REJECTED
The directors report submitted to the annual meeting of the company on the 11th September. The accounts which cover the year ending last December 31, show a loss of assets worth £32,865 due to the fire, which totally destroyed the Theatre Club, and its entire contents. An insurance claim made by New Brighton Football and Athletic Club has been repudiated by the company's insurers.

TOWER THEATRE CLUB
MOLYNEAUX DRI
NEW BRIGHTON
Telephone No: 051-639 598

Forthcoming attraction

The Bobby Vee Show

on Tuesday, 25th September
Tickets available 85p

ENTERTAINMENT EVERY
THURSDAY - DISCO
RIDAY - DISCO & TOP GROUP
SATURDAY - CABARET
SUNDAY - DISCO

Excellent selection of 1st Class F
Available Every Night

"RAKERS' RETURN"
New Brighton A.F.C's Luxury Social Club
TOWER FOOTBALL GROUND. NEW 5982
Under new jurisdiction. Full Variety Shows Saturdays and Sundays
TONIGHT—
BACHELOR NIGHT (Five Exotic Dancers, plus comedian)
Saturday, 9th August—
JACK PEARSON (comedy/vocal)
BILL and MADGE (musical/vocal/comedy)
GEOFF DAVIES (dynamic vocal entertainer)
Sunday, 10th August—
BEACH PEBBLES (musical / vocal group)
Next Drag Night—Friday, 22nd August.

"RAKERS' RETURN"
(MEMBERS' CLUB)
MOLYNEUX DRIVE • NEW BRIGHTON 5982 • TOWER
NIGHTS YOU WILL REMEMBER
CHICK MURRAY & MADIE
TOMBOLA at 8 p.m.

TOWER GROUND DECAY
Following on from a call for action from Wirral Leisure Services
Committee, who want to stop the decay at the tower grounds and get
the place tidied up. Wirral's Director of Engineering, Mr Frank Rodgett,
said estimates for a tidying up operation were being prepared for
consideration by the council. This would include site clearance and
grassing of large areas, also temporary car parking.
Wallasey News 31st May 1974
Wirral World reported in September 1974 that the £15,000 clean-up
which began in July after the land had been bought earlier in the year by
the former Wallasey County, was now complete.
The 16 acre site begins at the promenade then rises to the site where the
Tower stood and rises again to a car park which is still in reasonable order.
Scrapped Cars and heaps of rubbish have been removed. The miniature
railway tunnel was filled with the dumped remains of stock cars. Now
it will become a shaded detour from the promenade. In its heyday, the
arcades beneath the arches of the cycle track used to ring with the sound
of slot machines. Now the arches are bricked up to provide useful storage
space for plant owned by the Recreation Services Department of Wirral
Metropolitan Borough.
Vandalism is still a problem in the area on one occasion a contractor's
tractor was taken on a joyride round the site and used to batter down the
wooden frames which filled the arches beneath the cycle track. The one
main asset of the site is the existence of established trees. Householders
in the area have been invited to fill in a questionnaire and express their
views to decide the future of the place.

Photograph taken of the cleared site.

It took over 13 years and hours of debate by the Council to decide on the fate of the Tower grounds The only good thing to come out of this débâcle was the council actually took notice of the local residents. The result River View Park, which has a community football pitch, swing and skate park . In 1997 Wirral Council made an unsuccessful bid for Millennium funding to build a new tower in New Brighton. How things go around in circles.

Strong opposition to the terms of the proposed sale of the Tower Grounds to Wirral Council is expected to be made today at an extraordinary general meeting of the New Brighton Association Football Club.

The meeting has been called to confirm the sale of the football ground and stadium to the council for £115,000, but a minority shareholding group feels the move could ultimately lead to the disintegration of the football club.

The minority group, Rakers Shareholders Association in a statement yesterday said it did not oppose the sale of the ground to the council in principle, but under the terms of the present agreements there was no provision for football to continue at New Brighton.

"In fact the Leader of the council, Councillor Malcolm Thornton, has said he wants the tower grounds site developed for new housing," said Mr Ken Almond, chairman of the Rakers Shareholders Association. Mr Almond, a former. chairman of New Brighton football Club, said the shareholders association was formed in 1972, to look after the interests of the football club following changes in the structure of the company.

"The same directors who are now attempting to sell the ground to Wirral Council were able in 1972 by using their majority vote. to prevent a contract by the previous board for the sale of the land to the former Wallasey Corporation.

"However the contract we negotiated with Wallasey was totally different in that, although the price was the same, the football was guaranteed together with many side benefits," said Mr Almond.

18 March 1976 Wallasey News

Wirral Council run the risk of having to settle for a second-best housing development on New Brighton Tower ground, if the land was put up for immediate sale, the director of development Mr Roger Shaw has warned. Wirral Council own more than 22 acres at the Tower grounds and adjoining Tower Stadium and about 16 acres are earmarked for housing. Mr Shaw points out in a special report that the present condition of the site could be a disincentive to potential developers particularly those likely to provide a high standard of design......

14th July 1977 Wallasey News

Vandals shatter a dream

by Geoff Barnes

DREAMS of a Wembley of the north super stadium at New Brighton have disintegrated into an ugly nightmare.

And now Councillor Bill Wells, the man who envisaged the showpiece arena at New Brighton Tower Stadium, has called for a probe into the way the area has been neglected since New Brighton FC left to take over new headquarters at Hoylake almost 12 months ago.

Councillor Wells had a vision of a prestige development capable of staging top international events in soccer, athletics and cycling.

The reality is a scene of devastation. Security fencing has been broken down, holes punched through walls, turnstiles demolished, and buildings shattered beyond recognition. Debris is strewn everywhere.

Councillor Wells, former leader of Wallasey Council, which initiated a local authority takeover of the Tower Stadium, said: "If Labour was still in control, this project would be well on its way to completion.

"It was a great opportunity wasted. There is an urgent need for a Wembley of the north, and here we had the scope to create just that.

"With the current economic state of the country, and the political climate on Merseyside, the scheme is obviously a non-starter. But the matter of the existing state of the stadium is something which needs serious investigation.

"I intend to find out why Wirral Council allowed a perfectly good sports ground like this to go to ruin."

New Brighton FC director Mr Ben Usher said: "It's a jungle now —the ground has been given no thought by the local authority.

"We knew that if we didn't have a watchman there, night and day, it would be vandalised.

"There were a lot of local amateur football teams after the stadium and it could have been let out to help the ratepayers; and the authority could have had £150 a week if stock car racing had been allowed to continue."

Stadium plan could mean jobs

A land reclamation scheme for New Brighton's tower grounds and stadium could bring a 100 per cent Government grant and a few more jobs to the area, Wirral Policy and Resources Committee has heard.

The council is to ask Merseyside County Council through its derelict land team to draw up a preliminary scheme for the site.

Coun. Bill Wells (Lab) paid tribute to the work done so far by Wirral's officers on possible future uses for the site, and said a derelict land scheme could well bring extra jobs for unskilled labour.

GRANT

In a report to the committee Director of Development Mr. Roger Shaw said such a scheme could take up to two years to prepare and carry out.

A Government grant of up to 100 per cent would enable landscaping to take place on the open areas of the site, so the housing land could be developed immediately the scheme was finished.

The committee decided to await the county team's preliminary report on reclaiming the land before agreeing on a method of developing or disposing of the site.

Keep Tower private says planning chief

Fears over Tower site

£10 million plan for Tower is still on

'Sell site' campaign fails

No council homes on Tower site

Council dwellings should not be allowed on New Brighton's plum Tower Grounds redevelopment site, according to Wirral Council's planning chief.

Only prestigious private units should be built there, and this would help lead to the rejuvenation of New Brighton as a high class residential area, claims Coun. Ken Jackson (Cons), chairman of Wirral's Planning and Development Committee.

Describing the Tower site as "unquestionably" the best in Wirral for housing development, Coun. Jackson said the houses built there must be "something special". His views go against the official council plans for the site, which when drafted two years ago called for mixed development—both municipal housing and private dwellings — on the site.

Firms' tender for prime homes site

Labour councillors launched a storm of protest over the sale of the prestigious Tower Grounds in New Brighton. The prime 10 acre site has been bought by Barratt Developments for an estimated ¼ million from Wirral Council.

But that figure was described as "disgraceful" by labour spokesman Coun. Jim Edwards, who claimed the site was worth a lot more….

But the leader of Wirral's Tories, Coun. David Fletcher, defended the deal. He said council officers were satisfied that the offer was a good one.

The land had been up for sale for the last two years, but had failed to reach its reserve price at public auctions.

Barratt's plans are to build more than 100 houses or bungalows on the former funfair and football ground off Molyneux Drive., with construction starting in September.

9th July 1982 Wallasey News

WALLASEY MP Mrs. Lynda Chalker has stepped into the heated controversy surrounding the future of New Brighton's Tower Ground boating lake.

After visiting members of Tower Action Group recently, Mrs. Chalker told TAG secretary Martin Hovden: "I cannot state any final decision until many more facts are available, but I am conscious of the competing needs and particularly the wishes of children who have enjoyed playing football on the drained boating lake this summer."

Mrs. Chalker pointed out the site was presently being used without council permission and that this was "a situation which had to be rectified as soon as possible."

She also said it was very important that the council weighed up the need for new housing and the income which they might get from the sale of part of the land for a housing development.

Mrs. Chalker added she would inquire further into details of the County and Borough Council's intentions for the plans and would discuss with the chairman of planning, Coun. J. Roberts, what sort of facility could be made available for young people in the New Brighton area.

330

A Tower of Cards
LAND SPECULATION?
New Brighton Tower at the time the tallest building in Britain was to be, during its short life, a catalyst for shady dealings and profiteering by a number of unscrupulous individuals. With a foundation of profiteering and with numerous political interferences from local politicians, with even the church getting involved it stood very little chance over time of being a success, unlike its neighbour situated on the Fylde coast at Blackpool. Both had gone through recessions, wars and fickle tourist trends with only one survivor. This is my interpretation of the financial arrangements that helped create one of the most expensive seaside amusements ever erected, and at the same time a marvel of engineering. The Victorians built wildly ambitious projects and this must surely rank in the top ten of their achievements, it only took 22 months to build. From the construction of the tower which started in November 1896 to the opening of the Tower in August 1898, with the grounds open earlier in Whit of the same year.

In the first instance New Brighton Tower was probably driven by property speculation. In the consideration of its potential financial performance, which contrasted with the sale price of the site? it has to be concluded that making a fast buck was the original plan. Mr Robert P. Houston being the mastermind behind the financial arrangements.

Numerous scams and shaky investment schemes had operated in seaside resorts like New Brighton. The boom in pleasure pier building during the 1860's and 1870's had spawned several disasters, and New Brighton had an Aquarium, Baths and Hotel Co., founded in 1872 to develop the site next to the Palace. The company collapsed in 1879 with almost total losses. Other disasters' followed with the New Brighton Graydon Wheel and Tower Company Ltd going the same way.

In 1830, a Liverpool merchant, James Atherton, purchased 170 acres of land at Rock Point. His aim was to develop it as a desirable residential and watering place for the gentry, in a similar way to Brighton, one of the most elegant seaside resorts of that Regency period – hence "New Brighton". Substantial development began soon afterwards, and housing began to spread up the hillside overlooking the estuary. The more desirable sites fronting the Mersey had been developed with large mansions in grounds such as "Rock Point", "West Bank", the "Woodlands" and "Kirkdale Cottage". In front of these, in place of the present promenade, were rocky areas and sands.

A syndicate was formed in 1895, to purchase the West Bank estate and resell it to a new company promoted to develop a Tower and Grounds. Mr R.P Houston, a Liverpool shipowner and Unionist M.P was a leading figure in both investments.

The Tower Estates Syndicate purchased West Bank for £30,000 and employed a firm of Manchester architects Maxwell & Turk to design a new development on the site. This was to include a Tower, 561 feet tall with a theatre and ballroom, an Athletic Ground and water chute in extensive grounds. The newly floated New Brighton Tower & Recreation Company where to have the benefit of the scheme and the purchase price was some £50,000, plus £125,000 worth of shares in the new company. The glowing prospectus outlined in detail a massive profitability, based on anticipated receipts of at least £84,000 p.a.. The massive profits from the sale of the land could be justified by the access to even greater profits secured by the package of land and redevelopment plans. Receipts were actually to amount to only £15,000 in 1908. The Tower Company succeeded in attracting shares from numerous small investors who were destined never to receive any dividends. The prospectus had been a mirage issued by Mr Houston, with the Company controlled by his business partners.

The construction of the Promenade in front of the Tower site, had been agreed by the local Council and construction began in October 1896. It is difficult to establish the motives of the Tower developers the promoters sought not only to gain from the original land sale, but to profit from the anticipated income and capital growth from the completed development. This was a pipe dream. Mr Houston the major shareholder, did not sit on the Board of Directors and thus did not draw fees, at times he was forced to prop up the ailing company with loans upon which he was, from time to time, forced to waive interest payments. The Tower itself was to have very mixed financial fortunes.

It was a scheme fraught with massive risks, the enormity of the structure, the maintenance, administration and ability to keep the public coming through the doors all had to be successful. Many reasons for the financial failure of the Tower have been put forward. Anticipated improvements in the ferry service, were not to materialise. The Promenades were not finished in time for the opening. Drink licences were heavily restricted at the Tower, while the policy of the local authority in Wallasey was aimed at the limitation of visitors to favour the promotion of seaside amusements rather than the attraction of a mass audience.

At first the Tower featured musical entertainment aimed partly at middle class visitors, which was to be rapidly replaced by the more popular seaside and music hall type amusements.

The Blackpool Tower, and Belle Vue operations provided a model for the entertainment complex to be formed at New Brighton.

Entertainments there combined the attractions of the circus, ballroom, music hall, theatre and seaside curiosities such as an "Olde English Village" and a menagerie, boating Lakes and the themed oriental exhibits.

The New Brighton Tower Company was incorporated in July 1896 with a secretary, R H Davy, previously secretary to the Blackpool Tower company.

The first entertainment manager was John Hollingshead, who had considerable experience in the growing field of Victorian entertainment. He was aged 70 when he took the post but by all accounts was full of energy. Formerly a journalist, in the 1860's, he had been manager of the Gaiety theatre in The Strand for 25 years.

The company were anxious to make money so the incomplete Tower was opened on Whit Monday 7th June 1897 with various attractions organised by Hollingshead. These included an open air dancing platform, for up to 1000 dancers, for which he obtained a licence in June. This overlooked a lake which was served by a water chute which opened in June. A zoo and menagerie were provided by a showman from Hamburg. Two seasonal attractions were imported James Hardy the modern Blondin, a Canadian tightrope walker, who specialised in cooking pancakes on the high wire, had walked across Niagara Falls in 1894; he was to return in 1898. With no safety net and hundreds of spectators below, it was truly a Health and Safety nightmare. Our tightrope artist was to met an untimely death at the Alexandra Palace the following year.

A "Burmese Village", comprising a troupe of entertainers from North Burma, arrived complete with bamboo huts, en route for Berlin. The Empire, then being formally consolidated, was a source of fascination. The rapid growth of professional football in the late Victorian period and amateur sports such as cycling and running, created a new opportunity. The Tower management had been trying to devise entertainment for the winter months. The New Brighton Football Club was founded in October 1896, and soon signed an international goalkeeper from Derby County; it was affiliated to the Football Association in 1897. A Cycling and Athletic Association was formed in March 1897, and amateur races, including several national championships, were organised at the Athletic Grounds Musical entertainment was provided by Granville Bantock, his music was influenced by folk song of the Hebrides and the works of Richard Wagner. Many of his works have an "exotic" element. It all started with a military band outdoors, then in 1898 he set up a dance band indoors. This became an orchestra which was to be host to such composer/conductors as Berlioz and Edward Elgar. This middle class attraction was complemented by the opening of the basement theatre, ballroom and rooftop promenade gardens.

During 1898 the "Algerian Restaurant" opened, with catering supplied by J Lyons & Co, their first venture outside London. The ageing Hollingshead was replaced by a new manager with many years experience with the Cambrian Railway Co. The Tower Theatre opened with a performance twice daily. To bring in the crowds advertising was placed as far away as Nottingham, Stafford and Leeds. A "Olde English Fairground" opened, featuring such oddities as babies in incubators and a "veriscope" of the Corbett/Fitzsimmons boxing match, among stalls let to various vendors.

The formal opening of the Tower Grounds at Whit 1898 was preceded by the construction of a Himalayan switchback railway, imported from the Brussels Exhibition.

The 25 acre site needed a private police force of 15 to supervise visitors. This impressive investment ran into difficulties with its suppliers and contractors. A range of cases was to be brought against the Tower Company, including ones by both the architects and the lift contractor. A jeweller and the Veriscope Company all sued for loss of trade due to misrepresentation. Failure to complete works at the promised time delayed the Towers opening date.

J Lyons made staggering losses on its involvement in the catering trade, and in 1898 withdrew at the end of the season. In 1900 Bantock the musical genius departed to become Principal of the Midland Institute School of Music, the orchestra reverted back to a dance band format. Massive changes in the character of entertainments followed, with the quality much reduced. The failure of the Towers profitability only helped to underline the fragility of the operation. With falling gate receipts and an increase in the grounds rent the New Brighton Tower Football Club was unable to continue. Closure was the only option as far as the businessmen were concerned. On the 4th September 1901 it was announced that the club would be unable to fulfil their fixtures. With the national sporting bureaucracy still undecided about the suitability of the athletic track, the future for the complex looked bleak.

A large investment took place in 1905 with the introduction of "Figure of Eight" Roller Coaster, near to the entrance to create a funfair atmosphere and hopefully some decent profits.

Another dismal report to shareholders was presented by the board for Christmas 1906, with a reported loss of £9,400 during the past year. The best thing the shareholders can do was to put the company into liquidation.

For the start of the 1908 season, and to try and turn around the Towers fortunes, Mr J. Calvin Brown was appointed to lead the management team. Mr Brown was the Walt Disney of the time with interests in various amusement parks, and a knowledge of what the public wanted. The Athletic grounds was put to use with the Cummins-Brown Wild West Show, but due to inclement weather this too became a financial disappointment. The Himalaya Railway was replaced with a scenic railway. The start of the First World War did little to help the Towers prosperity with thousands of men overseas. Mr George H. Appleton presiding at the ordinary general meeting informed the shareholders that after the outbreak of war the receipts fell off considerably and consequently the improvement shown last year had not been maintained.

In 1916 more troubles with the renewal of liquor licences at the Wallasey Sessions being refused for the Algerian Café. With the Ministry of

Munitions taking an interest in the mild steel on display in the form of the Tower, it was unsurprisingly another disappointing year. It was decided in January 1919 that due to lack of maintenance and the cost to maintain the structure that the Tower would have to come down. In the same month the inevitable happened reaching the end of their patience "The British and South American Steam Navigation Company" who happen to have advanced on the Tower mortgage twice as much as the property was worth, appeared before the Lancashire Chancery to secure the immediate foreclosure absolute against them.

The Tower Athletic Grounds had a new lease of life with the World Cycling championships held in July 1922. The construction of a boating lake in place of an ornamental lake , and some hot summers helped to transform the Towers Fortunes.

The Wallasey Act of 1927 allowed the local authority to expand its business interests, with a promenade extension, marine lake and a massive open air swimming pool, and the purchase of the pier for a sum of £12,000, this only helped to reinforce the idea that the Council was serious in developing the resort. It was during this period that The Tower Company had hoped to sell the business to the Wallasey Council, but the deal fell through. The start of the Second World War put a stop to the councils plans so the great boulevard from Seacombe to West Kirby was put on hold, Blackpool with its golden mile had nothing to fear.

The next decade was to have a devastating effect not only on the people but all the businesses alike the Great Depression had spread its ugly tentacles through out the land. The Tower company instructed Edmund Kirby and Sons surveyors to appeal the rate assessments. The board of the directors of The Tower Company offered the business up for sale to the council, the Finance and General Purpose committee made an offer of £80,000 which was rejected by the board.

Speedway was introduced for the first time, and to reduce maintenance the spires on the roof of the Tower were removed. New attractions and the Wall of Death came to the Tower Grounds. A move to reintroduce wrestling was warmly welcomed by the public and well supported.

After the Second World War, the popularity of New Brighton as a seaside resort declined dramatically.

New Brighton in the 60's was very different to the way it is now. The ferry brought an endless stream of day trippers from Liverpool to arrive at the Pier. It was a real seaside resort up there with Blackpool and Southport. Thousands of people from all over the country took a coach to visit the resort whilst some people actually came for their holidays! With a big outdoor fairground, as well as the Indoor Palace, plus numerous amusement arcades scattered along the promenade and up Victoria Road. New Brighton baths, the biggest outdoor pool in Europe. With the best pop groups in the world appearing on the Tower, and numerous live entertainment venues in pubs, and clubs. The New Brighton 'Tower' Ballroom was re-discovered and reinvigorated by Sam Leach the visionary Liverpool promoter whose one of many brainwaves it was to present 'Operation Big Beat' at 'The Tower'.

A five-plus-hours, multi-group extravaganza—'Rocking to Merseyside's Top 5 Groups'—The Beatles—Rory Storm and The Hurricanes—Gerry & The Pacemakers—The Remo Four—and Kingsize Taylor and The Dominoes.

The Tower Ballroom continued in use until 1965 by which time the entertainment had ground to a halt, and the Tower and grounds started to deteriorate and finally in 1969 it was destroyed by a fire.

The dealings of Mr Jadah Binstock and friends managed to squeeze the last drop of blood from the enterprise.

A planned Disneyland-type venture costing £400m called "Ocean Dome" followed by another ambitious "Pleasure Island" scheme in the 1960s complete with artificial lagoon and £10m development funding for the former Tower Grounds site also sank without trace.

But at long last the resort has a future and this is without the Tower and open air baths, we can only think of what if!

Appendices

337

Capt. W. H. Molyneaux, R.N., died at Rock Point, New Brighton, Liverpool. on July 26, in his 72nd year. He entered the Navy, Nov. 23, 1811, as a 1st class volunteer on board the Daphne, fitting for the Baltic, where he served at the siege of Danzig, and came into boat contact with the enemy's privateers off the island of Rupen. On board the Tagus, he assisted, on Jan. 6, ensuing, while cruising among the Cape de Verde Islands, in company with the Niger, at the capture of the French 40 gun frigate Cérès; and he subsequently, on visiting the Pacific fell in with Pitcairn's Island, the first time it had been touched at since settled on by the mutineers of the Bounty. In the early part 1816 he served in the Magicienne, East Indies, and the Minden. He was promoted, on his return home, to the rank of Lieutenant, and was subsequently appointed to the Jupiter, to the Niemen, three years on the Halifax station, as first to the Minden, whence he returned to England. and was paid off in August 1837; and, in a similar capacity to the Alfred. He was advanced to his present rank on the 23rd of the month last mentioned, and has since been on half-pay. His Captain's commission was dated July 21, 1858.

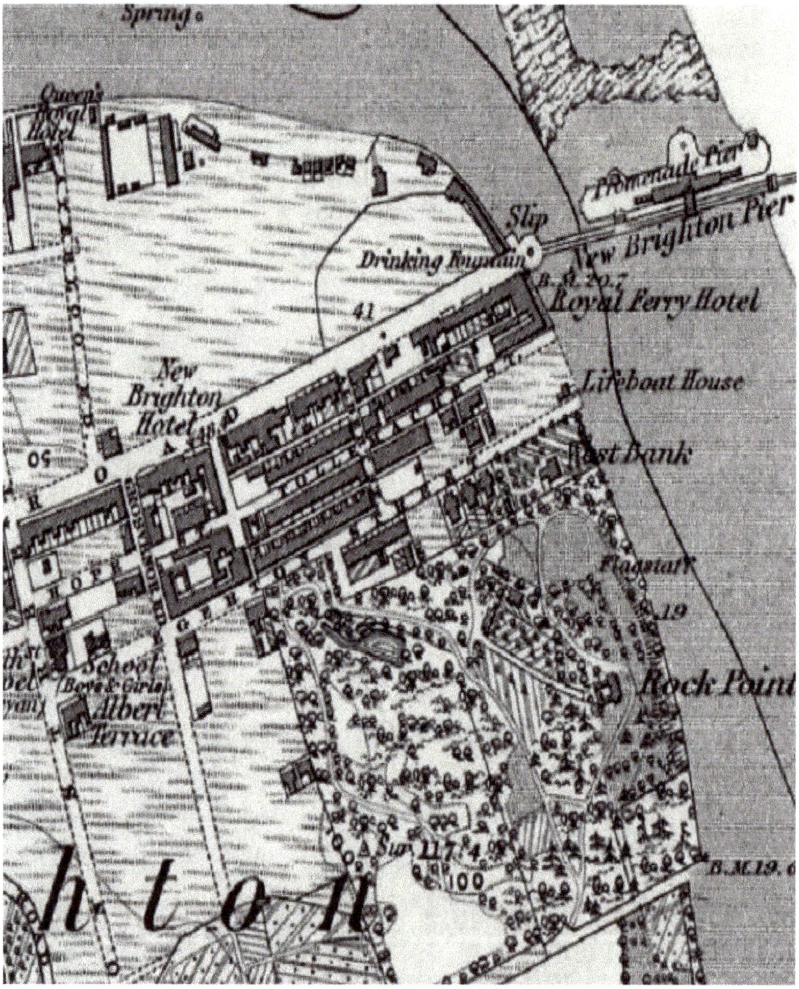

Molyneaux Estate - Rock Point 1882

338

THE NEW BRIGHTON TOWER and RECREATION COMPANY, Limited

Share Capital ………………….. £300,000.

Divided into 300,000 Shares of £1 each, of which 175,000 are 6 percent. Cumulative Preference Shares, which rank in priority to the Ordinary Shares both as to capital and dividend (as per Memorandum of Association annexed), and 125,000 Ordinary Shares, which are all taken by the vendors in part payment.

ISSUE of 175,000 SIX per CENT. CUMULATIVE PREFERENCE SHARES OF £1 each. Payable – 2s6d. on Application, 2s61 on Allotment, and the balance in calls of not exceeding 5s. per share at intervals of not less than two months.
By the articles of association, the Directors are empowered to issue up to £125,000 in debentures or debenture stock. It is not expected that more than £100,000 will be required and the Directors have obtained a reasonable offer to guarantee the subscription of this amount as required.

DIRECTOR
Philip H. Chambers, Esq., D.L., J.P., 2, Titbebarn-street, Liverpool, and Dee Fords, Chester.
Wilfred F. Anderton, Esq., J.P. (Director of the Blackpool Tower Company Limited Haighton, near Preston.
Ralph T. Newbold, Esq. (Director of the Manchester, Sheffield, and Lincolnshire Railway Company), 17, Water-street, Liverpool, and Ledsham-hall, Cheshire.
Domingo de Ybarrando, Esq., Tower-chambers, Liverpool.

CONSULTING ENGINEER.
Sir Benjamin Baker, C.S., ex-President of the Institution of Civil Engineers, Westminster.

ARCHITECTS.
Messra, Maxwell and Tuke, 41, Corporation-street, Manchester.

SOLICITORS.
Messra, Simpson, North, Harley, and Birkett, I, Water-street, Liverpool.

AUDITORS.
Messra, Harmond Banner and Son, Chartered Accountants, 24, North Johm-street, Liverpool.

339

BROKERS.
Messra, Henrey E. Hassell and Son, Queen Insurance-buildings, Liverpool;
Messra. Mareland and Chew, Leinster-chambers, St. Ann's-square,
Manchester; J. Clark Sharp, jun., Esq., Mansfield-chambers, St. Ann's
square, Manchester; Messra H. Bazelt Jones and Sons, Carzon-house-
chambers, Preston: Messra, Walter Park-hurst and Co., 59 Old Broad-street,
and Stock Exchange, London, E.C.

BANKERS.
Bank of Liverpool, Limited, and Branches, and their London Agents,
Messra. Glyn, Millis, Currie, and Co., 67, Lombard-street, E.C.; Manchester
and Liverpool District Banking Company, Limited. Liverpool, Manchester
and Branches; North and South Wales Bank, Limited, Liverpool and
Branches.

PROSPECTUS
     This Company has been formed to purchase the picturesque
freehold estate known as the Rock Point Estate, consisting of over 20
acres of beautifully-wooden land, situated at New Brighton, on the
Cheshire side of the river Mersey, opposite to the City and Docks of
Liverpool. It is intended to erect on a portion of the estate a tower of
550 ft. high, with circus, assembly hall, winter garden, promenade and
bazaar, restaurants, and refreshment rooms, and to lay out the remaining
portion of the property with cycle track, football, recreation and pleasure
grounds, suitable to the entertainment and tastes of all classes of the
public.
     The estate occupies the finest available site in the
neighbourhood of Liverpool, possessing great natural beauties, and
commanding views of town, decks, river, sea and country which are
unique. It is close to the ferry landing-pier, and a short distance from the
railway station; it faces the river; with an extensive river frontage, abutting
on the proposed promenade between New Brighton and Egremont,
part of which is already completed. The remainder is authorized to be
completed by an Act of Parliament passed this season
     The tower to be constructed will be higher and of more
elegant design than that erected at Blackpool, the Company owning
which has shown the most satisfactory commercial results, the present
market price of its Preference Shares (although neither cumulative
nor preferential as to capital) being about 50 percent premium. The
Blackpool Tower has no land other than the area covered by the tower
buildings, and none of the outdoor attractions which this Company will
possess, nor does it command the view of so many objects of interest.
The New Brighton Tower will possess many improvements upon that at
Blackpool and the buildings will be more commodious.

The tower will be furnished with four elevators of the most recent design capable of conveying about 2,000 people an hour to the top, from which there will be magnificent views of the River Mersey, the River Dee, the Irish Sea, the Welsh mountains, and other objects of interest. The buildings round the base of the tower will include, as stated above, a circus, interior promenade and bazaar, restaurants and refreshment rooms. The circus will accommodate nearly 3,000 persons, and will, by means of hydraulic arrangements, be convertible into a water show. Above the circus will be a large assembly hall for dancing, concerts, and other entertainments. The assembly hall will send 2,700 persons, with balcony accommodation for 500 more. Over the hall will be a large winter garden, lounge, and the elevator hall.

Active operations have been commenced, and the laying out of the football ground and cycle track is being pushed forward, and will, at an early date, be completed and produce income for the Company. The grounds, restaurants, dining rooms, lodges, stands, and other buildings, with the exception of the tower and main buildings, should be ready for the public by the next spring season, and the Architects estimate that the tower and other main buildings will be completely finished and ready for the following spring. It is proposed to erect covered-approaches from the entrances to the tower buildings.

The well-known Architects, Messrs, Maxwell and Tuke, of Manchester, who designed and superintended the construction of the Blackpool Tower, have been engaged for the past eleven months upon the designs, drawings, specification, and quantities, and in order to insure the best possible construction, the completed plans of the tower and buildings have been submitted to the eminent authority Sir Benjamin Baker, C.E., who reports as follows: -

To the Directors of the New Brighton Tower Estates Syndicate.

Gentlemen. – I have had the detail drawings and calculations for the above work under consideration, and have been able to arrive as sufficiently accurate results to give my opinion with perfect confidence as to the stability of the proposed tower.

Generally I may state that I have found the work well and ably designed, both as regards calculated strength and practical details. The modifications I have considered advisable to introduce are matters of detail, the nature of which has been indicated on the drawing by your engineer under my personal supervision, and the necessary calculations and revised detail drawings of the these parts will, I assume to carefully prepared by him and be submitted to me if thought desirable.

I have satisfied myself that the bracing bars and other parts of the structure are sufficient to ensure the complete stability of the tower during the most violent storms which can ever prevail in the country, and that the door arrangements, when modified as suggested by me, will also be satisfactory, having regard to the limitations imposed by the architectural requirements of the tower. – Yours faithfully,

(Signed)

BENJAMIN BAKER.

In addition to the attractions of extensive football grounds and cycle track, with grand stands, large cafes with open terraces and bandstands, the remaining portion of the estate will be laid out as pleasure grounds and gardens, with a picturesque lake. It is further proposed to build a large sunk aquarium on a novel principle, to be excavated out of the red sandstone rook. A large annual income is expected to be derived from the football ground, as it will be one of the best and most convenient for the densely-populated districts in the North of England.

It is surprising that there being no large open-air place of amusement in the neighborhood of Liverpool, the splendid position of New Brighton, as the mouth of the River Mersey, commanding a full view of the estuary, with the fleets of ocean-going steamers and sailing vessels passing as every side, its bracing sea breezes, and surrounding scenery, has not already secured for the public the advantages which this Company is about to provide.

New Brighton is in direct communication both by railway and ferry with Liverpool, and by railway with all the populous centres in Lancashire, Yorkshire Cheshire, Wales, Staffordshire, and the adjoining countries. Within an easy railway journey of New Brighton there is a population of over 10,000,000 which is looked to for patronage and support. During the summer months large numbers of excursionists and others from the manufacturing districts visits Liverpool and New Brighton, and with the attraction of the New Brighton Tower and grounds, it is expected that the number of visitors from the outlying districts will be greatly increased.

The number of passengers carried by the Wallasey Ferries to and from their three piers, exclusive of season ticket holders, in the year 1884-95 was 10,092,054. New Brighton is at present without any special feature of attraction beyond its position as a seaside resort year 129,814 passengers passed through the turnstiles to or from the New Brighton ferry steamers in one day during the holiday season. This is exclusive of those going by railway and road.

The Directors are assured, and they believe that the following is a very reasonable estimate of the revenue which this Company may expect:

342

RECEIPTS.	£	s	d	£	s	d
Admission to grounds, musical promenade, aquarium, & e.. say, 2,000,000 at 6d. (it is proposed that is, be charged on certain days)	50,000	0	0			
Admission to ascend tower, say, 500,000 at 6d	12,500	0	0			
Admission to circus, say, 300,000, at 6d...... (This is the price for the cheapest seats)	7,500	0	0			
Profits from football matches, concerts,	5,000	0	0			
Profits from sale of refreshments, rend from stalls and bazaar in buildings, automatic machines, and advertising,	9,190	0	0			
				£84,190	**0**	**0**
EXPENDITURE.						
Wages of staff	7,000	0	0			
Lighting	2,000	0	0			
Bands	5,000	0	0			
Artistes	10,000	0	0			
Office expenses	2,000	0	0			
Rates, taxes, insurance, Directors' fees, and other expenses	6,000	0	0			
				£32,000	**0**	**0**
Balance profit				**£51,160**	**0**	**0**

The total expenditure of the Blackpool Tower Company (exclusive of cost of liquor) for the year ending September, 1895, as shown by the balance-sheet, was £27,452 15a. 2s., and this sum includes chief rent, an item from which this Company is free.

	£51,160
4 ½ percent, interest on £125,000 Debentures fit all issued)	£5,625
6 percent, interest on £175,000 Preference Shares	£10,500
10 percent, interest on £125,000 Ordinary Shares	£12,500
	£29,625
Leaving margin for sinking fund, reserve fund, depreciation, etc.	
	£22,535

The owners of the ferries, the Wallasey Urban Council, being so impressed with the importance and advantages of this undertaking, at a recent meeting of the Ferry Committee resolved to grant to the Syndicate a return of 25 percent, of the ferry tools on persons visiting the grounds, from the date of opening the same to the public, and accordingly their clerk and solicitor addressed the letter as follows to a representative of the Syndicate: -

W. Danger, Clerk and Solicitors.
Wallasey Urban District Council.
Egremont, Cheshire, Clerk's Office, June 13th, 1896.

Dear Sir, - Your letter of the 10th inst. asking that in the event of the New Brighton Tower scheme being carried out a return might be made in the ferry tolls in respect of those persons using the grounds, was had before the last meeting of the Ferry Committee, when I was directed to inform you that when the grounds are opened the committee will be prepared to make you a return of 25 percent. – Yours truly,

(Signed)   W. DANGER.

On the estimated number of 2,000,000 persons this will amount to £12,500 per annum (the ferry toll being 3d. each way); this, added to the £22,535 margin shown above, would increase that amount to £35,535. As shown by the above estimates, there is, therefore, £47,535 of revenue behind the Preference Shares.

The freehold estate has been valued by the well-known experts, Mr. William Thomson, of Liverpool, and Messrs, William Wilson and Sons, of Manchester, who report as follows: -

To the Directors of the Tower Estate Syndicate.
Particulars and Valuation of the Rock Point Estate, New Brighton, in the County of Chester.

344

We have surveyed this freehold estate, which is situated near to the New Brighton Pier, and in close proximity to the New Brighton Railway. It contains 20 ¼ statute acres of land, exclusive of foreshore, and has an extensive frontage to the River Mersey. It is well wooded and beautifully undulating in character.

Owing to its position, views, and rock formation it is peculiarly adapted for the erection of an "Eiffel Tower", and the nature of the ground lends itself admirable to other purposes of amusement and recreation.

The foundation will be very inexpensive on account of the red sandstone rock being close to the surface on that portion of the estate where the tower is to be erected.

We have examined the plans which have been prepared by Messra, Maxwell and Tuke, Architects, of Manchester, for the purposes above mentioned, and are of opinion that when the grounds are laid out and the building completed, it will be a successful and very profitable undertaking.

We understand from the architects that the sum of £215,000 is to spent on the erection of the tower and other buildings to complete the undertaking.

Taking into consideration the site, position, natural formation, and advantages of the ground, and the money that will be saved in the foundations and excavations, we estimate the value of the land at the sum of one hundred thousand pounds (say, £100,000).

(Signed)   WILLIAM WILSON and SONS
             29 Fountain-street,
             Manchester.

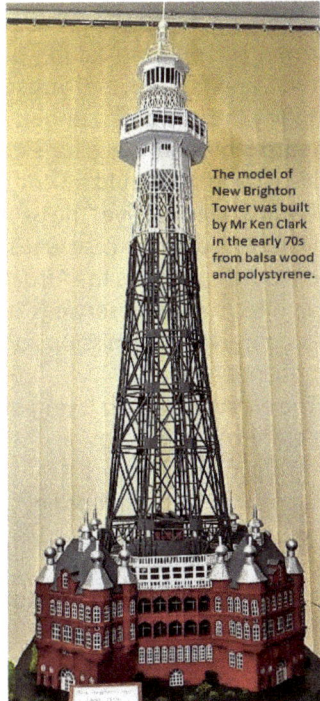

The model of New Brighton Tower was built by Mr Ken Clark in the early 70s from balsa wood and polystyrene.

(Signed)   WM. THOMSON.
             Values and Property
             Auctioneer.
             7, Cook-street, Liverpool.

8th July, 1896.

345

Maxwell and Tuke was an architectural practice in Northwest England, founded in 1857 by James Maxwell.

In 1895 the Tower Estates Syndicate commissioned Maxwell and Tuke to design New Brighton Tower. The company had previously designed the Blackpool Tower buildings and Southport Winter Gardens.

Walter Beer, began working on the plans in July 1895 a gifted engineer he was given the task of the design born on the 4th June, 1874, an old boy of merchant Taylor's School. From 1897 until his untimely death he practised as a consulting engineer at Westminster, and was engaged in the design and construction of electric railways, tramways, waterworks and other undertakings. He lost his life in the "Persia," which was sunk in the Mediterranean on the 30th December, 1915.

In 1893, and before the completion of Blackpool Tower the following year, both senior partners Maxwell and Tuck had died. The practice was then continued by Frank Maxwell as sole principal with the help of some of his assistants, and he continued to use the title of Maxwell and Tuke.

The architect first submitted plans to the Council in June 1896. The New Brighton Company was incorporated in July 1896 with a secretary, R H Davy, who had been previously the secretary to the Blackpool Tower Company.

In 1899 the architect sued the New Brighton Tower Company for money due for services, with damages for wrongful dismissal, and a curious statement of facts was made. The Tower Company proposed to build a tower and other structures on its land, at a cost of two hundred and fifty thousand pounds, and engaged Maxwell and Tuck as architect, agreeing to pay them five per cent on the cost of the work executed, with a reasonable allowance for extra labour in altering the plans, and agreeing also that they should be entitled, in addition to the five per cent from the Company, to receive "the usual architect's commission from contractors." Unfortunately, the case was settled out of court so we have no means of knowing what is the "usual" compensation paid by the contractors to architects for their services, it appears the company thought its architect had received commissions or remuneration to which the agreement did not entitle him.

The excavations and laying of the foundations for the tower were contracted to William Clapham of Stockport. Clapham's first major project was to make the roof garden on the Blackpool Tower in 1894. The primary contractor for the tower was Andrew Handyside and Company, based in Derby.

Wrought Iron vs Steel
The Bessemer process first patented in 1855, had been a slow learning curve for the pioneers of the process, and it was not until 1879 that Gilchrist and Thomas resolved the problems of phosphorous in the iron ore. The railway industry pioneered the early use of steel; this material was not suitable for structural uses although stronger it was insufficiently ductile. The Forth Bridge was the first major structure in Britain to be constructed of steel; and was completed in 1890.

In trying to establish why the architects Maxwell & Turk of Manchester, decided on steel instead of wrought iron, which had been the material of choice in the construction of The Eiffe Tower (1889) and Blackpool Tower (1891) it appears that cost was the major consideration. The designers of New Brighton Tower we're also famous for building many other major attractions in Britain including Southport's Winter Gardens and the Blackpool Tower.

No real chronology exists to explain the change from columns to steel stanchions and girders. The construction methods had to adapt to the changing materials with the introduction of more off site fabrication work to help reduce costs and delays, with engineers rather than architects being involved in the design.

It was only a matter of time before steel became cheap enough to replace wrought iron altogether. In the construction of New Brighton Tower a total of 1000 tons of mild or low-carbon steel was used, at a cost of £120,000, in comparison with Blackpool Tower which used over 2,500 tonnes of iron at a cost £290,000 to build.

The hostile environment and additional maintenance costs seem to have not featured in their considerations so without due regard for the protection of the steelwork from corrosion the project went ahead using steel which has more vulnerability to corrosion than wrought iron.

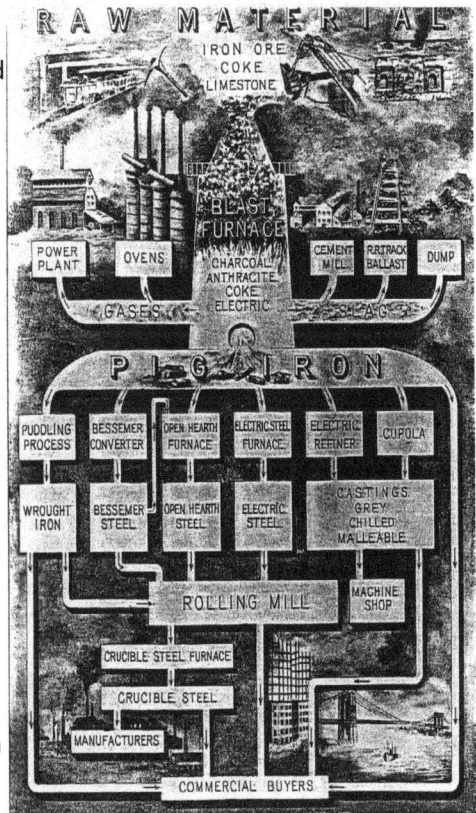

347

ELECTRIC LIFTS AT THE NEW BRIGHTON TOWER ENGLAND
The New Brighton Tower consist of central spire the base being surrounded by a promenade and theatre and other buildings of considerable height. The height from the ground level to the top of the flag staff is about 540 feet. The highest gallery accessible to the public is about 480 feet up. The lifts are arranged so as to make the journey up in two stages, the first being to the 80-foot platform and the second to one situated at 354 feet from the ground, the range of stroke of the lifts in this stage being therefore 304 feet. The highest galleries can only be reached by a staircase. The passenger lift to the first or 80-foot stage is two in number each being designed to carry 12 people and for a stroke of 80 feet, the speed 160 feet per minute.

They are placed one in each of two opposite corner towers of the building, and their arrangement is very simple.

The shaft is a solid masonry well, with three doorways opening to the several floors commanded by the lifts, and the winding gear is placed at the top directly over the well and carried on steel girders. It is of the type patented by the company (Anderson's patent)with a view to getting rid of the many disadvantages connected with the ordinary drum, which are accentuated in lifts of long stroke such as in this case. The electric motor, which is of the four pole type with slotted drum armature wound for 200 volts and provided with carbon brushes, drives a case hardened steel worm situated on the top side of a worm wheel, an arrangement which makes it easy to design the casing so that it is very simple matter to examine the worm at any time by merely lifting the cover, and it is but little trouble to get it out or to take the thrust bearing to pieces. The worm wheel is of phosphor bronze and drives a horizontal steel shaft having on it a cast-iron drum furnished with eight semi-cylindrical grooves, one side of which plumbs the centre of the cage and the other is nearly over the balance weight.

Underneath this drum and below the supporting joists is fixed a four grooved pulley by suitable bearing brackets placed on the skew. The four ropes leading up from the cage (each of which is competent by itself to sustain the whole load) are brought over four grooves of the driving drum, and finally down to the balance weight over a smooth-faced guide pulley, which in this case is necessary to bring them to the proper position. By this means an excellent grip is obtained of the ropes without the aid of V-shaped grooves, which tend to wear the rope; the ropes always lead off on the same position. The gear is of small dimensions, the size is the same no matter how long the stroke and any number of ropes may be used to both cage and balance weight without materially increasing the width of the drum.

The worm shaft is provided with a powerful magnetic brake acting on a drum on the shaft. The pressure on the brake blocks is given by an adjustable spring, and on starting the lifts the brake magnet is energized and thus takes off the brakes blocks against the spring. The magnet is enclosed on the bed plate casting so as to be protected from any damage. The switch is a simple type enclosed in a cast-iron casing and operated by the hand rope in the normal manner. This method is simpler than the automatic devices so frequently adopted and has the advantage that the speed of the lift may be regulated, a consideration which is often one of some importance, besides which it is less liable to get out of order. No difficulty is found in preventing the lift from being started too quickly if the switch is properly designed. To avoid any accident arising through the breaking or slipping off of the hand rope, emergency switches are fitted, working at each end of the stroke, so that in any case, when the cage reaches the limit of its travel it outs the main current off and so necessarily comes to speedy standstill, as the cutting off of the current brings the brake promptly into action. The cage is of ornamental woodwork, carried by the company's usual suspension frame and standard safety gear. Both cage and balance weight run on wooden guide rails. The wire rope attachment to the balance weight is made in such a way that the stress is equally borne by all the four ropes. There is also a goods lifts provided in this part of the structure, to work from the ground to the 80-foot level, which is designed to raise a load 15 cwt, at a speed of 130 feet per minute. It is arranged in a manner precisely similar to the passenger lifts just described, the only difference being that the cage is of a plain type to suit the work this lift has to do. The chief interest of the installation naturally centres in the two main lifts which work in the spire itself, and which take passengers from the 80-foot level to the 384-foot level or through a stroke of 301 feet. These are constructed to raise from 20 to 25 people, or say, from 3,000 to 4,000 lbs each at a speed of about 300 feet per minute; and owing to the unusual dimensions, position, speed and length of stroke, are necessarily in many ways special in their design. The chief novelty is that owing to the fact that the high building at the base of the tower was available for the purpose the balance weights have been kept out of the spire itself altogether and are suspended in a masonry well similar to those in which the already described lifts are placed; but in so much as the available height is much less than the stroke of the lift, it has been necessary to introduce a multiplying gear with a ratio of four to one, and of course a weight four times heavier than that which would be ordinarily required. The stroke, therefore, of the weights is only 76 feet.

The gearing is exactly the same type as that already described, the advantage of which with the unusually long stroke, is all the greater. It is, of course, much larger, the work done being about four times as great as in the other lifts, and in some particulars the details are modified on this account. The thrust bearing is separately attached, and is of a different construction, and the pressure of the brake is not given by spring but by a system of levers and a weight.

The four ropes pass up from the balance weight multiplying pulleys over four grooves of the driving drum, down over the skewed pulley, up again over the remaining four grooves of the driver, down once more to a guide pulley placed a little way down the weight shaft, along horizontally to the lifts shaft in the spire, round more guide pulleys and up a trunk at the side of the shaft to the top of the spire, where they lead over pulleys down to two corners of the cage, two ropes thus going to each corner, in which position they can be protected very largely from the effect of the wind, which in such an exposed position is a matter of some consequence. The cages are of a design suited to resist the weather which they necessarily have to encounter, and are provided with a powerful safety gear. The guide is of wood, and the cages are provided with rollers which run on the guide and cause therefore a minimum of friction, an important matter also on account of the side pressure when a strong wind is blowing.

The switch arrangements are in principle precisely the same as for the lifts already described only the switches are larger and the hand ropes are of wire, somewhat differently arranged so that they can be more readily controlled by the attendant under the special conditions obtaining. Emergency switches of similar type are also provided. Space is left in the tower for two more similar lifts to be added at some future time. The lifts have all been at work for some time, and have carried a great number of people.

The water supply of the establishment is provided for by a double bucket borehole pump, with 6 1/2 inch barrel and 26 inch stroke, drawing from about 55 feet below the surface, and pumping under a total head of 120 feet, driven by means of an electric motor of the same type as those used in the lifts through the medium of worm gearing. As the turning moment is uneven with this type of pump, a heavy fly-wheel is placed on the crankshaft to equalize it to some extent.

The current is supplied to the lifts and pump at 200 volts from a private generating station belonging to the tower company.

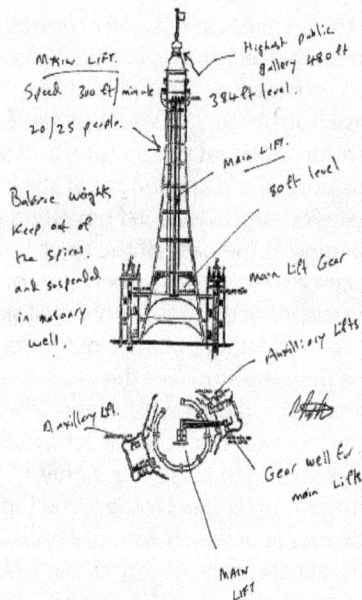

350

Tit-Bits

Tit-Bits was a mass circulation commercial publication which reached sales of between 400,000 and 600,000, with the emphasis on human interest stories concentrating on drama and sensation. With numerous competitions and promotions carried out in the Tower and grounds.

Yesterday was what is known as "Tit Bits" day on this side of the water at New Brighton Tower. On this particular day any purchaser of the weekly newspaper called "Tit Bits" can cut therefrom, a coupon of free admission into the Tower grounds, where several five-pound notes were advisedly lost in various parts of the buildings and grounds, and were afterwards found by visitors. A snapshot photographer was present, who took pictures of visitors, and these will from time to time appear in the newspapers, and the person recognising their own photo and proving the same, will receive five dollar gold pieces as presents. Six pictures will appear each week for six weeks. This move on the part of the Tower management and the "Tit Bits" proprietors resulting in an extremely large attendance, which proved very acceptable as well as financially beneficial to the various and sundry concessions in the park, all of them doing an exceptionally large business during the day.

"Tit-Bits" Gala Day
at the
New Brighton Tower
TO-MORROW, THURSDAY, AUG. 1.

The MERSEY and WIRRAL RAILWAYS and the WALLASEY FERRIES are kindly reducing their fares for this Great Day.

TOWER GROUNDS, THEATRE, BALL ROOM, MENAGERIE, &c., FOR

THREEPENCE,

AND A COUPON FROM EITHER "TIT-BITS," "TIT-BITS NOVELS," or "WOMAN'S LIFE."

Children (under 12, with Adults) Coupon only.
Children (under 3, with Adults) Entirely Free.

EVERY CHILD WILL BE PRESENTED WITH A PRETTY FLAG.

Mr. Tit-Bits will visit the Grounds and Sideshows during the day, giving money and handsome presents to persons carrying copies or making displays of "Tit-Bits," "Tit-Bits Novels," and "Woman's Life."

☞ LOOK OUT FOR MR. TIT-BITS. 🐦

GRAND FANCY DRESS BALL. TWELVE SPLENDID PRIZES FOR BEST COSTUMES REPRESENTING "TIT-BITS," "TIT-BITS NOVELS," or "WOMAN'S LIFE." All the Latest Music by the Grand Tower Orchestra.

THE GRANDEST DAY'S ENJOYMENT EVER OFFERED!
COME IN YOUR THOUSANDS!! ROOM FOR ALL!!!

Tower Grounds 1899 & 1911

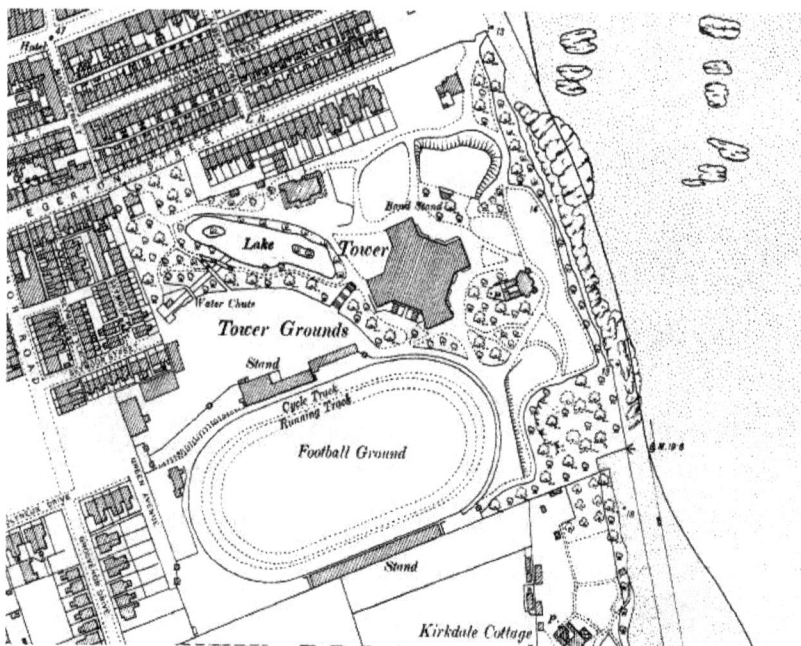

Tower Grounds 1899

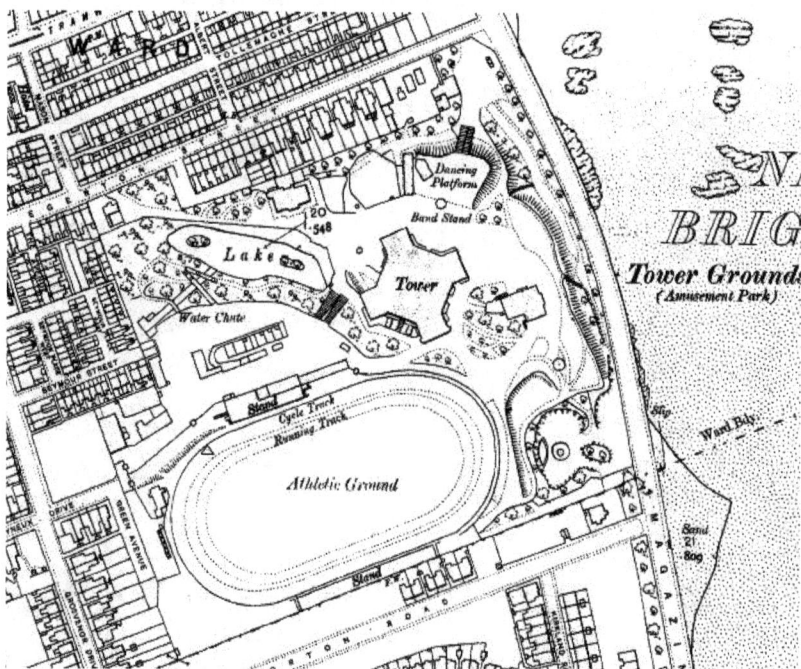

Tower Grounds 1911

Tower Grounds 1935 & Present

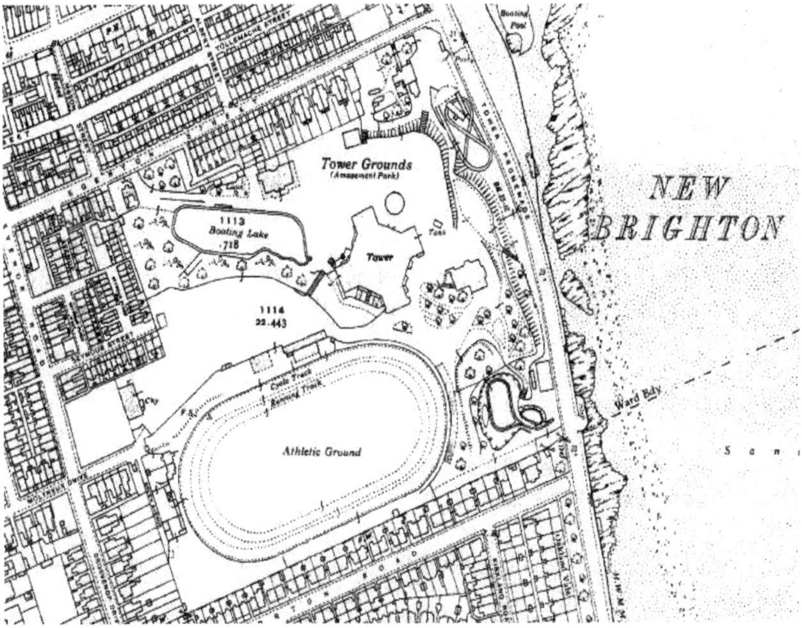

Tower Grounds 1935

Tower Grounds Overlay showing housing built over stadium

List of Companies associatted with New Brighton Tower & Grounds
Company No: 48380; Tower Estate Syndicate Ltd. Incorporated in 1896.
Dissolved before 1916.

Company No: 49767; Patent Switchback Steeplechase (Manchester
New Brighton and Isle of Man Concessions) Ltd. Incorporated in 1896.
Dissolved before 1916.

Company No: 98820; L A Thompson Scenic Railway of New Brighton, Ltd.
Incorporated in 1908. Dissolved between 1916 and 1932.

Company No: 49928; New Brighton Tower Football Club Ltd. Incorporated
in 1896. Dissolved before 1916.

Company No: 29851; New Brighton Club Ltd. Incorporated in 1889.
Dissolved between 1916 and 1932.

Company No: 49929; New Brighton Tower Cycling Club Ltd. Incorporated
in 1896. Dissolved before 1916.

Company No: 53073; New Brighton Chute Ltd. Incorporated in 1897.
Dissolved before 1916.

Company No: 10419; New Brighton Aquarium Summer and Winter
Gardens Company, Ltd. Incorporated in 1876. Dissolved before 1916.

Company No: 10418; New Brighton Aquarium Baths and Hotel Company,
Ltd. Incorporated in 1876. Dissolved before 1916.

Company No: 44099; Castle and Gardens (New Brighton) Ltd.
Incorporated in 1895. Dissolved before 1916.

Company: 8044; Brighton New Club Limited. Incorporated in 1874.
Dissolved in 1948.

Company No: 48861; New Brighton Tower and Recreation Company Ltd.
Incorporated in 1896. Dissolved between 1916 and 1932.

Company No: 50281; New Brighton Graydon Castle Great Wheel and
Towers Company Ltd. Incorporated in 1896. Dissolved before 1916.

Company No: 49927; New Brighton Tower Athletic Club Ltd. Incorporated
in 1896. Dissolved before 1916.

The licensing justices enjoyed great discretionary powers and regularly limited the opening hours or even curtailed the licence of the various premises within the tower. Below is the fame work of the law with regards to licensed premises.

1872 First introduction on restrictions in opening hours

1890 Public Health Acts Amendment, which empowered licensing justices to grant music, singing and dancing licences. They could also attach conditions to licences.

1914 In August powers to close public houses and to restrict pub opening hours were given to military and naval authorities. This power was extended to civil authorities shortly afterwards.

In October 1914 evening closing time in London became 10.00pm instead of 12.30am.

In 1915 opening hours were reduced from 16-17 hours (19.5 hours in London) to 5.5 hours and evening closing was 9 - 9.30pm.

The State Management System, as it was called, banned Sunday drinking, the consumption of spirits on a Saturday and the use of spirit chasers. Food, soft drinks and facilities for women were introduced to pubs. There was even a call for the Nationalisation of the brewing industry and pubs.

1921 Act set opening hours at 8-9 hours a day, with afternoon closing. And 5 hours on a Sunday.

1934 Licensing (Permitted Hours) Act, 'gave authority to licensing justices to extend the closing hour from 10 p.m. until 10.30. p.m. for part of a year should special circumstances or requirements dictate that it was in the public interest so to do to do

1949 Licensing Act special hours certificates introduced with a music and dancing licence.

1961 Extended the 'special hour's certificates for premises providing music and dancing.

1964 Licensing Act introduced Public Entertainment Licences issued by the Local Authority.

Because local authorities were responsible for defining the requirements of individual licensing applications it often took on a bizarre outcome.

During the 1920s, Wallasey Liberal Hall got a licence renewal only with the proviso that no saxophones were played by visiting jazz bands.

And the council used licensing laws to limit the number of so called undesirables from visiting the Tower.

.

ALLSOPP'S LAGER

Your medical man has perhaps recommended you to avoid all but light beverages, and experience may have taught you that you cannot digest a heavy beer. In ALLSOPP'S LAGER you will find a light, bright, sparkling beverage that you can digest and appreciate, as it is brewed exclusively from Malt and Hops, and absolutely free from Preservatives.

The cost is small. 2/0 per doz. Half Pints.
3/6 . Pints.

Main Tower Promotions
8th DEC 1965 The Yardbirds
9th JAN 1965 The Kinks
28th MAY 1964 The Searchers
30th AUG 1963 Southern Sounds 63, Brian Poole & Trem., Rolling Stones, TBC,CM
16th AUG 1963 The Searchers
26th JULY 1963 Northern Sounds 63, Billy J. Kramer & Dakotas, Freddy & the Dreamers, UT,EPT,JS,R4,4M,MPS,PMC,SWC,FSM
20th JULY 1963 Rory Storm and the Hurricanes
28th JUNE 1963 NEM Enterprises present Jet Harris & Tony Meehan, Billy J. Kramer & Dakotas, Billy J. Kramer & Dakotas, BT, FSM, TQC, 4M,
3rd JUN 1963 Whit Beat Show, Six Merseyside Sounds, DWP, IZ, RSH, TN, TR, CF
14th JUN 1963 'Mersey Beat Showcase'The Beatles, GP, plus 5 supporting Groups
10th MAY 1963 Rory Storm and the Hurricanes
20th APR 1963   Rory Storm and the Hurricanes
7th DEC 1962   The Beatles
1st DEC 1962   The Beatles
23rd NOV 1962 Art's Ball, The Beatles, LLew Hird Jazz Band, Billy Kramer
19th OCT 1962 Operation Big Beat 6th, MB, JSR4, UT, BKC, ST, plus four groups
12th OCT 1962 Little Richard, The Beatles, MB, BKC, DPM,4J, LCAS, BT,UT
21st SEP 1962 Rory Storm's Birthday Night The Beatles, RSH, BKC, B3, BDT
14th SEP 1962 - Operation Big Beat 5, The Beatles, RSH, GP, BKC, 4J, MB
17th AUG 1962 Leach Entertainments present The Beatles, BJC, LCAS, FF
27th JUL 1962 Joe Brown, The Beatles,SM, BT, SDD, 4J
21st JUL 1962 The Beatles,
13th JUL 1962 The Beatles at Tower Ballroom,
29th JUN 1962 Operation Big Beat 3, The Beatles, B3,4J, KC5,KTD,UT, TS, JTHC, LCD, The Trance.
28th JUN 1962 Jet Harris & Tony Meehan
21st JUN 1962 Star Show, The Beatles, Bruce Channel, BT, ST, 4J
25th May 1962 Big Beat Night, Rory Storm and the Hurricans, KTD, LCD, SWC,
17th May 1962 Bob Wooler presents Jerry Lee Lewis, plus 11 star groups
5th MAY 1962 Gene Vincent at Tower Ballroom, only appeared the once
6th APR 1962 Emile Ford & Checkmates, The Beatles, GP, HCS, RSH, BT
2nd MAR 1962 'Mad March Rock Ball' The Beatles,
23rd FEB 1962 The Beatles
16th FEB 1962 The Beatles
15th FEB 1962 The Beatles, Terry Lightfoot and His New Orleans Jazzmen.

RADIO CAROLINE CLUB BALL
◎ **ZOWIE 1** ◎
NEW BRIGHTON TOWER HALL
NEW BRIGHTON, NEAR LIVERPOOL
8th DECEMBER, 1965 ★ 7 - 11 P.M.
FREE - FREE - FREE TO CAROLINE CLUB MEMBERS
YARD BIRDS ★ THE 4 PENNIES
BRIAN POOLE AND THE TREMELOES
THE HONEYCOMBS ★ TWINKLE
PAUL & BARRY RYAN
CARRY FARR & THE T BONES
MARK LEEMAN FIVE ★ BILLIE DAVIS
RONNIE JONES   THE V.I.P'S
& THE BLUE JAYS ★ THE VAGABONDS
ALL CAROLINE CLUB MEMBERS WISHING TO TRAVEL WITH THE GROUPS PERFORMING
CATCH THE 12.30 P.M. TRAIN FROM EUSTON STATION, LONDON
Entertaining on the Train — The Rolling Kind

26th JAN 1962 The Beatles

19th JAN 1962 Pre-Panto Ball The Beatles

12th JAN 1962 Twist at the Tower, The Beatles,Turner & the Bandits, Strangers,RSH

26th DEC 1962 Boxing Night Big Beat Ball, The Beatles, Tony Osborne & Band

15th DEC 1961 The Beatles, RSH,DS, The Big Three and Case re-unite

 8th DEC 1961 The Davy Jones Show, Davy Jones, The Beatles, RSH, GP, EPT, R4,

1st DEC 1961 Big Beat Sessions, The Beatles, RSH, DRJ, DS,KTD, SDD,

24th NOV 1961 Operation Big Beat 11, The Beatles, RSH, GP, R4, EPTT, FF

10th NOV 1961 Big Beat, The Beatles, RSH, GP, R4, KTD

24th JUN 1961 Echolets, Dane Lawrence, The Tony Osborne Band,

15th JUN 1961 Northern Entertainments presents Beat Night Screaming Lord Sutch

27th MAY 1961 Ricky Valance, Lucy Strikes,

11th MAY 1961   Nero and the Gladiatots

Key: RSH Rory Storm & The Hurricanes, GP Gerry & The Pacemakers, R4 Remo Four, BKC Billy Kramer with the Coasters, KTD Kingsize Taylor and the Dominoes, MB Mersey Beats, 4J The 4 Jays, BT Big Three, SM Statesmen, TBC Tommy Bruce and the Bruisers, CM The Checkmates. UT The Undertakers, ,EPT Earl Preston and the T.T's ,JS Johnny Sandon,,4M The Four Mosts, MPS Mark Peters and the Silhouettes, ,PMC Peter MacLaine & The Clan, SWC, Sonny Webb & The Cascades, FSM Freddy Starr and the Midnighters, TQC Tommy Quickly and the Challengers, SDD Steve Day and the Drifters, HCS Howard Casey and the Seniors, DRJ Dale Roberts and the Jaywalkers, DS Derry and the Seniors, EPTT Earl Preston and the Tempest Tornadoes, FF Faron and the Flamingoes, LCAS Lee Curtis and the All Stars, BDT Buddy Dean and the Teachers, DWP Derry Wilkie and the Pressmen IZ Ian and the Zodiacs, TN The Nomads, TR The Renegades, CF Carl Francis, DPM The Dakotas with Pete MacLaine, LCAS Lee Curtis and the All Stars, JSR4 Johnny Sandon with Reno Four, ST Strangers, KC5 Kansas City 5,TS The Searchers JTHC Johnny Templars Hi-Cats, LCD Lee Curtis & The Detours, LCD Lee Curtis and the Detours, , SWC Sonny Ward and the Casuals

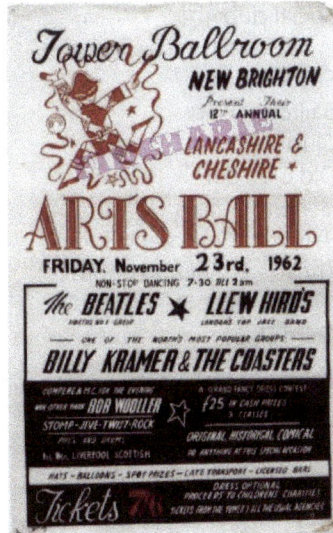

New Brighton Tower
Extracts from a survey undertaken in the early '60s

Basement

General Stores.
Electrician's Shop
Plumbers Shop
Staff Canteen
Boiler House
Theatre Dressing Rooms
Theatre Stage

Ground Floor
Waxworks
Amusement Arcade
Snack Bar (Theatre Passage)
Theatre Entrances
Social club Stillage
Ballroom Cloak Rooms

First Floor
Ballroom Cloak Rooms
Theatre Balcony
Social club

Second Floor
Ballroom Flat
Club Toilets
Old Club Bar
General Offices
Ballroom Cloaks and Toilets
Theatre Projection Rooms

Third Floor
Void

Fourth Floor
(Ballroom Level)
Ballroom
Ballroom Cafe
Soda Bar
Cigarette Kiosk
Dressing Rooms
Committee Rooms
Stage
Pink Room
Manager's Office
Entrance to Ballroom Flat

Fifth Floor
(Ballroom Balcony Level)
cloakroom (disused)
Blue Room Bar
Baronial Hall
Baronial Hall toilets

Sixth Floor
Void

Seventh Floor
(Roof Level)
Roof Cafe
Storage Turrets (3)
Chair Lift Terminal
Roof Telescope (Site of)

Basement to First Floor
Tower Theatre

Whilst there is adequate accommodation for all purposes of
entertainment, there is an unusual amount of superfluous space.
The general decor is poor and the annual cost of maintenance is high.
The whole premises are served by a hot water central heating plant
which has become inefficient and almost obsolete. Gas heaters and space
heaters are also used.
The inner building is octagonal in shape with multi-storied blocks
situated at the compass cardinal points.
The building is faced throughout with Red Ruabon brickwork and
supported by part of the steel work originally constructed for supporting
the tall tower.
Basement
Maintenance Stores are mainly situated within the outer perimeter of the
main walls, construction of stone and concrete with steel
with the steel foundations of the original steel structure of the old steel
tower.
There is no natural light or ventilation and there is general dampness
throughout the basement.
Ballroom
The ballroom is considered to be one of the two largest in the North of
England. Octagonal in shape, spring wood block floors supported by
8 steel pillars 4'9" x 4'3". There is a fireproofed false suspended ceiling.
height about 30'
The Algerian Cafe, at the date of inspection these premises had been
disused for about four years and were in a state of abandonment and
completely unusable.
The Lakeside Cafe & Bar seemed to be in use.
Also garage used by ice cream vendor. Also ten lock up garages
Self-contained flat at rear of Rock Point Restaurant occupied by Mr
Roberts, Managing Director of New Brighton Tower Co, ltd
Egerton Lodge a two storied detached red Ruaban Brick, with slated roof.
House in a poor state of repair and having all main services. Occupied by
a Mr W. Bedson for life, an ex employee of New Brighton Tower Co.

COUNTY BOROUGH OF WALLASEY FIRE BRIGADE
RESEARCH REPORT
NEW BRIGHTON TOWER BUILDINGS, WALLASEY

1. **Date, Time and address of the premises concerned**

Saturday 5th April, 1969 by Police radio to Police Headquarters at 0507 hours relayed to Fire Brigade Headquarters at 0508 hours.
Address:- Tower Buildings, Tower Grounds, New Brighton, Wallasey, Cheshire.

2. **Trade or business carried on**

Place of public entertainment consisting of ballroom, theatre, waxworks, museum, amusement arcade and licensed bars. At present only one small section occupied.

3. **Place and Time of Origin**

The severity of this fire, together with the collapse of walls etc. was such as to render the analysis if its origin and build up extremely difficult. The manager of the Tower and his staff had left the premises at approximately 2030 hours after a routine security check of the principal entrances to the building. The stage area was not included in this inspection and in fact was last visited some three days before the fire for the purpose of setting switches in a brick built switch house containing three phase 400 volt equipment, situated against the rear wall which governed supplies to the Tower building and the fairground surrounding it. The Tower roof was opened to the public on Friday for the first time this year as a vantage point for sight seeing, reached externally only be means of a "chair lift" which consisted of an endless chain of cars on cables travelling from the ground on the North side of the Tower Grounds to the roof of the building.

At approximately 0300 hours the New Brighton Lifeboat coxswain who lives some few hundred yards away from the Tower Building was awakened by crackling and banging. He arose and checked the street outside but seeing nothing amiss went back to bed. It is presumed that this noise was due to the developing fire. At 0405 a Police Constable on patrol in New Brighton smelt smoke in Victoria Road, and commenced a search of the area. From this point on, some statements from members of the public resident in the streets adjacent to the Tower Grounds imply that smoke and flames were visible from 0415 hours onwards. However, close examination and interviews reveal various anomalies and confusion in times which seem to indicate that in fact this was much later. The constable called for assistance to his control to search the area and, after alerting householders in Victoria Road and Tollemache Street, the Police finally came to Egerton Street and the Tower Grounds and discovered a severe fire in the stage area West tower of the Tower Building. The Brigade were then informed and the call was logged at 0508 hours in Brigade control.

On arrival at the incident, just prior to the wall collapse, the fire was showing principally in this West tower therefore, from subsequent investigations, the stage and loft most certainly was the seat of the fire. From the degree of involvement noticeable to the joint attendance, it is reasonable to suppose the origin of the fire was at least midnight if not earlier.

The first attendance consisted of a pump, pump escape, turntable ladder and General Purpose Van from Wallasey Fire Brigade. On arrival at the incident a sever fire was visible in the windows of the stage area with large volumes of smoke issuing from the top level. The officer-in-charge radioed "make pumps 10, turntable ladders 2" and established the G.P. Van as a central unit in the Tower car park.
He then approached the building down steps leading from the car park immediately adjacent to the western tower, and after reconnaissance, returned back up the steps. On reaching the car park he heard a muffled crump and turned to find the whole of the external gable of the west tower building collapsing outwards. At 0518 he orginated a further assistance message "make turntable ladders 4". At this time the Assistant Divisional Officer arrived at the fireground and assumed command, and at 0520 hours made pumps 20. The collapse of the external wall had had the effect of opening up both the tower theatre level and tower ballroom level through to open air allowing the severe fire in the stage left section to surge unopposed into the main building. After assessment by the Assistant Divisional Officer, and having regard to the poor water supplies in the area (a large lake immediately adjacent having been drained some three years earlier despite requests from the Fire Brigade). It was obvious that most of the water would have to be provided by relay from the Marine Lake on the promenade some third of a mile away. Immediate provisions were made to institute some three relays and an officer delegated as relay officer. Three jets from pumps fed from hydrants were got to work to try to reduce the large volume of fire opened up by the wall collapse. Two turntable ladders were also at work initially at this end as the lie of the land and the wall collapse made close fire fighting at ground level difficult (See plate I).
At 0610 the first relay was in operation and was feeding a turntable ladder and ground monitor on the north western side.

At 0535 hours the Chief Fire Officer assumed command of the incident and at this stage it was apparent that the fire had gained a secure hold and owing to the nature of the building and the acute water shortage the theatre and ballroom sections would become a total loss. Roof collapses were already taking place and as the general state of the building before the fire was one of neglect a decision was taken to permit entry to the building only on the southern tower. By 0620 hours the second relay was completed and was supplying water for a twin branch on the north western side and a ground monitor on the western side. Throughout this time the fire was spreading rapidly and had quickly involved the whole of the theatre and ballroom (See plate II). At 0635 hours information was received from the Tower Company staff that a number of compressed oxygen and dissolved acetylene cylinders were present in the offices situated at fifth floor level in the north tower. At 0642 an informative message was issued by the Chief Fire Officer and about this time the expected explosion of the compressed gas cylinders took place. Entry had been made but now into the southern tower but roof collapses and blocked staircases had limited access to the theatre balcony level and two unattended ground monitors were at work in this position. Liverpool Fire Brigade were requested to attend the fire ground with their heavy water unit which arrived at 0640 hours. At 0703 pumps were made to 25 to provide a fourth relay and at 0720 the third relay was in operation and was supplying a twin branch and a ground monitor on the north eastern side of the building. At 0800 hours a senior officers conference was called and it was decided that firefighting operations would still remain external except for the sourthern side as more serious roof collapses had taken place. Relief crews from all supporting Brigades would be requested. Fire fighting continued with the institution of a fourth relay which supplied water from redeployed turntable ladder and ground monitor on the eastern side of the building.

At 0900 hours the effect of fire fighting was beginning to tell and crews were being relieved at their positions by fresh personnel. At 0932 the situation was judged to be under control and the stop message circulated. Appliances and personnel were released.

Before & After

Direction of Photograph   Photographs courtesy of Ken Clark

363

Bibliography

New Brighton Tower - Football Club History Database.
The Builder (1896). University of Michigan. p. 159.
The Development of Steel Framed Buildings in Britain A. Jackson, (1998).
Helmets,Handcuffs and Hoses, The Wallasey Fire Brigade Noel E Smith.
Construction History. 1880–1905, The Construction History Society.
Musical Times. Granville Bantock, Musical Times Publications. Jan.1909.
New Brighton: The Tower Ground: 1933–1935, The National Speedway Museum.
Kennedy, Michael (1960). The Hallé Tradition: A Century of Music.
Yesterday's Wirral 5 Boumphrey, Ian; Boumphrey, Marilyn (1988).
Bantock At New Brighton   By Stuart Scott
Bass Ratcliff & Gretton Excursion to Liverpool & New Brighton July 1904
The Inviting Shore, A Social History of New Brighton Anthony M. Miller
Rise and Progress of Wallasey E. C Woods & P. C Brown 1974
Mr C. L. Weller notebook photographs, drawings and blueprints for the construction of the New Brighton Tower. Also included are several newspaper clippings about workers who fell to their deaths during the construction in 1897. In his notes, Weller talks about these deaths and some of the photographs show the scenes of the accidents.
Central Library Wallasy: 29 Volumes of Newspaper Cuttings from November 1896 – July 1950. Saved from the Fire in 1969.

Extracts from numerous vintage newspapers including:
Belfast News-Letter, Nelson Evening Mail. Dundee Courier, Leeds Mercury, Manchester Courier, Liverpool Mercury, Daily Post, Wallasey News, Era,

Sixteen Decades In Wallasey

Roy Dutton

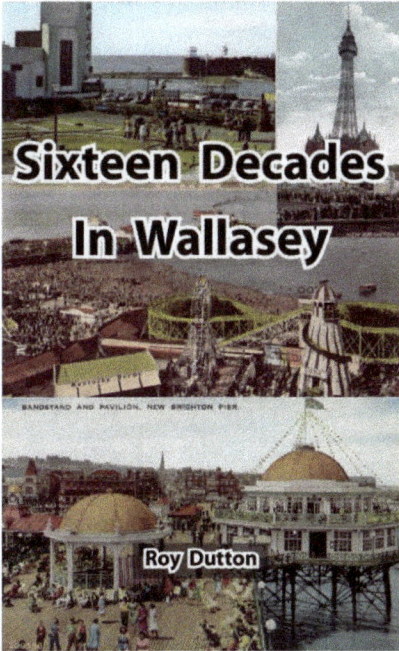

Reminiscences of New Brighton and Liverpool. The constant procession of ocean-going liners up and down the Mersey was a real spectacle. Wallasey has eight miles of promenade, fringed by golden sands with children's talent contests "Joytime" in Vale Park. The Tower Grounds, rides, skating and a figure of eight. We even had a circus and a zoo. The New Palace indoor amusement park was the largest in England. Tommy Mann's miniature railway operated in the Tower Grounds next to the Promenade. Trips on the Royal Iris, the ferries and a magnificent pier. And don't forget the largest outdoor swimming pool in Europe. What a place to grow up in! It was my Disneyland and on my very own doorstep.

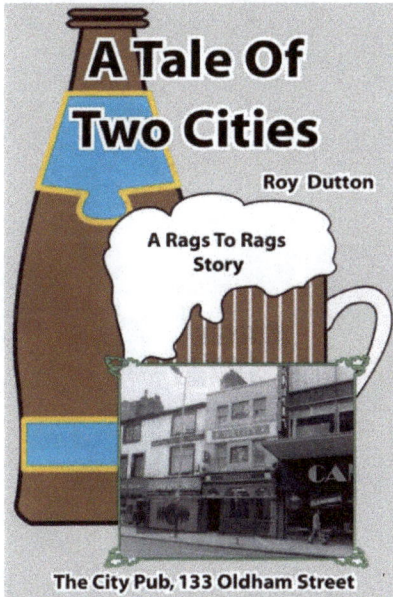

A Tale Of Two Cities

Roy Dutton

A Rags To Rags Story

The City Pub, 133 Oldham Street

A tale of two cities is the story of our tenure of the City Pub, its history and the characters that crossed its doorway. Followed by a dip into the smorgasbord of Manchester's glorious past, from the clubs and pubs that have faded into history. To the buildings and places lost in the passage of time. With contemporary news paper cuttings of events and the people that helped shape the city of Manchester. I hope you enjoy the tale of two cities as much as I have in compiling it.

www.ingramcontent.com/pod-product-compliance
Lightning Source LLC
Chambersburg PA
CBHW060348100426
42812CB00003B/1166